PERSPECTIVE

A
Book
By
Charles D. Gaines

www.PerspectiveAmerica.com

PRESS

PERSPECTIVE
by Charles Gaines

Printed in the United States of America

ISBN-13: 978-1-60034-727-6
ISBN-10: 1-60034-727-4

www.xulonpress.com

CONTENTS

—⚊—

PERSPECTIVE
By
Charles D. Gaines

ACKNOWLEDGEMENTS

"For what thanks can we render to God for you in return for all the joy with which we rejoice before our God on your account.
(I Thessalonians 3:9)

I wish above all to acknowledge our Creator, Lord and Redeemer who's Spirit gives us life, light, hope, peace and joy. He delivers us from the curse of death and the deadly and destructive disease of human deceit that holds every man separated from the saving grace of God in its grasp.

It was the Spirit of God working through the lives of a hand full of men joined together by divine appointment that lead to the birth of our nation. God gave to them the vision of a new nation whose citizens would have a passion for God and for liberty. They were inspired to separate themselves from an oppressive European government and establish a new nation in which charity, liberty, self government, equal justice for all, free religious expression and free enterprise were its guiding principles.

Our Founders shared a vision of a nation of people who walked humbly before a super-intending God. I wish to acknowledge these precious, wise, morally courageous and humble men who declared boldly to a stunned world they held certain truths regarding the lives of human beings to be self-evident and God given. First among those truths was that "all men are **created** equal". This was a radical and powerful idea confirmed in the heart and soul of every man even though that perspective was contrary to a world view in which rights were distributed to people by governments based upon social position, wealth and race.

I wish to acknowledge the remnant of Christian believers who continue to Trust God, spread His message of grace and function as the fullness of Christ in the land. We have inherited God's blessing in large part due to their prayers, sacrifices and efforts.

I want to acknowledge a giant of a man in my eyes who has had an eternal impact upon my life and the lives of many others. He is my Brother and my good and loyal friend Ken whose love and encouragement have made this possible.

Another good and faithful servant of God I wish to acknowledge is my Pastor Donald Shelley of Church of the Highlands in San Bruno, California. He patiently guided me early on in my Spiritual pilgrimage.

I wish to also acknowledge my loyal friend Charlie Sweeney, a reformed liberal thinker, whose loyalty and his detailed knowledge of American History and his deeply held respect and honor for his country and for those men and women who serve our country in the military has inspired me to listen and in listening I have learned much from him.

There are many others who have touched my life and the lives of millions of Americans for the cause of truth and good that deserve acknowledgement. I owe so many so much!! Among them I wish to acknowledge David Barton for his tireless attempts to protect the history, tradition and heritage of America by constantly and consistently being an example of salt and light. His powerful and cutting edge "Wall Builders" ministry has brought clarity to the struggle of discerning between secular humanism and our historical Christian foundation and tradition..

David has led the charge in exposing the deceit and destructive impact of secularism in the public education system and in the Judiciary. His works has had a significant impact on my perspective as well as the perspective of millions of Americans. He has awakened many to the subtle reality that secular humanism is not a neutral or objective force, but rather the force of anti-Christ. Its supporters and adherents are setting a deadly course for America.

America needs a host of men like David Barton to stand up and reveal the truth and the destructiveness of secularism. His work must surely be acknowledged here. Thanks David.

Another Spiritual giant in our times I wish to acknowledge because of the impact his ministry has had on my life is Dr. Charles Stanley. He is truly one of the great Christians and bible teachers of our age. I, and perhaps millions of others, have learned much about the character, grace, will, sovereignty and charity of God through his "In Touch" ministry.

I also wish to acknowledge D. James Kennedy of the Coral Ridge ministry. His unrelenting battle against the deceit of secularism and cultism and the devastating implications of Satan's lie that has captured the hearts, minds and imaginations of many of our leaders and citizens of this modern culture has kept me, and millions like me, alert and engaged in the battle against the encroachment of evil and deceit. He is a clear and distinct example of Gods admonition to be salt and light. Thank you Dr. James Kennedy.

I wish to acknowledge the ministry and leadership of Dr James Dobson who works tirelessly to interpret for us the implications of the good and the foolish choices we make individually and collectively as a nation. He has been one of the nations most influential spiritual leaders in the effort to guide parents as they attempt to raise up their children in the nurture and admonition of the Lord. He is a distinct example to the church of the ministry of salt and light.

I want to also acknowledge the leadership and contribution of Dr. William Bennett. He has defined in his writing the moral questions of our times and exposed the destructiveness and utter deceit of liberalism and secularism. His wisdom and judgments are on target and timely. I have learned much from his books and commentary. Thank you Dr. Bennett.

I, like many other American patriots, am deeply indebted and grateful for the research and writings of Peter Marshall and David Manuel in their incredible books "The Light and The Glory" and their follow up book "Sounding Forth the Trumpet". I simply add my thanks, I am grateful. Certainly their perspective and their clear and vivid illumination of the truth regarding America's birth and history leaves little room for the arguments of the secularist social reformers who deny God's role in the foundation, character and tradition of our national existence. Their writings clearly contrast the destructive meanderings of the liberal and evil deceit of secularism in which America has become trapped.

Among these watchmen at the gate of the conservative cause whose wisdom I wish to acknowledge and whose contribution to liberty and our free enterprise system cannot be ignored is a man who (tongue in cheek) presents himself as the professor of conservative thinking, Dean of the Institute of Conservative Studies who sits daily behind the EIB mike in New York City attempting to vigorously fend off the liberal attack against America. Thank you Rush!

Finally, it is essential to acknowledge the distinct clarity of message and leadership of America's current President, George W. Bush. He is indeed one of the great leaders of our time. George Bush is a man of faith and character who God has raised up among us to lead and guide us and to help awaken us to our need to return to our Spiritual roots and heritage. Men of faith love him, however, the liberal and secular world hates him.

President Bush is the CEO of America. He is America's general manager and quarter-back! The liberal secular media, the liberals in the Democratic Party and a secular court system are trying to derail his leadership. We have chosen him above all others to lead the team that governs our nation. However, the judiciary and the liberals among us have ignored the voters and they want to boil him in oil! President Bush's moral courage and steadfast example brings hope to America because it is a reminder to us that God is still in charge and working through His appointed ambassadors to awaken and guide America.

Our President's vision and commitment to transport the liberty, opportunity and prosperity of democracy to the peoples of the world has to be close to the heart of God and far more important than many of the domestic issues many of our citizens and our politicians are preoccupied with that cannot be fixed by a secular government.

Finally I acknowledge my loving and supportive family that have tolerated me as I sometimes seemed pre-occupied with attempting to bring perspective to the insanity of a secular humanist culture at what I consider to be a very critical time in our history.

I acknowledge Lois, my wife of 51 years, who has patiently endured many hours listening to me speak and debate these perspectives from every platform afforded to me. I am thankful for her attentiveness and interest demonstrated week after week and year after year as she has listened to me speak with great passion about these things from the pulpits afforded me. Most of the thoughts and attitudes expressed herein I have rehearsed in her presence in the privacy of my office in our home. Without her caring and the many practical expressions of her love this book would have never come forth.

DEDICATION

—ɯ—

Ephesians 1:18-19
"I pray that the eyes of your heart may be enlightened, so that you may know what is the hope of His calling, what are the riches of the glory of His inheritance in the saints, and what is the surpassing greatness of His power toward us who believe"

*P*erspective is dedicated to those American patriots who continue to fight the never-ending struggle against the deceit and evil that competes for the heart, soul and Spirit of America and to the cause of returning the people of America to a consciousness of and a passion for our Spiritual heritage of one nation under God.

I dedicate *Perspective* to the memory of the brave who have sacrificed, and continue to sacrifice, so much in the effort to sustain and protect our liberty and precious heritage so it might be experienced for generations to come. America has historically been the land of free because of the brave.

I dedicate *Perspective* to the church, the body of Christ, which God has given to mankind to help light our path and carefully guide our ambassadorship to His kingdom under the inspiration of His Spirit in pursuit of the wisdom and fulfillment of His divine purpose.

Perspective is dedicated to the reinstatement of, and respect for, those precious biblical values that made America good and developed the character that made her strong and gave her vision, purpose, direction and inspiration.

Finally, I dedicate *Perspective* to my immediate and extended family. First to my wife Lois, the true matriarch of the Gaines family, who raised our family during those years when I was flying all over the world as a member of our armed forces joined in the constant fight to keep America secure and preserve the unalienable rights and principles of freedom, liberty, justice and human dignity declared by our founding fathers to be the principles that offer the highest hope for any human government and for all men of good will. Lois is a true patriot and a great encouragement to all who know her even though I doubt she has ever thought of herself in that light.

Her life has been a model of loyalty and service to her family dedicated to doing what she feels must be done for the good of the family. Lois is truly exemplary of the mothers who share membership in what has become known as "the greatest generation". They have been the backbone of family life in our nation in the best American and biblical tradition.

Lois has past on the faith, spirit, loyalty, love and those Spiritual values that build wisdom, character and charity in the hearts and minds of her children and grandchildren. The lives of mothers and wives like Lois define what has been historically good about America. They have upheld the values that have kept America strong and good during difficult times. The mothers of her generation interpreted God's role for them in life to honor and love God, their husbands and their children in the true sense of biblical love.

Lois has exemplified in her life a committed effort to live according to God's revealed will for her life, as defined by the scriptures, demonstrated in her family relationships. It sounds like a big job requiring much sacrifice? You bet it is but the benefits of her sacrifice manifest themselves in the lives of her children and grand children and these benefits are enormous.

Next, I dedicate **Perspective** to my children who must live and raise their families in the secular humanist and materialistic culture that has evolved because of our abandonment of God and His wisdom.

First I dedicate **perspective** to my oldest son Timothy who shares my most precious faith and conservative views. God has given Tim a gift of wisdom and grace that enables him to positively influence many while interacting with men of diverse views and values without compromising his belief. I am grateful to God for His wonderful grace that allows Tim and I to share a very special father and son relationship of mutual respect rooted in God's love. I recognize that I have not earned the right to this kind of relationship; it is another gift of God's grace. I am deeply thankful for a son like Tim. I am proud of the person he has become and I love him very much. It is necessary to take this opportunity to tell him so.

I also dedicate **perspective** to my daughter Laurie Ann who is the apple of my eye. I am thankful for her heart that wants her father to be, and somehow believes that he is, the best and wisest and most honorable man in her life. My professional life caused me to miss much of Laurie's childhood and I was therefore not much help in those times when she needed me most. Laurie has had to pay a huge price in this life trying to make marriage work while she preservers believing that God knows and cares and *"works all things for good to those who love Him and are called according to His purposes.* I hope *perspective* will help inspire her and her children to an even stronger faith and to continued good citizenship

I dedicate **perspective** to my youngest son David, whose heart is tender for our Lord and whose Spiritual courage and perspective on life is grounded in a deep faith in God. I am thankful to God for the relationship David and I share and for the man David has become despite my neglect when he was growing up. David is a man of good conscience and has great favor with his fellowman and surely with the Lord. God has used David to teach me many things about myself helping me to mature in my faith to a deeper appreciation of God's people. I love David deeply and pray for God's continued blessing upon the work of his hands. I must take this opportunity David to tell you so.

Finally, I dedicate *perspective* to my precious grandchildren who are part of the generation in whom the future of the nation rests. The culture and predominate thinking of the society in which they are growing up is far removed from the America created by the inspiration of God through the work of our founding fathers. I am thankful to God for His grace that has guarded the hearts, souls and lives of these nine grandchildren while they have grown up in the midst of a great moral crisis in a society that is walking in great deceit and rebellion against God. However, thanks to the mercy and grace of a wonderful God each one of these precious grandchildren has responded to God's call upon their lives and has accepted His saving grace. What a glorious gift God has given the Gaines family.

They are Matthew, Jennifer, Ryan, Katie, Spencer, Cari, Emily, Nathan and Taylor. I leave *perspective* to each of you as a legacy revealing my faith, values, ideas and experience to encourage, help guide and perhaps inspire you. I hope it will help build your faith and somehow make you wiser and more alert to the working and subtle wiles of evil and deceit that works in the world and resides in the nature of fallen man. I pray it will also lead you to recognize the importance of becoming alert and engaged Christian Americans.

INTRODUCTION

—m—

"There is a way which seems right to a man,
but its end is the way of death." (Proverbs 4:12)

"THESE ARE THE TIMES THAT TRY MEN'S SOULS; THE SUMMER
SOLDIER AND THE SUNSHINE PATRIOT WILL, IN THIS CRISIS, SHRINK
FROM THE SERVICE OF HIS COUNTRY; BUT HE THAT STANDS IT NOW,
DESERVES THE LOVE AND THANKS OF (EVERY) MAN AND WOMAN.
TYRANNY, LIKE HELL, IS NOT EASILY CONQUERED; YET WE HAVE
THIS CONSOLATION WITH US, THAT THE HARDER THE CONFLICT, THE
MORE GLORIOUS THE TRIUMPH. WHAT WE OBTAIN TOO CHEAP, WE
ESTEEM TOO LIGHTLY; TIS DEARNESS ONLY THAT GIVES EVERY THING
ITS VALUE. HEAVEN KNOWS HOW TO SET A PROPER PRICE UPON ITS
GOODS; AND IT WOULD BE STRANGE INDEED, IF SO CELESTIAL AN
ARTICLE AS (HUMAN) LIBERTY NOT BE HIGHLY (ENOUGH) RATED
(TO CALL US TO BATTLE)"
Thomas Paine, December 1776

Perspective reveals what I believe to be true about those things which most affect our lives and the lives of our fellowman for now and eternity. Liberty and a walk of faith, much like eternal life, demand the price of alertness, sacrifice, endurance and a constant unrelenting battle against the forces of evil.

Perspective is dedicated to the worthy cause of urging every reader to carefully and seriously consider the nature and value of liberty before casting a vote for any political leader or before supporting any legislation, public policy change or social program that increases dependence on government, removes individual accountability, denies the role of discipline in any family or society, removes God and the incentive to do what is right.

Perspective is dedicated to the cause of placing God on the thrown of our lives and exposing the deceit of liberalism and to the outright rejection of secularism. *Perspective* is dedicated to reducing our citizen's dependence on government and to stopping the head-long destructive trading of individual freedom for government dependence that further restricts liberty.

If you have read the acknowledgement and the dedication you have no doubt concluded that I am a Christian patriot whose perspective tends to be conservative. Before you set the book aside I would like to acquaint you with my philosophical perspective.

I am a Christian, an American and a conservative in my perspective in that order. I have discovered that conservative idea's and ideals seem to more nearly parallel truth and biblical principle than do liberal ideas and ideals. However, conservative philosophy without the leading of the Spirit of God can be just as spiritually bankrupt as liberal philosophy.

Unfortunately, the spirit in which conservative thought is presented sometimes seems lacking in charity and grace, which are essential ingredients that make its ideals and expectations reachable and effective. Nevertheless conservative ideals tend to be those ideals that are biblically based and more closely reflect God's revealed wisdom.

I believe conservative ideals tend to be the right ideals, however, sometimes the implementation of these ideals require the application of grace. Calling something black does not encourage it to become white. At any rate, whether ideals are conservative or liberal, without God's grace, His wisdom and Spiritual guidance both of them administered by men of fallen natures will prove to bring destructive results.

However, the liberal perspective seems to me to be so fraught with deceit and lacking in truth, wisdom and intellectual honesty it is not a tolerable perspective to wise men.

During one of the Presidential debates Kerry attempted to convince America that, like our President George Bush, he was also a man of faith. In his deceit he went on at great length to explain that his faith didn't effect how he thought or acted professionally. John Kerry obviously doesn't have a clue about what faith is or how the walk of faith impacts you and your acts regardless of the role you are playing in life. He seriously and foolishly tried to sell the idea that he could make decisions as a leader contrary to and completely setting aside the beliefs he professed to be his deepest held beliefs.

This deceitful idea is the most revealing of any of the blindness and arrogance resident in Spiritual deceit. Bill Clinton suffered from much the same kind of deceit. Kerry told us how important his faith was to him and then in the same discussion he went to great lengths to explain that his faith was not as important to him as his political considerations. He said his faith did not impact his legislative decisions as a United States Senator nor did it impact how he performed his Senatorial duties. If that is true then the only conclusion wise men can draw is that Mr. Kerry is not a man of faith and beyond that he is a very foolish man, certainly not fit to be a Senator or our President.

The secular world will scream "JUDGMENTAL" at this discussion of Mr. Kerry's obvious hypocrisy. It will clearly not be politically correct. Sorry folks, there is a great deal of difference between discernment and judgment. The man who lacks discernment is a fool. The one who determines the ultimate fate of the sinner is the one who either condemns or forgives. That one is God.

What is condemning to America is not that fools exist who attempt to sell foolish notions born out of deceit and present to us false claims for personal political gain, but that almost half of the American voters can be hoodwinked by such deceit.

Ironically, Kerry applied the same twisted logic while discussing his stand on several other issues throughout the Presidential campaign. He presented to America the idea that separation of Church and State was a more fundamental, important and relevant issue than the will and ways of God. The fact that the world is arrogant, indifferent, misguided and deceived men like Kerry can say almost anything and deceived followers will accept it. More than 43% of America said they would vote for him, according to the polls. This should scare us enough to awaken us to the condition we find ourselves in as a nation.

Unfortunately, there are obviously millions of professing American Christians who are just as deceived and hypocritical about who they are and what they believe as Senator Kerry. Some of them no doubt voted for him. Fortunately Senator Kerry was defeated in the election by a man of faith who does make decisions and judgments according to his deepest held beliefs. The world, and particularly the liberals of the world, hates him for his faith.

The bible says that Gods Spirit dwells with the man of faith and opens his eyes to the will and wisdom of God and also to the deceit of man. God's Spirit does not reside with the man of the world and therefore he is left trapped in his deceit. The Holy Spirit is a gift promised exclusively to the believer. Without the Spirit of God dwelling within to guide us we must be guided by the conviction and charity of other men and/or by the dictates of our own appetites and pleasures. Man does not enter the world as a believer.

We are living in an era when the measure and value of biblical character, the value of the family unit, moral accountability, personal integrity and spiritual values once cherished and recognized as the foundational values of America and essence of life in America, in and out of the church, have come to be despised as we become more and more a secular culture. Life in America today is measured by a standard of measure that does not consider individual character, moral courage, accountability, Godly wisdom, faith or truth as necessary or important qualities to be desired in our leaders. In fact we have a culture that perceives these values as bigoted and detrimental to what is best for America.

On the thrown of human life are the appetites of man and secular thinking, which are controlled by the mind and passions of man inspired by his pleasures and the unbridled spirit of evil. Most Americans profess they believe there is a God but many no longer honor God and certainly do not obey Him or walk according to His Spirit.

In fact we have moved so far away from the witness of the Spirit of God in our lives that our culture considers those who honor God and attempt to walk according to the Spirit of God living by biblical principles as bigoted, divisive and destructive enemies of the state. They see the state as the God of America to which they are becoming more and more dependent systematically relinquishing their resources and liberty not understanding the trap they are building for themselves and for the generations to follow. America tends to consider the Creator of the universe subservient to our secular interests, our laws and our government. Sound stupid? That's because it is stupid. It is deceit manifesting its most effective destructive work through the minds of men. Unchecked, it destroys liberty and invites tyranny.

We who profess to be Christian have stated that we are committed to obey His admonition to be salt and light to the world and to rise up our children in the nurture and admonition of the Lord. We have long since rejected our calling and His admonition. We, therefore, are harvesting the fruit of the rebellion and evil we have sowed. We are destroying our children by raising them up in secular schools and it is clearly obvious to those who see that we are, for the most part, blind to the destruction we are planting and what it will bring down upon us.

It should be clear that America must make a dramatic change in direction! We can no longer allow the world or a secular judicial system to define the meaning, purpose and nature of life in our nation or the role, content, purpose and definition of education for our children. God has already defined these things for His people in His word. As a Christian society our laws, the God we worship and the public incentives rewarding good behavior must express our Christian value system and its guiding principles.

We in the church, and our entire nation, must humble ourselves before our Creator and plead with Him to help preserve our liberty and our most holy faith from the destructive effect of the deceit that is overtaking us. We must seek His forgiveness, His mercy, His guidance and dedicate ourselves to getting the church and our nation back on course.

Jesus was clear about his position regarding the foolish, evil and destructive ways of the world and of organized religion. The thinking of the church in regard to hiding from the relentless on-slought of evil is foolish. The world is dedicated and fully committed to destroying any symbol, evidence or witness of Christ, His church and His followers and it is foolish to attempt appeasement by staying low profile. Satan is after us and he will destroy us if we don't wake up and engage the Spiritual battle. The spiritual battle against darkness and evil is the reason the Church exists in the earth!!! The church is placed here as God's ambassador to reach into the very midst of the devils playground and rescue millions from his deceit and grasp. God has been fighting this battle for thousands of years and we don't have to worry about protecting Him or His promise to protect His Church. He has stated that the "***gates of hell shall not prevail against His Church***" and I expect He will keep that promise if we begin to act like we are in fact a part of His Church. We don't have to worry about Him protecting us as we loyally and consistently do His bidding.

Each new generation within the church tend to occupy themselves in the debate as to whether the bible is indeed the inspired Word of God and whether speaking in tongues and other Spiritual gifts are for today etc. These are not profitable speculations in light of the testimony of the word and the work to be done. The gifts of the Spirit will be manifest in our efforts. So long as there is a world to be rescued the role and the gifts to the true Church will remain unchanged. The question is not "where are the gifts?" but rather where is the church?

In the meantime the enemy has indeed come in like a flood and our society does not recognize him and they have welcomed him as an angel of light. Now we worship him as god. We, like Eve in the Garden of Eden, bought into the lie of secular humanist reasoning and are becoming trapped in our own deceit.

The wisdom our government, and much of the church, has chosen to follow is secular humanist, which is anti-God! Many Christians foolishly think there is a satisfactory alternative to the word and will of God. They have been hoodwinked into a way that seems good to them; however, the Lord warns us in His word that it is a way that leads to death and destruction.

We have become trapped in our dependence on a secular government. Think about it folks, the government bureaucracy you are depending upon to protect your God ordained rights and liberties and to deal right and justly has declared itself an enemy of God and separated itself from accountability to God. Do not be foolish, your government does not love you, it cannot protect you from evil, it cannot protect you from life's struggles and it will abandon you without a thought or consideration if another cause or political interest more beneficial to its cause attracts it.

Only God loves you and can do these things. If you think government will be loyal to you and will not abandon you when it is easiest for them to do so then you have not lived very long or you are very naïve or just plain foolish. Government responds to the loudest voice that has the greatest political impact. It does not react to right or to justice because it is a secular bureaucracy that has adopted secular values, secular philosophies and laws that cannot discern right and wrong.

The government of today is working to create and enforce those secular ideals that conform to secular philosophy. We have appointed deceived secular humanist leaders and Supreme Court Justices who in their deceit have slowly and deliberately removed God from the governing process and from our traditional way of life. The ultimate end to this utter insanity is the complete destruction of our way of life. The public expression of our Christian faith will come to its inevitable end if this insanity is not stopped.

There is a contingent in the United States Senate that are fully dedicated to voting against any candidate for the judiciary that professes to be Christian. Why do you suppose they would do that? They say they do so because it's the constitutional thing to do. Really!! If the majority of our nation decides its Christian then our nation is Christian.

Whether we are Christian and chose to enact laws that reflect our values is clearly constitutional and it is out of the jurisdiction of the court to decide whether or not we are Christian. These deceived men insist upon secularism because they hate Christ and are totally intimidated by Him. God says in His word they recognize their utter sinfulness and deceit and don't want their foolish and evil ways to be exposed by the truth.

We are trading our future and our hope for a perceived smoke and mirrors wealth financed by individual and public debt. They, and we, sold out our nations industrial economic base to the nations of the world. When we had given away millions of jobs along with our industrial base we became a nation of consumers rather than producers and we traded capitalism and free enterprise for socialism in order to finance an increasing level of poverty and dependence. We elected to adopt government dependence rather than having to be a productive, responsible and accountable people.

We have traded our distinctly Christian heritage for a foolish notion of religious diversity we foolishly and proudly proclaim as the secret to America's greatness. Thinking we are wise we have become utter fools. We divided ourselves up into special interest minority groups to compete for political power, public resources and prominence at the expense of our fellowman to satisfy our own special individual appetites and agenda's.

We have long since abandoned the merits of righteousness, moral character and self-discipline because our flesh rebels against the discipline they demand. Rather than confront evil and encourage abstinence we teach our children to protect themselves from sexually transmitted disease with condoms.

We promote the merits of the abomination of the homosexual lifestyle and think we are doing the right thing to teach our children that homosexuality is good and an acceptable lifestyle. We have outright rejected God's assessment of homosexuality. We have brainwashed our people to accept sin and perversion as normal and, in fact, a right somehow guaranteed by our constitution.

We reject the concept of right and wrong, good and bad or yes and no. Our courts have adopted and forced upon society a politically correct philosophy of utter deceit. The courts find themselves continually engaged in the process of attempting to protect those who sell perversion and pornography holding firm to the foolish judgment that it was the intention of the founders that the First Amendment protect them.

Ironically, at the same time the same courts move aggressively to remove the expression of our faith from public arena. This movement by the courts is clearly contrary to our constitutional guarantee to the free public expression of our faith. The court justifies their position by saying that the admonition to not make laws that prohibit the free expression of faith applies to the congress and not the judiciary. Crazy? I expect the founders wanted to protect the peoples right to publicly express their faith since that is what they declared!

We live in a culture and are governed by a spiritually blind court that will not tolerate God but protects evil and perversion.

Only a Spiritually blind man cannot recognize that America is beginning to reap the harvest of the Spiritual neglect, rebellion and indifference of spiritually blind people. I can only suggest that it is now time to turn humbly to our Creator and God in prayer and supplication and ask Him to deliver us and light the way. I believe that God is beginning to bring judgment upon our nation.

With each new generation the truth becomes more hidden and the rich Christian heritage of America's founders and the early settlers is understood, appreciated and known by a smaller segment of our population. The foundational values of our Christian heritage and the Christian faith become more perverted with each generation and we sink deeper into rebellion, worldliness and sin within the organized church.

It is up to all who consider themselves followers of Christ to make the light of our Christian faith to shine as brightly as we can for as long as we can in hopes that some may see and recognize the light and be delivered from the deceit of evil and the grasp of the devil.

One of the most effective diabolic tools used to bring about the onset of deceit is a "luke warm" or watered down religious faith and a sleepy church. Those who are men of faith who do not stay alert and on the cutting edge of God's will soon find themselves becoming molded by their appetites and the ways of the world.

The impact of deceit is gradual and persistent as it works every angle to mold our society into adopting its foolish premise. That premise is that man is naturally good and is his own God. The premise is that the Creator is manufactured out of the mind that is seeking a psychological escape from reality. The premise is that the bible is not the inspired word of God but rather a book presenting the religious views of men throughout history.

The secular humanist attempts to put God in an intellectual box or bottle, like an aspirin, which he can partake of whenever he feels the need to ease his psychological pain. America needs a clear look at its beginnings, a stark look at where it stands today and clear vision of where it is headed if God does not intervene.

The hundreds of social and economic issues that face our nation were not the real issues in the 2004 election. What was and remains at issue is leadership and character! The 2004 Presidential election was in part the response of a people beginning to understand they must begin to elect courageous leaders of faith and integrity with strong moral character that defines who they are and guides them in every decision and action as they face the incredible challenges of leading a confused and rebellious America in an evil and lost world.

I have read many accounts of our Presidents words, life and actions and have concluded that he is a man who recognizes that we are a nation under God with a purpose that goes beyond more prosperity to satisfy our fleshly appetites and lusts. He recognizes we have a mission to our own people and to the world we live in to bring liberty to oppressed peoples and to protect us from the arm of terrorism. Because of his leadership and humility before God our President Bush has been used to do more for the people in Iraq and the Middle East in the past year than all the missionaries throughout the centuries have done.

The church now needs to respond to the call with Christian missionaries who will now have an opportunity to spread the Gospel in Iraq and the surrounding communities. The people of Iraq are witnessing the meaning of bringing salt and light and deliverance. They have been given the opportunity now to experience liberty and deliverance from physical oppression. It remains to be seen how that will effect or impact spiritual deliverance. Spiritual awakening and deliverance is the work of God and His Church. He works His works through individual and corporate lives according to His will. America is but a tool he is using in Iraq and around the world to open the door for millions of people to be delivered. Our people cannot grasp the vision!

Clearly President Bush has proved himself a man of faith. He is a man of character who can be trusted to do what is right because of his faith and that's good enough for me. In fact that's as good as it gets!!!

Most serious minded men of conscience would have to agree that man's calling and ultimate purpose in life is to do our Lord's will, give Him glory by the way we live, to worship Him and to fellowship with him. Knowing and obeying the will of God is as good as it gets in this or any other world. Anyone who rejects that notion is obviously a fool and ought to be rejected outright from any kind of leadership and certainly from national leadership of a Christian nation.

One of the weaknesses of our system of government that has become more apparent over the past 50 years is that the appointment to the Supreme Court of secularist judges allows secular, anti-God, special interest groups to circumvent the vote of the people and even the legislative branch of government. We have failed to challenge the scope of the authority of the judiciary and they have discovered they can in fact legislate by going around the legislative body or the Executive branch to the Supreme Court to force their secular agenda on the nation even when the vast majority of Americans reject outright their agenda. The Court is not accountable to the people. Those on the court have lifetime tenure and it only takes the vote of 5 men on the court to set or change the direction of our nation.

Therefore, America has another problem that is even more pressing than the election of a President. That problem is keeping the judiciary within their jurisdictional boundaries and stopping activist secular federal Judges from attempting to legislate the systematic destruction of our nations values by changing the constitutionally based laws of the land. Five (5) people on the Supreme Court (5 constitutes a majority of the 9 members of the court) can control the direction of our nation regardless of the direction and values the people and/or their legislative representatives desire. The Supreme Court has legally removed from consideration America's historic reliance on the wisdom & will of our Creator and demanded that our laws and code of justice become totally secular and separated from our Christian faith and tradition.

This sounds good to the person who translates that to mean that keeping the legal basis as secular is the only truly objective approach to justice. However, what we must not overlook is that secularism is not a neutral alternative to biblically based principles of justice. Secularism is as anti-God as Satanism! The United States is in a very scary situation because a very few activist Judges, (five Supreme Court Judges) have within their grasp the control of our nation and the lives of millions. They determine the laws that will rule the land. They have created the abortion industry, stopped prayer in school, removed the ten commandments from public institutions, ignored the constitutional protections against government interference in religious expression and ignored the traditional and biblically based values that have historically lead our society.

The court has advanced the porn industry light year's through some foolish, so-called, free speech decisions. These decisions have increased the perversion and crime associated with pornography under the guise of protecting "Freedom of Speech". They have determined totally out of context that in America anyone can say anything anywhere and or dress, undress, publicly perform sex acts or act anyway they choose in public because the court has concluded that they have that right under the constitution. Is this lacking in wisdom? The Supreme Court has done more damage to America than any army could ever do.

These decisions are totally out of the context of the Freedom of Speech amendment to the constitution. Common sense and the historical record dictates that such a conclusion is totally out of context with the intentions of our founders. It lacks wisdom and context and has proven to be utterly destructive given the fallen nature of man. Only a fool, or another pervert, would support the proliferation of pornography or fight to protect the perversion it fosters under the cloak of "freedom of speech" protection.

I grant that developing a legal standard that determines to the satisfaction of a majority of our citizens what is and is not porn might be a challenge in a culture as diverse as ours. No one ever suggested it was easy, however, it is still necessary. Most children have it figured out. Perhaps we need to ask some of them.

What a tragic situation we as a nation have allowed ourselves to fall into!! The thing even more tragic is that neither our people nor our legislative representatives, or our President for that matter, have chosen to fight vigorously to expose and/or defeat those destructive decisions of the court through the impeachment process. The Court has become the God of Government and therefore of America and they have become decidedly secular.

The character and beliefs of those who we appoint to the highest court in the land are vital issues. They cannot be compromised. In fact they are the most important issues to be considered by the President and the Senate Judiciary Committee when they are appointing Supreme Court Judges, or for that matter any Judges. We either judge according to the constitution and the will and way of God or we judge according to the way and will of Satan.

Perspective is intended to reflect my perspective about God, mankind, liberty, the governing process and the nature of the American dream. I have attempted to reveal a glimpse of the danger and destructiveness of the deceit in the hearts of those public leaders who deny Christ and more specifically the deceit in the hearts of those who profess belief in God and in America but live and act and speak in concert with the world.

Perspective finds its foundation and authority from the word of God and my biblically based faith and many years of life experience. It is presented in an attempt to reveal the vivid contrast between the secular humanist perspective that is overtaking our nation and the biblical perspective and there effect on current events, social issues, the church, government, leadership, our judiciary, our legislature and the executive branch of government as well as government at any and every level.

Perspective is dedicated to contrasting the foolishness and destructiveness of the acts and decisions of those in national and local leadership in the government who attempt to lead America without the benefit of God's Spirit, His Word or His wisdom to guide them.

Discussing and presenting a biblical perspective to the many challenges that face the nation, the church, the family and our individual lives is at the heart of **"Perspective"**.

Sincere minded Spiritually reborn Christian patriots must somehow be awakened and begin to present a distinctive in our thoughts, attitudes, actions and words which displays a wisdom and authority of supernatural origin and glory if we hope to ever see the Church (and therefore America) Spiritually revived and returned to her divinely appointed purpose, direction, glory and destiny.

We, as a nation, must somehow re-acquire the vision God gave to those who founded our nation. The Church must re-acquire the vision our Lord had for His Church when he revealed it as the **"fullness of Christ"** in the earth.

Our current President, George W. Bush, is a beacon of hope to Christian patriots and to the governing process, however, the liberal secularists truly hate him with a passion and that hate is polarizing America. It ought not be surprising to men of faith because Jesus declared, **"if they hated me they will hate you also"**. We are witnessing that hate in spades.

The democratic process is giving way to the demands of a government dependent culture whose character is indolent and its focus is pleasure and its appetites. Truth is not an absolute in the secular culture. Our people have adopted government as the golden goose that can provide for them whatever they demand, need or desire. They have discovered they can get what they want by simply voting for it or voting for the candidate that promises them whatever they want in return for their vote. In doing so we have fallen into a terrible trap of government dependence and social entitlement. We are foolishly and deliberately exchanging individual liberty for government dependence.

Liberty is becoming usurped by the oppression of a bureaucratic government. We are heading in that direction "hell bent for destruction" as we drive along the road oblivious to what is happening to us who are wrapped in luxury and our radio's blaring with worldly nonsense so we can escape reality. Our federal and state governments have grown in scope, size and power well outside the limitations of their constitutional role and there is nothing on the horizon that will limit that growth and dependence.

Our capitalistic free enterprise economic system is being systematically replaced by socialistic economic policy. We view the accumulation of capitol as evil rather than the only path to economic deliverance for our society from the grip of poverty. The rich who provide the jobs and the opportunities for the poor are characterized by our society as the enemy. The lazy and indolent are being characterized as the victims of someone else's actions or inactions. The government dependent have been taught that the taxpayer somehow owes them something they have not earned and /or are not willing to work to obtain or achieve.

My generation took our faith and way of life for granted. We dropped our guard and in doing so we sold America out to secular humanism, which was well hidden from view for those who did not have ears to hear or eyes to see. We developed a sense of religious dignity which has sense overtaken the mainline denominational churches which deny the power and authority of God and of our most precious faith.

The generations that have followed adopted a mind mush philosophy of life that litigates against the role of accountability, responsibility, discipline, faith and moral courage. They have considered holiness as bigotry and justice as arbitrary. This utter nonsense has destroyed our public school system, our children, our justice system, our family values, liberty, free enterprise and constitutional government. It has relegated our faith to superstition, our bible to a fairytale and our faith to secular humanism.

The culture that has evolved has adopted a secular humanist religious view to lead us which has removed God and ultimate truth, as defined biblically, from the education process, from government and from the public arena and from public discourse. This secular culture considers the Christian community as enemies of the state. Christians have been labeled as bigots and radicals whose ideas are so dangerous they must be isolated from public debate, the political and the governing process for the good of the nation.

In abandoning the faith of our fathers we have removed Godly character as the true measure of a man. Instead we have chosen to define and recognize man's worth and measure in America in terms of financial success, academic achievement, social status, popularity and physical beauty. In our collective lust for worldly things and sexual expression our pleasures and materialism have become our God and ourselves have become our principle focus.

To keep our make-believe economy growing and to maintain our materialistic lifestyle we must continue to promote a continual increase in public, corporate and individual debt. It appeals to us because it is impossible to afford our lusts or to finance them on a cash basis. The more we have the more we must have! It is impossible to earn enough to finance the fulfillment of our lusts and appetite's, therefore; we must borrow against our future earning power.

Just as the biblical parable has warned, we are indeed building our house of straw upon the sand and signs of an impending storm are beginning to appear! We will surely reap the result of the foolishness we have sown. In our incredible deceit we do not see our problems and we remain astonished at the prospect of ever experiencing national collapse. It is inevitable unless we dramatically reduce the size and scope of government and accept the responsibility for disciplining or paying the price for our individual and collective appetites.

I am asking you to invest the time to read and consider the *perspective* presented herein, test the spirit in which it is written, and take up the cause to actively help preserve the faith, truth and our liberty which offer's our people the best hope.

Join me in this vital struggle to reveal biblical truth and wisdom. I urge you to become aware, proclaim and courageously defend it at every opportunity, insist upon its guiding principle and Spirit in the public arena and, last but not least, work diligently to convince our people that we must humble ourselves under the mighty and merciful hand of our sovereign God whose way will prevail and whose truth will ultimately judge us.

If we do not chose to follow after the law of the Creator who and what law are we going to chose to follow? What star are you prepared to hang your life and ultimate destiny on? The Lord has said, **"You either gather with me or scatter against Me".** There is no middle ground. We either follow the will and Spirit of the Lord or we will destroy ourselves and many influenced by our example and leadership.

Perspective is a compilation of my faith, experience, hopes and whatever wisdom God may have given me through the study of His Word and the prompting of His Spirit. It reveals what I believe and therefore defines who I am and what I believe about life and the issues that surround it as well as the issues and ideas that guide or sometimes misguide our nation.

PERSPECTIVE

A
Book
By
Charles D. Gaines

Ephesians 2:10
*"For we are His workmanship,
created in Christ Jesus for good works,
which God prepared beforehand,
that we should walk in them."*

SECTION I

BIRTH WITH DIVINE PURPOSE

—ᏔᏔ—

CHAPTER ONE

A GREAT BEGINNING

—ᴍ—

*"I am the Lord, I have called you in righteousness,
I will also hold you by the hand and watch over you, and I will appoint you as
a covenant to the people, as a light to the nations" (Isaiah 42:6)*

At the time this Old Testament Scripture was written to God's chosen people, Israel, it was obviously not intended to suggest the distinctive purpose and vision our Lord had in mind for the American nation, which would come along several hundred years later. However, history, hindsight and the Spiritual discernment to perceive the unveiling of His plan provides the vista from which we clearly see His workings through His people to capture prophetically the mandate God had in mind for America.

Columbus died in 1506 never really understanding what he had discovered. Nevertheless he spoke great tales about the lands he had visited and the riches available for the taking. The stories of Columbus mission and the experiences of his crew captured the imagination of Europe. They were welcome stories to a Spiritually void world. The dark ages had ended during the fourteenth century and the plague had run its course wiping out almost one-third of Europe's population.

Europe was ready for a new hope and welcomed a time of Spiritual awakening, economic growth and prosperity. Europe had begun to experience a measure of economic growth because of the opening of some trade routes to the African coast and there was a revival of the Arts that had laid dormant for several hundred years. However, the new world offered great potential for not only trade but for new land acquisition and expansion.

The Monarchy's of Europe and the Papacy became increasingly restless at the potential of gaining riches and power. They recognized they must expand trade and land holdings to build new nations if they were going to enjoy new power and riches. There was a division causing war and land disputes between the various monarchs' of Europe and between the monarch's and the Church.

The people of Europe were seeing cultural changes come they did not approve of and they were experiencing both government and religious oppression. Old Med-evil Europe wanted deliverance from oppression but they did not endorse the cultural change necessary to bring about that change so they fought it. Those who sought and welcomed the change wanted more of it. There arose anti-Church sentiment in this new culture, in part because of a corrupt and oppressive church, which would ultimately lead to bloody conflict that even the Pope could not control.

Those who lived in the port cities of Europe began to enjoy the benefits of and see the opportunities and potential of foreign trade. However, most of Europe still saw the world as the community of nations that surrounded the Mediterranean Sea. The two mighty political forces that divided western Europe were the nobility and the papacy. They struggled continually for dominance over the land and the people who were simply pawns enslaved by the struggle.

Europe was alive with ambition and political and religious unrest. It was without a rudder and was threatened from every side. The people found themselves hopelessly trapped by the political ambitions of the nobility and the papacy. The inordinate taxes levied by the monarchies and the church destroyed any incentive to conduct legitimate business or to be productive. They were slaves of an oppressive religion and of the monarchs. They were forced to survive outside the law and when they were caught they were severely punished and even executed. In the meantime the Turks carefully watched a divided, confused, oppressed and weakened Europe. They saw it as a plumb to be picked.

Italy found themselves endangered by the political ambitions of Kind Ferdinand II of Spain who was also engaged in driving back incursions from Portugal, the papacy and the old Roman Empire. Spain was also actively engaged in expelling the Moors from Granada and the Jews from Spain. The Moors were Muslims who remained in Spain when their ancestors had invaded Spain in the eighth century.

The people throughout Europe were anxious to see who would ultimately become the dominant power in Europe. It seemed to the Mediterranean community of nations that either France or Rome might emerge as the Continent's dominant power. Great Britain and Spain had strong monarchs and they seemed to be prospering, however, they were logistically and physically removed from the center of power in Europe.

The Rome of Caesar and Nero had collapsed, however, the heart of Europe was still dominated and seemed likely to continue to be dominated by the Papacy of Rome and its repressive religious practices. However, Rome had an access problem to central Europe because whatever prosperity was to come to Europe would be dependent upon access to the sea. The road system in Europe was virtually nonexistent. The roads built during the hay-day of the Roman Empire were in ruin.

The populations all across Europe were increasingly becoming slaves to warring monarchs and to a corrupt religious system. They were taxed by the monarchs and by the church beyond their ability to pay. The King could and would confiscate whatever he wanted and the Church was little better. They were slaves and justice was at the whim of the King and/or the church. Self-determination and individual liberty were only unattainable dreams.

As new discoveries were made by exploration and trade routes opened sea trade and travel began to flourish. Great Britain with its access to the sea began to see new and exciting worlds opening up to them on three continents. So did the other monarch's of Europe as did the Church as well, however, their ability to participate lacked focus, organization and adequate seaports. The people were more than ready to throw off med-evil Europe. Exploration and expansion became the excitement and absorbed the energies and activities of the day. Exploration of sea routes to Asia and Africa offered incredible riches and new opportunities. A new trade route to Asia and lands to the west became rumored about Europe who was preoccupied at the moment with a new route around the Cape of Good Hope to Indies and the riches of the East African Coast.

Columbus, an experienced Sea Captain born in Genoa in 1451, made a trip to Iceland in 1477 where he heard great stories of Leif Eriksson's discovery of a land to the west, which he named Vinland. This land was perhaps a part of what we now know as North America. No one knew how far west these lands might be from Vinland and the "flat earth" contingent was not particularly excited about travel much beyond the then known world. Columbus sought counsel from two sources regarding his plan to explore further west. The first was a scientist and theologian Cardinal Daily who believed the earth was round, that its land mass exceeded the volume of its oceans and that the sea to the west was relatively small. He was wrong about the landmass and the size of the sea; however, he was right about the world being round. The second source was a Florentine astronomer and cartographer Paolo Dal Pozzo Toscanelli, who believed the Indies were just a short distance from Europe.

It was commercial concerns and the instinctive desire of the human spirit for liberty from political and religious oppression that determined the course of history. Columbus set about to put together an exploration to the west. He and his associates could not finance the exploration and he recognized that Italy, his native country, did not have the resources to underwrite a major expedition into the unknown world. Therefore, in 1484 he approached King John II of Portugal about funding a voyage west until they hit land or fell off the edge of the world. The King was preoccupied with internal affairs and did not share the vision of Columbus.

So Columbus set out for Spain to meet with Queen Isabella who was anxious to make a foothold in Asia and enjoy the treasures of trade with Asia. At the time Spain was still occupied in a concentrated effort to eject the Moors, nevertheless, the Queen decided to help support the expedition.

An interesting agreement was forged. Isabella of Spain named Columbus Admiral and guaranteed him one-eighth of the profits realized from the venture. Isabella agreed to put up one fourth of the money and the balance would come from several Italian bankers. Queen Isabella would also provide Columbus with three ships. The 60-ton Nina, the 55-ton Pinta, and the 120-ton Santa Maria. In addition the Queen gave Columbus the right to govern any islands or main lands he might discover. The expedition was undertaken under the supposition that its mission was to discover a clear route to the Indies by sailing west. However, Columbus believed the legend that a wealthy land lay somewhere between Europe and Asia and the Queen declared to Columbus that his foremost mission was to convert whatever heathens he might discover in that land to Christianity as Christianity was perceived in 1492.

On August 3, 1492 Columbus and his crew of eighty-seven men departed Palos, Spain and headed for the Canary Islands where they picked up the trade winds and sailed due west. On October 12th he sighted the Bahama Islands and landed on Watling Island, which he named San Salvador. From there he sailed on to Cuba and then to Haiti where he traded with the natives and persuaded some to return with him to Europe. He called these native inhabitants Indians thinking that he had landed in the Indies.

Columbus returned to Spain in March 1493 with ships logs that reflected that he had reached China and Japan and found great wealth in them. The people of Europe believed his stories and Spain began to legalize their claims in the new world. Pope Alexander VI granted Spain possession of all lands to the south and west not held by other Christians as of Christmas Day, 1492.

Ignoring the rest of the then known world, Spain and Portugal decided in 1494 to divide the potential Spoils. A line of demarcation was struck at the meridian 370 leagues west of the Cape Verde Islands. East of this line everything belonged to Portugal and west of it all discoveries belonged to Spain. This, of course, meant that Spain would get the America's and Portugal would get all of Africa plus the tip of Brazil. Unfortunately Great Britain, France and the Netherlands were not a part of this agreement. They would be heard from later and the wars and treaties between them over the spoils of exploration and exploitation set the stage of the next two and a half centuries

Soon after Columbus discovery wealth from the new lands and from the African coast as well began to pour into Europe. Throughout the Sixteenth century expeditions to the new world flourished. Settlements were established by Spain along the eastern costs of Central and South America. Gold was seized from the native people and sent back to Spain. These adventurers would come to be known as conquistadors (soldiers of fortune) whose principle interest was the gold. Throughout the next century they plundered central and south America and made brief journeys into the South Western regions of North America.

In the meantime Great Britain, France and Italy were making other explorations and discoveries. The Italian Navigator Amerigo Vespucci, from which the America's got their name, journeyed to the mouth of the Amazon in 1499 and proved that South America was not a part of Asia.

In 1513 Balboa crossed the Isthmus of Panama and discovered the Pacific Ocean. At the same time Juan Ponce De Leon sailed north to what we know as Florida where he made the first Spanish landing in North America. Diego Velasquez completed Spain's conquest of Cuba and other Spaniards landed on the west coast of Central and South America.

Explorations continued up both the east and west coasts of central and North America. However, they only moved as far north as Virginia on the eastern coast because the explorers were distracted by a vast Gold discovery in Mexico in 1519. Explorers entered Mexico and overran the Aztec Empire of Montezuma. The Aztec's numbered some five million when Hernando Cortez entered Mexico. Interestingly, they discovered established cities of 100,000 or more. The capitol city of Tenochtitlan was inhabited by 250,000 people making it more than twice the size of any city in Europe at that time. These natives were a superstitious people who perceived Cortez as some sort of God to which they must yield whatever resources they might have. At any rate Cortez ravaged this advanced civilization. His excursions made Spain the wealthiest nation in Europe, therefore Spain continued to concentrate her explorations in central, south America and what we now know as Mexico.

North America and the Orient were left by Spain to explorers from Britain, France, Portugal and the Netherlands. It must be noted however that before abandoning North America the Spaniards made some significant incursions into North America. Narvaez landed in Florida and began his quest for a fabled city of Apalache, which legend held to be a city of vast riches. He pressed on as far as the gulf of California. Virtually all his party was lost except four men who returned to Mexico in 1536 full of stories of vast prairies, gold and vast wealth. These stories reached another explorer, Hernando de Soto a Spanish conquistador who obtained a patent to establish a colony in Florida. He arrived in Tampa Bay in 1539. He eventually pressed north through the Carolinas to the Mississippi River to what is now Tennessee. He then moved on to what we now know as Arkansas and Oklahoma. He died in 1542 but his expeditionary force moved on.

An exploration into North America was attempted by Francisco Coronado, the Governor of the Spanish province of New Galicia, who set out in search of the mystical city of Cibola and its supposed seven cities of gold. He set out from North-west Mexico in 1540 and headed into the Southwestern part of North America exploring what we now know as Texas and New Mexico and then turned east into Kansas. He returned to Mexico in 1543 failing to find the mystical city or the gold, however, he had considerable insight and information about the interior of the Southwestern part of North America. Spain continued her explorations into South America making her the dominant power throughout Central and South America.

In the meantime most of central Europe was embroiled in religious conflicts. Martin Luther, a professor of divinity, nailed his ninety-five page theses to the door of the court church of Wittenberg, Germany. His note on the door of the church put Christ and His Word on the throne which shook the foundations of Christendom in Europe and shaped the nature and character of the kind of Christendom that would be introduced into the new world. The Catholic and the Anglican church would have a definite presence in the new world, however, the predominant religious movement would be protestant and led by followers of Christ rather than followers of the Pope or of church doctrine. Meanwhile the Monarch's of Europe struggled with internal affairs and the Church pursued their endless religious wars between the Papacy and Protestantism.

By 1570 England, France and the Netherlands had begun to take a serious interest in the New World potential. They were willing and anxious to make a financial commitment to its exploration and exploitation. France was financially the largest and strongest of the three nations. The Netherlands needed room to expand and was better positioned financially than England, which had neither the natural resources, the industrial base or the banking power of the Dutch.

While Spain had plundered two continents France had been pre-occupied battling with the Holy Roman Empire at home. Some interesting things were happening in Britain that occupied the mind and heart of her monarch King Henry VIII who was in trouble with the church over the issue of divorce. In order to justify a divorce and remarriage, he took full advantage of the protestant reformation. He instituted some radical religious policies that antagonized Catholics and Protestants alike. Henry died in 1547 and was succeeded by his nine-year-old son Edward VI who died six years later.

His elder and devoted Catholic Mary prevailed in an attempt by the protestant church to take over the throne. She became queen and became married to King Philip of Spain. Mary died in 1558 and was succeeded by her younger sister Elizabeth who reigned for some 45 years. She turned Britain into the economic superpower not only of Europe but of the world.

Elizabeth was a capitalist. She allowed private companies to be formed for the express purpose of exploration finding not only gold, but opportunity for investors and for Britain to expand its hold on new lands with natural resources. The early explorations by Britain turned up little, however, she finally sponsored some expeditions to North America by Sir Walter Raleigh. He sold the queen on the idea that he would find passage to the Orient and open its markets. He also declared that he would provide access to the stores of gold and natural resources North America had for the taking.

In 1585, Sir Walter Raleigh landed on the shores of what we know as North Carolina from where he returned and reported to the queen of the vast riches he had discovered. She sent him back to establish a colony at Roanoke, Virginia, which was named after Elizabeth, the virgin queen. Unfortunately, this new colony ended in disaster due to poor leadership and under-funding. The project was larger and more complex than he had anticipated. However, his efforts whet the interest of Britain in the potential of the new world and soon the Queen in consort with private investors joined together to form company's that would explore the new world and establish colonies wherever possible.

Other countries (Spain, France and the Netherlands primarily) took notice and decided they must participate in the bounty to be gained from exploration of the new world. It was just a matter of time until these nations came to blows over which lands and which bounty was theirs. Britain's newly found might and wealth proved too much for Spain and France. Queen Elizabeth's fleet destroyed the Spanish Armada, which abruptly ended a century of rule over a large part of the new world by Spain. Six years later France under King Henry IV became unified and powerful enough to make its presence known in the old and the new world and the clash between the two powers, Great Britain and France began and lasted almost two centuries.

However, it was not England's powerful navy that brought her the upper hand in establishing successful settlements in America and around the world. It was the power of free enterprise working itself out through the trading companies who worked in partnership with the nobility of Great Britain.

As early as 1555 the Muscovite trading Company began to establish settlements in North America. The Levant trading Company had established a monopoly on trade with Turkey and the Barbary trading Company held a charter for North Africa. In 1588 Queen Elizabeth bestowed the rights to American trade to the Guinea trading Company. In 1600 the East India Trading Company was formed and was granted a fifteen-year monopoly on British trade with countries between the Cape of Good Hope at the southern tip of Africa and the Strait of Magellan between Tierra del Fuego and the South American mainland.

By 1610 the East India Company had expanded to nineteen facilities at settlements around three continents shipping exotic spices and fabrics. They searched desperately for a northwest passage to the Indies, which they did not find, however, what they did find was that the North American Coastline was suitable for agriculture and therefore colonization.

What on the surface appeared to be failure to find the passage to the Indies turned out to be the best thing that could have happened for Great Britain. They decided to settle for establishing settlements in North America, which ultimately proved to be far more profitable than gold and tea from China. They set out to populate and develop the potential of the New World. So in 1606, Britain's King James I (who succeeded Queen Elizabeth) issued settlement charters to two groups of merchants whose capitalist tendencies would ultimately give birth to a nation. The first of these Trading Companies was the Virginia Company of Plymouth who received the rights to explore, settle and exploit what became known as New England. The second Trading Company was the Virginia Company of London, which was granted rights to the south of New England. The Virginia Company of London settled Jamestown, which became a disaster under the leadership of Sir Thomas Smythe, however, Great Britain was not discouraged and sent Captain John Smith to take command.

Captain Smith whipped the Jamestown colonists into an enthusiastic force and set about negotiating fruitful agreements with the Indian tribes of the region. In time he established several colonies. The secret to his success was owed largely to the colonies embrace of the principals of capitalism. Rather than allowing the colonists to draw their sustenance from the common stores he insisted that they work and produce and each receive his share in direct proportion to his production. By the summer of 1609 Jamestown had grown into a thriving community of farmers living off the land and trading with the natives. In 1612, Virginia found a cash crop in tobacco and by 1620 they were exporting 40,000 lbs of cured tobacco leaves a year.

It was indeed the tobacco leaf that would provide the economic base of what would ultimately become the United States of America. However, it also introduced plantation slavery to help with the backbreaking work involved in cultivating tobacco. In 1619 a Dutch ship landed at Jamestown and unloaded the first load of 20 black Africans to work in the tobacco fields of the New World.

The Plymouth Company landed in 1607 in Maine and established its first settlement. It came upon hard times as well. By 1620 the Plymouth Company and its settlement was in shambles. The Company continued in an attempt to recruit new settlers. They finally found an eager group of religious dissenters from East Anglia who referred to themselves as pilgrims who had relocated themselves in the Netherlands to escape persecution for their beliefs. They were Protestant Separatists of humble backgrounds who had given up Anglican worship in the mid to late 1500's because they recognized the corruptness of the Church was beyond reform. **They were followers of Christ** who met secretly and when caught were fined, imprisoned and even executed, which prompted their flight to the Netherlands and ultimately to the new world and the religious freedom it provided them. They were decidedly English and wanted their families to grow up as Englishmen and they jumped at the opportunity to go to the new world and establish a British Colony there. The Virginia Company offered them stock in the exploration Company if they would join them in settling the New World.

So fate and the winds of the north Atlantic landed them (not in Virginia) in Cape Cod aboard the Mayflower in 1620. They established a small community they called Plymouth after the name of their point of departure from Britain. The Mayflower remained in port for the winter as protection from the elements for the pilgrims. Many died and more came the following year. It was indeed a struggle to survive, however, Plymouth survived and succeeded ultimately because of the nature of the pilgrims who eagerly established friendly relations with the regions native Americans who introduced them to new crops such as corn. At any rate Plymouth continued to grow strong and new settlements begin to spring up throughout the region.

In 1628 the Puritans established a colony in the new world and the Massachusetts Bay Company was formed in England and new loads of Puritans soon arrived in New England. **The first governor of the Massachusetts Bay Company was a smart young lawyer John Winthrop. He declared the driving vision of the colonists; "We shall be as a city**

on a hill. The eyes of the people are upon us, and so the eyes of the world were indeed on them.

They had little use for royalty and soon begin to revise their charter and reorganize themselves into a more democratic constitution for governing the colony. It provided for the governor and his assistants to be elected annually by the stockholders (each colonist was a stockholder of the company) at a general meeting. **Every adult male church member had a vote. They were virtually all members of the church. Unless they were members of the church they had no voice in government**. They set up courts, passed laws, levied taxes and established a militia. By 1634 each town in the Massachusetts Bay Colony elected representatives to the general assembly, which was the first step in establishing what would become known as a bicameral legislature little more than a decade later.

Despite the aristocracy of the leaders of the British colonies self-governance and individual liberty characterized most of the ensuing British colonies founded through royal charters. Lord Baltimore settled Maryland in 1634 as a refuge for British Catholics who faced persecution at home. A group of English nobles formed an expedition to settle the Carolinas in 1663. James, Duke of York, took control of an area seized by the English from the Dutch in 1664 and named it New York in honor of himself. He granted 5 million acres to his friends Lord John Berkeley and Sir George Carteret on which they founded what we now know as New Jersey. They were capitalists in that they offered settlers land, religious freedom and a democratic assembly in exchange for a small fee.

Another colonial founder was William Penn a proselytizing Quaker. Charles II, 1681, in payment of a debt owed to Penn's father granted him East Jersey where he could join the rest of the Quaker contingent of settlers. In 1682 the state of Delaware was added to his company grant. What became Pennsylvania proved to be a great economic and social success attracting not only Quakers but by 1700 some 21,000 Catholics, Lutherans, Baptists, Presbyterians and a few Anglicans who were willing to work together for the common good. The common doctrine they all subscribed to was the belief that the Native Americans rightfully owned the lands in the region. This made for an enduring peace for the settlers.

The hand of God and the inalienable rights of human liberty and self determination was the force inspiring and moving prominently in the New World in very tangible ways. The writings and rhetoric of the day declared it to be the way of the future of the new world. In 1682 William Penn's "Frame of Government" guaranteed freedom of religion and civil liberties for every citizen. It created a representative assembly and a system for the fair distribution of good land to new arrivals. One of its tenets stated **"Any government is free to the people under it where the laws rule and the people are a party to the laws."** Penn described these settlements in this way; **"Our wilderness flourishes as a Garden."**

The Colonial empire spread up and down the coast, however, Britain began to face strong competition from the Dutch. The Dutch pursued the establishment of new colonies in the new world and evolved into a world power during the seventeenth century by establishing colonies in the America's and, in concert with the Portuguese, opened Japan to trading with Europe. The Dutch East India Company formed in 1602 established a monopoly on Oriental trade. It became a mighty trading company that made it the best performer on the Amsterdam Stock Exchange. Other Dutch trading company's such as the "New Netherlands Company" which was awarded by the Dutch government grants that gave it a monopoly on commerce in the Americas.

Eight years later the Dutch West India Company was formed and took over the New Netherlands Company and was given a charter to establish colonies and conduct trade in the America's and on the west coast of Africa below the tropic of Cancer. The new company grew rapidly expanding out across the Western Hemisphere. They established the small colony of New Amsterdam in the New York Harbor and other colonies up the Hudson River, in New Jersey, in South America and throughout the Caribbean. The Dutch began to dramatically cut into British trade in the New World. In addition, the Netherlands was able to gain advantage because Great Britain was involved in a civil war. As a result of the war the monarchy fell in 1648 to the forces of Oliver Cromwell, who had King Charles I beheaded. Cromwell established his Puritan government, which ruled until 1660, two years after Cromwell's death.

Before the advent of Cromwell's takeover, the northernmost British colonies in the new world had united into the New England Confederation for the purpose of halting Dutch expansion in the new world beyond New Amsterdam and the Hudson Valley. They were successful until the British became pre-occupied with its civil war. The Dutch moved in and began to take over British markets. The Monarchy was restored in 1660; however, by 1688 the parliamentary leaders could no longer tolerate the Monarchy of King James II primarily because of his open Catholicism. They removed him and invited his Protestant daughter Mary and her husband, Dutch ruler William of Orange, to take joint command of the British throne. This began the bloody removal of monarchs.

Seeds were being planted in the new world that would change the face of government and plant the seeds of the American Revolution. It was John Locke's **"Two Treatises of Government"**, which denied the divine right of Kings. He set forth his model of government, in which citizens would have the right to overthrow rulers who violated their natural (divine) rights to life, liberty, and property.

Its interesting to watch the fundamentals of our constitution being formed in the governments, lives, minds and hearts of the colonists more than a century before the nation of the United States of America would come forth.

The British colonists had begun to take exception to Britain's micro-management, taxation and unreasonable control over their commerce. They became more and more inspired by the exposure of the myth of the **"divine right of Kings"** prominent in the old world. Exports from the colonies of wool, yarn, cloth, paper and iron were stopped and became forbidden to the colonies by mother England. By 1700 the colonies were operating at a huge trade deficit. By 1760 that deficit became an average of $5,000,000.00 per year, which was huge in 1760.

In 1733 Britain had imposed a duty of twelve cents per gallon on molasses. It was a tariff put in place to end the trade between the colonies and the non-British counterparts in the West Indies. Rather than comply the colonies reverted to smuggling.

From the moment the first English colony was established in New England in 1620 there was a general recognition among people throughout the world that this new land and its people were planted there by divine appointment with a divine purpose. They were driven by the search for human liberty, a new religious freedom, passion and zeal having discovered, due to the bold proclamation of Martin Luther, that God's grace and not men's religious works brought men into the kingdom and that the keys to the kingdom of God was based on relationship to him and not on works for the religious cause. This new religious doctrine smacked of liberty and the right given to God's creatures to choose their destiny. These pilgrims, settlers and colonists in the northeast were, in large part, Quakers and Protestant followers of Christ rather than members of a particular sect or denomination.

This new Christianity with its freedom from religious oppression and persecution was turning the world upside down. It brought the hope of liberty and deliverance, which was imbedded in the heart of every man, to this world. There was now such a place in the World where followers of Christ could live and experience liberty from religious and political oppression where they could make a new start. This new world became recognized as the promised land for men who loved liberty.

America was an escape from the old world, its Kings and the religious intolerance of a corrupt Church. This new world became the land of and for the gentile believers much like the land in the middle-east biblically defined and historically viewed by Christians and Jews as the land God promised to the Jewish people as their home.

However, all was not well in this new world. The Netherlands was moving aggressively to colonize and take over the markets established by Great Britain in the new world. The colonists were flagrantly ignoring the navigation and tariff acts. Neither Parliament nor the crown did anything about it early on because they deemed the crackdown and discipline of these unruly and rebellious misfits, who migrated to this new world, would bring more trouble than it was worth and it would stir up a struggle between the colonies of Great Britain, the Netherlands and the French. However, as the trade with the new world became more promising and profitable, particularly with the incredible increase in the fishing and whaling industry, they could no longer ignore the rebellion against the tariff acts.

Britain and the Netherlands continued to establish colonies along North America's eastern seaboard from Maine to Georgia. France founded settlements in eastern Canada and from there settlers began to expand south into the Mississippi Valley. Relations between the colonists from each of these three nations were tense and often erupted into battles over fur trading and fishing rights.

In the meantime a coalition created by Great Britain, Austria, Spain, Holland, Sweden and Germany in 1688 attempted to stem the tide of Frances expansion under Louis XIV. It was called the League of Augsburg. It did not work and it was disbanded in 1697. Skirmishes erupted in India and Africa. In America skirmishes broke out between British and French colonists forcing Great Britain to dispatch a task force of troops to its northern settlements to help them fight the French. The French sent troops to Canada to mount an expedition to the south.

In the meantime there was a war in Europe, which finally ended in 1697 with the treaty of Ryswick, under which France agreed to recognize Queen Mary's husband, William of Orange, as king of England. France also agreed to abandon its claims to the Rhineland in central Europe, negotiate a favorable trade pact with the Netherlands, and allow the Dutch to install garrisons in the Spanish Netherlands to protect them from potential French attack's.

This treaty had an impact in America because of the effect of the constant confrontations between the French and English colonists. It brought about the declaration of a status quo among the colonies of the Northeast. However, the treaty provisions were not acceptable to the British Colonists. The Colonists saw the cavalier attitude of the Crown in regards to the need to protect the colonist's interests in the new world to be intolerable. Wars continued to erupt in Europe despite the treaty. Battles also erupted once again in the colonies. The French continued to push down the Mississippi establishing settlements and being confronted by British Colonists that had pushed that far west. The British continued to move from Pennsylvania and Virginia into the Ohio Valley increasing the contacts and conflicts with the French.

By 1754 the British colonies decided they must become united in their desire and cause to remove the French, who early that year had taken the fork of the Ohio River, where they built the formidable Fort Duquesne, near the present day city of Pittsburgh.

The French intrusion was intolerable to the British and Governor Robert Dinwiddie of Virginia sent three hundred troops to the area under the command of a twenty-one-year old lieutenant colonel George Washington. This excursion began what would become known as the French and Indian war. The effort failed however, which made way for the French occupation and domination of the region.

The war and unrest in the colonies spread to Europe. In 1755, General Edward Braddock was dispatched to the Virginia colony to take command of the British forces in America. He was killed in an attempt to retake Fort Duquesne. In Europe this began a protracted conflict what became known simply as the Seven Years War, which lasted from 1756 to 1763.

Early on the French made great gains in the colonies primarily because the colonists could not depend on Great Britain to protect their interests and because they would not unite in the battle. They chose to only engage the battle when their own colony or settlement was threatened.

However, in 1757 when William Pitt became England's Prime Minister he had a broader vision of the potential of British holdings in the new world and concentrated Britain's military and naval forces and efforts on the problems in the colonies. The tide began to change in the colonies and the French began to be defeated at every turn. General James Wolfe captured Quebec and in 1760 Canada fell to Britain's General Jeffrey Amherst. In the meantime, the colonial forces under the command of Robert Rogers took Detroit and all other French territories in the Great Lakes region.

France sued for peace in 1763, which ended both America's French and Indian war and the Seven Years War in the treaty of Paris. Under this treaty Britain took possession of all of France's American possessions except the West Indies and a few small Islands. Unfortunately, the French and Indian war continued in the Mississippi Valley under the leadership of the Ottawa tribe's chief Pontiac.

Once the common foes of Britain and the Colonies were defeated the interests of the colonies, which were independent of the Crown began to draw them apart planting the seeds that would lead to the revolution. The colonists had considered themselves to be British even though they had planted themselves in a new setting. The foundational culture, moral, religious and political beliefs of the old country were still evident in the new world, however, over two centuries the colonists had become Americans having created their own culture and a love for independence and freedom.

The separation between the new world and the old was inevitable because the colonists were no longer a part of the society or the culture of the old world. They had become hard working adventurers who dared to take a chance on finding liberty and opportunity in an unknown world. They had done the work and made the sacrifices to build America and they were not about to give it up to greedy aristocrats who considered the colonists and the colonies as their property.

The reliance on faith in God, the demand for bravery, the sacrifice and the adjustments necessary to build a new world had transformed this people into an entirely new Western civilization distinct in character and set apart from their ancestral Europe.

There were minor differences between the colonies, however, this new society had faced and adapted to circumstances together under the guiding Spirit of God which matured them and left them with far more in common than they had in common with the old world. **Their belief in Jesus Christ, in limited government, common law and free enterprise were the fundamentals upon which they had built a new culture and out of which would evolve a new nation.**

America, while civilizing rapidly, was still largely a wild and untamed place. It had British roots but the tree trunk and its various branches were distinctly American. However, many of the new world Americans were well educated and well read in philosophy. However, the few colonies built around the utopian fairyland of academia without experience so prevalent in the old world were soon to fail.

Americans were looking for education that produced something. Experience in the new world had taught them that the colonies that succeeded were built by those colonists who had embraced the challenge and survived the physical and psychological impact of the ocean voyage and the environment and the practical circumstances they had to deal with in the new world. Education was important in America; however, American intellectuals were far more mature and down to earth than their European counterparts. A strong faith, good ideas built on biblical truth and justice, common sense, proven integrity and a willingness to be held accountable would bring men into a leadership positions in the new world. In the old world leaders were, for the most part, products of academic theories applied without experience or accountability, which seldom worked in their attempts at application in the real world.

American leaders and intellectuals avoided advocating broad progress or sweeping reforms because societies move slowly and reforms without foundation often do not prove out. Besides that, reforms among the small colonies would be put to the test almost immediately before the promoter of the reform or idea had time to run and hide from the result. There was almost immediate accountability, which tends to force leaders to act wisely and be very careful about what they say and the decisions they make. The truth was important and sought after. They had observed the old world's philosophies, and for the most part, determined and rejected the ones, which had proven not to work.

America wanted the economic security of living under the guidance of the crown; however, they did not want the discipline and accountability it demanded. In 1763 Britain recognized that it was necessary to teach these young misfits a lesson in economics. They were not carrying their part of the financial load of protecting and providing for the treaties and agreements made with the native Americans by the leaders of the various colonies. Chief Pontiac, of the Ottawa Indian tribe, was accused by the settlers of attempting to drive them east of the Appalachian Mountains. The British board of trade proposed what became the Proclamation of 1763, which decreed that the Indians would be allowed to keep the region beyond the line of the Appalachian mountains and that white settlers would not be allowed to cross into that region.

The colonists ignored the order and began migrating into the Ohio Valley. Angered by this defiance, the British Prime Minister Greenville saw fit to order British vessels into American waters in search of smugglers. When they discovered smugglers they chose to punish them through courts they established in America. The verdicts were rendered by royally appointed magistrates rather than colonial juries. Often these smugglers were from the colonies and were treated harshly and unfairly by the magistrates.

Britain also instituted new duties (tariff's) on a broad range of products and they forbade colonists from issuing money. That was the straw that broke the camels back so far as the colonists were concerned. Men like Samuel Adams began to appear on the scene with strong complaints and declarations that their regions (colonies) would not tolerate such treatment. By 1764 the complaints and threats of the colonists became so strong that English Parliamentary support for the colonists began to grow. The support of English citizens in Europe for the colonists began to grow also because of the English companies that had trade interests in America and did not want those interests disrupted.

The Prime Minister of England ignored the complaints however and in 1765 instituted the stamp act which levied a tax in the colonies in the form of stamps that had to be purchased and affixed to newspapers, legal documents, marriage certificates, diplomas etc. The protests were not as severe in the colonies as was expected. This prompted concerned, alert and wiser men like Benjamin Franklin to warn the colonists *"They who give up essential liberty to obtain a little temporary safety deserve neither liberty nor safety."*

Patrick Henry, a young lawyer, also rose to the occasion and evolved as spokesman for the colonies farmers against the stamp act. He spoke to Virginia's house of Burgesses that this act violated the colonist's rights as Englishmen. Henry made a passion filled speech in which he said, *"Caesar had his Brutus; Charles I his Cromwell, and George III may profit by their example."* When a few British loyalists shouted that his words were treason, Henry responded, *"If this be treason, make the most of it".* English newspapers carried the full content of Henry's speech angering the crown and the Prime Minister.

Nevertheless, representatives from nine of the colonies were fired up by Henry's eloquent words and convened the Stamp Act Congress to fight the stamp act legislation. Talk of revolution arose at the very first session of the congress and a group evolved called the sons of liberty whose purpose was to discourage and harass the distributors of stamps. Pennsylvania representative John Dickinson summed up the prevailing mood of the congress when he presented a series of declarations, which denied the British Parliament the right to impose taxes on the American colonies. The arguments of many were far more radical, however in the end Dickinson's resolutions won the day.

In the wake of colonial trade legislation the value of England's exports to America had fallen from 1764 to 1765 prompting members of Parliament from thirty British constituencies to call for immediate repeal of the Stamp Act. After much debate the King acquiesced and the stamp act was repealed with the condition that England would have the right henceforth to levy taxes. This would all lead to the eventual replacement of the new Prime Minister with a new Prime Minister, William Pitt who was a strong supporter of the colonists. Unfortunately, the colonists saw all this as a weakness rather than an act of conciliation on the part of England.

Soon William Pitt was replaced by another Prime Minister Charles Townsend who was committed to forcing the colonies to pay their fair share of the costs of the empire. He took control of the American economy and levied taxes on imports of tea, paper, paint and glass to finance the salaries of civil servants stationed in America to look after British interests. Despite the opposition of parliament and the colonies Townsend's program became law in

1767 and a Board of commissioners of the Customs was established charged with enforcement and collection. They were also empowered to try cases without the benefit of juries. This inflamed the colonists and the talk of rebellion became more prominent.

The British Government was angered by the intransigence of the colonies and installed a new secretary of state for the colonies, Lord Hillsborough, who denounced the Americans as treasonous conspirators and he dispatched troops to Boston.

At the time Benjamin Franklin was living in London as colonial representative to Great Britain. He called this move as "perverse and senseless". This move goaded Boston to put further restrictions on British imports. This new boycott by the colonies of British imports proved to be effective. British frustration spilled over in June 1768 when the HMS Romney attempted to seize within the port of Boston, the Liberty, an American ship used by Boston merchant John Hancock in his smuggling operations in the West Indies. The residents of Boston responded by rioting and beating custom officials. This prompted Lord Hillsborough to send two more regiments of British troops to Boston to help keep the peace.

All of this came to a head when it was revealed in 1769 that all of Townsend's tariff's had returned only 3,500 lbs to England while the trade boycott had cost England 7,300,000.00 lbs. A new Prime Minister was appointed in 1770 and Townsend's program was repealed.

However, a group of citizens who did not recognize England's move to remove the tariffs as a move toward reconciliation attacked the Boston courthouse. British soldiers, goaded beyond endurance, began to fire killing five people and wounding several others. This became known as the Boston Massacre and it was the first blood shed of the American Revolution.

The rebellious attitude that had spread throughout the colonies was somewhat defused when knowledge of Great Britain's conciliatory actions prompted by Lord North became known. Therefore, in 1770 Boston's merchants lifted the trade boycott on British imports. England's East India Company was on the verge of insolvency, however, its London warehouse held more than 17million pounds of tea. If these stores of tea could be sold the company could survive. Lord North concocted a plan to sell the tea in America at lower prices than those offered by smugglers like Hancock who brought the goods in from Dutch possessions in the West Indies. The plan failed, however, because the Sons of Liberty were convinced that Lord North's plan was a subterfuge. Therefore, on December 16, 1773 Hancock and Sam Adams directed a group of Sons of Liberty disguised as Indians to board the British tea ships in Boston Harbor and dump their cargo overboard. The British were so outraged they closed the port of Boston until the colonists would agree to pay for the lost tea. The colonists refused and the bill was never paid!

The very next month, Lord North introduced the Massachusetts Government Act to suspend the colony's legislature, which became law in May of that year. He also introduced a new Quartering Act as well as the Administration of Justice Act, which provided for trials in Britain of any colonial officials accused of capital crimes.

The colonial protests caused a firestorm out of which emerged a brilliant young planta-tion owner, Thomas Jefferson, who published his "Summary View of the Rights of British America" which took issue with the English Parliaments right to legislate colonial matter on the grounds that *"The God who gave us life, gave us liberty at the same time."*

On September 5, 1773 representatives from every American colony except Georgia met in Philadelphia at what became known as the first Continental Congress. Radical members called for trade embargoes while more moderate members, like John Jay of New York and Joseph Galloway of Pennsylvania supported a strongly worded protest. All agreed that some significant action had to be taken.

Joseph Warren of Massachusetts introduced the idea of the creation of revolutionary colonial government. The resolution passed. Next he put forth the idea of forming a Union between Great Britain and the Colonies, under which each American colony would control its internal affairs but would accept England's rule in all other matters. It was defeated by one vote and the Congress resolved that they would accept the Declaration of Rights and resolves that conceded British rule but asserted American rights including Locke's right to "Life, Liberty and Property" as well as the right to self government on internal matters and taxation.

King George was infuriated and declared that blows would be required to decide whether America was a subject or was independent. The British commander in Boston, General Thomas Gage, was ordered to strike a blow at the rebel colonists. Gage learned their whereabouts and sent troops to seize them.

It was that very night that Boston Silversmith, Paul Revere rode the twenty miles to Lexington to warn the leaders and everyone along the way that the British were coming. When the British troops reached the town on April 19, 1775 they encountered an armed force of seventy, some of them "minute men", a local militia formed by an act of the provincial congress the previous year to be ready to fight on a minute's notice.

The tensions were high and tempers short on both sides, but it was the British troops who were advancing to form a battle line when a shot rang out. No one knows to this day whether it was from a British or colonial musket. At the time neither side realized this was the first fired in the American Revolution. It was followed by volleys of bullets that killed eight and wounded ten Minutemen before the British marched on to Concord and burned the few supplies the Americans had left there. On their way back to Boston the British faced local farmers who were organized into an army that outnumbered the British 5 to 1 and shot at them from every house, barn and tree on the way. By nightfall the casualties numbered 93 colonists and 273 British soldiers. Sam Adams exclaimed to John Hancock, "What a glorious morning for America".

The next few weeks were filled with confusion as to what had taken place and its implications. Some considered that a few radicals had taken control of the Massachusetts government and entered on their own into a war with Britain. In essence, that was true, however, this group was not a rag tag group. They consisted of a well-organized and trained group of 10,000 troops and the number grew rapidly.

On the heals of this action, Massachusetts dispatched a young Connecticut officer Benedict Arnold to attack and capture Fort Ticonderoga on New York's Lake Champlain. At the same time the Connecticut leaders sent Ethan Allen and his militia of "Green Mountain Boys" on similar missions.

The Massachusetts Government dispatched its delegates to the Second Continental Congress, in hopes of finding enough common ground with its fellow colonials to convince them to join in the rebellion against the British. They met in Philadelphia on May 10. 1775 on the same day Arnold and Allen captured Fort Ticonderoga. **John Adams of Massachusetts called for a Declaration of Independence"** at the meeting.

The movement required leadership! John Adams set out to find someone who could symbolize American Unity, Heritage and tradition and was competent to lead. He found just such a man in George Washington, whose service in the Seven Years War had made him one of the most experienced military officers in the colonies and whose tenure in the Virginia's house of Burgesses had established him as an implacable foe of British rule. Adams proposed naming him General and Commander in Chief of the Colonial Army.

It was the same day, June17, 1775 that marked the first major battle between colonial and British forces in Massachusetts. It became known as the Battle of Bunker Hill, even though most of the battle took place on a neighboring hill called Breed's Hill. The British took the hill after being driven back three times. They lost 1000 men while the colonists lost 400. The colonists soon ran out of ammunition and supplies and the British kept coming until they overwhelmed them.

The problem in the Second Continental Congress back in Philadelphia was that many of the delegates to the congress still considered themselves loyal to the crown and to Parliament. Therefore, on July 4th, 1775, exactly one year before the declaration of America's independence the delegates adopted the "Olive Branch Petition " in hopes the colonies might reconcile with the mother England. Those delegates who insisted on America's independence started out as small in number, however, that changed rapidly.

In January 1776 Thomas Paine published his "Common Sense" that declared the underlying reason for breaking away from the old country was for the creation and formation of a new civilization. He declared that Europe was corrupt and tainted by its past. America was young, fresh and pure with a new vision and purpose. He contended that those who sought reconciliation with the mother country were therefore not only timid but also foolish, an example of "perfect independence contending for dependence". His declaration was that "everything that is right and reasonable pleads for separation. The blood of the slain, the weeping voice of nature cries, it is time to part."

Passion often sells better than reason and in three months some 120,000 copies were sold and by the end of the revolution some 500,000 copies were printed and distributed which was enough for at least one copy of "Common Sense" for every family in America.

The British were defeated at Charlestown, Massachusetts and General Howe had retreated from Boston. More and more confidence was being gained in the colonial military against the much larger and better-equipped redcoat forces.

John Adams, in a letter to his wife, attempting to explain their success wrote, "There is something very unnatural and odious in a government a thousand leagues off. A whole government of our own choice, managed by persons whom we love, revere, and can confide in, has charms in it for which men will fight."

On June 7, 1776 Virginia delegate Richard Henry Lee proposed a resolution "that these united colonies are, and of right ought to be, free and independent states." After four days of debate a vote was postponed to line up support. In the meantime a committee was named to draft a declaration of independence into a formal resolution. The committee was John Adams, Benjamin Franklin, Thomas Jefferson, Robert Livingston and Roger Sherman. It was also determined that this congress would act as a provisional government until a more formal representative government could be established.

Each committee set out writing drafts of the independence resolution, however, they considered John Adams to be the most likely and ideal author of such a work as this. Adams declared he could not because *"I am obnoxious, suspected and unpopular. Tom Jefferson is much the otherwise"* and so the job rested with Thomas Jefferson to organize their collective thoughts and write the Declaration of Independence. He had substantial editorial help according to the historical record.

The draft declaration consisted of two main sections after the preamble asserting that the Americans were indeed revolting in actions, not just in word. The First section outlined Jefferson's argument that reflected in part the thinking of John Locke and others, that some truths are self evident, and among them are life, liberty and the pursuit of happiness. It declared that the foundational purpose of government is to protect these rights and should the government fail to do so it must be overthrown, which was precisely what was taking place in 1776. The second section of the draft was devoted to an unprecedented indictment of King George III and making it clear that colonists no longer consider themselves Englishmen but an independent people opposing foreign rule of any kind.

On June 28th, 1776 Jefferson's draft was presented to the Continental Congress, which debated and edited it. John Adams wrote to his wife Abigail, that: "the second day of July, 1776 will be the most memorable epoch in the history of America. I am apt to believe that it will be celebrated by succeeding generations as the great anniversary festival. It ought to be commemorated as the day of deliverance, by solemn acts of devotion to God Almighty. It ought to be solemnized with pomp and parade, with games, sports, guns, bells, bonfires and illuminations, from one end of this continent to the other, from this time forward forevermore."

His prediction was two days off. **On July 4, 1776 the Continental Congress formally approved the declaration of Independence by a twelve to zero vote.** Every delegate to the Continental Congress represented a colony willing to sever ties with England. Copies of the declaration were distributed across America and on July 9, 1776 a copy reached George Washington in New York where he was preparing for a British attack. The Battle for independence had really just begun.

It would be a long and hard war with the tide of the war on the side of Britain until France joined the colonial side of the battle. The tide began to turn and late in the decade Washington was victorious at a decisive battle at Sarratoga and then once again at Yorktown. **The war ended with the Treaty of Paris in 1783 negotiated by Benjamin Franklin and a New Nation was born.**

The United States of America is not even mentioned in the scriptures so far as I can determine. However, **men of God working under the leading of His word and the inspiration of His Spirit congregated in America according to God's divine purpose and made a bold declaration to the world of men's unalienable rights to life, liberty and the pursuit of happiness. That declaration would begin the war of independence and would henceforth turn the world upside down.**

This hand full of men created a constitutional republic that adopted a democratic form of government. The new republic was designed upon the foundational belief that men are endowed by their Creator with certain unalienable rights. America's government would be specifically dedicated and uniquely constructed to the cause of protecting those rights and to governing the nation according to the revealed will of the Creator. The people it governed would be a people humble before a superintending God and dependent upon His protection, provision, guidance and mercy.

The world's governments, businesses and churches saw this new land as potential new markets for their products as well as new lands for expansion and a source of new wealth. The Church became threatened and intimidated by the radical idea of religious freedom. They saw organized religion as the only route to God. They rejected the idea that Christianity was not fundamentally about religious observance and obedience to a religious social order but rather about individual relationships to the Creator.

Old world religion worked from the presumption that men were changed from the outside and it therefore tried to change men from the outside by forced religious observance and laws, however, Christ and the Spirit of God changes the hearts of men from the inside.

Religious men who have not experienced the necessary Spiritual rebirth can modify there habits or attitudes for a time however they cannot change themselves adequate to meet God's standard of holiness because they are victims of pressures from without and within they cannot overcome without the power of God. Their life condemns them and becomes a virtual "hell on earth" and a hypocrisy lived to satisfy the religious social requirement.

So it was in the old world. These pilgrims came to America to escape religious persecution and the frustration of religious oppression. The Kings used religious oppression through the churches and the government to control the masses.

Organized religion saw the new world as an opportunity to expand the size, power and wealth of their religious movements. The church was excited at the prospect of spreading the Gospel message among the native Americans, however, they thought it essential to maintain the same religious oppression over the people in the new world as they attempted to maintain throughout Europe and Spain. The colonist would have no part of it.

The American colonist was indeed a new breed of cat! They were not typically religionists but rather followers of Christ. Religion in that sense meant they were individually responsible for their relationship with God and accountable to God for their actions and inactions. They were born again believers who were followers of Christ for the most part who had severed their ties to the Anglican and the Catholic Church. Many of them were not tied to the various denominational doctrines of the mother church or the moralistic pride they found associated with the institution. They were, for the most part, indeed a religious people in the context that they were predominantly Christian believers, followers of Jesus Christ, and they would not tolerate the political religious oppression and persecution of the Church of England and /or the Roman Catholic Church.

The Church of England and the Roman Catholic Church viewed the American religious movement as the rebellious and heretical act of an undisciplined people. Certainly they had reason to believe it. However, it's interesting and appropriate to note, for example, that the people of Maryland, in a representative assembly of its citizens, passed a significant act protecting Christians from the power of religious Puritanism. It was the Toleration act of 1649, which guaranteed, *"no person professing to believe in Jesus Christ shall be in any wise molested or discountenanced for his or her religious practice or expression."* They saw the need to protect Christians from the persecution of the Church.

The foundation on which the United States of America would come to rest was: *"We hold these truths to be self-evident, that all men are created equal, that they are endowed by their Creator with certain unalienable rights, that among these (not limited to these) are life, liberty and the pursuit of happiness. That to secure these rights, governments are instituted among men, deriving their just powers from the consent of the governed."*

A radical new idea of Christianity even though it was clearly revealed in the new testament scriptures and a new Constitution, which would take its form and substance from the principles and truths of the bible, would manifest themselves in the character and nature of the people of this new world.

Those Americans who hold a liberal anti-Christian world –view continue the absurd argument over just how Christian (as apposed to deists, Unitarian, agnostic, atheistic, secularist etc.) our founding fathers really were. They would have us believe our founding fathers were not Christian believers at all and in fact were concerned with keeping Christianity and biblical principles out of public affairs and out of our governing documents. The historical record clearly supports the opposite.

History, and the writings of the founding fathers themselves reveals they viewed America's foundation established with a distinctive biblical view and that Christianity, whether or not they were strict followers of their professed faith, was the only religious view they approved is obvious to anyone who is not utterly prejudiced against the Christian faith. Only a deceived anti-Christ mind and heart would or could interpret anything different from the historical record.

Our national constitution would take much of its wording from the constitutions of the independent states which had sprung up over a century of immigration to the new world primarily from Spain and Europe. Emigrants formed various colonies that would ultimate become the original states of the United States of America.

This was indeed a divinely inspired document that declared liberty to be the God given right and gift given by the authority and will of God to every man. It would provide for a federal government of, for and by the people mandated with the security of the people from outside incursion and the arbitrator and protector of individual rights granted under the constitution. The government would be the administrator and the implementer of the public mandate.

The people of the United States would be a self-governing people that would govern through the election and the voting process. The election process would be the vehicle by which the people would elect leaders who were distinctively men of character, faith, wisdom and moral courage. They would take an oath to follow after the revealed will of God and represent the collective interests of the people in the administration of the governing process.

These elected representatives would enforce the revealed will of God and the people through representative government establishing laws that expressed the will of the electorate and met the constitutional test of liberty and justice for all. A Supreme Court was established to administer that test.

The institution of government would be specifically required to secure our nation and our people from encroachment from either inside or outside by the prompt and thorough enforcement of the law within and by establishing a militia properly equipped, trained and managed to meet any apparent outside threat. The government would be required to represent and protect our interests among the council of nations of the world. It would protect the social order and the very foundation of rights, justice and authority built upon biblical principle. It would administer justice and take care of the day-to-day administration of government. The vote of the electorate would be the process by which the United States citizen would reflect its approval or disapproval of the governments and/or its leaders direction.

An impeachment process would be put in place by which any government leader or Judge who refused to lead according to the will of the people or who proved not to represent the values of our people or proved to be incompetent to lead or refused to conduct himself according to the law of the land could be removed from office.

The settlers and founders who colonized America, after much consideration and debate, begin to recognize the need for a central government, however, the vision the founding fathers had of the role of central government, although vital, was to be limited. For example, it would not be the responsibility of government to raise or educate their children, nor would government be responsible for their health or welfare. The government would have a very limited role in the conduct of business or control of interstate commerce. Government would not subsidize various products, services nor would it administer the free enterprise system except to protect it from foreign and criminal interference.

Government would not have authority to control religious expression nor would it create a state religion. The scope of the federal government would be the protection of the unalienable rights expressed in the constitution and to administer justice when it involved national issues that could not otherwise be settled between the states.

The principal purpose and foundation of the government would be its role in protecting individual life liberty, free enterprise, religious freedom and to protect our people and secure our borders.

Articles one, two and three of the Constitution would establish the three branches of government and provide for the separation of powers and the establishment of three sovereign branches of government, each with separate responsibilities, whose collective mantel was to establish and protect the rights guaranteed by the Constitution.

The constitutional pre-amble and the history that precedes it, is profoundly significant because it reveals national authority and power, the historic circumstance, the religious belief and value system as well as the Spiritual condition and practice of the colonists and the founding fathers.

The issue for the early settlers of America was not riding themselves of the influence of Christianity in their lives and government but, rather, protecting and establishing its foundational role as the moral standard and code that would guide the social order and philosophy by which this people would live and be governed. In fact, universally established throughout the individual colonial governments, in the formation of the individual states constitutions, was a revealing requirement that each candidate for public office must meet. For example; **Article VII, Section II from the 1796 Tennessee constitution says,** *"No person who denies the being of God, or a future state of rewards and punishments, shall hold any office in the civil department of the state".*

Interesting, controversial and confusing to our generation is another seemingly contradicting article, Article XI, Section IV of the same constitution, where we also find written some curious language which states, *"No religious test shall ever be required as a quali-*

fication to any office or public trust under this state." Is this statement that rejects any religious test in direct conflict with the requirement for any man running for public office to believe in God and His sovereignty to qualify to govern in the affairs of men in Tennessee? Historical research reveals that it was not! The Supreme Court in their current decision to separate God from government did not do their homework and therefore they made a wrong decision regarding qualifications for public office under the constitution.

In virtually all the states constitutions we see established the requirement for belief in God to hold public office as prescribed in Article VII (above) and at the same time a prohibition against a religious test in Article XI.

How are we to interpret this seeming contradiction? Are these in fact a contradiction? To answer that requires an understanding of the historical context. What is the historical context of these articles? Is holding a belief in Christ the religious test of the type prohibited by Article XI, which incidentally appears as Article VI of the constitution of the United States, which states, *"No religious test shall ever be required as a qualification to any office or public trust under the United States?"*

To interpret this apparent disparity we must turn to the historical record and to the writings of the founding fathers. The truth is clearly revealed in the clear context of their individual testimonies on how they saw these governing documents and the conduct of government in light of how the colonists viewed organized religion and their Christian faith. Prominent among their writing is the stark contrast between the perspective of the followers of Christ and the intolerant perspective of the religious establishment. Many prominent leaders of that day wrote much about how they saw the governing process with Christ the head of this new society as apposed to the Anglican Church and its various denominations and/or the Roman Catholic Church.

Many modern self-proclaimed anti-Christian historians have singled out Thomas Jefferson as the founding father who championed their cause of secularism. Unfortunately the Supreme Court of the United States missed the boat and because they did not seek the truth they allowed secularists to decide the future of government for America. The case for secularism and the division between church and state based on the sentiment and writings of Thomas Jefferson is a misguided cause. The courts conclusion can only find merit by taking his remarks out of context. In order to understand the intention and context of freedom of religion as guaranteed by our constitution it is necessary to read Thomas Jefferson's writings, as well as the other founders, in the context they were written.

In 1781 Thomas Jefferson wrote a book entitled "Notes on Virginia" discussing several subjects. Prominent among them are his remarks critical of the state's tolerance of the religious intolerance of the Anglican Church. The Virginia assembly had passed several laws in the 1600's, which reflect many of the Anglican Churches prejudices. By the time of the American Revolution Virginia, having seen the benefits of religious tolerance in neighboring colonies, declared freedom of religion as a natural right. Jefferson's argument is that a man's religious opinion does not impact his civil right. His point is that all men are created equal and in a free nation he has certain rights that ought not be removed from him because of his religious opinion. The leadership of the nation is not a civil right. It is given to men who qualify as leaders and have the favor of the people.

Jefferson goes to great lengths to discuss the workings of the Spiritual conversion of men and how the Spirit of God gives the faith that He requires of us to believe. It is this distinctive truth that finds men at various levels of Spiritual discernment and maturity and that regardless of their station and level of Spiritual growth their maturity demands freedom of choice and the right to self-determination. The rest being up to the dissemination of the biblical message, the education and inspiration through the word of God, the circumstances of life and the gentle persuasion and example of the lives of followers of Christ.

The concern here, of course, is that the church in concert with government authority might dictate where, when and how we worship God and what biblical doctrine we chose to follow. When we consider a religious test from the perspective of the 21st century secular humanist perspective it comes to rest on the false idea that its meaning is simply a test of determining whether or not a candidate for public office is Christian, Atheist, Muslim, Buddhist, Satanist, Hindu, Catholic etc. On the foundation of this assumption rests the popular politically correct judgment against any attempt to discriminate against any particular religious affiliation of a candidate for public office.

Our courts have wrongly concluded the intention of this statement relating to a religious test was to deny the need for belief in God to hold public office. The court concluded the statement was to prohibit the state from requiring a candidate for public office to be a Christian believer. However, it is clear as crystal this was not the issue the colonists were dealing with at all. As a historical fact the candidacy for public office in virtually every colony demanded the public recitation of the following oath. *"I_____do profess faith in God the father and in Jesus Christ His only son, and in the Holy Ghost, one God, Blessed for evermore; and I do acknowledge the holy scriptures of the old and new testament to be given by divine inspiration." (Delaware 1776)*

History reveals that Christianity was not the religious test in question because the governing documents of the states required that anyone who aspired to hold public office must be Christian and practice the Judeo Christian ethic much like the age, educational, residential and other requirements.

The religious test, which was unacceptable to the states and to the founding fathers of the United States, was a religious test to determine and require a candidate for public office be part of the intolerant religious establishment of the Anglican Church or to be a member of any particular denominational affiliation of the Anglican Church or the acceptance of a particular religious doctrine to be a candidate for public office. However, it did require that any man who held public office declare publicly that he was a follower of Jesus Christ.

They did not wish to establish a particular religious denomination of the Anglican Church as the church recognized as the only orthodox Christian religious affiliation by the government. They came to America to escape religious intolerance and they did not want to rise up the same potential for such intolerance in the United States.

It was to be acceptable for a candidate for public office to be a member of any orthodox Christian denomination so long as he was a follower of Christ. What it prohibits is discrimination against a candidate because he might be Baptist, Methodist, Presbyterian, Lutheran, Episcopalian, or any other orthodox Christian denomination.

History makes it clear that the state was not intending to separate itself from its Christian foundation or to open the door of national leadership to heathenism, atheism, Satanism or cultism. Our Supreme Court managed to do that in the twentieth century.

In fact, any thought of a Muslim, Hindu, Buddhist, Satanist, atheist or secular humanist holding public office anywhere in the United States of America would cause the early republic to raise up in arms. It would be a cause for all out war then and it still ought to be according to the constitution. **Christianity was as inseparable from their lives and the government of the United States as was the constitution itself** because it defined the character and nature of Americans as a society of people whose religious faith was the foundation of their social order and was their most passionate belief.

Biblical New Testament Christianity was to be the faith and wisdom that would guide our nations leaders. It not only provided hope it provided the foundational principles which establish the laws that would guide their lives, their government, their commerce, their justice, their morality, their institutions of education and their individual decisions.

Anyone other than a follower of Christ attempting to gain public office was determined unfit to hold that office. Any public leader attempting to attack Christianity publicly was considered in early America as unpatriotic. Attacks against God (the God of the Christian bible) were considered unconstitutional and considered by Americans to be a direct attack against the nation and its people because the New Testament scriptures defined whom Americans were.

While the rights of citizens were broad, the right of public service and the public exercise of authority were considered to be an extension of who they were and what they believed and it was a right only extended to those who were distinctly Christian.

It is indeed inspiring to read the historical record because we discover this requirement to hold and demonstrate the existence of Christian faith by every candidate for political office was required by every state constitution and in fact, it was a mandatory part of the constitution of every state that applied for inclusion as part of the United States of America

Roger Sherman holds a unique and distinguished position among the founding fathers because he was the only one who signed all four of the nations major founding documents. (1.) The Articles of Association – 1774; (2) The Declaration of Independence – 1776; (3) The Articles of Confederation – 1777; (4) The Constitution of the United States – 1787.

He had an intimate knowledge of the debates, discussions that lead up to the development of these documents as well as the intent and meanings of their wordings. Sherman's view toward Christian influence in the governing process is clear in the historical record. In February 1776 he was placed on a committee with Adams and George Wythe of Virginia for the purpose of developing instructions for an ambassador group to visit the Canadian government. An important part of the instructions reads: *"You are further to declare that we hold sacred the rights of conscience, and may promise to the whole people, solemnly in our name, the free and undisturbed exercise of their religion, and that all civil rights and the right to hold office (in government) are to be extended to persons of any Christian denomination."*

Another of the founders with extensive knowledge of the constitution was John Jay who became the first chief justice of the Supreme Court. In fact, John Jay, James Madison and Alexander Hamilton authored the federalist papers, which presented the case for and the scope and nature of the proposed central government. John Jay was one of the three men most responsible for the ratification of the constitution and was selected by George Washington as the first Chief Justice of the Supreme Court. Listen carefully to what he had to say about the importance of Christian leadership in the government of this newly formed republic. *"Providence has given to our people the choice of their rulers, and it is the duty as well as the privilege and interest of our Christian Nation to select and prefer Christians as their rulers."*

John Jay, in the Federalist papers, noted the religious make up of our collective population: *"I have as often taken notice that providence has been pleased to give this one connected country to one United people descended from the same ancestors, speaking the same language, professing the same religion.."*

The historical record from each and every era up to the current era clearly reveal and establish the United States to be distinctively a Christian Nation. Any attempt to alter the historic record is intentional and driven by evil intent. The writings of the founding fathers confirm this truth. Christianity was more central to our identity than our union. Samuel Adams once described America's greatest enemy. *"A general dissolution of principles and manners will more surely overthrow the liberties of America than the whole force of enemy. While a people are virtuous they cannot be subdued; but when they lose their virtue they will be ready to surrender their liberties to the first external or internal invader. If virtue and knowledge are diffused among a people they will never be enslaved. This will be our greatest security…..(therefore) we must impress the minds of men with the importance of educating their little boys and girls, or inculcating in the minds of youth the fear and love of God and in subordination these great principles; the love of country and, in short, leading them in the study and practice of the exalted virtues of the Christian faith."*

Samuel Adams instigated the "Boston Tea Party", an uprising against unreasonable taxation, signed the Declaration of Independence, called for the first Continental Congress in 1774 and served as a member of those congresses until 1781.

John Witherspoon, in addition to signing the Declaration of Independence, was a member of the Continental Congress for six years where he served on some 100 congressional committees. He was president of Princeton University where many men of national prominence, presidents, vice-presidents, Supreme Court justices, cabinet members, senators and congressmen, were trained. It's exciting to hear what he said regarding politics and Christianity: *"It is the man of piety and inward principle, that we may expect to find the uncorrupted patriot, the useful citizen and the invincible soldier. God Grant that in America true religion and civil liberty may be inseparable and that the unjust attempts to destroy the one, may support and establish both...what will follow from this is that he is the best friend of American liberty, who is most sincere and active in promoting true and undefiled religion, and who sets himself with the greatest firmness to bear down profanity and immorality of every kind. Whoever is an avowed enemy of God I would not hesitate to call him an enemy of this country."*

Patrick Henry was largely responsible for the adoption of the first ten amendments to the Constitution, which has become known to us as the "Bill of Rights". He was the driving force behind the first Amendment, which reads, *"Congress shall make no law respecting an establishment of religion, or prohibiting the free exercise thereof; or abridging the freedom of speech, or of the press; or the right of the people peaceably to assemble, and to petition the government for a redress of grievances."*

Please listen carefully to his words regarding Christianity and the State: *"It cannot be emphasized too strongly or too often that this great nation was founded, not by religionists, but by Christians; not on religions, but on the Gospel of Jesus Christ! For this very reason peoples of other faiths have been afforded asylum, prosperity, and freedom to worship here".*

Its interesting to note that one of Patrick Henry's grandsons, William Wirt Henry, remarked when speaking of his grandfather Patrick, *"He looked to the restraining and elevating principles of Christianity as the hope of his country's institutions."*

James Madison, more than any other, because of his efforts and debate at the constitutional convention became known as the "chief architect of the Constitution". He was one of the authors of the Federalist Papers. He served eight years in congress, eight years as Secretary of State and eight years as President of the United States. He was trained at Princeton University under the leadership of John Witherspoon.

Princeton University's profession of biblical truth was the foundation upon which it was created; it publicly declares, *"Curse be all learning that is contrary to the cross of Christ".* James Madison's proclamations concerning the relationship between God and civil government are clear: *"Before any man can be considered a member of civil society, he must be considered as a subject of the governor of the Universe. Religion is the basis and foundation of government."*

Madison believed the future of America rested not on the constitution but on the ability of us to conduct ourselves according to the will of God. Listen to his declaration: ***"We have staked the whole future of American civilization, not upon the power of government, far from it. We have staked the future of all our political institutions upon the capacity of mankind for self government; of the capacity of each and all of us to govern ourselves, to control ourselves, to sustain ourselves according to the ten commandments of God."***

It is fit to ask the question, 'how could it be, with every evidence to the contrary, that a court in America in the case of Stone vs. Graham ruled it unconstitutional for students to see the ten commandments displayed on school property? A court who would make such a ruling is so out of touch with the intentions of our founders and the foundational truth and faith upon which our nation stands, or they are so committed to perpetuating the lie, they are unfit to serve on any court or in any position of public service in of the United States of America. The decision to secularize government could only be the conclusion of deceit, ignorance or evil intention. The tragedy is that the Executive or the Legislative branches of government did not challenge the decision, nor was it challenged by the Church.

As I am writing *"perspective"* I am watching on television the progress of coalition troop's sweeping through Iraq and at this moment occupying the Baghdad International Airport, the streets of Bagdad and one of the Palaces of Sadaam Hussein in central Bagdad. Meanwhile, I am watching Iraq's Director of Information broadcast on Iraq's State run television that coalition troops are not anywhere near Bagdad and that the war we are observing on the five separate American broadcast networks, plus any number of European networks are presenting a staged war that is the product of Hollywood illusion.

Obviously, the Director is either ignorant of the truth, mentally deranged or his intentions are to deceive. Clearly his broadcasts are an attempt to deceive and inflame the surrounding Arab nations against coalition forces and to manipulate Iraq's citizens to rise up and fight even though the war has been lost.

It is the same kind of deceit the liberal contingency and the Supreme Court consistently attempts to use to circumvent or deny the truth in order to destroy the Christian foundation and Heritage of America contrary to that which is clearly established in the historical record. Those who participated in the courts decision are either fools or liars and deceivers or all three. The decision comes forth from an insane and preposterous perspective at best and it is a deliberate lie with an evil intended perspective to remove God and Godliness from America.

Governor Morris, a Pennsylvania delegate to the Constitutional Convention, was responsible for translating and transcribing ideas from the convention floor onto paper. In that sense he wrote the constitution. He also served in the Continental Congress, helped write the New York state constitution and served later as a Senator from the state of New

York. He also served as an ambassador to France, whom he encouraged to move toward a self-governing nation. He said in a letter to the French government, *"Religion is the only solid basis for good morals; therefore, education should teach the precepts of religion and duties of man towards God."*

John Adams, who recommended George Washington to the congress as the appropriate candidate to fill the role of Commander and Chief, personally urged Thomas Jefferson to accept the responsibility for directing the drafting of the Declaration of Independence. Adams signed the Declaration of Independence and served in the Continental Congress. He was also a minister to France and, along with John Jay and Ben Franklin negotiated the final treaty, which ended the War Between the United States and Great Britain. He wrote a three volume work entitled, "A Defense of the Constitution of the Government of the United States" which, was a work written to help in the ratification of the constitution by the individual states. John Adams served two terms as Vice-President under George Washington and was elected the second President of the United States. He was the first President to live in the "white house".

Having been an ambassador to the French government he declared publicly that a republic, such as the United States government, could not be successful in a nation such as France, which was inhabited by 30 million atheists. He states that atheism and widespread immorality would defeat the French in their effort to produce a stable and lasting government. His analysis has proven to be right. His proclamation was that the two ingredients of Christianity and morality make American government distinctive and powerful. In 1798 he wrote; *"We have no government armed with power capable of contending with human passions unbridled by morality and religion. Avarice, ambition, revenge, or gallantry would break the strongest cords of our constitution as a whale goes through a net. Our constitution was made only for a moral and religious people. It is wholly inadequate to the governing of any other."*

In regard to the inclusion of Christianity in politics and public affairs Adams said: *"Statesmen, my dear sir, may plan and speculate for liberty, but it is religion and morality alone which can establish the principles upon which freedom can securely stand. The only foundation of a free constitution (and a free people) is pure virtue….religion and virtue are the only foundations, not only of republicanism and of all free government, but of social felicity under all governments and in all the combinations of human society."* Clearly, the second President of the United States was not confused about the role of Christianity in government, in politics or in public affairs.

Alexander Hamilton was a captain in a New York artillery unit who later became secretary and personal assistant to George Washington. After Washington became President he appointed Hamilton as the first Secretary of the Treasury. Hamilton served as a member of congress and called for the constitutional convention to which he served as a delegate. He was one of the authors of the Federalist Papers, which gave understanding and purpose to the idea of central government and the newly proposed constitution.

Hamilton proposed the establishment of a "Christian Constitutional Society" for the purpose of promoting the relationship between the two factors that had been most influential in America and American government. He wanted to support the Christian religion and its relationship to the constitution of the Untied States. He wrote in an address to be delivered by George Washington at a farewell address; *"Of all the disposition and habits which lead to political prosperity, religion and morality are indispensable supports. In vain would that man claim the tribute of patriotism, who should labor to subvert these great pillars of human happiness? The politician ought to respect and cherish them. Reason and experience both forbid us to expect that national morality can prevail in exclusion of religious principle…whoever that is a sincere friend to America can not look with indifference upon attempts to shake the foundation of the fabric."*

John Quincy Adams at the age of 14 years received a congressional appointment to a post in the court of Catherine the Great of Russia. He later became Ambassador to Russia and also served as Ambassador to Britain and to France. In a letter to his son Adams wrote: *"It is essential my son that you should form and adopt certain rules or principles. It is in the bible you must learn them and from the bible (learn) how to practice them."* He was Secretary of State under James Monroe and was elected the sixth President of the United States. He also served in the House of Representatives where he saw no allowance for the separation of the church of Jesus Christ and the government of the United States. Listen to his remarks: *"The highest glory of the American Revolution was this; it connected in one indissoluble bond, the principles of civil government and the principles of Christianity."*

Noah Webster, most frequently associated with the dictionary bearing his name, was one of the founding fathers. He was a soldier in the American Revolution. He served nine terms in the Connecticut general assembly, three terms in Massachusetts's legislature and four years as a Judge. Webster held unmistakable convictions regarding the relationship between Christianity and government. Note carefully his remarks: *"The religion which has introduced civil liberty is the religion of Christ and His Apostles, which enjoins humility, piety and benevolence; which acknowledges in every person a brother, or a sister, and a citizen with equal rights. This in genuine Christianity and to this we owe our free constitution of government. The moral principles and precepts contained in the scriptures ought to form the basis of all our civil constitution's and laws. All the miseries and evils which men suffer from vice, crime, ambitions, injustice, oppression, slavery and war proceed from their despising or neglecting the precepts contained in the bible."*

Webster was known for his extensive efforts in establishing sound education in America. He was known as America's schoolmaster. He authored textbooks, resource books, spellers, history books and many more. He and his extensive works recognize that the principles, which had given birth to the Nation, must be translated to future generations in order to insure continued national success and survival. His notion was that education must become the guardian of true Christian and Republican principles. He recognized the quality of our governing would be dependent upon the quality and focus of our education. He warned that Christian principles must be inseparable from education. He wrote: *"In my view the Christian religion is the most important and one of the first things in which all children, under a free government, ought to be instructed. No truth is more evident to my mind than that the Christian religion must be the basis of any government intended to secure the rights and privileges of a free people."*

In one of his textbooks Noah Webster wrote: *"It is extremely important to our nation, in a political as well as religious view, that all possible authority and influence be given to the scriptures for these furnish the best principles of civil liberty and the most effectual support of republican government. The principles of all genuine liberty, and wise laws and administrations are to be drawn from the bible and sustained by its authority. The man, therefore, who weakens or destroys the divine authority of that book may be accessory to all the public disorders which society is doomed to suffer."*

These founding fathers expressed the sentiment and vision that inspired virtually all the founding fathers and expresses their stand and intentions regarding the relationship between our government and Christianity as well as education and Christianity.

Ever since the first settlers came to Plymouth the world has beat a path to the doorway into America with the hope of making this new world of God given free enter-prize and individual liberty their home. America has historically been the envy of the entire world.

The worlds populations try every scheme they can think of to set foot on these shores. Millions are willing to literally sacrifice their lives for a chance to escape the oppression of government and world poverty just to experience a touch of the American dream. That American dream was based on the foundation of the sovereignty of our Creator and two pillars which promoted and offered the best hope for mankind. Those pillars were a constitution that protected those unalienable (God given) rights and the freedoms that make life tolerable and a government of, for and by the people it governed.

God surely had a plan and purpose for the creation of this new nation whose government would be a unique government of, for and by the people governed. It would be distinctively Christian in its character and would be governed by Christian principles. Its people and its leadership would be predominately Christian.

It would be a nation whose doors would be open to those seeking individual liberty and political freedom. However, America was never intended to become like the world in which it was planted. America was intended to be a conduit through which God could deliver many from the oppression of worldly governments and a people who would bring salt and light to a lost world.

There was a divine hand on the creation of the American Nation. Wherever we see a divine hand in the creation process we can rest assured that creation is for a divine purpose and will be subject to God's sovereign will and judgment. God was on the scene long before the Declaration of Independence or the constitutional convention out of which this new nation was born.

For almost 150 years prior to the advent of central government America was a land of several colonies or states whose governments were independent of each other each with their own constitutions and sovereign governments. It's amazing to learn that constitutions of all these colonies held to the Lex, Rex tradition of Rutherford. They were, loosely speaking, on the same page Spiritually. The concepts of the constitution that formed this federal union were not unique to the writings of the constitutions, but rather a compilation of ideas from the same Spiritual script.

It took over a century to communicate and coordinate the Spiritual and political vision that would establish these "colonial states" on the same page legally, spiritually, emotionally and administratively. As the scriptures teach us, our Lord sees a thousand years as one day so a mere century or two in light of eternal matters is not very long in the ultimate scheme of things.

America's uniqueness is found in the vision of leaders who recognized that America was born into the world for the purpose of spreading and sustaining a divine vision of purpose, hope and liberty. America matured into a nation of ambassadors to the Kingdom of God and therefore a bastion of liberty, equality and justice for all men. Deceit and evil work hand in hand to destroy the work of God and His followers.

CHAPTER TWO

LIBERTY,
AN UNALIENABLE RIGHT

—m—

"The Lord is the Spirit;
and where the Spirit of the Lord is, there is liberty."
II Corinthians 3-17)

Liberty, the right of individual determination, is a foundational aspiration that gives life meaning, pleasure, purpose, direction, hope and opportunity. It is the environment in which dreams can and do come true. Liberty is an idea that releases in men the inspiration to explore possibilities and the hope to endure. Liberty provides a spark that inspires the very heart and soul of every human being. It gives every life value and potential. Life without liberty is a sentence of oppression and slavery. Liberty does not exist without the right of a person to determine the path he will take. Patrick Henry expressed that yearning best when he declared, **"give we liberty or give me death"**.

Our founding fathers declared this yearning to be God given. The Scriptures confirm it and our very being resonates to its call. Liberty has to do with choice. Inherent in an environment of choice is the necessity to accept the responsibility for the consequences of the choices we make. Also inherent in choice is the opportunity to share in the blessings of wise choices and the consequences of bad choices. Walking the walk of liberty requires courage, discipline, moral character, sacrifice and charity. Liberty is not for the indolent or the coward or for the rebellious. Liberty is a walk of faith to be enjoyed and appreciated.

Free choice is indeed a blessing. Men were created to be free morale agents and to make free choices. History reveals clearly that free men are the most creative, productive, successful and happy men on earth. Oppression, dependence, slavery and religious intolerance demoralize and depress man. Men were never created to live in the bondage of slavery. Free choice, even when men suffer the consequences of bad choices, produces the best result and offers the best hope for mankind. It is also the best way because it is the only way in which man learns from his choices.

The men who founded our nation were followers of Christ who abhorred the oppression of a tyrannical government and of religious intolerance. They were dedicated to the proposition that all men were indeed created equal and they inherent in God's creative plan was the right to liberty and the pursuit of self-determination.

Unfortunately every time man makes bad choices and is not required to suffer the consequences of his bad decisions he tends not to learn and he loses a little portion, sometimes a big portion, of his liberty. A nation where Liberty flourishes is a land where liberty is protected. It is a nation where the citizens recognize its value and stay vigilant to any incursion against it. Liberty can only be sustained by a nation of courageous people who are willing to confront and fight against anything or anyone who might attempt to take it away. Thomas Jefferson in his "Summary View of the Rights of British America" declared; *"The God who gave us life, gave us liberty at the same time."*

From the very first steps onto the shores of the new world this blessed land was viewed by the entire civilized world as the land of renewed hope and opportunity. What it was to become was not known, however, its very existence excited the hearts of all men. The new hope for liberty in a new land was inspired in part by a new revelation that had come to the heart and mind of Samuel Rutherford, a Presbyterian Minister, who expressed the implications of his revelation in 1644 in a book entitled *"Lex, Rex or, The Law and the Prince."*

Rutherford was inspired by the scriptures. Scriptures such as the scripture quoted above taken from II Corinthians 3:17. **"The Lord is the Spirit; and where the Spirit of the Lord is, there is liberty."**

The world would never be the same! Rutherford asserted that the basic premise of government and therefore, of law, must be the Word of God as these principles are revealed in the Holy Scriptures rather than the secular words and attitudes of man.

He directly challenged the idea of the divine right of Kings. He declared the law of liberty to rise far above the right of Kings. His inspired writing said to mankind that all men, even Kings, are governed by the law, which is handed down from God himself and nether Kings nor governments are above it. His foundational contention is that God exists as Creator and Sovereign ruler of the world, indeed the universe, and all that it contains. None can escape His purpose or judgment and that all men and nations will be judged by His Word.

Rutherford died before his concepts were implemented as the foundational truth that would guide the Spirit of this new republic, however, his revelation lived on to profoundly influence the creation of American government. His declarations became foundational in the writing of America's Declaration of Independence and ultimately the constitution.

Government based upon the premise of Rutherford's "Lex, Rex and the absolutes of Scripture was realized and fully appreciated by colonial America primarily through the influence of John Witherspoon and John Locke. (A Federal Union by John Hicks; The Bible and the Dawn of the American Dream by John Whitehead)

As noted earlier the Constitution of the United States is distinctive primarily because it defines its foundational purpose as protecting those rights that make it distinctive among all the nations of the world, which it believes and declares to be unalienable. It describes these rights in the Declaration of Independence as endowed by the Creator and common and indeed vital to the life of every human being.

They are rights that define the character and inherent value of every man and of the constitution and of our nation, which cannot be alienated from the mind and heart of human existence by governments or through any other jurisdiction or even by the rebellious acts of individuals or people groups. These sacred rights as stated include, but are not limited to, life, liberty and the pursuit of happiness. It was and remains the primary purpose and responsibility of government to secure and protect these God ordained rights from any and all enemies. Unfortunately, our government has forgotten and has not carried out its divine mandate.

The Declaration of Independence established in Congress July 4, 1776 declares that America is established on the basis of certain divine truths; "*We hold these truths to be self evident, that all men are created equal; that they are endowed by their Creator with certain unalienable rights; that among these, are life, liberty, and the pursuit of happiness. That, to secure these rights, governments are instituted among men, deriving their just powers from the consent of the governed; that, whenever, any form of government becomes destructive to these ends; it is the right of the people to alter or to abolish it and to institute a new government". We, therefore, the representatives of the United States of America, in general Congress assembled, appealing to the Supreme Judge of the world...for the support of this declaration, with a firm reliance on the protection of Divine Providence, we mutually pledge to each other our lives, our fortunes, and our sacred honor.*"

The nature of the liberty related to in our constitution was defined clearly by John Winthrop, a twelve-term governor of the Massachusetts Bay Colony. He was a religious man in the sense that he was a follower of Christ. He coined the notion that liberty is the proper end, object and mandate of all authority.

John Winthrop declared there to be a twofold idea of liberty each having distinctively different motivation and application. One is natural liberty, which is a desire common to man and beast and all other creatures. He stated that this kind of liberty is to do as we please. It is very appealing to the flesh and appetites of men. It is liberty to do evil as well as good. He said regarding this kind of liberty, "*This liberty is incompatible and inconsistent with authority, and cannot endure the least restraint of the most just authority. The exercise and maintaining of this liberty makes men grow more evil, and in time to be worse than brute beasts. This liberty is a great enemy of truth and peace*".

The second liberty, which is the liberty guaranteed by the constitution and ordained by God is civil and moral in *"reference to the covenant between God and man, in the moral law, and the political covenants between men themselves. This liberty is the proper end and object of authority, and cannot subsist without it; and it is a liberty to do only that, which is good, just and honest. This liberty you are to stand for, with the hazard of your very life, if need be. Whosoever crosses this is not authority but a distemper thereof. This liberty maintained and exercised in a way of subjection to authority; it is of the same kind of liberty wherewith Christ hath made us free. The women's own choice makes such a man her husband; yet, being so chosen, he is her lord, and she is subject to him, yet in a way of liberty, not of bondage; and a true wife accounts her subjection to her husbands authority her honor and her freedom…Such is the liberty of the Church under the authority of Christ. His yoke is easy and sweet. If we stand for our natural corrupt liberties and will not do what is good you will not endure the least weight of just authority.." (John Winthrop 1630)* This is the liberty found in obeying the God of the Ten Commandments and it is the character of the liberty declared in the declaration of independence.

It is true that many Americans misunderstood and misunderstand today the nature of the liberty they subscribe to. They also misunderstood, and misunderstand today, the responsibility of the governing authority that must govern with the same love and attitude with which our Lord governs His Church. Therein is the unalienable right of men to the liberty to do what is good and right in the sight of God. It is liberty from the selfish and evil inclinations of the flesh not the liberty to satisfy every whim of the flesh. That, my friend, is why inherent in the American dream is the God of America who is the only true God, the Creator and sustainer of all life and the redeemer of man from the sin so natural to his fallen nature. Therein is the liberty spoken of in the Scriptures. It is the only true liberty.

At any rate, tied to the land of Israel and its people was the plan and purpose of God as revealed in the Scriptures. In similar fashion, tied to this new world was a hope, which had its foundation, inspiration, spirit and authority in God's word and His Spirit. It was the divine gift to every American citizen to experience the God ordained unalienable right of freedom from oppressive government, religious or social oppression and the right to self-determination.

The vision, hope and purpose encompassed in God's deliverance from the curse of sin, the trap of deceit and the power of satanic oppression, gives to men the sense of divine calling and purpose. His deliverance is from sin and not authority to sin at will.

More than half of the immigrants into this new land were inspired with this divine calling and purpose. Contrary to much of today's evangelistic effort and religious rhetoric salvation is a divine holy calling. It is regarded as such by our Lord, declared as such in His word and it was regarded as such in the early church. It was also regarded as such by our founding fathers and the majority of the early settlers of America.

God's grace gave a people a nation and a government that would protect individual liberty and the right to self- determination, religious freedom and free enterprise that offered virtually unlimited opportunity. It was not a liberty from discipline it is a liberty that is inherent in the discipline that recognizes that my liberty ends where it infringes upon the liberty of another.

Prior to the vision out of which the Declaration of Independence of this new world came forth was the Governing process and philosophies predominate among the nations of Europe. The civilized world to that point had historically been governed by Monarchy's. The people were considered slaves of the Monarch. They were made to recognize that position as their role in society. The attitude, which prevailed throughout most of the world regarding the governing of nations, was the divine right of Kings. It was a generally accepted idea that men were not capable of governing themselves without the sovereign hand of a King who was somehow ordained as a direct ambassador to the nation from God or "the gods" and who was therefore wiser and more noble than the people and was therefore given absolute power over the lives of men and the affairs of state.

Tied to this new Declaration of National Independence and freedom from the oppression of the old world was the right to enjoy individual liberty which would allow men to live and pursue the future according to the will and provision of God and the philosophy of the right to self determination. The only limitations to be placed in the way of individual liberty was that no man would have the right to injure his neighbor except as necessary to protect his family, his property or himself or to stop criminal activity as defined by the laws of the land.

The America dream remains today the dream of every man anywhere and everywhere. That is so because God's will for all men, even for those who fail to recognize God's calling upon their lives or for those who do not recognize, understand or appreciate the profoundness of God's saving grace, is that they might have the right to experience liberty.

The liberty our Lord decrees establishes every man a free moral agent, which suggests man is free to make moral choices albeit some of his choices may not be wise choices. He alone can determine the path on which he will walk. Along with that liberty comes the responsibility to make the right choices and the suffering the just penalty for making the wrong choices. For man to make choices suggest that he is free to make both good and bad choices.

Our society has foolishly established its hope on the presumption that men will chose to make honorable and just choices. That presumption assumes that a majority of men are men of good conscience and character. Unfortunately, that is a foolish presumption. The bible declares that all men are sinners by nature and come short of the glory of God. God has given, however, all men the right to choose for himself the road upon which he will walk. He has commanded the Church to give clear warning to all men of the danger of the wrong choices and the destructiveness of the wiles of the world in which he walks and to offer him wisdom and God's hope of deliverance in His name if men will humble themselves and accept His deliverance and saving grace.

We easily forget that man is not the author of liberty, God is! Man cannot guarantee it or even protect it without God. Perhaps one of the great problems we have in transporting the democratic process to nations of the world is that we tend to leave out the very foundation upon which our nation and way of life is built and is sustained. That, of course, is the problem we are having in America as well. Our way of life and liberty and our constitution will not work well in a secular society. Why? Simply put, God says, *"there is a way which seems right to man, however, it is the way of death".* God is the foundation and sustainer of our way of life as envisioned by our founding fathers, expressed in our constitution and confirmed by the Holy Scriptures.

The Monarchy model of governing had great efficiency's in governing men of fallen natures and was therefore not without merit. Experience and history has proven clearly that natural man is selfish, deceived and inherently evil. He will lie, cheat and steel to satisfy his needs, desires and appetites at the expense of others if necessary unless he is given strong incentives to act otherwise. The strong make slaves of the weak and the rich and powerful take advantage of the poor and oppressed and the poor steel from the rich.

In a lost world filled with sinful men justice would become perverted unless someone with the power, wisdom and authority to bring balance and final judgment to serve as arbitrator between men. A powerful and wise Monarch was therefore seen as necessary to lead, govern and administer justice. That idea is true in every group of people who will not or cannot accept the responsibility to govern themselves. A leader, or group of leaders, who have discernment, vision and authority to decide the most practical and righteous course of action and implement it must ultimately lead and act as arbitrator between the selfish interests of fallen man.

However, the Monarchs were typically not men of God nor were they necessarily wise men. They were also men with fallen natures and lustful appetites. They paid homage to evil Gods or to no God at all. Their God was typically the God of this world, Satan, or they were Gods that did not exist. They therefore inevitably became corrupted by their power and wealth and inevitably enslaved and oppressed their people. Men throughout recorded history rebelled instinctively against the oppression of the Monarchy's and they were constantly looking for a way and a place of escape where they would be free to live in peace and the right to determine the course of their lives and benefit from the work of their hands.

Men the world over longed for a place where self-determination and individual liberty was the rule and the common experience. There were experiments with democracy for centuries before the existence of the United States of America; however, none existed in the context of liberty existing as a God given gift and right previous to the United States of America.

Unfortunately, most Americans today fail to recognize the implications; the calling, the responsibilities and the disciplines required for America to remain a free people and we are therefore systematically losing those associated freedoms. If America does not wake up we will soon find ourselves as slaves to another oppressive government.

In the sixteenth, seventeenth and even the eighteenth centuries the idea of a time and place in the world where men were given the right of self-determination and citizenship in a nation not governed by an oppressive Monarch was a radical idea to say the least. In fact it was a pipe dream that seemed more like the hereafter promised by the Christian bible than the "here" of worldly existence.

There had been experiments with democratic rule. One of the more notable historically was the Nation of Greece. There experiment failed because it was secular and ruled by the minds, lusts and appetites of men. Their democracy was secular and therefore perverted by the deceit and fleshly appetites of men of fallen natures. The foolish thinking of men not guided by righteous inspiration and truth, special interests, sin and corruption destroyed the democracy of Greece. To control and govern fallen men it found it must take away their freedoms. To finance its special interests and socialist programs it found it had to tax the people beyond their ability to pay. Their tax and spend welfare policies bankrupt the nation. It found itself not only ineffective and cumbersome but also impossible for the secular mind of man to find the wisdom, courage or authority to govern and control men of fallen natures and evil appetites.

We are experiencing the same problem because we have removed God and His wisdom, way and will from the governing process. Our Supreme Court has thrust upon us a secular humanist government bureaucracy that will ultimately destroy America. Without a moral code and a righteous Spirit to guide the people a democratic form of government will not be able to govern this or any nation. They too will find they must systematically remove freedoms to maintain order.

America this very day is naively attempting to transport liberty to the people of other nations without transporting the author of that liberty. In fact we are losing our own God given liberty because we, as a government, have also forgotten and rejected the author and Spirit of liberty and have adopted a secular governing philosophy, which by its nature is anti-Christ.

Democracy with all its elections will not make a people free without the Spirit of God to guide the hearts and minds of the people toward goodness and charity. Liberty through democratic government cannot be put in place simply because we want other peoples to experience it because democratic government by itself does not secure liberty. Liberty requires the Spirit of liberty, which is charity and righteous judgment. Charity finds its source and power in the Spirit of our Creator and Lord and not in the secular minds of men.

Secularism is a myth. In its purest form there is no such thing as secular judgment. Man is not a robot. He judges according to what he believes to be true. There is no such thing,

71

as it relates to the thinking and judgment of men, as secular. According to the Scriptures we are lead in our thinking and judgments by either the Spirit of God, by our appetites and pleasures or by the Spirit of the world. Secular does not mean objective. When the court decided that the most just way to govern such a diverse nation was through a secular government they signed the ultimate death warrant on the nation created by our founding fathers as the United States of America. We cannot be a nation that protects liberty by rejecting its author and sustainer.

Clearly, heaven on earth is a myth! Fallen man cannot reach the perfection necessary to equal the perfection of the glory of God. Beyond that, God has another plan. However, He has described a way to live our lives among a people of faith who enjoy His blessing and experience His peace, love joy and protection. Perhaps we might call it a paradise, of sorts, on earth created to bless His people and testify to the world of His glory until he delivers us from this life. It must be a place in which the people trust in Him and honor his word and revealed will. It requires a people whose laws, system of justice, government and leaders are endowed with the Spirit of charity, righteousness, justice, moral courage, wisdom and mercy. They must be a people who trust in a God who guides and inspires them to a love for and commitment to that which is right, best, fair and just for their fellowman. They must be a people who insist that government does the right thing and not simply the most convenient or popular thing. Clearly we must never become a people who place their trust and confidence in secularism or on the minds of secular or evil men.

Wise men, awakened by the Spirit of God, recognize that the nature of man is fallen leaving man to be lead by his lusts, appetites and pleasures. Mans nature without God is clearly revealed by Gods word to be selfish, destructive and inherently evil. The world rejects this idea, which is a vital truth essential to recognize if we are to conclude we are in need of a deliverer. If God is indeed God, among other things, He has all knowledge, power, wisdom etc. He knows what is best for us and His will for us is therefore best for us. Why would we want to reject His will? Rather foolish wouldn't you say! Yet we do reject it every day and we are collectively rejecting Him and His will as a nation. We would have to describe a people who live like this as foolish at best.

When we speak of a Savior surely we must recognize that our circumstance is one from which we must be delivered and our natural condition is one that places us at odds with God. In this condition we are unable to meet God's standard and therefore we cannot please God, therefore, we must be saved because of this unacceptable condition we are in. The condition and the circumstance we are in are destructive. If we chose to continue in this circumstance and condition God has said we will perish.

Government leaders in all governments of the world tolerate religion (not necessarily God) because they have come to recognize that religion, which emphasizes the fear of judgment (outside the context of Gods love and grace), which is religion without humility before God and without the guidance of His Spirit, is, however, helpful in holding the evil instincts of man at bay and therefore useful to governments to help control societies.

However, the Christianity of the new covenant as revealed in the new-testament scriptures changed the entire panorama of religious attitude once man came to recognize its profound implications. Governments and some of the religious institutions determined they must expose that part of the bible that furthered their cause. Reading the bible undermined the authority and power of the oppressive self-serving use of religion by the church and the Monarchy's to control the masses.

The Scriptures declared clearly that the King was no longer God and, in fact, must also humble himself before the only true God and allow his kingdom to be governed by those same promises, principles, truths and judgments of the scriptures that deliver men from the bondage of oppression caused not only by individual and collective sin, but also from the oppression of religionists and tyrants. This caused many problems for the religious and for the governments.

God's has declared for the world to see and experience that man was His finest creative effort and his plan for man included liberty from the penalty of sin, liberty from bondage to a fallen nature, liberty from the oppression of religious institutions and governments and the right to self-determination. However, he also declared that liberty and self-determination are impossible objectives without the convicting authority and loving kindness of His Spirit to guide and inspire men toward goodness. This revelation is and was the inspiration and foundation of the government of the United States of America!

God's grace, once discovered, realized and declared to the world by men such as Martin Luther, began to turn Europe upside down from a political and religious perspective. Kings became fearful, intimidated and jealous of Christianity and its King Jesus Christ. As Kings began to lose control over the lives of Christians, whose ultimate loyalty was to God the sovereign of the universe, Kings and governments saw themselves with no choice but to declare war on Christians and Christianity or lose their kingdom, power and wealth.

When men begin to humble themselves before God and became "born again" according to the scripture text of the new-testament gospels a new discovery and deliverance was opened to the hearts and minds of men. A new "goodness " and purpose and freedom began to express itself in the lives of men. A new love for God and for ones fellowman began to direct the actions of men. Conviction against evil actions and attitudes and forgiveness for those who offended drove men toward acting rightly and justly toward his fellowman.

That new Spirit brought new love, commitment, unity, liberty, peace and hope. It brought a new vision of life's purpose and ultimate destiny. There was a new hope on the horizon that recognized men delivered from the deceit of evil and secularism could discern God's will and that God's Spirit humbled their hearts and they became willing to walk in such as way as to insure and protect each others liberty and right to self determination. The new covenant revelation that delivered man from the condemnation of sin and the power of deceit began to bring an entirely new life and perspective to the idea of religion and governing.

The Monarchy's of Europe and their associated religious institutions were indeed threatened. In fact, much of Europe's organized religious institutions discouraged there people from reading the bible and some even forbid it. The religious oppression government used to control the people was being challenged by deliverance of the Gospel of Jesus Christ and the loyalties and commitments of Christians to the only true God.

Of course the traditionally religious, which comprised the majority of the organized church in Europe, were not encouraged to read or study the scriptures. They were lead by the church leaders as apposed to the scriptures and therefore they were not lead by the truth and power of God's word. The organized church therefore stood in rebellion against the gospel message and the people trapped in organized religion were without deliverance or vision. Such is still the case in much of the world. The institutions that comprise the world council of churches are typically not a part of the Church of Jesus Christ revealed in the new testament scriptures. This fact brings great confusion when we consider the distinct roles of church and government.

For a nation of people to arise under the inspiration of God able to govern themselves by means of human government founded on faith dedicated to God's purpose and will was a radical idea! Inherent in mans creation was dependence upon God, the only truly sovereign monarch who was holy, all knowing, all powerful, all wise and perfectly just.

Human government requires at least three ingredients to work effectively and preserve liberty! **First**, the only Monarch must be God Himself whose will and purpose is expressed to His people through His Spirit and word. **Second,** His Spirit must indwell its leaders and inspire righteousness, justice, charity, wisdom and the obedience of the heart. **Third,** the governed must possess the same Spirit in order that they are led to humble themselves before the law of God and of the land and the government that God uses to protect, guide and unite the efforts of His people for righteousness sake. God gave man the freedom to chose and promised man that he would benefit or be cursed by the choices he made. Man's nature is fallen and his spirit must change if he is to respond willingly to God's will for his life. Only God's people enlightened by His wisdom and inspired by His Spirit will live and act out of the influence of His love and grace toward each other in such a way as to demonstrate His wisdom, His grace, His justice, His mercy, His love and His glory. This incredible truth inspired John Jay, the first chief justice of the Supreme Court to declare to America that this new and distinct form of government of, for and by the people will only serve to govern effectively a Godly people who chose to walk humbly before God.

This distinctive process had to be carefully instituted by the constitution and must insure that checks and balances, which would ultimately give man the best hope of justice and righteousness being enacted, were in place and could not be easily altered by government in fact or context. The government of the new republic would rest firmly on the foundation of God's sovereignty in the governing process and in all the conduct of the affairs of men. America would be a Christian nation, one nation under the hand and inspiration of the God of the Christian bible. Any enemy of the bible was indeed an enemy of America. The power of America would be her Spiritual oneness in mind and heart before God and clearly not her spiritual diversity!!

"We the people of the Untied States, in order to form a more perfect Union, establish justice, insure domestic tranquility, provide for the common defense, promote the general welfare, and secure the blessings of liberty to ourselves and our posterity, do ordain and establish this Constitution…"

CHAPTER THREE

GOVERNMENT OF, FOR &
BY THE PEOPLE

—m—

There are two vitally important distinctions that set the government of the United States of America apart from the government of any other nation. Those distinctions are clearly spelled out in our founding documents. The first distinction is that it is a government subservient to Gods sovereignty and, second it is a government of, for and by the people.

The final authority in the governing process is intended to be God as His will is accomplished through the collective conscience of a Spiritually discerning people united together for the purposes of God and for the common good of those who are humble before Him.

The preamble of the document that declares America an independent nation defines the intentions, purpose and essence of our nation. It spells out our creed and our character as a society of people and as a nation among nations of the world. It reads, *"When, in the course of human events, it becomes necessary for one people to dissolve the political bands which have connected them with another, and assume, among the powers of the earth, the separate and equal station to which the laws of nature and of nature's God entitle them, a decent respect to the opinions of mankind requires that they should declare the causes which impel them to the separation. We hold these truths to be self-evident, that all men are created equal; that they are endowed by their Creator with certain unalienable rights; that among these are life, liberty, and the pursuit of happiness. That to secure these rights, governments are instituted among men, deriving their just powers from the consent of the governed;"*

It doesn't take much discernment to recognize that if the citizens (at least the vast majority of citizens) and those men chosen to govern this new nation were not faithful, loyal, courageous, alert and wise Christian men led by the Spirit and wisdom of God this experiment in liberty, peace, justice and the pursuit of happiness would ultimately fail.

77

Those well intended and God ordained freedoms would be lost to the lusts and appetites of the fallen natures of men, despots and heathens who naturally walk according to the dictates of their lusts, appetites and pleasures. We are indeed experiencing the inevitable deterioration that comes when men ignore their responsibilities to govern or when men move away from God.

A nation without God and in rebellion against His will is destined to become morally degenerate, selfish, divisive and cruel dependent upon more and bigger government that spends itself arbitrating between the selfish interests of natural man and providing the essential control over the open expression of the lusts and appetites of the fallen nature of men. Ultimately America, or any nation without God, is destined to failure in the sense that its depravity will destroy its freedoms and its ability to function efficiently and effectively, which ultimately leads to economic and moral collapse, poverty, slavery and uncontrollable evil.

Our Supreme Court in its incredible moral blindness and secular humanist arrogance has taken it upon itself to reject Gods sovereignty and His influence in and over the governing process, our public education system and the social order of our nation. We are therefore witnessing the agonizing deterioration of the goodness and moral character of a nation of people. We are beginning to taste the death that governed and destroyed the Soviet Union.

We are also beginning to uncover the vulnerability of the democratic process as we watch it systematically fail because it has been placed in the hands of a people who have lost the vision and focus and rejected God. They find themselves without the Spiritual foundation or Spiritual guidance and wisdom that are the foundation and sustaining source of true liberty.

Our declarations as a government and as a people become more form than substance and our national character continues to deteriorate rather than to grow in strength and righteousness. Only a blind man cannot recognize that a democracy and/or representative government void of God is no challenge to the passions and unrestrained evil of men who are without the leading and protecting hand of our Creator. Our hypocrisies are increasing and the true evil of our fallen natures is becoming more evident. The declarations of our leaders become meaningless chaff that blows away with tomorrow's meaningless declarations. Our government leaders cannot be trusted to do what is right and our courts judgments are no longer wise, righteous or just.

Democratic government in a secular nation is relegated to an endless process of arbitrating the various selfish interests and evil issues that arise when the appetites and pleasures of its citizens compete for power, wealth and acceptance in the arena of ideas, attitudes and heathen or pagan religious belief systems.

There are certainly many vestiges of the great heritage of a God led government of, for and by the people, remaining today. However, America is crumbling from within because it has adopted evil and abandoned righteousness and the guidance of our Creator and

Protector. We have adopted secular humanism as the God of America and we have chosen secular humanist leadership guided by deceit to inspire and lead us. Secularism gets its inspiration directly from Satan, the God of this world, who works his will and way through the fallen nature of men who are not humble before God.

We are discovering in our attempts to transport democracy to the Middle East that it involves much more than objective idealism and/or simply holding an election and installing a form of democratic government. Freedom is inseparable from the sovereignty of God and a philosophy of life led and inspired by the wisdom and courage of the Spirit of the Author of liberty.

The source and key to the glory of America's democracy is God and His people. The magic and mystery of the American government of, for and by the people is God and His wisdom resident in and worked out through the hearts and minds of His people. The dependence upon this supernatural power is expressed in our founding documents. For the democracy and liberty of any republic to survive requires a predominant Spiritual presence in its citizenry to protect its freedom and sustain its goodness and justice.

There are several nations throughout history who have adopted a democratic form of government only to find it impossible to administer in an atmosphere of secularism, selfish interests and evil religious cultism. As I mentioned in an earlier chapter, the Greek government of biblical times is one of the most notable examples of failure of a secular democracy. Their secular humanist government and the pagan religious practices that found their source of power in the minds of men and the passion for lust and appetite for pleasure found in the fallen nature of man led them to a moral depravity unparalleled in the civilized cultures of the world. Its people became dependent upon government and morally depraved. The taxes were beyond the people's ability to pay them causing their economy to collapse. A government dependent society immerged and an inefficient and huge government bureaucracy had to be financed. Government became so large and costly it enslaved and destroyed them economically through taxes levied to finance government dependence and the inefficient government monster.

The principal lesson we should have learned from these various social and political government experiments is that Secular humanist government and the liberty promised by democratic government are indeed enemies of the truth unless they are dependent upon the wisdom of God. Freedom is a gift of God and not a condition created by the cleverness of political manipulations generated in the minds of secular men.

Jon Jay, the first chief justice of our very first Supreme Court, knew and boldly declared that democracy and secularism would not work together because of the deceit of humanism, which is inspired by the appetites, pleasures, lusts and pride of the fallen natures of men. When secular humanism is predominant within the society it will destroy freedom and justice to satisfy its lusts and appetites. It will ultimately destroy the faith, character, courage, justice and wealth of any society it controls. It will destroy itself and all who follow after its deceit.

The glue that holds representative government together is God and his love shed in the hearts of the men governed that leads them to hold sacred Christian character, moral clarity, mutual charity and respect for the desires, rights and needs of their fellowman. Without this Spiritual foundation a democratic republic is no better than any other form of government. Our Supreme Court has leveled a decisive blow to America. Deceived men are working diligently to destroy the Spiritual foundation in America and the Church is not providing the salt and light to lead us out of this delusion.

The secular humanist believes and promotes the naïve concept that it is the competing interests of the special interest groups doing battle in the political arena that makes democracy work. They therefore worship this diversity as the key to community. It is true that the democratic form of government and its processes holds out the best promise for men so long as all competing special interest groups are similar in size, resources and political power. However, when special interests do not possess the same political power a secular democracy will not protect the needs and interests of those without political power.

There is no form of government known to man that works perfectly. However, Democracy works better than any other form of government so long as those governed are men and women of conscience and character who walk humbly before God. The point is that it takes much more than a democratic form of government to insure liberty, justice and tranquility to any people.

America is witnessing the rejection of the one that makes democratic rule work. We are witnessing the crumbling of the power and influence of the vital foundational promises of our founding documents. Representative government is becoming a cesspool of power seeking nest-builders looking for a ticket to ride who are without moral courage to challenge the attempt by the Supreme court to create a secular humanist government to rule over a society of secularism, atheism, humanism, and Anti-Christ religious cults.

It is more and more apparent that we are becoming a people without moral authority or Spiritual leadership. Our government leaders are without the wisdom, character or moral courage to lead righteously. We see ourselves free falling into national disgrace, however, in our deceit we find ourselves unwilling or unable to take the necessary action to change our tragic circumstance.

Rather than confront the lie and expose its deceit we find ourselves attempting to live by a new moral and social code of political correctness, which hides from the truth for the sake of social politeness. It is an idea of hypocrisy born out of the deceit of the secular mind. We are becoming slaves of the deceit of image rather than substance, which is the product of perverted secular humanist minds.

We see the influence of money and power determining the course of the nation because we can no longer see a beacon of light to guide us into truth and righteousness. We find we are left without a foundation by which we establish or measure good and evil, right and wrong or Justice and injustice.

Life's purpose and the principle national purpose of America have shifted from Spiritual maturity and human liberty to material success, national diversity and the acquisition of political power. Material success and political power in a society of evil and deceit is acquired at great cost to ourselves, our families and those foundational values that have sustained and identified our society. The attitude we have adopted is that reaching our selfish goal justifies our selfish and evil acts. In short, it seems necessary to repeat that this or no other government can withstand or overcome the passion and the works of the evil that lies in the heart of natural man. Only a sovereign God can deliver and protect us from that kind of evil! American government has rejected God!

From a political perspective our diversity has brought our nation to a standstill in its progress toward liberty and justice and the realization of those unalienable rights spoken of in our constitution.

Not long after the 9-11 tragedy one of our citizens wrote an editorial that was published in one of our nations newspapers that reveal the misguided thinking of our culture regarding the political correctness of our diversity. He wrote, *"I am tired of this nation worrying about whether we are offending some individual or their culture. Since the terrorist attacks on September 11th, 2001 we have experienced a surge in patriotism by the majority of Americans. However, the dust from the attacks had barely settled when the "politically correct" crowd began complaining about the possibility that our patriotism was offending others. I am not against immigration, nor do I hold a grudge against anyone who is seeking a better life by coming to America. Our population is almost entirely made up of descendants of immigrants. However, there are a few things those who have come to our country, and even those born here, need to understand. The idea of America being a multicultural community has served only to dilute our sovereignty and our national identity. As Americans, we have our own culture, our own society, our own language and our own lifestyle. This culture developed over centuries of struggles, trials and victories by millions of men and women who have sought and fought to maintain our freedom and our culture. We speak English, not Spanish, Portuguese, Arabic, Chinese, Japanese, Russian or any other language. If you wish to become part of America learn the language. "In God we trust" is our national motto. This is not some political slogan. We adopted this motto because Christian men and women, based on Christian principles founded this nation. This is clearly documented. It is certainly appropriate to display this motto on the walls of our schools and the institutions of government. If God offends you, that's your problem not ours, and I suggest you consider some other part of the world to make your new home, because God is the centerpiece of our culture. If the stars and stripes offend you, or you don't like Uncle Sam, then you should seriously consider a move to another part of this planet. We are happy with our culture and have no desire or plan to change it. We really don't care how you do or did things in your country. This is our country. Our First amendment gives every citizen (not every person) the right to express his opinion and we will allow you an opportunity to do so as well. But once you are done complaining, whining, and griping about our flag, our pledge, our national motto and our way of life, please take advantage of another right while you still have it, the right to leave!"*

The vast majority of Americans share his sentiment! However, very loud and obnoxious minorities of deceived Americans who want to destroy everything that is or ever has been American have the ear of the press in America and their secular and socialistic message continues to gain inroads into our national culture. Their deceived and foolish thinking dominates our public education system. We have appointed such men to high position in our government and in our public institutions of higher learning, our law schools and to our federal courts. Their perverted secular thinking continues to set the course of our nation and our children's future.

The obvious question is how long will America continue to be the sanctuary of freedom and justice if we continue to allow secular humanists, socialists, a liberal minority and our Supreme Court to re-write our history, set aside our Christian heritage, ignore the plain meaning of our constitution and destroy our children and our value system, indeed our very foundation

As millions have said, "when will someone do something to protect and secure our constitutional rights as American citizens?" The next time you consider that question perhaps you ought to look in the mirror. You and I are the ones appointed to lead the battle in our homes and communities. Perhaps you have overlooked the fact that we are supposed to be a self-governing nation? When will we begin to examine the concept and begin to accept the responsibility of citizenship of this self-governing nation? Perhaps it is a concept beyond our understanding and capacity to grasp and we are therefore unable or unwilling to govern ourselves! That's the conclusion our government has come to.

In America, we have traditionally celebrated Christmas because it was a symbol of our individual and collective charity toward our fellowman as followers of Christ. The polls tell us almost 90% of Americans profess to be Christian. Christmas is the celebration of the birth of Christ, who is the centerpiece of God's grace and our most precious faith, during which we display all that is good about the spirit of America.

However, our courts have decided that since Christmas is distinctively a Christian holiday and isn't celebrated by all other religions in America we cannot publicly cele-brate the Christmas holiday because it might suggest a breach in the separation of church and state and it might offend other religious observers. It's enlightening to note that the protests and court actions are not typically prompted by other religious observers, but by atheists and secular activists and judges who hate God and His people. If atheists chose not to participate, if agnostic secular humanists chose not to participate, if other religious followers chose not to celebrate Christmas that is up to them. No American Christian has ever forced anyone to observe our Christian tradition.

I am not aware of a single case in which our government attempted to interfere with the public religious expression of any other religious group belonging to any recognized world religion. Heathens, homosexuals, atheists and perverts of every sort fill the public streets of urban communities in America with parades of naked bodies and sick expressions of their perversion. Our government protects that expression under the guise of freedom of speech and freedom of religious expression. Doesn't it strike you as strange that Christians are denied the same freedom of speech and religious expression in the public forum? If it doesn't I believe it should!

Whether the courts, the government, the atheists, secularists, perverts and God haters like it or not the majority of people in America profess to be Christian. American people are Christian and Christmas is a traditional Christian holiday during which we celebrate our Christianity and our Christian heritage. The people who chose to live in America or who migrate here may come here so long as they come here legally with the understanding they are entering a Christian nation into which they must assimilate. They are choosing to join the culture of a Christian nation and **this Christian nation is not joining their culture.**

The attitude that the United States of America is a culture whose foundation and deepest beliefs and values are evolving, rather than fixed, is horribly wrong and tragically destructive. The beliefs and biblical Spiritual foundation of followers of Christ was established 2000 years ago and clearly revealed in the Christian Bible. Faith in God and His will for His creation is not subject to political debate and does not change with time or cultural change. It is not an evolving process. God is the same yesterday, today and forever according to the scriptures. The Scriptures are clear and the secular idea that we change these beliefs to accommodate the fickle minds of a rebellious and diverse culture is Spiritual suicide for that society and therefore it is insanity.

The secularists have decided that we must avoid the spiritual battle between God and Satan. To do that they have decided they can make everyone happy with a weird sort of ungodly spiritual diversity attitude and a "don't ask and don't tell" mentality. We suffered a very unwise and Spiritually blind President who tried to do that with the introduction of homosexuals in the military. Rather than confronting the problem declaring that homosexuals are not eligible for military service he created a destructive and ungodly mess for the military and for America.

This liberal nonsense is an attempt to create a fools paradise of peace when there is no peace. There is no blessing in Spiritual diversity. The Scriptures remind us that one lump of leaven leavens the entire loaf. Our liberal secular humanist friends who have lost site of the Spiritual dimension that has made America who she is have adopted the notion that our greatness is found not in our spirituality but in our ethnic and spiritual diversity. They are utter fools!! Unfortunately we, as a society, are accepting that spiritually devastating notion.

The Ultimate situation, from their perspective, is that we abandon religious, and particularly Christian, observance and practice and evolve into some "ally ally altson free" perfect cesspool of diversity. It is a stupid and spiritually blind perspective because the Lord has said that those who do not gather with Me gather against Me. However, the wonderful national diversity crowd wants to hypocritically destroy who we are and have us forsake what we believe and the observance of our faith for the sake of what they consider a higher cause. They want us all to hold hands and walk off the cliff together! As someone once said, they are telling us to go to hell while attempting to make us look forward to the trip! Therefore, it is not acceptable to celebrate a Merry Christmas in the public forum in America because it is a celebration of the birth of Christ.

Consider for another moment this idiocy!! We have sacrificed Christmas for what? So we will not offend heathen religions, atheists and secular humanists that are anti-Christ? Are evil, atheism, and all the other isms so dear to us that we dare not offend them by the free expression of who we are and what we believe? What will it take to awaken America to the devils ploy, which is to destroy us and our precious faith? Why does it have to be Seasons Greetings at Christmas? Is it because the appearance of freedom is so dear that we are willing to support evil to avoid protecting the author and sustainer of true freedom? Is it because we are afraid to do battle with the buffoons that work for the ACLU who want us to believe the constitution demands that we abandon who we are for the sake of the secular cause? Is our faith so shallow that its public display can be stopped simply because some misguided or heathen court says we must?

Doesn't the constitution declare that our government is a government of, for and by the people? Folks, we govern this nation!! Those secular bureaucracies that manage the institution of government are simply people we appoint and hire to administer it. When are we going to make it clear to the heathens, atheists, cults, anti-God perverts, political hacks and secular humanists they do not govern America? When do we decide to make it clear to the Judiciary that they are not a legislative body and therefore they do not govern America? Supposedly some 90% of us believe in God and more than 70 % believe that Jesus Christ is indeed the savior. Where are all you believers when it comes time to exercise your belief and responsibility as a citizen. If you exist wake up and smell the coffee folks!! Think about the implications of your faith and values and register who you are at the voting booth. When are we going to wake up and begin to accept the responsibility of government? We must never relinquish the public expression of our precious faith nor should we ever allow our government or the Judiciary to prohibit the public display or change officially our public Christmas greeting to accommodate the Season's Greetings preferred by the anti-Christ. This is not a battle about signs in the public square or how we can decorate store windows! This is a battle between good and evil! Wake up and recognize we are in the midst of a spiritual battle for America! Perhaps you haven't noticed that we are losing that battle.

We agree with the freedom of people to celebrate their religious faith according to their tradition. They are free not to observe Christmas if they do not wish to. They do not have to enter into the Christian and American tradition if they chose not to. They may call Christmas whatever they wish, however, since the vast majority of Americans are Christian, at least culturally, and traditionally recognize Christmas as Christmas those who do not call it Christmas will just have to wake up and smell the coffee. We are and have always been a distinctly Christian nation and with God's help and a Spiritually alive people that will never change.

We must take whatever action necessary to protect the free expression of our faith in the public forum and in our public schools. In fact we should be insisting that teachers teach our children the scriptures and we must put a stop to referring officially in our public schools to Christmas vacation as winter break. If a student wishes to call it winter break we Americans have no problem with that. However, we do have a problem with school administrators and teachers in the public institutions of this Christian nation who are being hired and paid with our tax money to decide Christmas is not constitutional and therefore its winter break.

The majority of Americans traditionally recognize this holiday as Christmas. That's what it is and if we wake up and recognize the battle lines between God and Satan and we aggressively enter into this spiritual battle Christmas is what it is going to be! This is America both public and private. We are Christian and therefore that is what we must be. Anything less is denying our faith and mocking our God. The Spirit of the God we serve according to the scriptures determines who we are. We are Christians and no apology is necessary.

The battle is real folks! It's not a figment of the imaginations of a few Christian zealots.

Folks prayer is vital, however, prayer that is genuine demands action. *"He who watches the wind will not sow and he who looks at the clouds will not reap."* We must wake up to the battle and draw a line in the sand if we value the faith we profess, the America of our founding fathers, and/or the liberties millions have sacrificed their lives for. We have the opportunity to govern! Lets do it!!

Blessed is the man who listens to me, watching daily at my gates, waiting at my door-posts. For he who finds me find life, and obtain favor from the Lord. But he who sins against me injures himself; All those who hate me love death. " (Proverbs 8: 34-36)

We must place watchmen at the gates of America if we value our faith and our freedom. We must create watch groups who carefully observe the signs of the times and the activities of the judiciary and of our government. We must expose those who are constantly attempting to usurp our liberty and those who promote perversion and evil. We must inform our citizens and begin aggressively flooding the court system with cases that protect and establish our value system. We must begin to fight fire with fire. We must begin by joining the battle by filing multi-billion dollar class action discrimination lawsuits against institutions, organizations and special interest groups that are working to infringe upon our liberties and limit the free public expression of our Christian faith.

Sound radical! It is, however it is essential if we wish to preserve our liberty and the right to practice our precious faith in America. We are in a spiritual battle to the death! Lets don't give up and lie down and die. Lets engage the battle!!!!

We need to bring such pressure of accountability against our government and our Judiciary that every time a public representative or a judge opens his mouth or makes a decision he feels the weight of accountability to a higher government of, for and by the people and an even higher judge, our Creator and Lord.

We have gone so far to avoid offending the pagans, heathens and fools in our culture that we have allowed them to work through the judiciary to destroy our heritage and what is good in the traditional American culture. The historical and biblical truth is waning with each new generation and we do nothing. We have lost site of who we are and what molds our character and protects our spirituality. We declare ourselves to be a nation under God so lets begin to think and act like it, promote it and express our faith publicly and at the polls. Finally, when does this evil inspired offense against America begin to be register in our conscience and begin to inspire us to make a difference in how we govern and who we appoint to our courts?

This historical constitutional Christian republic is profound in concept, divinely inspired and can only be sustained and appreciated by those who recognize and are committed to its divine guidance and political strengths. We must become alert to its vulnerabilities and remain alert to attacks against it and we must be ready to go to battle for those divine principles on which it was founded and sustained. In the Spirit of Winston Churchill we must never, never, never, never, never, never, never, never, never forget that America was and is a "NATION UNDER GOD" and we must never let the enemies of America and/or God forget it either.

We must once again become a government of, for and by the people as it is envisioned in our constitution. We must view an attack on our constitution, our faith, our flag, our liberty and our tradition as an attack by the enemies of America and of God.

CHAPTER FOUR

A NATION UNDER GOD
OUR NATIONAL HERITAGE

—m—

"Blessed is the nation whose God is the Lord, The people whom He has chosen
for His own inheritance. (Psalm 33:12)

I understand that atop the Washington Monument is an aluminum cap upon which two important words are inscribed. Those two words are "Laus Deo". They are perched on top of this 555 ft monument facing skyward toward the heavens and the father of our nation who overlooks the capital of the United States of America. They are Latin words with profound implications! Laus means "Praise be" and Deo means "God".

The construction of this monument began in 1848 and it was inaugurated and opened to the public in 1888. From atop this magnificent structure visitors take in the view of the city, which is divided into four major segments. Interestingly to note that the layout of the city is in the form of a cross. The White House is located to the north, the Jefferson Memorial to the south, the Capitol to the east and the Lincoln Memorial to the west.

Leading from the base to the top of the Washington Monument is 898 steps and 50 landings. On each landing we find undeniable evidence of our Christian heritage. The Holy Scriptures adorns the walls of the landings.

In point of fact, every government institution in Washington is adorned with Scripture and several, such as the Supreme Court, with the Ten Commandments. Bible scriptures and the prayerful words of our founders are found engraved on virtually every government institution and monument in the capitol city. Biblical inscriptions adorn the capitol buildings of virtually every state capitol in America. It would seem impossible for anyone to offer up an acceptable defense against the obvious intentions of the founders to establish the United States of America a nation under God.

Yet in their incredible deceit the Supreme Court accepted the arguments of evil men or utter fools who declared the doctrine of separation between church and state as the doctrine our founders intended and the doctrine our Constitution supports.

Our first President, George Washington, declared the foundation of America in his incredible prayer over the republic as "One Nation, under God". His prayer, the writings and declarations of our founders, the historical record and the physical evidence that abounds in our nations capitol points in the opposite direction from the secularist and atheistic attitude of separation of Church and State declared by the Supreme Court to be the law of the land. Their ruling was not a matter of constitutional interpretation because no such an idea or its implications is found anywhere in our constitution or the founding documents. The ruling could not have been based on historical fact or president because the historical facts and presidents would have clearly led them to rule against secularizing our national government. The ruling could not be based on the intentions of our founders because the writings of the founding fathers refute any such notion.

Yet this highest court in the land saw fit to set the stage for the destruction of our nation with this foolish and far reaching ruling based solely on the out of context arguments of foolish lawyers and the secular bent of the court. Our foolish secular culture proudly points to this egregious unfortunate ruling as the legal basis for the aggressive destruction of our Christian Heritage. They celebrate our secularism as though it is a big step forward for the cause of diversity. What foolish people! America has no greater enemy!

The irony of this decision is its tragic implications and consequences for millions of Americans and perhaps even more millions in the world who have looked to the United States of America as the example of God's calling and His blessing on a people. The United States is still envied by billions of our world's citizens who dream of liberty. A majority of the citizens of virtually every nation in the world would give up their citizenship in their nation of birth for an opportunity to be a citizen of the United States of America.

In fact, outside of secularism, keeping our borders secure from intruders is one of our most pressing domestic problems. America historically has been the only glimmer of hope to a dark and lost world that is getting darker. The glimmer of hope, however, is getting dimmer because we have listened to fools tell us that we need to follow after the ways of the world and we have allowed them to lead us to abandon the ways of God.

As someone said a long time ago, ***"America is great because America is good. When America ceases to be good she will cease to be great."*** He was right! We are systematically abandoning He that made us good and we are losing our greatness and we are inviting the judgment of God. We have traded our goodness for evil and we have traded our wisdom for foolish myths and we have traded our faith for trust in the minds of men. We find glory in men rather than God.

The Scriptures teach us, *"Unless the Lord builds the house its builders labor in vain. Unless the Lord watches over the city, the watchmen stand guard in vain."* (Psalm 127:1)

Perhaps you didn't know that 52 of the 55 signers of Declaration of Independence were orthodox and deeply committed Christians. The other three all believed the Bible was divine truth and believed in the God of the Scriptures. They all believed in God and they all believed in God's personal intervention in lives of men and the events of History. They were not perfect men but they were believers.

This small group of men who formed the Congress of the United States also formed the American Bible Society. Immediately after they declared Americas Independence. The Continental Congress voted to import, purchase and distribute 20,000 copies of the scriptures to the people of this new nation. Amazing isn't it! When is the last time you can remember the United States Congress voting to provide bibles to anyone?

Patrick Henry, who is known as the firebrand of the American Revolution against British oppression is remembered best for his words, *"Give me liberty or give me death."* In our current textbooks in public schools all across America these words are deleted. The entire context of the message this phrase was quoted from reads, *"An appeal to arms and the God of hosts is all that is left us. But we shall not fight our battle alone. There is a just God that presides over the destinies of nations. The battle sir, is not to the strong alone. Is life so dear or peace so sweet as to be purchased at the price of chains and slavery? Forbid it almighty God. I know not what course others may take, but as for me, give me liberty, or give me death."*

Patrick Henry was indeed a Christian. The following year, 1776, he wrote these words, *"It cannot be emphasized too strongly or too often that this great Nation was founded not by religionists, but by Christians; not on religions, but on the Gospel of Jesus Christ. For that reason alone, people of other faiths have been afforded freedom of worship here."*

Thomas Jefferson, the man who atheists, pagans, heathens and anti-God separation of Church and State activists point to as the author of the constitution and the champion of their secularist cause wrote these words on the front of his well worn bible; *"I am a real Christian, that is to say, a disciple of the doctrines of Jesus. I have little doubt that our whole country will soon be rallied to the unity of our Creator."*

In an incident written down by hand and now kept in the Library of Congress, the Rev. Ethan Allen told the story of how a friend of Jefferson encountered him on the way to Church with his red prayer book under his arm. The Friend asks where he was going. Jefferson responded. *"To Church Sir, no nation has ever yet existed or been governed without religion that has ever been given to man and I, as chief Magistrate of this nation, am bound to give it the sanction of my example. Good morning, Sir"*

Although Jefferson did not express his faith as forthright as many of the founders he seems to have shared Washington's views on the usefulness of the religion. He permitted the Capitol to be used every Sunday for the largest church service in the country. He spoke of himself as Christian and insisted that he, as apposed to many professing Christians, understood the Christian faith more fully. He has been accused of being everything from atheist to deist. However, for the Anti-God wing nuts it might be interesting to note that Thomas Jefferson was chairman of the American Bible Society, which he declared in his writings to be his highest calling and most important role.

America's second president, John Adams, was not a deist. It appears that he was a Unitarian or perhaps a nondenominational Christian. He stated at one point to those who questioned his orthodoxy, *"Ask me not whether I am Catholic, or Protestant, Calvinistic or Armenian. In so far as they are Christian, I wish to be a fellow disciple with them all."* In dealing with the question of attempting to govern people of unethical and evil behavior his view was that it would be very difficult for the United States to sustain free institutions unless the behavior of its citizens were not guided by Christian principles. He wrote, *"We have no government armed with the power capable of contending with the human passions unbridled by morality and religion….Our Constitution was made only for a moral and religious people. It is wholly inadequate to the government of any other."* It might be interesting to note that John Adams was the first president to occupy the White House. He had this prayer inscribed in the formal dining room:

I Pray Heaven to bestow
The best of Blessings on
This House
And on all that shall hereafter
Inhabit it. May none but Honest
And Wise Men ever rule under this Roof!

John Quincy Adams, the son of John Adams, was president from 1825 to 1829. He declared that he read three chapters of the Bible every day, which incidentally, is the same number of chapters our current president George W. Bush reads. Every night before going to sleep John Quincy Adams recited a child-hood prayer his mother had taught him; "Now I lay me down to sleep. I pray the Lord my soul to keep; If I should die before I wake, I pray the Lord my soul to take."

The successor of John Quincy Adams was Andrew Jackson who was another daily bible reader who read three to five chapters daily. Jackson become deeply awakened to the meaning and implications of his Christian faith late in life. On his deathbed he stated, *"Death has no terror for me…What are my suffering compared to those of the Blessed Savior? I am ready to depart when called."*

Throughout the nineteenth century until Abraham Lincoln every president professed Christian faith. Some were more devout than others. James Polk (1845 – 1849) was

Calvinistic to the point of not permitting any work performed in the White House on Sundays.

Abraham Lincoln has been used by the same liberal anti-God secularist wing nuts as an example of a President who was not Christian and yet was an American hero. There argument stands primarily on a statement Lincoln once made regarding his mental reservations to various theological assertions. However, any Christian believer who declares that he has never experienced mental reservations regarding the doctrines and implications of his faith is either intellectually dishonest or has a very short memory. In Lincoln's writings he remembers fondly the Christian moral instruction of his mother, Nancy Hanks Lincoln. Lincoln was president of a divided nation and he was very sensitive to the further division that might be caused by his endorsement of any particular Christian denomination. Lincoln was, however, a Christian believer. President Lincoln always prayed standing up. Lincoln was once asked by a parishioner why he stood up when he prayed. He replied, *"When my generals visit the White House, they stand when their Commander-in-Chief enters the Oval Office. Isn't it proper, then, that I stand for my Commander-in-Chief."*?

Rev Phineas Gurley of the New York Avenue Presbyterian Church, where Lincoln regularly attended mid-week prayer meetings, was a friend, pastoral counselor and prayer warrior for President Lincoln. He relates that Lincoln was driven many times to his knees in prayer (figuratively speaking) by what Lincoln said was the *"overwhelming conviction that I had nowhere else to go. My wisdom, and all that about, seemed insufficient for the day."* Lincoln was a humble man that kept him from boasting about his triumph in anything and certainly in his Christian walk. Perhaps we remember best his retort to a Pastor who expressed the hope that the Lord would be on the side of the Union. Lincoln replied, *"I am not concerned about that, for I know that the Lord is always on the side of the right. But it is my constant anxiety and prayer that I and the nation should be on the Lord's side."* Lincoln's words declare that he possessed a profoundly Christian view of life. A brief visit to his memorial and a review of his second inaugural address there inscribed will confirm his trust in God and his Christian perspective.

Our Presidents down through the nineteenth century were predominantly Christian. That is because the nation was predominantly Christian and it was a nation born out of Christian faith and Tradition. Anything other than a devout Christian leader to lead a Christian nation was not something even considered by America.

Rutherford Hayes (1877-1881) was a devout Christian who made a public point of his faith. His wife was referred to as "Lemonade Lucy" because she would not allow tobacco, alcohol or card playing in the White House.

James Garfield in 1881 and William McKinley in 1901 were devout Christians and were both assassinated in office. McKinley stated in 1899, *"My belief embraces the divinity of Christ and a recognition of Christianity as the mightiest factor in the world's civiliza-*

tion." After McKinley was shot and his assailant was captured, he said, *"Be easy with him boys"….."Good-by all, good-bye. It is God' will. His will, not ours, be done."*

McKinley's Vice President and successor was Theodore Roosevelt, a man who would not pass the muster of Christian fruit inspection by evangelicals of his day or ours. He rejected outright the doctrine of justification by faith and outwardly declared and promoted a works-based righteousness. His argument was based on the words found in the epistle of James, *"Be ye doers of the word, and not hearers only".* Yet he was a religious man and a strong believer in Church and regular church attendance.

After Theodore Roosevelt Americas Spiritual umbrella began to disappear. They elected Howard Taft over the outspoken fundamentalist Christian William Jennings Bryan. Taft was a Unitarian. He said, *"I believe in God, I do not believe in the divinity of Christ, and there are other of the postulates of the orthodox creed to which I cannot subscribe."*

Taft's successor was Woodrow Wilson, the former president of Princeton University. He was a devout Presbyterian and Calvinist Christian believer. He emphatically declared, *"I believe in divine providence, If I did not, I would go crazy.."*

Franklin Delano Roosevelt was not a religious minded man, however, he concluded his inaugural address in 1933 with the prayer, *and "In this dedication of a nation we humbly ask the blessing of God, May He protect each and every one of us and May He guide me in the days to come."* America was beginning to shift from its dependence upon God and from the faith in divine destiny.

Harry Truman was Roosevelt's Vice President and his successor. Roosevelt died in office at the beginning of his fourth term. Truman was an outspoken Baptist who had little regard for religious display. However he carried with him at all times a prayer which began, *"Almighty and everlasting God, creator of heaven and earth and the universe, help me to be, to think, to act what is right, because it is right. Make me truthful, honest, and honorable in all things."* He was the President who in 1952 signed a joint resolution of Congress creating the National Day of Prayer. It became law in 1988 under President Reagan.

In the 1950's a conservative Protestantism reflected in the life of Eisenhower became the Spiritual mood of America. The President added the phrase (confirmed by the congress) "One Nation Under God" in the Pledge of Allegiance to the flag and the words "In God we Trust" on the nations Coinage. This time was the end of the age when mainline Protestant denominations were evangelical and orthodox from the theological perspective. The institution of church began is slide toward the apostasy we observe today.

America began a dramatic change in its direction away from dependence on and belief in a superintending God. Leading the parade of this change was the exciting figure of John F. Kennedy who America chose to be President over Richard Nixon. Kennedy offered America youth, wit and intelligence and a President that was for the first time, a Roman Catholic. Many Americans were concerned about electing a Catholic President, however, they had little reason to be because Kennedy's Catholicism was more form than substance or manner. The real problem was Spiritual. America was beginning to die Spiritually.

Kennedy was perhaps the first president whose worldview was essentially secular humanist. It was the introduction of the idea that there really isn't such a thing as evil and therefore no spiritual penalty for evil. The idea was promoted that whatever we wished to do we could do through the application of dedication and effort regardless of God's plan. Man was the measure of all things. Kennedy was a practical man but lacked insight into anything Spiritual. America was changing and the change was not good!! It was a move toward secularism. The good that came out of the 1960's was the extending civil rights to African Americans. Kennedy's romantic interludes proved his morals were similar to his pet dog. His leadership was appealing to an age of people who wanted to hear that man was indeed the measure of all things and whatever man wanted to do he could do and that God was window dressing that had little relevance in the new age.

Kennedy was assassinated in office and Lyndon Baines Johnson, Kennedy's Vice President, became President. He attempted to implement Kennedy's civil rights initiative, however, Johnson soon realized that civil rights, as just and necessary the cause, had a large contingent of players underlying its move who were seeking black power and the overturning of core institutions of American life. He had a tiger by the tail. America was moving away from God and was in an out of Control Spiritual free fall into oblivion. The Sexual revolution, experimentation with drugs and New Age weirdness with its perverted sense of spirituality ripped through the spiritual fabric protecting American culture leaving her soul exposed and vulnerable to the worst perversions of the flesh of man.

Nixon was the next president and his presidency was overshadowed by the disgrace of Watergate. Although Watergate was wrong and needed to be exposed it was in fact far less troubling to America's spirituality, considering the entire scope of things, than the fact that the Church remained silent at the collapse of the spiritual character of our Presidents or of the governments overall collapse of integrity. Nixon's character, or lack of it, was a foreshadowing of the condition of a Church in apostasy. He professed to be a religious man, however, his religion did not effect his actions, attitudes or decisions when the chips were down.

In the late 1970's there arose a so called "Jesus Movement' where its adherents ran around in thongs and adorned themselves and their person after the manner of a citizen of Palestine 2000 years ago. This move welcomed the likes of Jimmy Carter, a southern Baptist, who spoke openly about being born again. President Carter was undoubtedly sincere about his faith. He taught Sunday school and did not drink alcohol and his secret service code name was "Deacon". Carter said in an interview after the fact, *"The country at that time was searching for someone who would publicly profess a commitment to truth and integrity and the adherence to moral values concerning peace, human rights, the alleviation of suffering. I put forward these concepts, which are very deeply ingrained in my own character and motivations."*

Even though the people wanted a "born again" Christian's leading in the seventies, Carter proved to lack wisdom and discernment and he was too indecisive in crisis situations to lead. His quandary over moral truth and equivalence proved he was in need of spiritual wisdom and of knowledge that would give him the vision and determination to lead the nation. He was generally ineffective as our nations chief executive.

In 1980 the nation was ready for someone with down-home common sense wisdom, the moral courage of his convictions and a sunny disposition who believed in the vision and destiny of America. Such a man was Ronald Reagan a Christian believer who recognized that the purposes of divine destiny were being worked out though the United States and he was able to communicate that vision to a majority of the voters. It was his spiritual convictions, above all else, that drove him to denounce the repressive nature of communism. He recognized that we were all bit players in a divine drama. In 1980 he said about America, *"For we must consider that we shall be as a City upon a hill. The eyes of all people are upon us. So that if we shall deal falsely with our God in this task we have undertaken, and so cause Him to withdraw His present help from us, we shall be made a story and a byword throughout the world."* He took this figure of speech from Massachusetts Governor John Winthrop (1640). It was nevertheless appropriate and on point in 1980 as it is today.

Reagan was a great President. He began to arouse and expose the liberal anti-God hate that we see at work in politics and government today. That hate has gained great inroads into our culture because we did not recognize its danger and we lacked the courage to fight and defeat it. Now it has taken over our government and is rising up a secular humanist culture that legislates its agenda and controls our response through a deceived Supreme court, self-indulgent introspective legislative bodies and a spiritually dead and indifferent society.

George H. Bush, our next President could not articulate Reagan's vision for America because he did not have it. Bush was a religious person who surrounded himself with Christian leaders such as Billy Graham who was a regular guest at the White House during the Bush administration. Billy Graham was an evangelist. God used him mightily and still uses him to this day. President Bush (Senior) did not possess the passion of vision or purpose that is apparent in the calling of God on the life of a man called into the leadership of a nation. President Bush was the leader of a fickle people who hailed him as King after delivering Kuwait and they were ready to throw him out of office a few months later when the reviving economy demanded endurance, diligence, discipline and patience. Qualities long since gone from a fast food – drive by American culture.

Following George H. Bush was the kid from Hope Arkansas who just wanted to be President, Bill Clinton. Clinton was a supposed Southern Baptist who seemed well versed in the Scriptures but void of the power they offer to protect from the lusts of the flesh. He was a deceived and politically ambitious man who was comfortable with the evangelical

Christian community; however, his faith was more image than substance and had little power over his life.

I received a letter revealing the remarks of a man who was reported to be part of the secret service Presidential detail in the White House for many years. He confirmed the Kennedy & Marilyn Monroe relationship the press never seems to get enough of. He reveals what we all suspected regarding Bill and Hilary Clinton's liberal agenda, lack of character and failed marriage relationship. I was amazed at some of his comments; however, I was particularly pleased at his remarks regarding the character of some of the other Presidents he served. I have quoted his remarks for your information and perhaps enlightenment.

Regarding the Clintons he said, *"President Clinton was much more amiable than his wife Hillary. Even the Secret Service would cringe at the verbal attack antics that Hillary would use against her husband, then President. We were embarrassed for his sake by the manner and frequency in which she verbally insulted him. Even behind closed doors Hillary would scream and yell so loudly everyone could hear what she was saying. She was arrogant and orally abusive to her security detail. She forbids her daughter, Chelsea, from exchanging pleasantries with them. Hillary Clinton was continuously rude and abrasive to those who were charged with her security. They did their job but they all "loathed" her and wanted to be assigned a different detail. Many of us felt sorry for President Clinton and wondered why he tolerated it. It was crystal clear that neither of them liked or respected each other long before the Monica Lewinsky scandal. Theirs was a marriage of convenience."*

"Chelsea was much closer to her father than her mother, even after the Lewinsky scandal which hurt her gravely. Clinton had a charisma, however, he always displayed an air of superiority towards his security detail and aides. We believed uniformly that he was disingenuous, false and that he did nothing without a motive that in some way would enhance his image and political career. We did respect him, unlike his wife Hillary, but we did not like him and nobody trusted him. He was polite, but not kind."

Regarding Al Gore, Clintons Vice President, he stated, *"Al Gore was the male version of Hillary Clinton. They were friendlier toward each other than they were towards the President. They were not intimate, however, they were close in a political way. Tipper Gore was generally nice and pleasant. Al Gore, like Hillary, was very rude and arrogant toward his security detail. He was extremely unappreciative and would not hesitate to scold us in the presence of our peers for minor detail over which we had no control. He looked down upon us in disgust."*

Regarding George H. Bush he said, *"Bush 31 and the current President Bush made it a point to thank and they take care of the aircrews who flew them around and both of them made it a point to stay home on holidays, so the aircrews and security people could have a day with their families.*

Last but not least he said they who served all love our Current President Bush and his family: Listen to these words:

"Everyone in the Secret Service wants to be on First Lady Laura Bush's detail. Without exception, they uniformly concede that she is perhaps the most nice, kind, and genuinely good person they have ever had the privilege of serving. While Hillary patently refused to allow her picture to be taken with her security detail, Laura Bush doesn't even have to be asked, she offers. Laura Bush doesn't just shake hands and say,' Thank you' Very often she will give members of her detail a kind-hearted hug to express her appreciation. There is nothing false about her. This is her genuine nature. She is a breath of fresh air. Her security detail actually loves her as a human being. They joke often that comparing Laura Bush to Hillary Clinton is like comparing "Mother Teresa" with the "Wicked Witch of the North". Likewise, the Secret Service considers President Bush to be a gem of a man to work for. He always treats them with genuine respect and always trusts and listens to their expert advice. They really like the Crawford, Texas detail. Every time the President goes to Crawford he has a Bar-B-Q for his security detail and he helps in serving them their meals. He eats with them, sits with tem, and talks with them. He always asks about their families, the names of which he always remembers, and he of course, knows each of them by their first name, and calls them by their first name as a show of affection. We believe that he loves his security detail and that he is deeply and genuinely appreciative of their service. They could not like, love, or respect anyone more than President Bush, and most of them did not know they would feel this way until they had an opportunity to work for him and learn that his manner was genuine and consistent. It has never changed in the years he has been President. He always treats us with the utmost respect, kindness and compassion."

The above comments were forwarded through Dick Sprowl, a military Chaplain and close friend and associate of their author, a Secret Service Agent.

Finally in regards to our present President George W. Bush it is clear he is a "born again " believer. He is indeed a breath of fresh air in Washington; however, every anti-God liberal in Washington hates him passionately, which is perhaps the most sure testimony that he is the real thing. Perhaps our Lord is revealing to us His call to America for our collective awakening. Only time will tell, however, our heritage is clearly Christian and the revisionist historians who want to hide the truth and destroy our heritage have to deliberately lie to construct their humanist maze of distortion. However, they are able to find many deceived followers ready to accept their distortion and promote their destructive cause.

George W. Bush is candid about his Christian faith. He speaks frankly, freely and unashamedly of the influence his faith has on his character, his decisions and his vision for himself. It is what gives his life purpose and direction. The vision he has to spread liberty and freedom to the entire world is clearly a missionary vision drawn directly from the bible and inspired by the Spirit of God.

He recognizes the divine hand of God as sovereign in all of life and particularly in the calling on America and her people. He believes we are blessed by God with our abundance and with the opportunity as the most powerful, most influential and the most prosperous people in the world and we therefore have the responsibility and calling to spread the freedom we enjoy to the world wherever the providence of God may lead us to do so. God has made him the leader of the free world. His vision for our nation is to reach out to other nations to help protect millions from the tyranny of evil dictators much like our mission in Iraq.

George W. Bush has done more to help the oppressed peoples of the middle east, Africa, and the oppressed peoples around the world since 2001 than has the combined efforts of all the leaders and nations of the middle east, or anywhere else for that matter, and the combined efforts of missionary work, the United Nations or the bureaucratic foreign policy initiatives of appeasement agenda's throughout the last 50 years. He has brought more of the glory of God to the attention of our nation and the world than the organized church. We ought to be indeed grateful that our God has given us such a leader. However, he is limited in the effectiveness of our national efforts in the Middle East by the foolish and destructive criticism of the Anti-Christ liberal agenda and the political ambitions of those in the legislative branch of our government.

Unfortunately, America we are exposing our spiritual deceit and our self-serving attitude if the media polls are accurate. We are a fickle people who have been conned into the liberal thinking of the deceived. We declare we are Christian, however, our attitudes and actions tend to dispute our confession.

I have presented this brief rundown on the spiritual condition of our nations Chief Executives to give us a clearer view of the heritage of our nation and of the change from the evangelical leadership of our nation to its secular humanist turn away from God.

President Bush could well be the last effort our Lord will make to awaken America. The prophetic implications of his leadership are overlooked by our people. There does not seem to be a sensitivity or response to God's grace at work among us by our people. We seem to be becoming more and more selfish, secularist and atheistic. For those of you who wish to take issue with the historical record I simply suggest it is worth checking out. The historical record is relatively easy to discover for any who have the desire and determination to seek after the truth.

In 1782, the United States Congress passed this resolution: *"The Congress of the United States recommends and approves the Holy Bible for use in all schools"*

On July 4, 1821, President Adams stated, *"The highest glory of the American Revolution was this; it connected in one indissoluble bond the principles of civil government and principles of Christianity."*

Calvin Coolidge, our 30th President of the United States reaffirmed this truth when he wrote, *"The foundations of our society and our government rest so much on the teachings of the bible that it would be difficult to support them if faith in these teachings would cease to be practically; universal in our country".*

Interestingly, William Holmes McGuffey the author of the McGuffey Reader which was used for more than 100 years in our public schools of which over 125 million copies were sold before its use was stopped in 1963, wrote regarding the foundation of our nation and the divine authority that sustains it: *"The Christian religion is the religion of our country. From it are derived our notions on the character of God, the great moral governor of the universe. On its doctrines are founded the peculiarities of our free institutions. From no source has the author drawn more conspicuously than from the sacred scriptures. From all these extracts from the Bible I make no apology".* Our 16th President, Abraham Lincoln, referred to McGuffey as the "Schoolmaster of the Nation."

Of the first 108 universities founded in America, 106 were distinctly Christian, including the first, Harvard University, chartered in 1636. In the original Harvard Student Handbook, rule number 1 was that students who were seeking entrance into Harvard must know, or learn, Latin and Greek so they could study the scriptures.. It reads, **"Let every student be plainly instructed and earnestly pressed to consider well, the main end of his life and studies is, to know God and Jesus Christ, which is eternal life, John 17:3; and therefore to lay Jesus Christ as the only foundation for our children to follow the moral principles of the ten commandments."** This is a far cry from any part of Harvard's educational goals or curriculum today.

James Madison is thought by most scholars to be the primary author of the Constitution of the United States. Madison wrote and warned his associates in his speeches, *"We have staked the whole future of our new nation not upon the power of government; far from it. We have staked the future of all our political constitutions upon the capacity of each of ourselves to govern ourselves according to the moral principles of the Ten Commandments."*

No matter the convincing proofs of our Christian foundation and heritage, those whose will is set by the Spirit of the world hates God and they hate the church of Jesus Christ and any or all who are a part of it. In their deceit they refuse to humble themselves before God. They consider secularism as objectivity and therefore fair, just and good. They view Godliness and truth as bigotry and therefore evil and bad. They march to a different drummer. They will not be convinced no matter what proofs are presented because their rebellion springs from their will and their hearts, which are either deceived or evil or both. They are destroying America and causing pain and suffering to many. They mock God in an effort to hide their evil deeds from exposure by the truth. However, whether they deny or refuse to acknowledge the truth or not, does not change the truth nor the fact that they will ultimately be judged by it.

So long as the Godlessness in the culture in which we live is allowed to grow and politically control our society we will find that more deceived people will enter the ranks of this current secular culture. Their commitment to removing any influence or evidence of God's influence on our society will continue to grow stronger until we arrive at a time when one or another Court ruling forbids the public expression of our Christian faith.

Perhaps you are thinking – Oh! "they can't do that! Our Constitution forbids it! So it does, however, it also forbids the governments interference in the public expression of our Christian faith. It did not stop the court from taking prayer out of school, removing the Ten Commandments from display in our schools and from many public buildings or stopping prayers at commencement exercises or before high school athletic activities in public schools.

Our people have chosen to blindly follow after the spiritually dead foolish reasoning of these supposedly honorable men and women supposing they know what is best for us. So in our deceit we follow along like a bunch of lemmings without a clue about where all this will lead. Well, my friend that is not how it's supposed to be! God gave us a mind so perhaps it is time we begin to use it. To those born of His Spirit he gave us his Spirit to help guide us so perhaps it is time to begin to listen to Him. He gave the Church to the world to be salt and light so the world might be delivered from deceit so perhaps its time for the church to become the salt and light it is called to be.

The most startling decision to come out of the Supreme Court was the presented to declaration that the constitutional limitation against the constitutional prohibition forbidding the making of laws to prohibit the free public expression of our faith does not apply to the Court, only to the legislature, therefore they have the legal authority under the constitution to prohibit it.

What a bunch of poppy – cock!! They see no problem with ignoring the spirit and intent of the founders who recognized the danger of the government's suppression or control over free religious expression. We need to rise up as a nation and throw these foolish anti-God and therefore anti-America liberal Judges out through the impeachment process and have these devastating decisions reversed.

The Lord says in His word regarding the rebellious *"they are without excuse because "that which is known about God is evident within them; for God made it evident to them. For since creation of the world His invisible attributes, His eternal power and divine nature, have been clearly seen, being understood through what has been made, so that they are without excuse. For even though they knew God, they did not honor Him as God, or give thanks; but they became futile in their speculations, and their foolish heart was darkened. Professing to be wise, they became fools.."* Their rebellion is a matter of the will.

Those in rebellion against God hate the truth. Jesus said, *"And this is the judgment, that the light is come into the world, and men loved the darkness rather than the light; for their deeds were evil. For everyone who does evil hates the light, and does not come to the light, lest his deed should be exposed."* (John 3: 19-21)

Clearly when America was born it was born a new nation under God. Clearly God's grace reaches around the globe. However, he raised up America to be an example of His blessing and grace to the world. A small group of believers grasped the vision. There is a remnant of believers scattered throughout the globe who are His true Church. The Scriptures reveal that there are also some who have tasted the Spirit of God and have become caught up in secularism and this evil culture in which we live. They are spiritually luke warm, which God says he hates. God is still speaking to their hearts and minds and perhaps some of this group will be awakened and return to there Spiritual ancestry and recommit their lives to their role in God's divine plan.

Today I boldly petition God to bless Americans and America and guide our goings and comings. My mind and heart asks how I should expect a just God to continue to bless, protect and prosper a people who have rejected Him and rebelled against His will and mocked the atoning sacrifice of His son. My prayer is that we might be delivered from deceit and death inherent in this evil.

Clearly, according to the Supreme Court, God is no longer welcome in the governing process or in the American culture. They have also decided it is no longer fit to teach our children to know or humble themselves before God. The Godless and deceived revisionists of the Judiciary are busy erasing truth from our History books and the public arena. Our public education system Is now lead by secular humanist leaders and educators who eagerly present the lie of secular humanism to our children because it enables them to hide the truth and create a culture where they are not judged by the truth or the revealed will of God. The fallen nature of man seeks a place where he can justify his utter sinfulness. He grasps hold of the secular humanist arguments against America's Christian roots and heritage and the vital role of God in mans deliverance and the biblical concept of human liberty.

The United States has historically been an attraction to peoples from virtually every nation. Was it the character and nature of a people under God? Was it the Spirit of freedom whose foundation is found in those unalienable rights given to men by the Creator? Was it simply the economic potential of free enterprise? Was it freedom from the religious oppression of the Anglican, Catholic churches in Europe? Was it simply that everyone has to be someplace and there was the promise of plenty of space in America? Was it an escape from the law in Europe? Whatever it was it continues to call to the people of the world because people are entering America's southern border at such a rate we are unable to secure our borders let alone protect us against all enemies foreign and domestic. Currently, our greatest enemy is spiritual and its impact is domestic. We cannot help the world if we continue to allow America to be destroyed by the influence of the world.

History teaches us there is an inherent goodness, happiness, peace and justice found among people whose passion is their Creator? What did the man mean when he said, ***"America is great because America is good? When America ceases to be good America will no longer be great?"*** What was it about America that made her good and greatly respected among the nations? What uniqueness made America the home of the free and the brave? Clearly it was not the lust and selfish interests of the flesh of man. No, indeed! It was the Word and Spirit of God working its way through the conscience of man.

The dream of prosperity and secular humanism is attractive to those who hate God and His kingdom. It is little more than a slogan to cover the evil intent of the flesh. Secularism is evil and it is not the America of the American dream and vision given to our founding fathers by the Creator.

Americans have historically proven to be a creative, innovative, industrious, prosperous, courageous, generous and just people. Did our national character arise because those men who discovered and later settled this land possessed some special insight into life that was impossible to find or reproduce anywhere else on earth or by any other people?

The scriptures may reveal the source to us. They declare that the fruit of the Spirit of God is *"love, joy peace, patience, kindness, goodness, faithfulness, gentleness and self-control.."*

Did America's commitment to the inestimable value of a single solitary life and the commitment to protect and nourish that life above all other interests come from secular interests or from the Spirit of a God of love and grace?

Historians tell us it was the concept of unalienable rights of individual freedom from oppressive religions and governments that inspired our founding fathers who believed that liberty was a gift from God. It was this idea that made the United States of America the most attractive to men and has historically drawn all men to these shores.

History reveals that the expedition that discovered this land almost 300 years before there was a United States of America was exploring with an evangelistic mandate. It also reveals beyond any reasonable doubt that the men who established the colonies and eventually founded our nation were Christians. History also reveals that America's education system was exclusively and distinctively Christian. We know from a review of the various state constitutions that the political leaders of the various colonies were required to be Christian to hold office. In summary, a review of American history clearly reveals that America was ordained from the very beginning by our Creator to be "one nation under God", even though our pledge of allegiance did not include the phrase "under God" until the twentieth century.

Someone has said the evidence of Spiritual inspiration is the fruit it produces in and through the lives of those so inspired. There was indeed a Spirit in America that was infectious. It was God's Spirit! Our founding documents declare God's wisdom, glory, purpose and sovereignty. The lives of the colonists and the laws of the land demonstrated their religious faith because they revealed the way they chose to live, the words they spoke, the values they held dear and an almost universally proclaimed and sought after abiding relationship with God.

Virtually every institution of learning that sprang up in the new world was founded by Christian men as a distinctly Christian institution founded for the principle purpose of teaching young people to know, love, appreciate, discern and follow after the will and purpose of God and accept His gift of deliverance and salvation. These institutions understood the principle goal and ultimate destiny of life. They were not confused or distracted by worldly interests. The principle focus and primary goal of education as revealed in the founding documents of each of these institutions was to be the knowledge of God and Humility before His Spirit and word.

One of the most senior and formidable statesman at the constitutional convention, Benjamin Franklin, in a reminder and an admonition to his associates who were in heated debate absorbed in the incredible task of creating our Nations founding document declared his belief and dependence upon the leading of a sovereign God in founding this new nation: *"I have lived sir, a long time, and the longer I live, the more convincing proofs I see of this truth; that God governs in the affairs of man, and if a sparrow cannot fall to the ground without His notice, is it probable that an empire can rise without His aid? We have been assured, sir, in sacred writings, that except the Lord build the house, they labor in vain that build it, I firmly believe this."*

Andrew Jackson, speaking of the bible and its influence in the founding of America, declared: *"That book sir, is the rock on which our republic rests."*

As we look back at the roots of this nation the historical record makes it crystal clear to any intellectually honest student of history that America was born a Christian nation of people dedicated to God's purposes. The record speaks for itself! The power and uniqueness of the American dream is found in the vision divinely imparted to the framers of our founding documents and to our early leaders who recognized that America was born into the world with a divine and profound role in a lost and perishing world.

Our founders were convinced beyond any doubt that God's purpose was to raise up a nation dedicated to Gods will and purpose that would give God glory and men liberty, justice and the opportunity to pursue happiness in this life. America clearly began as a nation of ambassadors to the Kingdom of God and therefore a bastion of liberty, equality and justice for all men. America began as A Nation under God!

We find incontrovertible historical evidence that even before the advent of the declaration of independence, the constitution, the supreme court and the debate surrounding the issue of separation of church and state, or before the advent of a national government or a national president that the search for biblical wisdom and truth was evidenced in the affairs of state, the governing process, laws of the land, the lifestyles of the people and the leadership of America's early leaders.

Biblical truth was the foundation for all laws and judgments and depended upon for guidance by the vast majority of the people. The issues of life were dependent upon, centered around and directed by the Word of God and the wisdom it presents. Life, character, values and social order was defined by biblical truth.

The preponderance of history reveals that men and women of this budding nation turned to the preachers, prophets, biblical teachers and the Word of God to help them interpret where they must stand on the issues of their day. Out of biblical wisdom and Spiritual leadership was born a nation and a national tradition dedicated to the glory and purposes of God. It is indeed a precious and priceless tradition and legacy in which Christ's glory, character and purpose was demonstrated and lived out through the lives of sincere believers and patriots.

Someone has determined that the average senior colonial, which included most senior colonials, would have heard some 7000 sermons in his or her lifetime totaling nearly 10,000 hours of concentrated listening to the gospel of Jesus Christ and the wisdom of God expressed in the bible. I am not sure how accurate these numbers are, however, the point of course is that our early citizens were raised on the word of God.

As the Apostle Paul told the Romans *"do not be conformed to this world, but be transformed by the renewing of your mind, that you may prove what the will of God is, that which is good and acceptable and perfect." (Romans 12:2)*

That renewing comes from the study of the word of God, which *"is living and active and sharper than any two-edged sword, and piercing as far as the division of soul and spirit, of both joints and marrow, and able to judge the thoughts and intentions of the heart." (Hebrews 4:12)*

I believe it's important to note that contrary to the typical pulpit of today, God's grace was highly regarded by the church and its dignity, essence and price were fully appreciated, exposed and it was not peddled cheaply. Church was most certainly not a "pep-rally" fueled emotionally by singing what someone has referred to as "7-11" songs. 7–11 songs are songs with seven words sung eleven times in an attempt to build an emotional frenzy typically interpreted by many to be the moving of the Holy Spirit.

The early church was distinctly separate from the world it ministered to. There was an open invitation to men and women of the world. However, it did not invite worldliness into the church in hopes of somehow drawing the worldly to the church somehow trapping them into submission to God. Attempting to make the worldly more comfortable and unchallenged by the character and purpose of God, by religious surroundings or by the truth, which the world is in rebellion against, reflects our utter failure to understand that none comes to Jesus unless the father calls him. Salvation is of God and if there is anything we ought not do it is to attempt to remove or disrupt the distinctiveness of the working of the Spirit of God and the power of our Christian faith from the gatherings of the Saints.

On the contrary, the early church was distinctive in its message, its environment, its example, its truth, its love and its power. When lost men were seeking the Lord and came to the gathering of the church they were not looking for more of the world wrapped up in a little different wrapper and served up with a few mentions of Jesus Christ or God the father in a religious setting. They were looking for the distinctive character, power, purity, dignity, love, truth and the glory of the God of the bible who promised salvation and Spiritual rebirth to the repentant heart.

For early colonials the gathering of the Church was a time when men were forced to look soberly through the eyes of the Creator at their innermost being. It was a time when men submitted their pathetic pride and sin to the scrutiny of God the Holy Spirit in an attitude of repentance.

The great joy which comes from spiritual cleansing, divine forgiveness and blessing and the conversion of the heart came unto them as they begin to recognize that God truly forgives, restores and receives unto Himself the repentant sinner.

The music played and the hymns sung in the early church setting, which incidentally are still available to the church today, was anointed and spiritually powerful expressions of truth, praise and worship which explained and expressed the passion of men's utter dependence on God's mercy and grace and on God's faithfulness to deliver the repentant heart from condemnation and deceit.

Pastors and teachers were not motivational speakers selling self-esteem, formulas for overcoming and/or secret formulas to material prosperity. The Pastors and ministers of the early church in America were sincere repentant believers humble before God and His Word. They were ambassadors of the kingdom who clearly understood the heart of God and the fallen nature of man and could readily discern the difference. They understood and believed in the power of God to work miraculously through the gospel message of repentance and regeneration.

The typical Sunday worship service found ministers and teachers delivering sermons directly from the thrown and heart of God, which drew the populace into a Spiritual world that was more compelling and immediate than their physical surroundings. These men of God and their messages not only directed men toward salvation in Christ but also lighted the way for men to live temporal life, make decisions on issues effecting life here and hereafter. They were inspiring men and women to trust God to provide a national prosperity whose foundation was God's provision, protection and blessing experienced by a faithful and obedient people.

A brief review of the teachings of the ministers of the early days in America's development clearly reveal that the messages were profound, hard-hitting, and convicting bringing repentance, reform and liberty to the hearts and lives of listeners who understood their utter sinfulness and their need for the truth and God's forgiveness. Men sought after it no matter the cost or sacrifice it required.

America's government leadership, unlike the leaders of any other nation before its time or since, was comprised in essence of Christian colonials whose lives were influenced, inspired and indeed directed by sermons from the Word of God delivered by Spiritually appointed and anointed preachers more than any other influence or form of oratory.

The colonial Christian preacher and his sermon became the prophet, the newspaper, the video, the internet, the community college, the social therapist and the principle purveyor of truth and its application all wrapped up in one package, to our citizens.

These early preachers and teachers were clearly men dedicated to the glory of God and they relied principally on the wisdom of the Word of God and the Spiritual guidance of the Holy Spirit. Their discernment, wisdom and authority were born testimony to by the hearts of men because they were gleaned from the un-compromised Word of God. The halls of our government and all its deliberations echoed the truth and purpose of God as its guidance in dealing with the issues of the day.

The vast majority of colonial Americans would not countenance the teaching or leadership of secular humanists, atheists, perverts or pagans, or for that matter, much of what we today refer to as the church. Teaching not grounded in and consistent with the teaching of the Word of God was considered blasphemy and a devastatingly destructive force to be confronted and reckoned with. It was seen clearly as the enemy of the people and would not be tolerated.

Clearly Christian faith was the primary influence on all aspects of life in colonial America. The leadership of the nation at all levels of government worked diligently to seek spiritual wisdom and protect God's gift of this most precious faith from intrusion and erosion.

There is every evidence that even as late as the nineteenth century America remained a deeply religious culture, in the sense the majority was Christian, that lived under the careful guidance of God through the efforts of Godly leaders and ministers called to deliver truth and wisdom to fallen men and women. Christians were kept accountable and aware of their great need and of God's incredible grace available only through His son Christ Jesus mans only savior!

I am not suggesting there were not ungodly men and despots attracted and welcomed to these shores, however, I am suggesting their actions and attitudes when demonstrated to not be Christian were despised publicly and privately. Evil men and despots were a minority of the population and their despotism was easy for a predominantly Christian and spiritually alert society to discern and protect against. Immorality, evil and injustice were looked upon with disgrace and were not tolerated by society. Justice was sure and swift and administered without apology.

In early America the events of life and liberty were perceived not from the secular humanist vantage point but from God's viewpoint with His declared purpose foremost in the hearts and minds of our leaders and most of our citizens. All events of life, no matter how seemingly mundane or random, were seen as a part of God's providential design. The outline of God's plan and pattern was drawn from the bible and interpreted by believers and by truly called and committed Christian leaders of that day.

The result was that the people came to perceive themselves not as religious exiles and right wing radicals isolated and out of touch with the hearts of the people and left out of the debates of the issues of the day. They saw themselves as God's people called to become the fabric, salt, light, essence and spirit of a new society living on the cutting edge of Gods purpose and every issue of life in America. To them God and His will and way gave purpose, meaning, hope and dignity to human life. To early Americans God was the center-piece of the human race and all it touched.

It is abundantly clear that our forefathers and a vast majority of Americans who settled in the new world and founded this nation considered the United States of America to be a new nation under God.

Biblical truth was the foundation of all law, authority, and judgment. Biblical principles were depended upon for guidance by a vast majority of the citizens. The issues of life were dependent upon, centered around and directed by the Word of God and the wisdom it presents. Life, character, values and social order was defined by biblical truth.

The preponderance of history reveals that men and women of this budding nation turned to the preachers, prophets, biblical teachers and the Word of God to help them interpret where they should stand on the issues of their day. Out of spiritual biblical wisdom and leadership was born a nation and a national tradition dedicated to the glory and purposes of God. It is indeed a precious and priceless tradition and legacy in which Christ's glory, character and purpose was typically demonstrated and lived out through the lives of sincere believers and patriots.

The evidence is overwhelmingly against the idea that the vast majority of America's founding fathers were not professing Christians or that the Nation they envisioned, and ultimately created, was not founded on Judeo Christian principles, morals and values. Their writings clearly point out that they considered their deliberations guided by God the Holy Spirit. The founders recognized and proclaimed to the world that without humility before the Creator, His grace to forgive them and His wisdom to guide them this experiment in individual Liberty and justice for all would fail miserably.

William Blackstone, an eighteenth century English jurist and lecturer at law at Oxford, was considered America's foremost authority on Law and every law student of virtually every law school in America or England had to study Blackstone. His commentaries on law were considered to present the foundational thesis of all law because it looked for its authority and guidance to the Word of God. In the first century of American independence his commentaries were not merely an approach to the study of law, but rather, for most lawyers they constituted all there was of the law.

Blackstone believed that the fear of the Lord was the beginning of wisdom. His commentaries began with a careful analysis of the law of God as presented in the Christian bible. Blackstone considered it self-evident that God is the source of all law whether found in the Scriptures or observable in nature. He was secure in the thought that there existed a personal, sovereign God who worked in the lives and governed the affairs of men. Blackstone was certain that in the eyes of those who founded the United States every right and every law comes from God. **He said the very words** *rights, laws, freedoms, are meaningless without their divine origin.*

The colonists argued in the Declaration of Independence that **"the laws of nature and of nature's God"** entitled them to independence and equal station among nations. The proclamation was that *"all men are created equal".* **That there Creator endowed them with** *"certain inalienable or absolute rights"*! It was self-evident to the colonists that without the Creator there would be no rights and no liberty.

The Declaration stands on the bases of three fundamental Judeo-Christian ideas: *First*, it professes faith in a Creator who governs in the affairs of men and establishes absolute standards to which all men are accountable. *Second*, it acknowledges that man is a fallen creature and cannot be his own lawgiver or judge and *Third*, God is the author of liberty. It is God to whom we must all look to for guidance and bring our appeal. Law in America was and is not what man says it is but what God says it is!!

John Whitehead noted in "The Rebirth of America*", "When the reformation swept over Europe, it put the bible in the hands of people, revolutionized concepts of government and set the stage for the American Republic. With the influence of Samuel Rutherford, John Witherspoon and John Locke, the Bible became the basis of United States Government and law."*

John Quincy Adams noted, " *The first and almost the only Book deserving of universal attention is the Bible."*

Abraham Lincoln, our sixteenth President, noted, *"All good from the Savior of the world is communicated through this book; (the Bible); but for the Book we could not know right from wrong. All the things desirable to man are contained in it."*

Calvin Coolidge another of our Presidents noted, *"The foundations of our society and our government rest so much on the teachings of the Bible that it would be difficult to support them if faith in these teachings would cease to be practically universal in our country"*

Woodrow Wilson noted, *"The Bible is the one supreme source of revelation of the meaning of life, the nature of God and the Spiritual nature and need of men. It is the only guide of life which really leads the spirit in the way of peace and salvation."*

Horace Greeley told America; *"It is impossible to enslave mentally or socially a bible reading people. The principles of the bible are the groundwork of human freedom."*

Almost every Ivy League school in America was originally established to train ministers of the gospel for the work of evangelism. Harvard was founded in 1638, eighteen years after the pilgrims fist set foot on Plymouth Rock. The Puritans who were well-educated colonists established it. Their story is still part of the record of Harvard, however, it is perhaps the only thing Christian about Harvard today. It reads in part,*"After God had carried us safely to New England, and we had built out livelihood, reared convenient places for God's worship, and settled the civil government; one of the next things we longed for, and looked after was to advance learning, and perpetuate it to posterity; dreading to leave an illiterate ministry to the churches, when our present minister shall lie in the dust."*

Its incredible to read that Harvard's founders and its early presidents and teachers insisted that there could be no true knowledge or wisdom without Jesus Christ. Harvard's "Rules and Precepts" adopted in 1646 included the following*; "Every one shall consider the main end of his life and studies to know God and Jesus Christ which is eternal life." "Seeing the Lord giveth wisdom, every one shall seriously by prayer in secret seek wisdom of Him." "Every one shall so exercise him-self in reading the scriptures twice a day that they be read to give an account of their proficiency therein, both in theoretical observations of languages and logic, and in practical and spiritual truths."* History records that fifty two percent of seventeenth-century Harvard graduates became ministers of the gospel.

Two of the great heritages of the American Nation are both gifts of the grace of Almighty God. The first is America's Christian heritage born out of the lives and faith of her founding fathers and early settlers. The second is her constitution, which created her unique form of government of, for and by the governed. It is a system of government carefully crafted by its framers under the sovereign hand of God to bring liberty, freedom, justice and opportunity to her citizens. God had a purpose for America.

God gave our founding fathers a supernatural wisdom and vision of the essence and purpose of human life that led them to bring to life in America a unique government that would protect the liberty and freedom of men while guiding their consciences and bringing into play the checks and balances, the disciplines, incentives and encouragement necessary to rightly direct the lives of men while introducing and promising to protect and secure those unalienable rights every man is endowed with by his Creator.

Both of these precious heritages, because of their Spiritual essence, are constantly under attack by Satan and his disciples and by the fallen nature of man. It was understood from the beginning that this new nation was indeed a blessing from the throne of the Creator given unto a people according to his purpose in the earth and it would have to be aggressively protected and carefully lead by Christian men of great courage, wisdom and faith.

It was recognized by the founding fathers from the very beginning that liberty was a radical idea in a world of men of fallen natures and it would demand vigilance and a constant willingness to do battle for it! Liberty and freedom was a bold goal and would extract a price in the form of sacrifice and suffering. Freedom would have certain risks and responsibilities associated with it. It could not exist without the leading and protection of a superintending God or sustained without the leadership of morally alert and courageous men of Christian belief and Character.

The risks inherent in such a bold venture as the America of our founding fathers were only risks if we abandoned our trust and dependence upon the creator. Early Americans were willing to take those risks and endure a level of trouble and danger to protect the precious gift and concept of individual liberty and a free society. They were men of faith who were assured God would sustain what they had planted so long as they were willing to humble themselves before him. Such risks and sacrifice would only be tolerable to men of faith who would depend upon their faith in God to protect them.

It's necessary to remind us that our humility is before God and not before the enemies of God. Our Lord revealed clearly how he feels about luke-warm followers. *"I know your deeds, that you are neither cold nor hot; I would that you were cold or hot. So because you are lukewarm, and neither not nor cold, I will spit you out of My mouth. Because you say, "I am rich and have become wealthy, and have need of nothing, and you do not know that you are wretched and miserable and poor and blind and naked, I advise you to buy from Me gold, refined by fire, that you may become rich, and white garments that you may clothe your, and that the shame of your nakedness may not be revealed; and eye salve to anoint your eyes, that you may see. Those who I love, I reprove and discipline; be zealous therefore, and repent." (Rev 3:15-19)*

Never forget, only a fool gives quarter to an enemy that has not surrendered! Our enemy has not surrendered and our luke-warmness is losing the battle because God has said that luke-warmness is offensive to Him and he will not support it or put up with it from His followers.

Finally a positive note! NBC conducted a poll in April 2006 in which they asked whether we ought to retain the words "Under God" in our pledge and whether we ought to leave the words "In God We Trust" on our coins and bank notes? 86% of those contacted in the poll said we should retain "Under God" in our pledge and "In God we Trust" on our money. Lets begin to show up in the political poles folks!

A
Book
By
Charles D. Gaines

PERSPECTIVE

Romans 8:5-8;
" Those who are according to the flesh set their minds on the things of the flesh, but those who are according to the Spirit, the things of the Spirit. For the mind set on the flesh is death, but the mind set on the Spirit is life and peace, because the mind set on the flesh is hostile toward God…Those who are in the flesh cannot please God.

SECTION II

A NEW AGE OF DECEPTION

—⁓—

CHAPTER FIVE

A CHANGE OF PERSPECTIVE

—m—

"For those who are according to the flesh set their minds on the things of the flesh, but those who are according to the Spirit, the things of the Spirit." (Romans 8:5)

What happens to cause a nation to lose its Spiritual sight and moral compass and what must happen for that nation to regain it?

The greatest threat to our nation, and there are many, is not external. We are currently the most powerful nation militarily and economically the world has ever known. Our greatest threat is not physical danger from another nation or financial disaster. It is not the national debt or the trade deficit. It is not containing the threats of radical Islam or instability in the Middle East. It is not the nuclear threat from Korea and Iran nor is it domestic crime or poverty. It is not even racism, the environment, and it certainly is not global warming. It is not our growing dependence on foreign oil nor is it the threat of nuclear proliferation. It is not even drug dependency or government corruption. It is not even our growing dependence on government even though our addiction to that dependence will ultimately take away our liberty and bankrupt our nation. As important as any or all these issues might be if they are not addressed not any or all of them will destroy America or cause us to perish. Solving any one of these problems will not solve our most threatening problem because most of these problems are derivative in nature.

America's most urgent problem is the Spiritual suicide we are experiencing in our culture! Many, perhaps most, of the social problems we face find their roots in Spiritual death. Spiritual death is an eternal problem from which there is no escape and not even the most powerful government or wise men or all the wealth of the world can solve it. 100% of those who suffer from Spiritual death will perish according to the Scriptures. God is in charge of Spiritual life and death.

We, as a national government, through the ruling of our Supreme Court, have chosen to reject God from our public life. God has warned us that if we reject Him he will withdraw

His Spirit from us. *"It is a trustworthy statement: For if we died with Him, we shall also live with Him; If we endure, we shall also reign with Him; If we deny Him, He also will deny us; If we are faithless, He remains faithful; for He cannot deny Himself" (2 Tim 2:11-13).*

Your response may be that I have not rejected God! Perhaps not, however, if we have approved of our governments rejection of God and have not demonstrated our disapproval in the public forum or from the voting booth we may be as guilty for our government's rejection of God as those who have been active in making us a secular nation.

According to our constitution, America is a government of, for and by the people! We the people are ultimately responsible for what happens in and through the institution of government. We have elected our leaders and our leaders have appointed our federal judges. We have the power to remove anyone from political office that fails to do our bidding. Granted we are limited in our direct control of the day-to-day activities of the institution of government, however, our voices of approval and disapproval can be heard in the public forum and through the media. There is much we can do if we decide to do it. The institution of government in the United States of America has been forced by the Supreme Court to reject God and adopt secularism. The Executive and the Legislative branches of government have not challenged the Court. Likewise, we the people have not challenged the court. We have allowed the establishment of a secular humanist government that was let in quietly through the back door by the Judiciary. As American citizens you and I share the responsibility for the moral and cultural collapse of America if we do not take action to change the course of America.

The great tragedy of the 20th century for America was our change from a Christian Nation to a Secular Humanist nation among the nations of the world. Our government was legally determined by the Supreme Court to be secular. They established from this point forward a separation between church and state. The impact of that court decision has been devastating thus far and we are just at the beginning of our troubles.

If you are an American Christian you are most likely part of the silent majority watching Spiritual death overtake us. Spiritual death is a slow and subtle occurrence that escapes the notice of the luke-warm Christian whose Spiritual indifference and blindness hides their deadly separation from God. As Christians we cannot wait for the world to warn us because the world doesn't discern what is happening. They are Spiritually dead and do not have eyes to see. The world wanders around in a delusion! Many who profess to be Christian wander around in confusion wondering what is happening if they notice at all.

Choosing to separate the influence of the Spirit of God from the governing process can mean ultimate Spiritual suicide for the nation. God will honor our choice, which will lead to Spiritual death. This separation of the Spirit of God is a tragic judgment against any people because it releases us to our fleshly lusts and appetites and opens the door to the sovereignty of evil. Have we condemned ourselves to death as a nation? Is the evidence of our deceit strong enough to convict us?

The cry of the Psalmist must become the cry of America.. *"Create in me a clean heart, O God, and renew a steadfast spirit within me. Do not cast me away from they presence, and do not take Thy Holy Spirit from me." (Psalm 51:10-11)*

The spirit of this world hates God the Father, God the son and God the Holy Spirit. The deceit of the spirit of the world blinds men to the truth and works its evil through the selfish appetites that reside in the fallen nature of mankind. *"And you were dead in your trespasses and sins, in which you formerly walked according to the course of this world, according to the prince of the power of the air, of the spirit that is not working in the sons of disobedience. Among them we too, all formerly lived in the lusts of our flesh, indulging the desires of the flesh and of he mind, and were by nature children of wrath, even as the rest." (Romans 2:1-3)*

The deceit of Satan and his evil Spirit dominates the lives of those not born of the Spirit of God. He sneaks into every aspect of our very lives as a purveyor of light and presents a secular wisdom that seems so right to the minds of deceived men but the scriptures warn that it is a way that ends in destruction and death. *(Proverbs 14:12) "There is a way which seems right to a man, but its end is the way of death."*

Spiritual separation from God has opened the door for the spirit of the world to legally and therefore boldly manifest its rise in America in the last five decades. The proof is found in the rejection of God and His Church from government and the rise of secularism.

Secular humanism is a term that describes the natural response of the man who has made himself, his reason and his appetites his God. It also describes the thinking of the agnostic who cannot make up his mind whether he believes or not. It occurs when men chose to worship the creature rather than the creator. It results in actions, decisions and attitudes that seem good and right to the natural mind of man, however, it is the attitude that naturally springs out of the rebellion and deceit of the fallen nature of mankind. It is the enemy of our Creator. *"For who among men knows the thoughts of a man except the spirit of the man, which is in him? Even so the thoughts of God no one knows except the Spirit of God. Now we have received, not the spirit of the world, but the Spirit who is from God, that we might know the things freely given to us by God, which things we also speak, not in words taught by human wisdom, but in those taught by the Spirit, combining spiritual thoughts with spiritual words. But a natural man does not accept the things of the Spirit of God; for they are foolishness to him, and he cannot understand them, because they are spiritually appraised." (I Cor 2:11-14)*

The scriptures refer to it as the working of the flesh of man whose best and most honorable efforts are described as " like filthy rags" in the sight of God. The scriptures warn us about the relationship of the spirit of the world to the Spirit of God. Listen carefully, *"Do not love the world, nor the things in the world. If anyone loves the world, the love of the*

Father is not in him. For all that is in the world, the lust of the flesh and the lust of the eyes and the boastful pride of life, is not from the Father, but is from the world. And the world is passing away, and also its lusts; but the one who does the will of God abides forever. " (I John 2:15-17)

The scriptures teach us that nothing performed by the flesh pleases God. The flesh of man gets its inspiration and guidance from the eternal enemy of God and the fruit of the flesh form the character and leads to the inevitable and ultimate end of all men who reject God and rebel against His will. The scriptures refer to the fruit that comes forth from the flesh as ; **"immorality, impurity, sensuality, idolatry, sorcery, enmities, strife, jealousy, outbursts of anger, disputes, dissensions, factions, envying, drunkenness, carousing and things like these…and those who practices such things shall not inherit the kingdom of God" (Galatians 5:19-21).** We see the flesh of man and its effect manifest in many ways but nationally it is manifest in the secular humanist movement, which stands firmly and arrogantly against the sovereignty and Spirit of God and actively wars against the followers of Christ.

The flesh is arrogant and rebellious against God. It sets itself above God and rejects the will of God. The Scriptures teach us, **"the flesh sets its desire against the Spirit, and the Spirit against the flesh; for these are in opposition to one another, so that you may not do the things that you please…The fruit of the Spirit is love, joy, peace, patience, kindness, goodness, faithfulness, gentleness and self –control …and those who belong to Christ Jesus have crucified the flesh with its passions and desires" (Galatians 5:16-17, 22-24)**

The Spirit that led our founders and has led America traditionally is slowly but surely departing from us as a nation. The Supreme Court has determined that God's Spirit will no longer lead America. We have discarded and forgotten our rich Spiritual heritage and we have abandoned the wisdom and faith of our founding fathers. We have abandoned our Spiritual vigilance and rejected our Creator. We are rapidly becoming a secular nation reaping the result of our rebellion and neglect. We have chosen to trade individual liberty, constitutional freedoms and biblical faith for the ways of the god of this world. That god is the god of secular humanism and its intimate companion spiritual deceit. *"For those who are according to the flesh set their minds on the things of the flesh, but those who are according to the Spirit, the things of the Spirit. For the mind set on the flesh is death, but the mind set on the Spirit is life and peace, because the mind set on the flesh is hostile toward God; for it does not subject itself to the law of God, for is it not even able to do so; and those who are in the flesh cannot please God." (Romans 8:5-8)*

The deceit that is descending upon us is slowly and systematically destroying us and has led us to worship the creature rather than the creator and in our luke-warmness and spiritual slumber we have not even noticed the transition.

Secularism is indeed upon us. In our deceit we have created a burgeoning secular government bureaucracy that has replaced God and our need to live by faith and trust in

God. In our utter deceit and human wisdom we thought we were doing a good thing. At the alter of a government bureaucracy we are sacrificing our faith, our liberty, our resources, our families, the free enter-prize system and our right to self-determination.

In return for the sacrifice of liberty and faith in God we are promised secular humanism and government dependency. The Supreme Court has somehow concluded this is the right direction for America. We have convinced ourselves that in return for our dependence and loyalty to the institution of government it will watch out for us and take care of our every need. We have said we no longer need the wisdom of the Spirit of God to help guide us because we have a secular government that acts objectively and fairly to all no matter their religious bent. What utter nonsense!! Government cannot and will not provide physical and economic security let alone protection from life itself and from those tests of faith that come upon us to build trust in God and moral character. One would have to be spiritually dead to buy into the notion of secularism! Nevertheless, like many before us, we have also bought into the lie and it will destroy us.

What fools we have become. Perhaps you have not considered what and who this institution of government you have become dependent upon and pledged your life to really have become? It doesn't even know you exist unless and until it needs something from you or unless you become a part of some government investigation. It could care less about you or your problems. You are either a source for tax revenue or simply another administrative problem to government. You represent another expense and another control and management problem. You are simply another dependent slave that has to be led, controlled, punished and disciplined if you do not follow the millions of rules and laws they can selective use to control your life and activities. Government does not guarantee your liberty. In fact it limits liberty more every time a new government program or a new law is passed. The greater our individual or collective dependence on government the less liberty we enjoy and the more resources it must extract from us. From the governments perspective you and I simply replace some other dependent that has passed away. Our only value to government is the services we are called upon at times to perform and taxes our existence and activities generate. The government is not God, it does not honor God, it does not love you and it is not human and it doesn't even consider you. It is a secular humanist institution of bureaucrats that administer the law, the programs and policies that are supposed to reflect the just and best way to live and to improve your life and the lives of others. Without the direct oversight of the Spirit of God at work in the hearts and minds of government servants and their submission to the will of God and to the people they govern government is not a friend to you or to liberty. When government decides that justice and righteousness are separate issues it has alienated itself from the Spirit and the will of God.

I am amused by the humorous but profound remarks of one of our best Presidents, Ronald Reagan: In one of his speeches he remarked: **"The most terrifying words in the English Language are: I'm from the government and Im'here to help."** He also remarked, **"The nearest thing to eternal life we will ever see on this earth is a government program."** In a more serious context he reminded us that if government is not held accountable the taxpayer simply becomes **"someone who works for the federal government but doesn't have to take the civil service examination. If we ever forget that we are one nation under God, then we will become a nation gone under"**! No arsenal, or **no weapon in the arsenals of the world, is so formidable as the will and moral courage of free men and women."**

The institution of Government has an important but limited constitutional role. However, the power and glory of a nation is found in the character and nature of its people. Without the people insuring the role of government remains limited government will continue to grow and invade our liberty and absorb our resources until we have all become dependent slaves of an oppressive bureaucracy.

Most of us have never considered the fact that government has no incentive to limit its power or role. Government is people, buildings and paper. There is nothing honorable about the institution of government beyond the honor its people and its God bring to it. The people who work for government have no incentive to reduce the size, scope and influence of the branch or department in which they work. Most government employee's and elected officials are preoccupied with their future not yours and mine. Their motivation to serve is typically so they can keep their job. The point we must all come to grips with is that we the people must accept the responsibility to govern and limit the scope and role of government.

Unfortunately we have been so busy attempting to satisfy our own appetites we have chosen to assign government the responsibility of meeting our every need. We also expect government to protect us from having to mature and become responsible productive, alert and engaged American citizens. We have become another entitlement minded society. We are reaping from government dependence an indolent and dependent people living in slavery to a secular humanist government's growing tyranny. If we do not wake up and begin to govern the institution of government will consume us.

Government is systematically stealing our resources and our liberty while we eagerly turn over more of our liberty for what we perceive to be physical, social and economic security. We find excuses for allowing ourselves to become dependent because we do not have the moral courage to except the responsibility to take care of our families and ourselves or to govern.

We have somehow concluded that liberty and freedom from government oppression are not really an important or significant issue. In our blindness and indifference we have determined that freedom is not worth the price of having to accept responsibility for ourselves or for maintaining vigilance against any enemy foreign or domestic.

We foolishly think murderers, bank robbers, thieves and perverts perpetrate the only crime perpetrated against our people. However, the costs of the crime these hoodlums are engaged in is not even a drop in the bucket compared to the costs of the crime perpetrated against us in and by the institution of government. We have put our trust in a secular humanist government who is not loyal to us or what is best for us. We in our utter deceit have allowed and continue to allow this government to grow and solicit our dependence. We have this naïve idea that someone somewhere in government, perhaps some huge computer brain (and heart) is actively at work protecting our rights and taking care of our best needs and best interests. When put in perspective, isn't it a silly notion?

We have given over our constitutional responsibility of self-governing to a few politically ambitious politicians and bureaucrats who are looking for a ticket to ride. We have neglected our responsibility and we are losing our once great nation under God.

Living a life of foundational trust in God is not an acceptable way of life to a secular government or to a deceived, lazy, spoiled, wealthy, impatient and rebellious people who have decided God is not all that important because our hope, justice, protection and provision is provided by the institution of a secular humanist government.

Those who have suffered under the oppression and injustice of government tyranny or under the system of atheistic socialism or Marxist Communism recognize the value of freedom and how easily it can be lost. Most of them understand the price of not being vigilant. Those who have not experienced the bitter yoke of tyranny do not believe it can exist in America, therefore they see no urgency in fighting to preserve our liberty from the encroachment of a secular humanist government.

Likewise, many of our people have rejected the idea of the need to be Spiritual vigilant. Some are a spiritually dead and some are Spiritually lukewarm people who Jesus calls " ***wretched and miserable and poor and blind and naked".*** They foolishly take liberty and God for granted and unless they become awakened they are ultimately destined to lose both.

The scriptures teach us and experience confirms that trouble tends to avoid the wise and the vigilant, the prepared and the strong. It seems almost stupid to even debate it. Nevertheless our people don't seem to understand that our problem in America is not Guns it is spiritually lost people and a secular humanist government. Evil, spiritually dead, indifferent and indolent people are the nations, and every nation's, greatest problem.

Wise men recognize that we live in a world whose king is Satan and without God's protection and individual vigilance and preparation human government certainly cannot provide Spiritual or physical security. In fact, the very government who we depend on to protect our liberties is becoming the biggest threat to our liberty because it has declared itself the enemy of the God who is the author of liberty. Government is systematically robbing us of our liberty and our resources because of what we are demanding of it and our irresponsible stewardship!

Those of us who have had to fight for freedom recognize that in this world of evil and fallen men freedom, goodness, justice, love and peace do not come as part of the human package we are born with. The world is evil contrary to the declaration of secularists, idiots and atheists. The protectors of liberty have learned that those who become and remain free are those who stay vigilant and are willing and prepared to fight for liberty every step of the way. Liberty is a gift of God, however it must be accepted, valued and protected by men who receive it and recognize its value.

America is not the home of the free and the brave it is the home of the free because of the brave and because of a superintending God who goes before and prepares the way for us. Our only hope for remaining a free people is in the hands of the free and the brave and the grace of Almighty God who ordained that liberty is an unalienable right of every person.

Those who have had to pay the price of protecting liberty have also come to recognize that freedom to self determination and the protection of those liberties guaranteed by our constitution are much more valuable than any temporary false sense of physical or material security that may temporarily come from our dependence on a secular humanist government. One of the most powerful enemies of America is the bureaucracy whose unchecked power and ability to determine its own scope and size is unlimited.

We have institutionalized secular humanist federal and state bureaucracies that America worships. We run to it like a child runs to its mother anytime its hungry or is confronted with a problem or difficult circumstance it must face. Our government governs a lazy, lost, helpless, spoiled, selfish, indifferent and fickle people. Government finds itself all-powerful and free to set its own course and the scope and terms of its governing. It can extract money at will and can give or remove liberty from its citizens at will for the sake of its own agenda's without accountability because our people have chosen not to make government accountable. It is no longer a government of, for and by the people. We, as a society, have overlooked the fact that whatever power the institution of government has we have given to it and that whatever we have given to the institution of government we have taken away from the individual. We are losing our power to govern!

Most Americans are aware there is a great practical need to bring light, wisdom and clarity to virtually every aspect of our individual and national life. As a society we are exhausted with the debate over those social and political issues that work to continually divide us as a nation. Even though we see a great need for something or someone to straighten out the mess we find ourselves in spiritually and socially most of us do not have an understanding of the nature of the problem or how we got into the moral freefall and social quagmire that is destroying us nor do we understand how to fix or escape its grasp.

We find it more and more difficult to determine right from wrong and good from bad. In our confusion we chose to continue to support the same foolish and destructive secular humanist idea's that have worked to destroy us during this last half-century.

Many, perhaps the majority of Americans, fail to recognize that the answer and the resource to lead us out of this deceit is found in the grace of a superintending God and the wisdom God has revealed to us in His Word. There are many among us who even though they recognize the answer they refuse to humble themselves to God's sovereignty. Therefore a moral blindness and spiritual void continues to creep through our nation leaving a larger number of our citizens without a moral conscience and our nation without hope.

An anti-God insanity is being allowed to lead America that refuses to acknowledge and/or embrace the truth. We have allowed ourselves to become a people whose God is money, our appetites and our pleasures. We, as a nation, no longer have the discernment to recognize truth nor do we possess the moral courage to present it or fight to preserve it even when it becomes obvious to us.

The environment of evil and confusion in our culture is so pervasive we are over-whelmed by it. The Lord tells us in His word that we ought not be surprised at the fiery ordeal among us nor should we be surprised at the apostasy of the church and the false teachers that have arisen. *"But the Spirit explicitly says that in later times some will fall away from the faith, paying attention to deceitful spirits and doctrines of demons, by means of the hypocracy of liars seared in their own conscience as with a branding iron.." I Timothy 4:1-2)* The scriptures also warn *"For the time will come when they will not endure sound doctrine; but wanting to have their ears tickled, they will accumulate for themselves teachers in accordance to their own desires; and will turn away their ears from the truth, and will turn aside to myths." (II Timothy 4:3-4)*

In our efforts at understanding our dilemma we asked ourselves, how can this thing be happening to the mind and hearts of our people? How could a nation of people who have been so blessed by God choose to reject Him and become so spiritually blind?

There must be some concerted human effort at delusion that misleads and promotes an agenda for political, social or economic gain? Could there truly be some conspiracy among us that, even having some knowledge of the truth, denies the truth and proclaims the lie to justify or promote an agenda unknown to us? Our minds work to make sense of it. The scriptures teach us there is indeed a battle between good and evil: **"Our struggle is not against flesh and blood, but against the rulers, against the powers, against the world forces of this darkness, against the spiritual forces of wickedness in the heavenly places." (Ephesians 6:12)**

The world rejects the truth regarding a spiritual struggle and denies the problem and the dilemma we are in. It operates from the premise that if reasonable men have the opportunity to view the same circumstance and evidence with an objective understanding of it and/or if we were to view the same evidence or if we were exposed to the same truth we would arrive at the same conclusion. That notion is the secularist's fairyland. It is a totally false assumption. The rejection by some of the saving grace of God and the acceptance of others reveals the fallacious premise of the secularist. There is no such thing as an objective perspective short of the wisdom and will of our Creator.

The evidence that mans perception is heavily influenced by his will is overwhelming. What is it that controls his will? Without the Spirit of God man is controlled by his interests, appetites and pleasures. Nevertheless we tend to hold on to this foolish notion of secular objectivity in our public debate over vital issues that impact our very lives. How can we depend on objectivity when the evidence is overwhelming that men who are exposed to truth often reject it even though they know it is the truth? It doesn't make sense does it? Nevertheless that notion of secular objectivity is the foundation upon which America is establishing its future. We are reaping the harvest of this utter foolishness. Secularism is anti-Christ and it is not objective thought. It is a deceitful trap!

We have a spiritually divided nation. Secularists celebrate that diversity. We all do not march to the same drummer. Could God be turning America over to her foolish collective will. *"For since the creation of the world His invisible attributes, His eternal power and divine nature, have been clearly seen, being understood through what has been made, so that they are without excuse. For even though they knew God, they did not honor Him as God, or give thanks; but they became futile in there speculations, and their foolish heart was darkened. Professing to be wise, they became fools, Therefore God gave them over in the lusts of their hearts to impurity, …therefore they worshipped and served the creature rather than the Creator…." (Romans 1:20-32)*

It doesn't take much research to realize there is truly many fully informed intelligent human beings who live in utter rebellion against the truth and who hold utterly absurd perspectives with great sincerity and passion even though reasonable deduction would demand a different perspective or conclusion. What is even more befuddling is the endless list of supposedly educated person's, many hold high positions of professorship in our universities, who are trapped in utter deceit by absurd perspectives and philosophies. Deceit finds its way into every class distinction and is not limited to poor or the simple or the uneducated.

The question is obvious! What are the implications for society and what are we to do? The only solution to the problem of moral blindness is Spiritual awakening. Spiritual awakening is a gift only God can give. Listen to these words: *"But all things become visible when they are exposed by the light (truth) for everything that becomes visible is (the) light. For this reason it says, 'Awake Sleeper, and arise from the dead, and Christ will shine on you. Therefore, be careful how you walk, not as unwise men, but as wise, making the most of your time, because the days are evil. So then do not be foolish, but understand what the will of the Lord is" (Ephesians 5:13-17)*

Moral degeneracy comes upon a people because of their rebellion against God according to the scriptures: *"For even though they knew God, they did not honor Him as God, or give thanks; but they became futile in their speculations, and their foolish heart was darkened. Professing to be wise, they became fools,…and just as they did not see fit to acknowledge God any longer, God gave them over to a depraved mind, to do those things which are not proper, being filled with all unrighteousness, wickedness, greed, evil; full of envy, murder, strife, deceit, malice; they are gossips, slanderers, haters of God, insolent, arrogant, boastful, inventors of evil, disobedient to parents, without understanding, untrustworthy, unloving, unmerciful; and although they know the ordinance of God, that those who practice such things are worthy of death, they not only do the same, but also give hearty approval to those who practice them." (Romans 1:21-22, 28-32)*

According to the Scriptures we are without excuse and our feeble attempts at assigning truth to "someone's opinion" is obviously a fool's paradise. For the man who denies the Scriptural presentation has two major problems that are equally as profound as the truth itself. First his conscience recognizes the truth and therefore he knows; and second, he has no source or authority from which he is able to rationally support or justify his attitude or position. It is a matter of his will! The Lord speaks of such a person as a fool and so he or she is! Are we becoming a nation of fools?

Nevertheless, we have produced a culture lead by the deceit of the flesh of fools who do not believe in a sovereign and living God who created and sustains all things and who is able and willing to deliver them from the price of their sin and from their utter deceit. In our deceit we instinctively introduce a subtle spin on circumstances, actions, attitude and idea's that amazes and often baffles even our own understanding. It is a form of madness that works among us to delude, divide and ultimately destroy us. No amount of human reason or persuasion seems able to penetrate this madness or lead men away from the ultimate destruction that is inherent in this human deceit.

As can be easily seen, this profound blindness goes much deeper than simply some misunderstanding, miscommunication by a group or individual not made aware of some pertinent fact or somehow exposed to slanted information. The malady is called **"Spiritual Blindness"** in the scriptures.

There are clearly two distinct spiritual camps that lead the thinking and conscience of mankind. These two groups of people can hear identical testimony and be presented with precisely the same facts or observe the same actions, attitudes or circumstances and conclude, and therefore respond, completely different even though the truth and the facts points clearly to the one correct response.

The scriptures, when presenting those truths that profoundly affect the lives and destiny of men, identify the disparity in thinking by addressing the truth it presents to those who have ears to hear and eyes to see!

God is identifying to us here that the majority of people do not have ears to hear and eyes to see. In fact His word presents a sobering reality: *"Enter by the narrow gate; for the gate is wide, and the way is broad that leads to destruction, and many are those who enter by it. For the gate is small, and the way is narrow that leads to life, and few are those who find it." (Matthew 7:13-14)*

What do you suppose the implications of these words are to the atheist, the cultist, the liberal or the secularist? Perhaps you think God is just kidding around? Since you cannot deal with or accept this reality you can take the course of temporary escape chosen by the majority. You can say that you disbelieve it! Regardless of the course you chose the truth will ultimately be your judge.

The world denies the reality of these two spiritual camps of thinking that controls the will, the reason and responses of men. These two camps come from two distinctly different, diametrically opposed, spiritual camps that therefore hold distinctly different perspectives and attitudes about life. They therefore produce two distinctly different worldviews. One perspective comes forth from the Spirit of God and His word. The second perspective comes forth from Satan who God refers to as the god of this world who is in rebellion against the Creator and at war in the heavens and on earth with His Kingdom. The world hates God and His Church. It will only tolerate the Church so long as the Church tolerates sin and rebellion and does not interfere in the destruction Satan and his angels have planned for God's creation.

Many foolishly suggest there is a third reality that arises out of secularism. It is an attitude that seems to men to be a middle ground. They find it comfortable to engage socially and a way for government to avoid the confrontation of spiritual reality. Therefore secularism enjoys the distinction in American thinking of being the most reasonable approach to life and the preferred approach to solving human problems. However, secularism is Satan's most subtle weapon of deceit through which he manifests his destructive reasoning. He disguises himself as a bearer of light and the mind that is not sharp and vigilant and the heart that is not prepared is easily deceived. The scriptures say it this way, ***"there is a way that seems right unto man, but its way is the way of death."***

The scriptures warn that Satan is far more cleaver than the most brilliant secular minds of men. So cunning is his deceit that it escapes mans ability to discern it or escape its grasp short of the divine intervention of God and/or the Spiritual rebirth that brings the revelation that changes the hearts and minds of men. Satan comes to all men as a bearer of light and truth. In mans deceit he becomes trapped by Satan. The most brilliant and objective reason of natural man is no match against Satan's evil manipulation, delusion and persuasion. In fact man's nature is fallen and in its natural state is under the power and inspiration of Satan's evil spirit and man is trapped in his sin. By himself man cannot escape his deceit. Even the best of the works of men without God are described in the scriptures as little more than filthy rags even though they might be very impressive to the secular humanist mind.

The battle we are engaged in is so profound it deludes us, however, its existence and impact is very real. Its impact on the human race is eternal in its scope and yet it touches every aspect of life on earth. God has provided the only deliverance through which man can escape the condemnation of sin and the mind of natural man cannot even grasp the wonder of that deliverance short of divine intervention. The Scriptures teach us that the nature of the battle is Spiritual..

Unfortunately the predominant spiritual camp in America has moved from the Judeo Christian world view to the secular humanist world view which is lead primarily by Secular humanist reason, (the reason of natural man). The Secular humanist perspective sees man at the center rather than God and it arrogantly and deceitfully considers its perspective as truly objective.

Secular Humanism attempts to explain the great philosophical differences of the two camps of Spiritual thinking by arguing that Secularism treats all religious views fairly and equally. What escapes many Americans is that the great spiritual battle of our time is not an intellectual debate but a life or death issue. We often see this battle as simply a struggle to come to some equitable agreement or create some objective intellectual playing field upon which the battle might be fought according to a set of gentlemen's rules. Folks, spiritual life and spiritual death are not Monday night football. There is no wild card entry and there is no other way into the kingdom than through Jesus Christ the Savior. That attitude of presenting a level playing field is a fool's paradise. Never the less
many deceived Americans buy into the lie!

Secular humanists see the Christian or biblical world view as bigoted and self righteous since it denounces all other ways to eternal life and Spiritual deliverance and it presents Christ as the only avenue to God's kingdom. Secular Humanism essentially denies any Spiritual reality and argues that tolerance, open communication, secular government and secular education will solve the foundational problems of our society and will bridge the great chasm between the various perspectives. That is also absurd. Secularism cannot lead men to repentance and Spiritual deliverance.

Those who hold the secular world-view believe that secular leadership, secular government and politically correct attitudes are the answer to America's problems and the best hope for the proper functioning of government and society. What do you think? Its absurd isn't it? The important question is what can you do and what do you plan to do about it?

The secular humanists and their foolish philosophy will ultimately fail because they reject God's wisdom and deny the fallen nature of man and therefore reject its implications. However, millions will be destroyed and America left smoldering on the ash heap of history if the church does not wake up and become the salt and light we are called to be. In their deceit Secular Humanists fail to recognize they are being lead by a satanic spirit. That satanically inspired Spirit permeates the very being of all men and women who are not born of the Spirit of God.

Undisciplined, or perhaps we should say unenlightened, men measure all things according to the selfish introspective thinking of secular humanism that makes man his own God. Unless there comes a profound change in the guiding spirit and therefore the perspective of natural man he will not only perish, from an eternal perspective, he will ultimately destroy himself and everything good that surrounds him in order to feed his selfish interests and pleasures.

Natural man, if he is to be protected from himself and from others like him with competing agenda's must be deterred from evil by laws or by consequences that promise to extract such a price for evil and lawlessness that he is not willing to pay it! The alternative is that he must somehow become transformed into a new creature who loves rather than hates his neighbor. Having to suffer the consequences a society levels upon his foolishness and evil will not provide deliverance for him, however, it will reduce the evil he engages in because of the penalty it extracts and it will reduce the negative impact of lawlessness on society in general.

The competing selfish interests of natural man tend to make democratic government seem theoretically to be reasonably workable in a society of competing interests until or unless an organized and active special interest promote a foolish or evil agenda. At that point a democratic government that otherwise tends to protect the interests and freedoms of all the people begins to fail.

The only moral code natural man recognizes is a code that meets the approval of his fleshly appetites and does not challenge his goal's, likes and dislikes and does not distract him as he works to meet those goals. That which is defined as good by natural man is that which allows him to exercise his pleasures and promote his goals, agenda and general welfare. That which is good, from God's perspective, are those things God describes as good that demonstrate His purpose, glory, grace and charity.

The only perspective that holds out hope for men or nations finds its source, wisdom, courage and inspiration from the Spirit of God. It is a perspective that recognizes man, in his natural state, has a nature contrary to God and His will and ways. It is a perspective lead by the Spirit of God that recognizes Gods love for man, however, also recognizes and acknowledges that man is hopelessly lost without the divine intervention of God's grace. It recognizes that man is a sinner, not simply because he sins but because his nature is sinful and therefore man instinctively works to satisfy his nature which is fallen and sinful, to justify his attitudes and actions, to fulfill his natural appetites and the ultimate goal of his actions are his pleasures.

God's perspective, reflected through the attitudes of redeemed men, humbles itself before God's Spirit and His word and manifests charity toward his fellowman. God's Spirit at work in men presents an attitude that works to promote Gods love, goodness and justice. It works to create within man moral character and courage. It does not seek its own but seeks the good of others. It submits itself to a moral code that serves as the foundation for the laws that best define the will of God, that encourage men toward goodness, that has no favorites in its discipline or protective effort and is administered in an arena of mercy, righteousness and justice. This perspective accepts God and His revealed will as the foundation of all authority and the definition and purpose of life.

Clearly communication and general education are important factors in the social development of men and nations. They are essential to industrial and economic development and they tend to improve the standard of living and dignity of the life of any nation. However, they become destructive factors when communication becomes perverted and education lacks Gods wisdom. It becomes secular and materialistic when it fails to teach men to know and humble themselves before the Creator and when it does not teach and inspire men to good moral character. Education has missed the mark when it does not teach man that his nature without God is destructive and he will ultimately perish short of the saving grace of God. Education has utterly failed us because it does not teach men that God clearly loves them and has made provision for their deliverance from ultimate destruction and the slavery of Satan's deceit and delusion.

Education to be useful and productive and good must recognize that truth is ultimately found in the biblical absolutes and not in the self-centered compromises found in secular humanist materialism and the political ambitions and arguments of unregenerate men who live and react in an arena of deceit & selfish interest.

Therefore, every, or any system of government, or of justice adopted by men for maintaining order and dedicated to protecting those unalienable rights under the rule of law must be very carefully crafted and administered under the careful guidance of Godly wisdom. The laws must be crafted and enforced under the same wisdom to insure the best chance of justice prevailing particularly in an environment of competing secular perspectives.

The nation lost its perspective when the institution of church lost its Spiritual leadership. Church begin to lose its saltiness and its perspective in the late 1950's. Church became an event and not a people and our society began a moral freefall in the early 1960's from which America has not recovered. During the last half of the twentieth century America was kept from complete self-destruction from within because their remained a remnant of believers and a number of cultural Christians who worked through the democratic process voting their conscience. That number is declining and the majority of new "so called" Christians do not believe the bible is the word of God and fewer consider it for direction in their lives.

Competing agenda's of the various self-absorbed groups have provided some checks and balances in the political struggle for control of the thinking, resources and efforts of our people and our government. However, evil has overtaken us because the number of anti-Christian citizens have increased in number and organized their efforts while the Christians have become more worldly and they have therefore set back and allowed the voice of evil to overtake our nation. We have not been taught and inspired by Church leadership to exercise the vital role to be salt and light in our communities and nation.

Certainly one of the great advantages of the democratic process is that a government of, for and by the people helps to provide a check against the impact of destructive perspectives so long as those on the side of good remain predominant, alert and engaged. However, a culture that rejects God naturally and ultimately turns to secular humanist reason to guide it tends to divide people into special interests. Secular humanists will chose secular government leaders and a secular government bureaucracy to administer government neither of which are lead by the Spirit of God. Such a government is destined to polarize a nation into its various special interests and agenda's in order to gain power and obtain government resources. Contrary to secularist thinking, secularism is not a uniting idea. Men choosing up sides to promote their special social interests will ultimately lead us to rebellion and anarchy. The poor will become poorer, the infirmed overlooked and the old removed.

Our destiny is inevitable unless America is spiritually awakened. Secularism will ultimately destroy all who follow after it because, as reasonable as it might seem, it is utter deceit. The flesh of man finds the ways of the world reasonable. Its spiritual influence is satanic. Sign's of the unavoidable disintegration that accompanies secularism is evidenced in our handling of almost every domestic social issue that plagues our nation today. Our goal has become some assorted attitude of fairness rather than righteousness and justice.

America finds itself divided philosophically, and therefore politically, between two apposing spirits. Interestingly, at the same time, we are bitterly polarized into the liberal and the conservative world-views. There are professing Christians in both the liberal and conservative camps. However, there is a profound difference between the "cultural Christian" often found in the liberal camp whose emotion and ignorance of the truth guides his religious bent and the Christian who holds a Spirit lead Christian world view. There are many in the conservative camp that are cultural Christians as well, however, their conservative instincts lean more heavily on the side of biblical truth and principle than do the cultural Christians in the liberal camp.

There are millions in America and around the world who are in love with the Christian idea of compassion and love. Love is a powerful force, perhaps the most powerful force. However, the love expressed by the world is not typically the love spoken of in the scriptures. The love of the liberal presents the notion that your all right – I am all right social philosophy, however, and it cannot abide the idea of the fallen nature of man and the necessity for repentance let alone the spiritual battle with deceit. The liberal mind tends to view discernment as judgment and they view love as a marsh mellow pillow that overlooks truth, reality, spiritual and social accountability, productive effort, discipline and God's inevitable judgment against sin and evil in favor of harmony and a perverted sense of fairness. They typically are secularist, however those who profess belief don't typically believe men must be "born again" of the Spirit of God to be delivered. They see natural man as good. They have been deceived by false teachers who are wolves in sheep's clothing looking for a crowd to notice and listen to them. They have offered God's saving grace as if it were little more than a cup of hot coffee to help you endure a cold day.

The typical call of some in the Pentecostal church is "come just as you are"! I love the sentiment because it reflects God's love for all men; however, it does not reflect the conditions of His grace. To receive the gift of God's redeeming grace you must accept the call upon your life to become a follower of Jesus Christ His son. You do not come with the idea of being forgiven of the baggage of sin you carry so you can go on with your life in the same manner and attitude you held previously. You must come with the idea that you must repent of your ways. It requires complete surrender. Come as you are! Yes you don't have to dress up nor is there anything you can do to prepare yourself to be presentable except to surrender!!! You don't come to make a deal with the God of the universe. You come in an attitude of humility and unconditional surrender. Spiritual rebirth is a calling to become a child of God and from that moment on an ambassador of His kingdom.

Salvation and deliverance from deceit requires Spiritual rebirth, which God offers to all who will receive it! However, salvation and deliverance is a profound and holy calling upon the life of the one being called to it. His offer of salvation demands unconditional surrender and complete trust. His call that gives man the faith to believe is a call to complete surrender and a reversal from our sinful ways and attitudes. Acceptance of that gift of God's grace is confirmed by the heart of the one who has accepted it and by the change in attitude, activities and character of the "born again" Christian.

A nation under God is a nation of people who have surrendered and whose God is their Lord. It is not simply a nation of people in love with the idea of love, peace, kindness and gentleness but do not know or love the Creator or His Christ.

The world cries out for a peace that is a simple cessation of armed confrontation. They would prefer the environment of the hypocrisy of physical security because they do not have a sense of the real spiritual battle for the lives of men nor do they have the moral courage to engage that enemy.

It is vitally important to recognize the fundamental differences between liberal and conservative thinking. The Liberal political mind-set is fundamentally secular. It is anti-American because it tends to be anti capitalism, anti- free enterprise and anti-Christ. It tends to be an attitude that promotes government dependence and supports the redistribution of wealth through taxation. In that sense it tends to be socialistic. In point of fact it tends to view those things that have historically been distinctively American as somehow wrong or evil. If liberals were left to pursue unrestrained their agenda America would be a socialistic and a bankrupt nation because of entitlement. Liberal philosophy translated into public policy would destroy liberty, isolate America further from God and destroy the very economic engine that creates the wealth that pays for the benefits they seek after.

It's ironic, and the height of deceit, that liberals tend to hate terms and idea's like profit, prosperity, corporate business and financial success when they are so totally materialistic in there attitude and their solutions to our social problems. They see the essential answer to most social problems is to transfer money, opportunity, status, jobs or materials from those who have earned them to those who have not. They tend not to give a thought to the fact that many who do not have – do not have because they refuse the discipline, sacrifice and effort it takes to have. They tend to deny the existence of the lazy and indolent and throw them all in the same bundle with the truly needy and deserving. They reject the notion that the rich become rich because they offer or provide a service or product that is in demand. In the American traditional understanding of economics 101 " they earn it"!!!

Unfortunately for America, the liberal idea is one of entitlement. It tends to be that because you exist you have a right to what some else has whether or not you earn or deserve it. The liberal approach to solving the poverty problem, or most any other problem, tends to be short-sighted and tends to overlook the need to provide not only temporary relief but to also provide the proper incentives, disciplines and direction given the reality of the fallen nature of man, to lead them out of their problem. Liberal thinking tends to give temporary relief that is never temporary and it tends to make people dependent upon, addicted to and subjects of handout programs on which they become dependent.

Both liberals and conservatives typically recognize and endorse the idea of charity for the needy. However, the conservative tends to want to determine who is needy and who is simply indolent. The conservative wants incentives that will help man help himself out of his indolence. Sometimes the best incentive to be productive is to suffer the consequences of one's indolence.

In the long run the conservative approach produces far better results and builds industrious nations and people because it is based on biblical principle. You do for a child a much better thing teaching him to walk rather than to continually run his errands for him. Like wise you do a much better thing for a man teaching him how to earn a living that providing him a living.

The liberal approach to solving the problem of poverty, opportunity and education not only bankrupts the nation it is diametrically opposed to what it takes to solve these problems in most instances. The liberal approach lacks wisdom just as removing discipline from the child and/or giving the child what he wants when he wants it. It ultimately destroys the child because it removes the necessary incentive to become accountable and provide for himself. It fails to teach the need to produce if we desire to succeed. It tends to take away the opportunity to mature in Spirit and character, survive in the real world and develop confidence that we are indeed able to compete if we are willing to work at it.

Perspective is written in an attempt to contribute salt and light to our nation in what I believe to be a critical time in our nations history. America has changed her perspective regarding God, government and life in general. Our new perspective is driven by an anti-God secularism and a destructive liberal mindset. This rebellion and deceit must be turned around if the America of our founding fathers is to survive. Liberalism and secularism are both Anti-God and therefore anti-American. They are very destructive to our people and left unchallenged they threaten our national existence because they have removed the wisdom and will of God from the public arena and the incentive and inspiration for the indolent and disadvantaged to achieve. They both teach our children secularism and to be irresponsible and unaccountable. Liberalism creates a government dependency that will ultimately bankrupt our nation. In addition it has encouraged great moral degeneration in America, which is destroying the character of our people. It has removed our since of vision and purpose and it has endorsed and actively promoted the idea of secularism. The two, liberalism and secularism historically are bunkmates that promote those destructive philosophies that weave themselves into the fabric of our national life.

Liberalism has taken over the leadership of the Democratic party and its utter deceit has destroyed the vision and credibility of the party. The party leaders cannot see what is happening to them. It is a perversion of the true charity and compassion, which has historically been the slogan of the "so-called" peoples or working-man's party. Its goal and agenda has become the destruction of truth and moral character and the promotion of its deceived and anti-God destructive social and political philosophies. Liberalism, and secularism, are not simply another point of view from some never- never land of objective thought, they are destructive and foolish points of view satanically driven. Liberalism is not Christian regardless of the professions of some of its adherents.

Conservatism is not another word for biblical principle nor is it necessarily Republican, however, Republicans are generally the more conservative thinkers. Far more conservative thinkers than liberal thinkers are at least culturally Christian. The true American patriots are found more often in the conservative camp. They are the avowed enemy of Liberalism for several reasons. The primary reason is Christ himself. The world hates God or His wisdom because His truth calls them into accountability and His wisdom exposes their foolish ideas. Second, conservatism does not offer a ticket to ride. Third, it holds man responsible for his actions and attitudes, and fourth, conservatives believe accountability is necessary to control evil and irresponsible behavior.

Interestingly, God has told us the discipline of children is essential to the development of the character of children and to spiritual maturity. God disciplines His followers who do not obey because discipline is an essential tool to growth and maturity. ***"All discipline for the moment seems not to be joyful, but sorrowful; yet to those who have been trained by it, afterwards it yields the peaceful fruit of righteousness." (Hebrews 12:11)*** Parenting clearly demands love but it also demands discipline if the child is to mature into a person of integrity and character. Decisions and actions have consequences and that lesson is best learned with a little butt warming from time to time rather than a jail term once you become an adult.

The predominant perspective that has led America historically has been conservative. Both the Republican and the Democratic parties had conservative thinkers. Democrats have been historically more progressive on social issues. They have been responsible for leading the charge against racism and have championed the cause of equal opportunity. The Republican party has been historically more inclined to "status quo" in government and social issues. The Democrats have been more reluctant to stand firm when the going gets tough and military action is warranted. They tend to be more self-absorbed and short term in their thinking. The Republicans have been more ready to stand firm and fight for principle. The Republican administrations have historically been trusted more by our allies to do what we say we will do than Democratic administrations. Individual moral character for political candidates for office has been historically more important to Republicans than to Democrats. The Democrats have historically associated themselves with the workingman even though the policies of the Republicans typically offer the workingman a more secure future. The Republicans have historically been associated with management, leadership and with business. History reveals clearly that conservative thinkers who are Christian believers are typically our nations most loyal patriots.

Part of the struggle between the republicans and the democrats is echoed in the historic struggle between labor and management. The differences in these perspectives are important to the democratic process, however, the democratic party has moved to accept the deceit of liberalism and they have chosen to be liberal's first, democrats second and American patriots last if at all. This shift is destroying America because it is inspired by a Spiritual shift. Liberalism is a major destructive force at work in America.

We have this foolish slogan thrown around by the liberal democrats that suggests they support the troops engaged in the war on terror in the middle east, however they do not support what the troops are doing. This, of course, is foolish hypocrisy. You cannot support the military engaged in battle and not support the military mission and do everything you can to help the military gain victory. Liberals public support of the troops is utter hypocrisy. Typically liberals hate and are intimidated by the military and they hate anything or anyone associated with the idea of support for our nationalism. They are typically globalist's in their attitudes and they are caught up in the support of issues such as global warming, saving the owls, the trees and supporting secular government because they see it as a more fair way of governing. This attitude alone exposes their utter deceit.

The twentieth century brought a major shift in the collective nature and character of our nation. We no longer regard what has been historically and biblically good as good, nor do we regard that which has been regarded historically and biblically as bad – as bad. We are losing our way! We have thrown out our moral compass and we now wander aimlessly in the desert looking for an oasis. God's Spirit, will and way is no longer our will and way. However, in the midst of this shift God has given to America a leader who listens to the voice of His Spirit. Unfortunately, the majority of our people are unable to discern the hand of God at work and have chosen to reject his leadership.

It has been my intention to bring an examination of, and biblical perspective to; life, current events, social issues, the church, government, politics, leadership, national and local decisions of our judiciary, our congress and our President to stimulate our thinking and bring to light the implications of our notions and our decisions.

CHAPTER SIX

PERVERTING OUR
NATIONAL HERITAGE

—m—

"Let us hold fast the confession of our hope without wavering, for He who promised is faithful; and let us consider how to stimulate one another to love and good deeds"
(Hebrew 10:23-24)

The framers of the constitution had experienced the tyranny of a government where individual liberty and civil rights were non-existent. All power was centralized in the Monarchy and the institution of government. They knew what it meant to be slaves without any right of self-determination. They were accustomed to seeing the few resources they were able to obtain through the work of their hands become the property of government. They were aware of the dangers of all power invested in centralized government.

We are only five generations removed from these founders, however, we have already forgotten. We are either ignorant, naïve or we have chosen to ignore the warnings, wisdom and faith of the founding fathers and of those immigrants who came from Europe to settle in America and enjoy its promise of liberty.

We continue to ignore history and the potential threat of a powerful secular central government. As a society we submit ourselves to more and more government dependence. We place our hope in the power of central government and we reject the lessons of history and of God who is our only hope. Therefore America is continuing head long into the same destructive and demoralizing quagmire of the tyranny of powerful and corrupt government in the old world. In our utter deceit we continue to expand the size, scope, power and oppression of central government and in our blindness we have chosen to make national government secular. In our blindness we congratulate ourselves for our wisdom thinking we have done a good thing. We have become fools and the path we have chosen is a dead end!

The tradition of America previous to WWII was small central government both in size and scope. We were a nation of rugged individualists who believed in God, liberty and the "free enterprise" system of capitalism. That tradition is gone and we have become a nation of people dependent upon government.

Central government has become a bureaucratic monster that must be dramatically downsized in scope, mandate and size if the America of our founding fathers is to survive. Americans, we just don't seem to get it! We continue as though investing more in this ever growing inefficient and corrupt bureaucracy and surrendering more of our rights to it is the right way to go. We have overlooked or forgotten that the money we dump into this enormous and growing inefficient bureaucracy is destroying our economy and the economic engine that creates wealth and jobs. It further restricts the liberty of our people. Big government diminishes the power and authority of our constitution and absorbs more and more of our resources and makes government dependent slaves of our people.

The continual Expansion of government and increasing of greater government dependence decreases our gross national product and our national economic health. In fact financing this huge government bureaucracy is the greatest drain on America's economy. We invest more in government than in any industry or productive effort in American and yet it is clearly the worst investment of our resources because of its growing number of programs and its gross ineptness and inefficiency.

The primary focus of those in national government today is to feather their own nests, to promote its own growth and to finance the increase of its power over its constituents. Government tends to respond to what we demand of it and American citizens foolishly saddle government with solving every social problem they encounter not realizing they are exchanging liberty and financial independence for dependence and ultimately slavery.

Big central government that is not strictly limited in scope and authority by the aggressive oversight of the governed is dangerous to any society and our founders understood that danger and gave us a constitution and mandate to self governing to help protect us from that danger.

We have foolishly chosen to ignore our founders and re-interpret the constitution to support our sin and deceit. In order to justify our foolishness we have had to redefine the constitution as a living document in order to make it whatever appeals to our cultural attitudes and appetites.

In return for not having to accept the responsibility of caring for ourselves and not having to concern ourselves with our own financial security, we have chosen to make government an arbitrator of every problem we face and the provider of the resource to meet every possible need.

Welfare programs and our grossly inept public education system are our largest government expenditures and both are failing miserably to meet their goals. Unfortunately many of those on welfare have decided that because they exist they are somehow entitled.

Entitlement has become the attitude of the day in America. Many of our citizens believe that the rest of us owe them something. There are layered generations of Americans whose sole focus is entitlement and they spend most of there waking hours trying to figure out how to work the welfare system to provide more for themselves.

Some of them don't seem to understand or care that they are responsible to change their circumstance and become productive members of society. Our political leaders don't have the political or moral courage to force those who are able to confront their problem. Most of the crime in inter city in America comes from the minorities who are sustained by entitlement welfare programs. The liberals would have us feel that their circumstance and criminal activity is the fault of the rest of us.

Certainly, we need to care for those among us who either physically or mentally cannot care for themselves. They are not at issue here! At issue are the indolent couch potatoes who feel they have a right to be taken care of simply because they exist and live in America. Many of them learn early in life how to milk the system and keep the politicians focused on their welfare with the threat to withhold their vote if they don't keep getting handouts.

Government at every level prides itself in being a "so called" equal opportunity employer institution. That would be admirable if they interpreted equal opportunity to be offering the same opportunity for equally qualified applicants who compete for the same job. Unfortunately, that is a million miles from how "equal opportunity" has been defined by the liberal contingency. Equal opportunity has been defined to encompass racial and gender quotas, which override and virtually ignore aptitude, education, experience and qualification. Unfortunately that definition has come to be accepted as public policy.

The result of the "equal opportunity" idea, which is a just concept dependent upon how you define it, is an incompetent and inefficient government bureaucracy manned by people hired by government because of their race rather than their competence. These people now administer public policy.

Giving those who are less prepared to compete in the job market a leg up is intended to help, however, this policy has proven to be misguided and destructive. It has created an inefficient and incompetent bureaucratic government at almost every level. It has also increased the cost of government off the charts and has brought any progress in efficiency in the management of the regulatory process in the private sector almost to a standstill.

Many of these "equal opportunity" bureaucrats are uninspired and not properly trained. They often tend to forget they are not there to be served but to serve and they typically are not properly supervised. They are simply not able to adequately and efficiency administer the process of governing.

In fact they often set counterproductive self-serving and misdirected administrative practices and policies that are not focused on better serving the public. Common sense guided by reason and logic has been removed from the process of governing.

If you are having a problem understanding what I am saying I invite you to visit your D. M. V. particularly if you happen to be a California resident. On the national level let me suggest a visit to your local Social Security Administration or the Franchise Tax Board or the Internal Revenue Service or your local building department. The mindless make-work bureaucracy's that inhabits these institutions sometimes make the three stooges look like intellectuals. Their incompetence adds needless billions to the cost of government, the cost of doing business and the cost of living.

It is impossible to assess accurately, however, if we were to take a national pole regarding the public's impression of the administration of our federal and state governments, a vast majority of Americans would most likely agree that government could be dramatically reduced in size and still conduct all its current programs with even greater efficiency with competent productive and well trained workers.

Who is to be blamed for turning America into this government dependent entitlement minded society from the rugged individualism of our tradition. Who is to blame for turning the institution of government into this inefficient bureaucratic monster and for setting aside our national heritage?

Perhaps we must look first to ourselves who approach government with our hands out demanding that government take care of us and provide for us. We must remember we have elected the political leaders that have led us down this dead-end street. Second, we must look to morally and Spiritually bankrupt government leadership. Third, the branch of government that has become the most destructive spiritually and morally of any branch of government is a secular Judiciary. This is the branch that should be working diligently to protect our constitutional freedoms. I think most Americans would agree that the Supreme Court alone has caused more Spiritual and moral destruction in America than all the wars we have fought.

Unfortunately we have made them, or allowed them, to become what they are! We have all contributed by insisting on forcing government to provide for our special interests and selfish demands no matter the cost to others. We have failed to live like responsible mature adults who fear and trust God. We have chosen a government bureaucracy to baby-sit us. We have an out of control judiciary that refuses to police itself and protect itself from unscrupulous lawyers and Judges. We have taken for granted our government, our freedom and our God. We have become government dependent. We have forgotten the lessons of history regarding big government and in our utter deceit we have rebelled against God and rejected His wisdom.

The historical record back through centuries shows the devastating results of vesting limitless power and control in central government. Our attitude is that it can't happen to America because our form of government protects us from that. This is total deceit because our form of government has and continues to change at the whim of a clueless legislature, a secular humanist judiciary and a morally degenerating culture. Those foundational protections guaranteed by our constitution have been and are being ignored or profoundly and systematically eroded by our Supreme Court and our legislature continues to pass more and more laws that take away liberty and increase the size of government.

We, as a society, are systematically surrendering to government the right to self-determination and our individual liberty. We surrender these rights because we don't want to be accountable and responsible and we refuse to deal with problems of life.

The kind of effort, wisdom and resources needed to do what we are demanding of our government and what our political leaders are promising are no-where to be found. However, we continue to think that government holds the key to better America so we continue along this destructive and foolish path, which will ultimately absorb America's resources and destroy its hope of Freedom.

America can look forward to bigger government, more taxes and more government intervention because that is what we are demanding of government. Kennedy was right, it is not what your country can do for you, it is what you can do for your country! Along with more government comes more government intervention and oppression, more taxation to finance government, and the concentration of power and wealth in the institution of government. This will continue to further erode our freedom and ultimately destroy our nation unless Americans wake-up, decentralize much of government, reduce its power and size significantly and limit its role to its constitutional authority as defined by our founding fathers..

The national heritage of America is one of a nation of rugged individualists who accepted the responsibility for their lives and the lives of their loved ones. They were religious people who lived by faith in a sovereign God and they worked because there was honor, dignity, purpose and reward for work. They worked because if they did not work they could not eat.

We were born and grew up a Christian Nation. Clearly there were people who migrated to America who were not Christian, however, they came here recognizing America was a Christian nation governed by Christians and its laws and social moral code was distinctively Christian. If they were to live here they would have to live according to this code and laws.

Our political leaders looked unashamedly and humbly to the God of the Bible to provide guidance in times of need and crisis. We were a nation of people who recognized that every thing good and descent in the character of a man found its origin in biblical truth and principle. Our laws of the land that defined our moral nature and our way of life was Christian. The inspiration of the charity that distinguished us as a nation was spiritual.

Virtually ever institution of higher learning in America was distinctively Christian. This is diametrically apposed to the condition today where virtually every public institution of higher learning is distinctively anti-Christian.

The virtue of our nation among the nations of the world was its Christian foundation and character. Its leadership was followed readily because of our nations moral authority and charity.

The last two generations of Americans have little true sense of history and therefore they have failed to acquire any appreciation of our national heritage. It will take a dramatic Spiritual awakening to begin to open the minds and hearts of the current generations to inspire them to receive the truth and grasp the vision.. Then it will take a massive re-education of Americans, who have been taught to believe the lie, if we hope to re-establish the foundation and the vision on which our nation once stood. God and His will and wisdom must be firmly planted in our hearts and minds if we hope to experience once again what we as a nation was intended by our creator to be.

Most Americans today consider believing Christian patriots, who believe the freedoms America has enjoyed and fought to hold are divinely imparted and distinctive from any other nation in the world because they have a foundation in God's will and word are part of a radical lunatic fringe which is bigoted, divisive, disruptive and destructive to America.

The current generation neither recognizes the problem nor do they appreciate the nature of the battle to protect liberty nor do they appreciate the contribution of those who have fought and continue to fight to protect those distinctive and precious freedoms they are foolishly and casually throwing away in ignorance, indifference and in Spiritual rebellion.

Our nations heritage is hardly a memory to this culture and the current generation. Liberal anti-God social reformers have rewritten the history that defines America's beginnings and progress until it no longer resembles America's heritage and tradition. They have decided they must make history politically correct and unfortunately they have the attention of our children and they have somehow convinced many Americans.

In their deceit and blindness they cannot discern the hand of our Creator. In fact, they have decided, the role of Christianity was not a positive force in the development of the character and nature of our people. The secularists and liberals have an agenda to attempt to prove that God had nothing to do with founding, sustaining or guiding the beginning and growth of the American nation. They are systematically removing the role of our Christian faith, which they consider bigoted and divisive. Certainly there are bumps in the road to maturity of America just as there are bumps in the road to Spiritual maturity in the lives of people.

Nevertheless, the heritage and history of our people reflects the working of the hand of a superintending God. That road to maturity is the heritage and tradition of America. From it we learn many lessons and we observe God at work among His people.

CHAPTER SEVEN

SECULAR MYTH'S

—〰—

"For the time will come when they will not endure sound doctrine; but wanting to have their ears tickled, they will accumulate for themselves teachers in accordance to their own desires; and will turn away their ears from the truth and will turn aside to myths."
(2 Timothy 4:3-4)

When we look at the lines on a road map that depict the roads we must travel to a given destination we are confident that we can proceed along those roads with reasonable assurance that if we follow the road we will arrive eventually at the intended destination.

Myth's can be compared to alterations of the lines and/or miss numbering of the roads on the map. The name of the road we intended to travel is not changed, however the road no longer leads to the destination we intended to arrive at. Myths are a deception that leads to the wrong destination. They produce devastating results if not discovered and corrected before we travel that road.

Altering the road map of life to deceive us travelers is a continuous work perpetuated by minds deceived and inspired by the spirit that leads the fallen nature of man. The flesh of man works endlessly to satisfy its appetites, pleasures and lusts. The flesh of man is the culprit within that hates God, rejects His wisdom and is the enemy of truth whenever that truth limits it in any way.

We create myths because they seem good to us and more comfortable and desirable to our fallen nature than the truth. The scriptures warn us; *"There is a way which seems right to a man, but its end is the way of death." (Proverbs 14:12)* Myths typically do not require the discipline and sacrifice the right road requires, however, if they are followed they typically lead to a destructive results and the wrong destination.

Faith, or belief, is a mysterious and not well-understood phenomena, however, it is a vital part of human life without which we have no foundation for hope. Atheists reject the idea of faith and have concluded there is no God. What I find interesting about their thinking is their conclusion has to be arrived at on the basis of faith since they cannot prove the absence of God. A man who knows of nothing or no one greater than himself lives under a code of myths. He is a lost soul who lives with an unsatisfied longing in his soul and therefore often lives a very anxious, angry, longing, and unhappy life.

The story goes that a noted scientist debated a noted Atheist who stood very confident in his unbelief over the issue of whether or not God exists. The foolish thinking of the Atheist was exposed when the Scientist asked the Atheist this question; "Of all the knowledge that man has come to know over the ages, what percentage of that knowledge would you say that you know? Would you say that you know 5% of all there is to know? The Atheist was startled but replied, "I am sure I don't know even 5% of all the knowledge that man has come to know over the ages." For the sake of this debate let us say that you know 5% of all that is known, which means that you do not know 95% of all that is known and yet you argue emphatically that you are sure there is no God.

The Atheist obviously found his position foolish and found himself in way over his head trapped by his deceit. His conclusions about God and Creation revealed his foolishness and arrogance.

The bible teaches us that God is the Creator and He is the foundation of truth, righteousness, hope, peace and liberty. Without God man is condemned by his deceit and limited is his assessment of truth to secular humanist reason and the wiles of the Devil. He sees life through the lenses of his natural mind and human appetites, which interprets reality as material and secular. What he doesn't see does not exist so far as he is concerned.

There are many realities that surround us that we cannot observe because of our physical limitations. Nevertheless they are true and do exist. One example might be radio magnetic energy that is around us constantly. We can prove it exists by simply plugging in a radio or television or cell phone and listening to or watching as the radio magnetic signal transmits sound and/or a picture that we can hear and/or see.

The example that is perhaps more to the point is our inability to see God. God is Spirit and we are unable to see the things of the Spirit. However, God speaks to our spirit and we hear His voice and follow His leading if we are born of His Spirit.

Man, in the foolishness of his deceit denies truth and creates in its place myth's to justify and make peace with his attitudes. Then upon these myths, which are typically lies that result from secular humanist thinking, he judges life and circumstances.

Without God there is no ultimate truth, which is a much-preferred perspective in the short term for the sinner. The problem with attempting to prove the existence of God to the atheist or the agnostic is that the instruments we must use to prove God's existence produce evidence that is not perceptible or acceptable to natural mind. God's existence cannot be proven with a thermometer, or a tape measure, or a spectrometer, or a magnetic detector or by touch. However, God declares that we are without excuse because His creation proves

His existence. Only when our eyes have been opened can we use Spiritual instruments to recognize the design, wisdom and power of His creation.

God has said in His word that without faith we cannot see Him. He also declared in His Word that without Spiritual rebirth we are without faith and we cannot, or will not, see His Kingdom. *"For by grace you have been saved (delivered) through faith; and that not of yourselves, it is the gift of god;" (Ephesians 2:8)* Faith is the gift of God according to the scriptures and His Kingdom is beyond the ability of the secular mind to grasp and it is beyond the works of man to enter.

"But if any of you lacks wisdom, let him ask of God, who gives to all men generously and without reproach, and it will be given to him. But let him ask in faith without any doubting, for the one who doubts is like the surf of the sea driven and tossed by the wind. For let not that man expect that he will receive anything from the Lord." (James 1:5-7)

Two of the foundational myth's generally accepted by many of our educators and many of our citizens is that **"Science proves that God does not exist"** and "**There is no evidence to prove that God exists".** Science is the very limited study of what God has created. It is not the study of the Creator. It cannot answer any of the questions regarding where the earth, the universe or life began. It cannot explain away a Creator! It cannot ever explain why, who or how all the various species of animals exist. It cannot explain life and cannot begin to explain the human mind. Science cannot explain fear, anger, peace, patience, kindness, goodness, faithfulness, gentleness, or self-control because they are Spiritual things. Neither can it explain idolatry, sorcery, enmities, strife, jealousy, outbursts of anger, disputes, dissensions, factions, envying, drunkenness, carousing, immorality, impurity or sensuality and things like this.

To the Spiritually reborn believer the statements of the atheist are ridiculous and the product of deceit and arrogance rather than science. As the song states, "**once you have seen the sun no one can tell you its not there".** Spiritual rebirth gives man the eyes to see and the ears to hear. The scriptures tell us, *"My sheep hear my voice, and I know them, and they follow me; and I give eternal life to them, and they shall never perish; and no one shall snatch them out of My hand. My Father, who has given them to Me, is greater than all; and no one is able to snatch them out of the Father's hand. I and the Father are one." (John 10: 27-30)*

Science does not create in only observes and studies what has been created. Our culture has adopted the assertions of men in the scientific community and latched onto a simplistic attitude that says, "I am free to believe whatever I will. What works for you may not work for me- each to his own god. From the Spiritual perspective mans deliverance from deceit is not according to his choice only.

We are accountable to each other and ultimately to God for what we say and what we do. Sincere and honest men and women consider the foundation for their beliefs, free-doms and statements before they declare or attempt to impose them on others. In a more profound since, those who do not speak and live truth contribute toward the creation of a society that disregards the importance of truth and personal integrity and produces an angry and evil society.

A society that overlooks the profound effect of falsehood and tolerates it as a way of life and expects it in common communication soon will find they are unable to discern between truth and falsehood or right and wrong or good and bad. Unfortunately that has become the norm in American culture.

For example, perhaps you have noticed that products and services advertisements are typically blatantly false and intentionally misleading. We have come to except the misleading advertising with little consideration or alarm and rarely attempt to hold the advertiser accountable. Perhaps you have noticed that the words of the typical person in our culture have become untrustworthy. People will say anything without ever a thought of accountability. To depend on someone to act or perform what they say they will do has no doubt become a very disappointing experience common to all of us. It is rare today to find a person or business that can be trusted to perform what they say or in the context of what they advertise. We do not see this as a sign of our degeneracy as a people.

Democracy requires a constant vigil against the infringement of the enemy, evil, villains and fools, all of which will destroy it. It requires vigorous protection of the rights of those who are out to protect it. However, it also demands a discernment and wisdom that is no longer apparent among our people. We no longer hold men accountable for what they say or how they act publicly. We have appointed and elected deceived men to set in judgment over us. They have become enemies rather than protectors of our constitutional rights. We have adopted the perspective that we are free to do and say whatever we want no matter where we are or the circumstance and the destruction it will create. The purpose of our laws and our rights is to protect our citizens against evil and not to protect the evil. We have distorted and perverted the meaning of our constitutional rights and we no longer have leaders who are willing or able to discern the difference. The truth and accountability are no longer politically correct and therefore no longer protected.

For man to declare that he believes one way or another demands that he has accepted some authoritative foundation to support his belief system. The only other reasons a man may declare that he holds a certain belief is to justify his attitudes and ways, or his appetites and pleasures. Sometimes we are simply misguided by misinformation or we are ignorant of the truth or we act out of our will. The deeper our sin and deception the more anxious we become to justify our attitudes and actions! God points out that all men are without excuse. God's word says, **"for the wrath of God is revealed from heaven against all ungodliness and unrighteousness of men, who suppress the truth in unrighteousness, because that which is know about God is evident within them; for God made it evident to them."** (Romans 1:18-19)

In light of that truth man must somehow justify his attitudes and actions lest he be revealed as the fool he truly is! Fallen mans response to evil and sin in his life is to attempt to justify himself by adopting a belief system that does not confront his sin and wickedness. In our collective deceit we chose to believe the lie because we cannot bear the truth. So we live the lie and turn to myth's to guide us. That, in spades, is what we are doing in America. We have set aside the divine principles that provided the foundation and acted as the guiding principles that sustained and blessed and inspired America to goodness and Greatness. We have traded the truth for the lie and have adopted myth's to guide us.

Some of the myths that occupy American thinking today and provide the foundation for the thinking upon which decisions have been made and continue to be made that guide our nation today are as follows:

Erin Luther, in an article entitled **"the myths that are destroying America"** written for the Arthur S. Demos foundations "rebirth of America" published in 1986 presented some myths that deceived Americans have accepted as truth. These myths now guide the critical and dominant thinking of many of our people and many of the leaders of our nations government as well as the Judiciary. They feed our deceit, cloud our judgment and lead us in the wrong direction. They will ultimately destroy the America of our founding fathers if there is not a Spiritual awakening.

First myth: "The Spiritual battle Isn't Real"!

The point of this myth is there is no such thing as a Spiritual battle to fight. It denies the influence of the spirit of the world and it denies the Spirit of God. The scriptures teach us *.."The Flesh sets its desire against the Spirit, and the Spirit against the flesh; for these are in opposition to one another." (Galatians 5:17)* Those who deny the Spiritual battle are unable to discern that America is rotting from the inside out because its people aren't able to recognize the Spiritual battle and they are not inspired to carefully and sincerely examine the truth or engage the battle.

I believe it is even more profound. Many people don't want the truth because the truth judges the intentions of the heart. We don't want to be held responsible for our attitudes, actions and unbelief. Beyond that millions, perhaps even a majority, lack the ability to discern the truth let alone possess the discipline and moral courage to walk according to it. Simply put, we have rejected truth and have become deceived in our thinking!

The church has played down the social Spiritual deterioration of our nation leaving the average Christian to believe Spiritual blindness is not a deepening national problem or, if it is, it is not all that significant in its implications. The attitude that seems to prevail is that God can change our individual or national direction anytime he wants to and therefore we really don't have a role to play in it. It's as if what we might do to seek, preserve and demonstrate the truth is not really God's calling upon our lives. What incredible deceit!!

Obviously, the fact that God has already revealed His will and continues to reveal His will to the hearts and minds of those who will listen with the declared intention and hope that we will act according to it somehow goes completely over the heads of many.

Our history has been and continues to be re-written and badly distorted by educators and social engineers who have built their lives around secularism and its destructive myths. They promote those myths because it justifies their worldly ways and it justifies their attitudes and social agenda, which do not include God or His wisdom.

Two worldviews are on a collision course. The battle lines are drawn between secular humanism and Judeo-Christian beliefs. Every man must at some point choose on which side of the battle lines he is going to stand.

The more comfortable place to be is to believe that the battle between good and evil, between the spirit of God and the flesh of men, is not real. That is the course we have chosen to take as a national government. It is the path of deceit and it leads to death!

The second myth: "Life Began By Blind Chance"!

In order for men to justify their sinful ways they must somehow deny the existence of a Creator and God. They must also deny the curse men without Spiritual regeneration (redemption) live under because of sin against God. They must in fact reject the idea of a God who is the Creator or even a sovereign higher power.

If they are going to justify abortion they must reject the idea of a sovereign God and adopt the idea that all life came about and is sustained by blind chance!! Sincere scientists have been forced to conclude *"evolution is a fairy tale for adults"*! The doctrine of evolution is in disarray and Darwinism has fallen on hard times. The big bang theory has proven to be nothing more than speculation at the very elementary level.

It doesn't appear that the moon and the sun and the planets have moved further apart for at least the last several thousand years, so if there was a big bang it has run out of bang. The question is, of course, what would stop the expansion in space where there is no resistance and no gravitational pull. The planets seem to be almost exactly the same distance from the earth that they were when we were first able to measure their distance away from us.

Who "rolled the dice" so to speak that got the planets rotating at a precision we cannot imitate. Besides all that, nobody seems to be able to explain, including those who have adopted and promoted the theory, where the original energy and matter came from or what or who would have caused the "big bang" that supposedly started it all and what filled space before the big bang? Who created the original mass and the space?

However, evolution is the creation theory (which is a contradiction in terms) endorsed by the government and the worldly culture we live in and by the vast majority of our public education institutions and by much of the scientific community. Erin asks the question **"how could impersonal forces acting randomly construct a universe whose planets rotate with such precision that we set our clocks and navigate by them?"**

It is obviously preposterous to believe that nothing times nobody equals everything that exists. Only a deceived and intellectually dishonest mind can believe and promote such non-sense! That is the power of deceit at work! Evolution is harder to believe than the idea of throwing every letter and word up in the air and having it come down a dictionary.

While Christians and the church has put their light under a peck measure and has taken a knap the enemy has come in like a flood and impregnated our society with this nonsense which now guides our scientific thinking regarding the origin of life and fills the minds of our children.

It is very late for America because the lie is so entrenched in the teaching of our public education system it will take decades to correct the damage and reorient the thinking of our teachers and our children to the truth even if they might be instantly inspired to set out upon a sincere search for the truth.

Huxley captures the idea in his response to the question of why evolution was so readily accepted. He candidly admitted **"the reason we accepted Darwinism even without proof is because we didn't want God to interfere with our sexual mores" I** have a notion he may be right.

Clearly America has decided it does not want any interference from the Creator so we have chosen to condemn ourselves ultimately by refusing to believe and trust in God. We have condemned ourselves and we cannot rise above our deceit unless God somehow chooses to intervene and change our hearts and minds.

The idea of eternity in hell is so fearful to us that we reject the idea there might be either heaven or hell. We dare not examine the truth and fall upon God's mercy to save us from hell. Therefore we adopt secularism to justify our lifestyle and we hide in our deceit by continuing to perpetuate the lie that God does not exist and life somehow began by blind chance.

Rejecting eternal damnation is not considered a threat in this culture. It frees men to do evil without an ultimate penalty. Life by blind chance is a myth that has no moral code to guide it and no destiny, no hope and no accountability beyond this life. That thinking justifies, "eat, drink and make merry because tomorrow you die." Secular humanism does not interfere with or limit this myth.

Third myth: "We can have morality without God or religion."

The first myth was that we don't have a problem; the second myth was that the universe and life is a product of blind chance; the third is that we can have morality without a righteous God.

Its interesting to recognize that we profess not to have a problem and we deny God as Creator and supreme in all matters, yet something inside us says and our experience dictates there is a moral code for us to live by that stands as a foundation for law lest we destroy each other. Since hate for God is the overriding passion of those without God their response must be that we can have a moral code without God or without His word or without His church.

Immorality is a notion that demands morality as its foundation against which it can be measured. The only way immorality can be justified is to change the moral code to fit our appetites, pleasures and lusts. The secularists do that by attempting to establish a moral code without God. The alternative is to adopt God's moral code and attempt to live by it else we see ourselves as intellectually dishonest. Our pride will not allow us to accept the truth so we attempt to create through our secular mind some sort of moral code that fits into the natural and denies the spiritual.

The Supreme Court helped to accommodate the secularist and the atheist by stepping up to the plate and removing the Ten Commandments, the foundation of America's moral code, from public institutions and from the public classrooms on November 17, 1980. The Court explained, in essence, that the Ten Commandments were plainly religious and if they are posted children will read them and if they read them they will meditate upon them and if they meditate upon them they may try to obey the Commandments and that would violate the Constitutional separation of Church and State.

What do you suppose they thought would give our society moral guidance if they destroyed the moral code that has historically led America? Morality and God's law are inseparable. The very basis of morality is the expressed and applied will of God. Without religion humanity is without dignity, without liberty, without peace and without purpose. Life has no purpose, meaning or direction without God beyond satisfying our fleshly appetites.

America has not yet reaped the full harvest of its transition away from its Christian tradition and worldview to the secular humanist worldview. There clearly remains a majority in America that holds a cultural Christian philosophical perspective and their remains a remnant of true believers who have not been overcome by the world. When religion, more to the point when God, has no more guiding influence over our moral values then evil values will become virtues. Men will call that which is good as evil and that which is evil as good. And so it is rapidly coming to pass in America!!

Fourth myth: "Whatever is legal is moral".

We must return to a sense of the rich history that clearly reveals America was born with a God ordained purpose and accountable to the Creator for the fulfillment of that purpose. The facts of the historic record teach us that God's Spirit working through the hearts and minds of our founders inspired the creation of the United States of America and biblical principle is the foundation, inspiration an aspiration of our moral code and therefore our laws and system of justice.

Our founding fathers were inspired by the Creator to establish a system of government on earth according to His will with the mandate to protect the God given rights He ordained for men and to administer the vision and purpose he would give us. America was a nation designed to be unique to any other nation in the history of the world. America was led to put into place a government that governs by the consent of the governed believers and governs by laws based on biblical principle expressing the charity, wisdom, dignity and expressed will of Almighty God.

The standard by which right and wrong was to be determined for Americans was and is the Christian bible. Our declared national purpose was to give God the glory as we demonstrate His character and will in all matters of life. The measure of a man would be the strength of his character, his sincere devotion to God, his charity for his fellowman and his obedience to God.

When the Supreme Court chose to consider America no longer accountable to God and only accountable to itself we took the bate and ended up in the trap of assuming that whatever we consider legal is also moral! So our legal code became our moral code. The secular humanist philosophy, fostered and given license by our Supreme Court, has and continues to lead our people into believing and accepting the lie.

We have rejected our moral code and therefore legality is no longer accountable to morality. We have made our moral code accountable to our legal code. We can change that code simply by changing the law. We have chosen to protect immorality with our legal system and accepted the idiocy that whatever we chose to make legal is no longer accountable to biblical morality.

The Supreme Court has decided there is no higher authority to which man must be accountable. They have concluded our government and our courts are not accountable to the Creator. They recognize no morality other than there own decrees.

Francis Schemer called what has happened in this regard in America as "sociological law" which is law based upon what a majority agrees to or what deceived Judges say it is. The belief that God exists and is sovereign in the affairs of men and nations was obviously foundational to the establishment of this republic and it's system led America. Virtually every law of the land found its founding principal and authority in the word of God.

Prior to the last 50 years the worldview held by the majority of Americans was distinctively Christian. Even though a majority of Americans profess some form of Christian faith, the biblical Christian worldview found in much of the church has been replaced with a quasi-cultural Christian view that tends to be secular humanist. It is a product of satanic deception allowed to crepe in upon a Spiritually lukewarm Church and an indifferent Nation. We, as a culture, have drifted into Spiritual blindness and we are no longer able to distinguish between the truth and the lie and we have lost the courage and character to care.

For example, where did the Supreme Court get the notion or the authority to establish as a part of our social thinking that a woman has a right to an abortion? Such a right is not found in the constitution and it is contrary to biblical truth and the leading of the Spirit of God! God has declared that human life is a divine thing and that we will answer to God for how we treat that life.

The right of a woman to abort a life because it fits her agenda or because it is inconvenient, embarrassing or that it creates a problem for her is the product of a secular humanist worldview. The Supreme Court got lost in the utter deceit of secular thinking. It has chosen to interpret the essence and character of the United States of America as secular. In this fog of human deceit the court decided it was constitutionally the thing to do.

Abortion right's is a product of their collective deception. The Court, in making this decision, crowned itself God, the giver of life and/or death and Emperor answerable to no one. The Executive and Legislative branches of government in ignorance, indifference and lacking in political courage chose to let this decision stand. The Church as well as the Executive and Legislative branches of our Government should have raised a public outrage like the nation has never seen. A few Christian ministries expressed their concern along with the Catholic Church leading the protest, however the response of the Church was what could be expected of a lukewarm church. The American people, except for a few Christian protestors, allowed the Court to get away with it. According to various poles this Supreme Court decision has led to approximately 30,000,000 abortions and continues at the pace of approximately 4000 abortions per day. The protests against this horrible practice have virtually ended and this evil has triumphed.

To remove the stigma of abortion we have adopted a politically correct term "Women's right to chose". The politicians on Capitol hill do not have the political courage to correct this horrible wrong. I am not God, but my guess is these men will get a chance to answer to God for this terrible evil.

Every person in our nation of sound mind recognizes that abortion is impossible to justify and that it is the ultimate act in rebellion against God's will and contrary to the values of the civilized world. It is a tragedy that makes the holocaust look like a Sunday school picnic. Abortionists and those having abortions know it is deplorable and un-Godly, therefore, in their shame they hide its practice from public site and awareness for the most part. Abortion is murder pure and simple and no amount of discussion or debate will ever take away the stench or the guilt of the legalized practice of this ultimate of sinful acts.

The secular humanist worldview opened the door to abortion, pornography and the sexual perversion that permeates the lives and values of this culture. It has removed the moral protection necessary for man to responsibly govern himself. Its only moral code is the appetites and pleasures of the fallen nature of man. Secular humanism creates the idea that whatever seems right to the deceived mind of the secular humanist must surely become legal. Whatever is legal meets the secularist moral code. Any religious moral standard is considered bigoted and must be removed from the law of the land and the public arena.

If there was ever a decision by any nation that was a stench in the nostrils of God it is this decision by the Supreme Court. No amount of political or legal patter or any attempt to market the idea or to act under the slogan "the women's right to chose" will change God's judgment against this nation and this nations leaders unless there comes a national repentance. We have no excuse. We know what we are doing and we have chosen to continue in our utter sinfulness. Our guilt demands that we reject God and so we have! How do you suppose God will deal with us?

The state, and for that matter any special interest group, can now use this secular humanist interpretation of the law and its application to justify virtually any action it wishes to practice, support or indorse. Secular humanism has no standard to guide it. It substitutes an arbitrary moral code or standard based on the appetites of the fallen nature of man for biblical morality. The Christian worldview and Christian morality is considered bigoted and politically incorrect by today's culture. We have reversed that which is right and wrong, evil and good. We no longer revere and respect moral purity and we find the public expression and practice and demonstration of religious faith unacceptable

If you are one who considers yourself "pro-choice" you have been sucked in by deceit. The evil of this idea and act escapes you and you are complicit in this horrible act against your fellowman and your Creator. The so-called "right to chose" is a myth! No one has the right to chose to murder the innocent regardless of the law of the land because man is called to answer to a higher calling and a higher law.

Fifth myth: "morality cannot be legislated!"

The next battle the secular humanist must confront is the book of law that reflects the Character and nature of a traditional Christian society. In order to do that the secular humanists develops and presents the idea that they are the ones who are truly broad-minded, neutral and pluralistic in moral matters. They say they are apposed to censorship, sectarianism and intolerance. They depict the Christian as the right wing religious fanatic who wishes to impose his will and his morality on society.

The ironic thing about all this is that it is God's revealed will they are in rebellion against. His will is the very will we are destined to live by in heaven and it is our prayer that His will be done on earth. I cannot imagine a better world here on earth than a world that obeys and honors and loves His will. The only way that will happen is if the hearts and minds of Americans are changed so as to humble themselves to follow after His Spirits leading and to establish a legal system and laws that reflect God's value's and will.

Perhaps it has never entered the minds of our secular humanist friends that all law is the imposition of someone's morality. That, of course, is why the statement, "you cannot legislate morality" is an absurd idea! Somebody's will is legislated every day! If it is not God's will why are we even considering it?

Today secular humanism has imposed and continues to impose its perverted sense of morality on government, education, the church and virtually every area of life in America! There is a concerted effort among secular humanists to erase the Christian worldview and God's morality from our national public life. Unfortunately, that movement is succeeding because most American's fail to discern the implications and/or are sound asleep spiritually.

Columnist George Will put it so aptly when he said, *"and it is, by now, a scandal beyond irony that thanks to the energetic litigation of 'civil liberties' fanatics, pornographers enjoy expansive first amendment protection while first graders in nativity plays (at school) are said to violate first amendment values."* The only truth that insures justice and liberty in our land is now considered the enemy of truth.

There is no such thing as neutral legislation. Every law imposes some form of morality on the society governed by it. The abortionists want to impose their morality on the unborn. Homosexuals and sex perverts want to legislate their views so they can flaunt and promote their life styles. Atheists want to legislate religious influence out of public life in America.

Those politicians in the House and the Senate who recognize the price that will be paid by America because of the secular move away from our creator and yet do nothing because of the political price it may extract will pay a terrible price ultimately.

The question is not "can morality be legislated?" The question is "whose morality is going to be legislated'? If you are of the mind that morality is not influenced by legislation how do you explain the incredible amount of time energy and money that is spent legislating it? The laws that are passed to govern our activities are themselves the prime example of legislating morality.

Law is far more than the standard against which punishment is meted out by a society. It is the standard of morality acceptable to a society and it is the light that guides a people toward those things that protect life, liberty and justice and the incentive to guide people away from those things that threaten liberty and life. It is the laws of the land that express the character, morality, values and lifestyle of the people they guide. The laws of the land are the example of what society says is good and acceptable or bad and unacceptable.

We are a nation of law. We recognize the need and value of righteous laws and therefore we will not tolerate lawlessness. Righteous and just laws provide the greatest opportunity for protection from oppression, from evil, from the destroyers of peace and tranquility; from the unjust imposition of the misguided or perverted will of another. The law helps to train and lead us toward righteousness, justice and Godliness and establishes for us a standard of sound principle and fairness in our dealings and interactions with our fellowman. Sound laws lead us toward good character, human dignity, justice and the protection of human rights. Just laws and righteous judges provide the only hope for peace in a world inhabited by men with fallen natures who require from time to time restraint from imposing their selfish will upon or at the expense of another. Morally just laws make men accountable for their actions and helps to instruct and guide us toward responsible citizenship.

Morality must be carefully legislated if people are to live in peace and harmony. History is clear that the only morality that works finds its foundational authority, principle and context in the Christian bible. If we are to legislate any morality it seems Christian morality is the morality we must legislate. It is the foundational morality of our nation and its laws and it provides the best hope to guide America.

Certainly, man makes his choice as to what he will believe. However, the society, with its laws, morays and values systems, in which he lives will make the choice as to how he must behave regardless of what he believes if he wishes to be accepted by and assimilated into that society.

Man is free to believe what he will, however, he must recognize that what he believes does impact how he behaves and how he behaves has consequences. If what he believes is foolish he acts foolishly and if he continues to think and act foolishly he becomes known and considered a fool. If what he believes has no basis in truth he is choosing to depart from his accountability to God and his fellowman. If he continues in his utter foolishness he will sooner or later run head long into trouble and will become a victim of the legal system that defines the life, the values and the standards of the society in which he lives. He will have to pay the price for what he believes and how he conducts his life. Our beliefs have consequences good and/or bad. The Scriptures teach us and our experience confirms that we reap what we sow!

One of the great benefits of being an American is the protected right to believe and espouse that belief freely without the fear of reprisal by governing authorities. However, false premises lead us down destructive paths toward trouble. Our search must always be for the truth in order to live by it because it will ultimately judge us and therefore finding and living according to it provides our best ultimate hope. Ultimate truth is a Spiritual matter and not a secular matter. It is not only our judge it is our light and inspiration. It illuminates the pathway in which we must walk. Until we find it we cannot walk in it!!

Myth number six: "The roles of men and women are interchangeable in society:"

The argument the world tries to make is that since the bible teaches that both men and women are created in the image of God, and that all men are created equal, they may interchange the roles assigned by God as they serve in the family and society. That is clearly a perversion of scriptural interpretation. The bible doesn't even hint that! The motive behind the world's argument is to persuade everyone to support a perverted notion of equal rights and equal opportunity in the work place, in the home and in the church.

In the biblical context of men and women having been created equal before God every sincere student of the word of God will say "amen"! However, the biblical context is that every man or women ought to have an equal opportunity to fulfill their God given role in the family and in society.

Some women, and men as well, may be angry with God and in rebellion against Him because of the role he has ordained for them to fulfill in society. However, their best hope of personal fulfillment is nevertheless found in recognizing the role God has created us to fulfill and then to pursue it!

Our maleness and femaleness has a distinctive undeniable identity and purpose, which has a physical, mental and spiritual dimension obvious to even the most casual observer. However, many have rebelled against the obvious and walk in a deception, which completely denies the biblical concept of being of equal value to God while also having been created for a different role.

Once again in our rebellion we have perverted the truth to promote a devastating attack on the distinctiveness of the genders. Its purpose is satanic which is to ultimately destroy the individual, the family and our society. It is another sign of human rebellion against our Creator.

The radical feminists who back the ERA movement want to end the institution of marriage as biblically established. They want to exchange that divine institution of family for an environment where men and women are free without prejudice to cohabitate like animals driven by their sexual appetites and selfish pleasures with no accountability to God or their fellowman. They reject the concept of the marriage covenant whereby a man and a woman enter into a covenant of commitment and mutual accountability before God.

Feminists, in their rebellion against God, see marriage as tantamount to the historical institution of human slavery. Shell Corinne, one of the leaders in the feminist movement, stated: **"since marriage constitutes slavery for women, it is clear that the women movement must concentrate on attacking this institution. Freedom for women cannot be won without the abolition of marriage."**

Even though the constitution of the United States is gender and color blind these feminists see no equality unless women are somehow free of the burden of their God given role of raising up the children, caring for a home, faithfulness or accountability to a husband and family or to anyone for their attitudes and actions.

The feminists insist they still want to have children however they promote the idea that the nurturing and raising up of these children doesn't have to be in the traditional home. Their mantra is there can be no equality so long as the woman is seen by our society as the homemaker.

From their warped perspective they demand that other institutions should raise their children so they can be free to pursue their individual ambitions. They want to leave the responsibility for the content and direction of their education to be the burden of the state. They reject God's calling to raise up their children in the nurture and admonition of the lord.

N. O. W. (the national organization of women) demands federally funded day care centers that provide around the clock, seven days a week day care. They insist it be provided for them, however, they want to force the taxpayer and/or their employer to pay for it. They sincerely believe that society must bear the burden of raising and caring for their children while they are at work or free to pursue whatever their interests or pleasures.

Lenin and every other socialist or communist leader or society has pursued this idea of the children being raised by and even becoming the property of the state. History vividly displays the tragic results of such foolishness!!

N.O.W. adamantly opposes the right of the church or of private industry to declare and encourage any differentiation between the roles of men and women. They view the refusal of the evangelical church to ordain women and homosexuals as contrary to the law.

They cry out for separation of church and state in the public arena when the church wishes to express the biblical world view publicly, however, they want to forget about the separation when it comes to trying to get the state to force the church to ordain women and homosexuals as pastors and priests of the church.

Where does the organized church stand on these issues? Many of the main line denominations are moving away from the biblical worldview because it is not a politically correct or popular view in some communities. They see their survival requiring a sort of political correctness and inclusiveness which is an idea alive and well in our society today.

The world council of churches, which includes most of the main line denominations, has moved so far away from biblical truth that it is wrong to even continue to identify them with the church of our savior Jesus Christ.

For the sake of political correctness and acceptance by the world they have seen fit to release a biblical lectionary that omits all gender based terms, including all reference to God as "He". I am happy to report that this movement is losing support. Membership in the main-line religious institutions is falling each year.

In our social rebellion against God's revealed will many of the mainline denominations under the same spirit have seen fit to ordain women and homosexuals as priests.

Our rebellion against the God given role of men and women in God's church, in social relationships, in the family relationship and in workplace relationships have further divided our nation and is destroying our families and the children of the next generation.

This apostasy in the church has come to pass because we have drifted away from biblical truth and have accepted the lie. That lie takes on many forms and is subtly being grafted into and perpetuated in every area of life in America. America is crumbling under the load of sin and rebellion. We have sown the wind and we are now beginning to reap the whirlwind.

Myth number six: "A fetus is not human"

Another associated myth that permeates our culture is: **"if abortion was not legal the abortion industry would simply go underground and millions of women would get abortions illegally through charlatan doctors or practitioners who would cause great damage and even death to women. Therefore we need to keep it legal so we can do the humanitarian thing by controlling the process.**

The incredible deceit that darkens the mind to accept the idea that abortion is the humanitarian thing to do is so foolish it is impossible to explain and harder to believe.

When abortions became legal in America the number of abortions increased dramatically. I have heard numbers like more than 100 fold. I honestly don't know how much the increase, only that it was overwhelmingly dramatic.

The idea that it is better to perform millions of abortions legally than to have 1000 performed illegally is total unadulterated non-sense. This argument could be made about almost anything that is illegal today including the laws against the use of drugs and prostitution.

Regardless of its obvious idiocy the abortionists won in the Supreme Court of our land! The cry now against those attempting to call America into accountability is **"abortion is legal in America...so what's the problem?"** It's a tragic testimony to our collective deceit and sinful life styles that any thinking adult would have to have this question answered for them. **If you are one who does not understand the problem let me suggest the deliberate calculated mass murder of children is the problem!!** This procedure as it is permitted today is seen as acceptable because of the irresponsible character of our society.

This kind of murder is such an abomination in the sight of God that it alone will ultimately destroy us as a society unless we repent and stop it! The abortion mills in America make Hitler's system of destruction of the Jews appear relatively minor!

We mask our foolishness with self justifying slogans like "*a women's right to chose*" as though the right to chose here supports a higher cause that somehow justifies the calculated murder of millions of babies.

We attempt to mask our shame by stating, **"a fetus is not a baby"**! This spin, of course, is designed to mask the shame and the truth of the scripture, which teaches us that God knew each of us before we were formed in our mother's womb. The scriptures teach **"for thou didst form my inward parts; thou didst weave me in my mother's womb." (psalm 139.13)**

The only way our society can accept abortion is if they can justify it by promoting the idea that **"a fetus is not a baby"** and **"a woman has a right to chose"**. This deceit is intended to mask the biblical and moral condemnation of abortion.

However, politicians need to get elected and to get elected they need the votes of women, therefore the politically correct response of politicians so they can enjoy the good will of the abortion crowd that gets larger every day. The political spin has become that in America, **"we support the right to chose."**

Politicians have found the abortion parade and they begin marching at the head of it proclaiming the glory of a land where a women can chose to have an abortion if she wants to. The political spin is that **"I am personally against abortion, however, I believe in free choice even though the choice one might make is the wrong choice."** With this spin they think they can keep from alienating the abortion rights voters while at the same time not alienating the **"right to life"** group.

In addition to God's view of this matter how about the perspective of the baby that is murdered or the father of the aborted baby? Doesn't the baby have any rights to be protected here? The baby must depend upon the morally responsible decision of the potential mother to protect its life.

Sexual perversion is a very serious problem in God's view. When it results in getting pregnant out of wedlock it becomes and even more serious matter. Abortion adds to the already tragic circumstance. Adding murder to this complicates even more this irresponsible act. What about the parent's judgment regarding the best course to take in the event of a teenage pregnancy? The courts have ruled that a female child can have an abortion without the parent's permission or even notification.

Many say, "Well there is a nothing definitive to prove a fetus is a human life"! There can't be any sincere argument if we look to God for our authority!!! If God's word is not your authority just what authority do those who argue against God find as their source of wisdom and authority. Clearly, The bible teaches that if we destroy a fetus we are playing God! Killing a fetus is thwarting God's plan and purpose in the life of the one being aborted. It is rebellion against His revealed will by the one seeking to have the abortion done and it is murder being committed by the abortionist.

In our secular cultural blindness much of our current generation sees the Christian "right to life" advocates as the enemy of the state rather than the protectors of life. Our culture sees no law higher than the state. They acknowledge no god other than the state and/or themselves.

The "right to life" groups are trying to discourage people from doing what is legally sanctioned because abortion will have life long and even eternal consequences. This group is portrayed in the media as enemies of the people! Ironic isn't it that people can be so deceived! Why would anyone have to take the time to explain the abomination of the practice of abortion? It is self-evident and there is no justification for its practice.

It's also interesting to consider that tobacco and alcohol and abortion are all legal. However, up to now the government doesn't finance tobacco and alcohol but it does finance the abortion industry. In fact, tobacco and alcohol finance the government.

We the people of the United States made them all legal! So long as they are legal and in demand there will be someone to manufacture and distribute the product or service. The way to destroy any of these menaces to society is to quit demanding their product or services!!

The mentality that continues to smoke, drink and have sex on demand and then demand restitution from the provider is pathetically foolish. This kind of thinking is moving throughout our society like the plague. Our people have determined that the choice to bring litigation against someone is not whether such action is morally justified but rather whether there is a good chance of winning!

What we should have learned is that since something is legal in America doesn't suggest that it is morally right or best for the people. We forget that when the laws of our society suggest that it is alright to raise, produce, promote and market a product or service then its use is considered to be harmless to the individual, morally sound and it will not generally be destructive to society.

Unfortunately for America, abortion rights say more about a pathetically confused and deceived Supreme Court and Americas citizens than it does about human rights. No one has the right to choose to murder! Only the most brain-dead and perverted mind does not recognize it! Since abortion has become legal the floodgates to abortion has opened. Now we proudly present abortion as a right. The utter stupidity of the Roe v. Wade decision should be obvious to every sincere thinking American. However the pro-choice proponents still argue that the answer is to keep it legal.

Surely we must see that this mindset has contributed greatly to the dramatic increase in divorce rates, teen pregnancy, out of marriage pregnancy rates and abortions. Today, among minorities in America it is said that more than half of the children born to minority women are born out of wedlock and as a cross section of all American women one out of three children are born out of wedlock.

The problem our government is focused upon is not how best to help limit this activity by identifying those standards of behavior, which are not acceptable. Pregnancy out of wedlock must once again be the evidence of shameful and unacceptable activity rather than just another medical condition. Children born out of wedlock must not continue to qualify the mother for greater welfare benefits.

Our governments approach is not leadership that raises expectations and expresses clearly that which is acceptable and unacceptable behavior, but rather they have decided that individual accountability is not the answer because it is unpopular to promote and difficult to enforce!

Solving the problem to a secular and liberal government is to find the money to provide financially for illegitimate children, promiscuous mothers and irresponsible fathers. Obviously this kind of non-sense exacerbates the problem by giving incentives to women on welfare to have as many children as they can since the size of their welfare checks are determined by the number of children they have.

Many who read this would perhaps think that I am some sort of cruel minded, cold-hearted person who has no concern for these children. They will see me as a Simon Lagree who would allow the babies to starve.

In response to this, let me say first that these babies are the parent's responsibility first and foremost. The government is not responsible nor is the taxpayers. The parents must be held accountable by society or this practice will not change. Second, we reap what we sow and our best course of action is to let those involved know that this behavior is irresponsible and not acceptable in this society and if you engage in it there is consequences. Third, the church must step in and provide direction, provision, education and spiritual guidance. This is a moral problem and not a government problem.

The absence of these laws and/or their enforcement speaks loudly about what we do or do not consider important! Making unconstitutional any law that prohibits abortion tells America that our society has decided to set aside the moral standard that demands the dignity of human life and the aborted babies right to life. Today it is said that 97% of all abortions occur simply for the convenience of the mother. We have become so callus that we have allowed abortion to become little more than another means of birth control.

Peter singer, in "pediatrics" wrote, **"We can no longer base our ethics on the idea the human beings are a special form of creation made in the image of God and singled out from all other animals."** Baby's bodies are sold by the bag by some hospitals, according to Erin, for all kinds of experimentation.

It is revealing to study justice Harry Blackmens explanation and justification for the infamous roe vs. wade decision. He said that the objection to abortion came mainly from two sources; the **first was the Hippocratic oath and the second from Christianity. He reasoned that they wrestled with the oath because it specifically prohibits abortion.... but they concluded that in the context of general opinion, "ancient religions did not bar abortion." As for Christianity, the court on the basis of separation of church and state dismissed its consideration.** This is beyond belief that such deceit and foolish thinking had a seat on the highest court of our land.

The highest court in the nation elected to throw out two thousand years of Judeo-Christian influence and chose to reach back into paganism as justification for abortion.

As a result of that decision more than 30 million unborn babies have had their lives deliberately terminated in this abominable practice of abortion. Abortion clinics have proliferated our landscape and have made abortion a big business in America. I would

Myth #7 "Our constitution has constructed a wall of separation between the state and the church which prohibits the public testimony of our faith and the free expression of our religious belief."

In fact, **<u>just the opposite is true</u>**! The constitution erects a wall of separation that prohibits the state from interfering in the free expression of religious faith and/or from establishing a particular Christian denomination as a state sponsored church!

The most elementary study of history will reveal clearly that when Thomas Jefferson spoke of a wall of separation between church and state his intended purpose was to prevent the creation of a state religion based upon the doctrine of one or the other of the Christian denominations prevalent in the nation. It was not intended to eradicate the Christian world-view and its influence from American government or public life

In fact, the author of separation between church and state was Karl Marx not Thomas Jefferson! Marx saw it as permissible to have Christian ideas so long as these ideas did not spill over to the person's lifestyle in society or to the presentation of religious views in the public arena or in the institution of government! Does the communist idea of church being separated from having any influence over the state ring any bells in your mind and heart as you view what's taking place in America?

Have you heard the expression "separation of church and state" recently? If you have been listening to the Supreme Court of America you have clearly heard it because it happens to be the court mandated new understanding of what has become known as the separation amendment of our constitution!! Actually there is no such amendment or language anywhere in our constitution or its amendments or in the bill of rights or even in the federalist papers that preceded the constitution. This is the creation of deceived and foolish men with an intention to create a secular government. The court has taken a statement out of context from a speech by Thomas Jefferson and used that phrase as the constitutional basis for creating a secular government in America.

How could we have allowed the enforcement of laws and court precedents, which eliminate any Spiritual influence from the governing of a Christian nation? Our department of justice has spread its foolish and misguided agenda to every public institution. The most disappointing part of this is that many Americans have blindly accepted and joined their voices in heralding this evil, foolish and destructive notion as though it was the founders and framers intention, and, therefore, ought to be blindly accepted and taught in every public school and every law school in the land.

Most of our teachers in public education have never questioned the courts edict. These teachers have been given the incredible responsibility of rising up our children in the light of truth, which in essence involves the nurture and admonition of the lord. God is the children's only hope just as he is our only hope and we have given over our children to secular humanists and atheists to educate and who knows what kind of blind guides and teachers to instill their bankrupt and destructive philosophies into the minds and hearts of America's children.

Most of our public school teachers have been hoodwinked because they and we have put our trust in leaders and a court of secular humanists that we blindly believed to be the last frontier of wisdom, truth, justice and honor, in America.

I can't forget the old saying that says, "If the student hasn't learned the teacher hasn't taught". It also implies that students learn from teachers. They learn more about life and truth from the teacher than they learn from the material the teachers present. That is why good and Godly leaders and teachers are essential to America's future.

At any rate, this supposedly honorable court is, for the most part, believed to be the true defenders of the constitution of the United States, and the depository of all wisdom and objectivity and depended upon to present true justice. This can only be true if they are each one men humble before God who seek his wisdom and serve to promote his truth and glory.

Unfortunately truth is illusive in a fallen world and God alone is truly the only one who is trustworthy in his objectivity regarding truth. It is his wisdom we as a people must seek if we are to judge righteously and regain our ability to discern the truth. The apostle Paul gives us positive guidance in this regard (**Romans 12:2**), **"and do not be conformed to this world, but be transformed by the renewing of your mind, that you may prove what the will of God is, that which is good and acceptable and perfect."**

How can we expect men who themselves reject God and His wisdom to act wisely and justly? How do we expect our children to grow up as well rounded, responsible, wise men and women of character if they are trained up by men with minds and hearts that are deceived and perverted?

The answer of course is that we can't expect our children to overcome the teaching they have been exposed to. They become a product of the environment from which they have come and in which they have been trained.

Myth number eight: "Pornography is a harmless adult pleasure." I would add to this myth another equally and perhaps even more harmful myth that our society has accepted: **"Pornography is protected by the First Amendment of our constitution"**!

It is only the blind that cannot see that America is rotting from the inside out and adrift in a sea of sensuality. More than 50% of all divorces in America occur because of adultery much of which is encouraged by pornography that permeates our media, our movie industry, our videotape industry, our television entertainment media, the Internet and virtually every form of live entertainment.

The arts have become more and more perverted and demand to be heard by stretching freedom of speech to include any kind of expression that can be dreamed up by perverted and evil minds.

We have been conned into accepting the idea that profanity and profane expression is protected constitutionally by the freedom of speech amendment. Beyond that they justify their profaneness because it reflects the world in which we live.

It's interesting to note that historically in America it has been against the law to express profanity or dress or act profanely in public. In our arrogance we have decided that those men and women who would limit public expression to good and wholesome words and acts were somehow less aware of the true meaning of the constitutionally protected freedom of speech.

What utter nonsense! Freedom of speech was clearly made a right to protect the individual who wished to express publicly a political view that was contrary to the popular view without fear of reprisal against him by the government. Profane words and expressions were never considered to be the constitutionally guaranteed right of any individual.

Our arts, our public discourse, our public dress and our entertainment have all become loud and lude expressions profanity and pornography. Attempts to clean up profanity and pornography draw a cry of "censorship" and our government either runs and hides from the battle or considers any kind of censorship to be bad as though it is unconstitutional to insist on moral, honorable, and respectable public expression!

Censorship is mandatory in a variety of areas of life. Man is not guaranteed the right to do anything or say anything to anybody he wants to without interference from society. There are clearly things that society will not tolerate. Our courts present the censorship of pornography and perversion as something so deeply protected constitutionally that we must simply allow the perversion to flow unabated.

Our Supreme Court judges, once again, have bought the idea that our constitution allows and protects as a God given the right to exhibit, express or expound on any kind of filth and perversion that mans little sick and evil heart wishes to bring forth and tries to sell to other sick minds and hearts. This nonsense has been sold to the American people as a constitutional protected civil right and the measure of the kind of freedom that has made America great.

They have overlooked completely the context of our constitution right to freedom of speech. There was never intended that America protect perversion and pornography. The constitutional protection was and remains a protection from the state that might other-wise bring reprisals against men who present unpopular political or philosophical points of view.

The founding fathers were not protecting profanity, sexual perversion, satanic ritual, or pornographic literature and pictures. The detractors scream, "Who sets the standard of what is to be censored from the public"? The answer is a "no-brainier"! The standard is set biblically and virtually any child above the age of twelve that has attended Sunday school can immediately identify perversion and profanity without coaching.

Contrary to the detractor's loud complaint, the problem is not identifying and labeling that which is perversion! The problem is man trying to find sanction rather than deliverance from his perversion!!

It's interesting how easy it is for Christian schools and the body of Christ to identify perversion. They seem to have no problem identifying and, for the most part, weeding it out of their communities and institutions!

The problem is simply that sinners wish to live in sin and justify their sin by labeling evil as good and good as evil. Therefore, our secular humanist government continues to swallow gnats while the elephants are trampling the land. That is to say, they are absorbed and distracted by their involvement in the wrong battles!! The problem is the sin nature of man that either has to be transformed or his actions have to be limited by laws and directed by the right incentives.

Our courts seems to be Johnny on the spot when it comes to identifying what is political and what is not, what is illegal and what is not, what sort of activity is taxable and what is not!

I doubt that defining and identifying perversion is nearly as big a problem as the damage caused to the lives of millions of Americans by allowing it to be promoted and sold on the streets, in the museums, through the media, through motion pictures and in the public schools of America.

Our reaction to the porn and perversion industry is another example of our deceit. We have bought the lie and we are reaping what we are sowing in the lives of our children!

The incredible myth that pornography and perversion, wherever it might appear, is constitutionally protected is foolish thinking. If we simply have the will and wisdom to do so we can legally, constitutionally and practically eliminate pornography from general public view and practice. We simply have to do it!

The world has been waiting these past years with baited breath for this highly enlightened judiciary of the twentieth and twenty first century to liberate our people from the oppression of truth and Godliness. We surely need to be protected from the impact of God's love for us and our fellowman. We must also be protected from those who fight against and expose evil and promote decency and the common good. We need to protect people from the practice of honoring God and enacting those laws that appeal to the highest character traits of men born in the image of God, which held our people in good stead for several centuries! We have become fools and what we have come to believe regarding freedom of speech is total rubbish!!

Believe it or not no sincere God fearing man of character whose agenda was to promote the common good of his fellowman was ever oppressed by the enforcement of any of these biblically based laws that previously guided our nation socially. Laws that distinguish between what is good and what is evil are fundamental and foundational to what is best for America. Those laws have a divine source and when we break them or reject there wisdom we have become fools and we always will suffer the consequences of our foolishness.

Believe it or not the same constitution governed us during those times and the law graduates who interpreted the constitution were just as bright and enlightened as the secular humanists we are graduating today who are being taught to reject God's truth and his wisdom and justice as the standard.

The deliverance America has supposedly experienced this last half-century has been deliverance from the constraints toward Godly character. We have given license to freedom for man to express and display the most base human instincts and his most evil and lustful desires in order that we might allow evil men the freedom to act evil and feel justified in doing so! The flesh rejoices in its deceit and arrogance ignorant of the price it will pay for its perverted and foolish ways.

We unfortunately reject wise men of principle and character and continue to appoint to life-long terms deceived, foolish and evil men to the courts of the land and we elect blind men and fools to positions of national and local leadership in government. Unfortunately the church has also allowed false teachers, fools and infidels into the pulpits of many churches.

We, as Christian Americans, must actively enter into the battle against pornography and deceit by encouraging and supporting those who have already organized efforts against it.

The national federation for decency has helped make important gains against it. Several cities in America have closed adult bookstores because the citizens have insisted that the laws against it be actively enforced. It requires that communities let their political leaders understand they will not tolerate it. Either it goes or the leaders and judges go!!!!

We have a modern music industry that has become profane to the core! It publishes and plays music with lyrics that reach to the deepest core of profane and pornographic expression. The rap industry is evil and totally out of control and yet the secular humanist government, federal and state, has shown no interest in attempting to censor the purveyors of this profane and vulgar garbage. Could it be that government looks the other way because most rap music originates from the African American minority and they are afraid African America will raise a political racist flag? Politically correct or not we must let the chips fall where they may! It is profane garbage, which is not protected under the free speech amendment of the constitution, and much of it needs to be removed from the public airways and literature.

My thanks and appreciation goes out to the "American family association" for their vigilance and encouragement. I salute their efforts in this regard!

Unfortunately, there are enough customers of profanity today who are deceived and addicted to the lusts of the flesh who support the continued growth of the evil and destructive smut industry. Therefore, it will require the enforcement of laws that prohibit the development, printing, distribution, display, or sale of pornography in all its forms. Once again none of this infringes upon freedom of speech as intended by our founding fathers.

Through the loud voice of an inspired church with leaders of wisdom and vision that brings forth true light our ship of state can begin to be "righted" if enough Americans are of a mind to rise up and be counted. Oh yes, there will be battle lines drawn and "hell to pay". However, we can still win if we really enter the race and begin to run the race to win instead of just dressing like and pretending to be runners. We have no choice if we hope to see our people awakened and our nation restored.

It hasn't been many years since the movie theater was taboo for the Christian. The movies we didn't want our children to see we parade today as movie classics. Christians today curse the industry and watch more and more of the trash the industry produces as though they were trying to satisfy some glutton's insatiable appetite that cannot be satisfied.

The Christian community began at one time to vote at the box office by selecting and seeing the movies that did not present pornographic materials or did not glorify abhorrent and evil activities nor presented the characters of such movies as heroes. However, we have essentially given up the battle and allowed our flesh to lead us. Drawing the line became too hard. Expressions like, "∴ the movie was good but there were a few bad scenes in it", began to justify our watching or going to the theater.

Or, "that is the way they all are today....as if to imply that if I don't go to this kind of movie I would never be able to go to the movie's!" Who cares—most movies are not something essential to any of our lives. On the contrary they are detrimental in many ways beyond just their pornographic aspects. The subtle philosophic humanistic message that is presented by Hollywood is often more detrimental than the porn since it is more difficult to discern.

Offensive materials have become more and more tolerated while we justify our activities by saying, "well there is nothing else to watch" or "we can't raise our kids in a cocoon". We have come to a time in our society where we are now often confused as to where the battle lines between good and evil entertainment ought to be drawn. If Disney produced it or if it has cute little animals in it we seem to give it a stamp of approval regardless of the message it brings. We have long since quit trying to discern humanistic, paganistic or atheistic themes. If it doesn't contain nudity, sexual suggestive scenes or outright profanity it is ok for our kids to watch over and over and over again.

The explosive power of sexuality has crept into our minds and hearts and pushed the battle-lines further down the path of sensuality. Once our appetites are whetted constantly we have become addicted. Our children also become addicted and its power leads us all into a cesspool of sensuality and soon we find that we have lost control of our own sense of decency and our ability to discern. Beyond that we have lost the capacity to guide our own lives let alone the lives of our children.

It is not uncommon for our children today to develop relationships with girl and boy friends with the full expectation that they ought to be allowed to live sexually active lives so long as they have "safe sex".

Those of us who see the foolishness and damage this kind of thinking produces are considered radical religious nuts totally out of touch with reality. The liberated community fully expects that we accept the idea that humans who live instinctively and act sexually much like animals "have arrived" and are living the normal lifestyle of single Americans. Those who object to this thinking on any grounds, particularly religious grounds, are narrow-minded and right wing religious radicals who want to oppress society with their rules.

Perhaps it is time we ask ourselves what good we have seen come from the exposure of perversion to the minds and hearts of our people? Then, in contrast, we ought to consider where following God's admonitions will lead us?

Myth number nine: **"The church should have no voice in government".** The heart of this myth is wrapped up in a myth, which states that, **"there is a wall of separation between the church and the state and that wall is to protect the state from the church"**

I have already addressed this idea briefly, however, I need to point out that in the early days of our national existence Christians took seriously the process of electing and appointing responsible Christian leaders in the government because they understood the implications in society. Our citizens recognized good and Godly leadership as essential to insure the protection of the freedoms the constitution guaranteed. The influence of the Church in the political process was considered essential and practiced without any thought that Christianity and politics should not mix.

Daniel Webster once wrote, **"Whatever makes men good Christians makes them good citizens."** Collectively and as individuals we must rise up and fight off secularism by becoming actively involved in the political process. We must fight for those candidates who demonstrate good moral character and come closest to believing the principles and ideals that the bible teaches us as truth and good. We must also fight against the election of and expose the hypocrisy and agenda of those candidates who hold ideas and philosophies that are secularist.

We must never forget that we elect the person with all his warts and his glory. He will make decisions that effect the nation based on who he is not on whether he is able to set his religious views aside in his decision making. We don't elect who the man says he is and what he looks and acts like in front of a television camera or radio broadcast, we elect and become subject to who he really is!

The church has been told by the government it must withdraw from politics and from active participation in the governing process and so it has. There are a few exceptions where spiritual leaders continue to work toward awakening Americans to their Christian heritage and to the spiritual and moral freefall America finds herself in. I thank god for them because they awaken and inspire me and others to get involved and become the salt and light we are called to be by making our voices heard.

Nazism triumphed in Europe in large part because the church voiced little opposition to Hitler's idea's, political methods and immoral behavior. Secular humanism has triumphed in America for the same reason. American Christians in our collective indifference and spiritual blindness have opened the door wide open to secular humanists that have grasped the opportunity and now have solid control of government, public education and the political process in America.

Whittaker chambers once wrote, **"Humanism is not new. It is, in fact, man's second oldest faith. Its promise was whispered in the first days of the creation under the tree of the knowledge of good and evil: "ye shall be as gods."**

A
Book
By
Charles D. Gaines

PERSPECTIVE

Romans 1:21-22
"For even though they knew God,
they did not honor Him as God, or Give thanks;
but they became futile in their speculations, and their foolish heart was darkened.
Professing to be wise, they became fools,"

SECTION III

CAUSE

—⁓—

CHAPTER EIGHT

THE CULPRIT WITHIN

—ɯ—

"If you are living according to the flesh, you must die; but if by the Spirit are putting to death the deeds of the body, you will live." (Romans 8:13)

When wise men recognize a problem their thinking typically turns toward finding a solution. Finding a solution sometimes requires a careful examination of the problem, its impact and its cause or causes. Fools, even well-intentioned ones, often ignore the problem or attempt to solve it before they really understand the problem or its true cause. This often makes the problem and its impact worse rather than better. Attempting to implement clever solutions to problems that do not exist in the attempt to fix complex problems that do exist and whose cause is rooted in deeper issues is common.

Unfortunately when we fail to understand the real problem we not only fail to solve the problem we condemn ourselves to continue to face the same problems over and over again. When national leaders make foolish, albeit sometimes earnest and well intentioned decisions that do not address the real problem it often condemns the people because it leads them into the same traps, or even worse traps, because as a society we fail to discern the true problem and/or learn the real lessons from previous mistakes.

Perspective is the relation of parts to one another and to the whole! Perspective is written in an attempt to contrast the secular humanist and the Christian world-views, their foundations and the implications of each as they impact our people and our nation. It is necessary to understand the Spirit, wisdom, or lack of wisdom, and the world view that arises from the foundation of both the Christian and the Secular perspectives. These foundations guide and inspire from each of these perspectives in the constant competition for control over the minds, hearts and souls of all men.

Perspective examines the nature of man and the deceit that traps him in the calamity he finds himself in. I have attempted to expose those destructive philosophies, myth's and destructive ideas and attitudes that have woven themselves into the fabric of our national life, which have a devastating affect on our individual and national existence.

Some wise person has warned us that those who ignore or misunderstand history are destined to repeat it. History itself confirms his wisdom. We must recognize there is no glory in ignorance or its bunkmate's evil and deceit. They are destructive and costly and what is even more devastating, they are self-perpetuating and deadly. Our Lord warns us to be *"wise as serpents but gentle as doves"*.

Ignorance and deceit are like evil in the context they need no discipline or self-restraint to acquire them. They are a malady that comes upon us naturally. Ignorance, to a point, can be corrected with knowledge, however, deceit cannot. Deceit is a Spiritual problem that allows us to observe and experience events and either fail to recognize their significance or to misinterpret or reject the lesson they teach or both. By the very nature of deceit it mocks truth and despises wisdom. Wisdom brings light that we might see and ears that we might hear and understand. Ignorance of the truth can be corrected through a learning process. The bible tells us, *"'..Do not be conformed to this world, but be transformed by the renewing of your mind, that you may prove what the will of God is, that which is good and acceptable and perfect."* The truth revealed here is that if we study the word of truth as God's Spirit leads us we will come to know the truth. We will come to be wise in the context of recognizing and knowing the wisdom and will of God. If God's Spirit has not defeated our will we will never come to know the truth no matter how much knowledge we accumulate. Deceit is a matter of the will and the will is matter of the spirit of a man.

We must somehow come to grips with the truth about the division between the kingdom of the world and the kingdom of God and how they each manifest themselves in the acts and perspectives of people.

The Scriptures teach us that the world hates God. The spirit of the world and the Spirit of God are mortal enemies. The spirit of natural man is the spirit of the world that works its deeds through the flesh of man. It is not simply the deeds and foolishness that men do and say that condemns him it is his spirit that condemns him because his spirit is in rebellion against God. Mans spirit determines his will and therefore his perspective. The spirit of natural man must die and man must become a new creation born of the Spirit of God to be delivered from the condemnation in which he naturally exists. His spirit has been severed from God because of sin and that spirit must die for man to live Spiritually.

As a people we must somehow come to grips with the reality that the spirit of a man is who he is! The spirit of the world and the Spirit of God each produce a will and character that are distinctive and observable. The scriptures describe these character attributes as Fruit of the Spirit. *"For if you are living according to the flesh, you must die; but if by Spirit you are putting to death the deeds of the body, you will live." (Romans 8:13)* Jesus tells us that *"It is the Spirit who gives life; the flesh profits nothing:" (John 6:63)*

Wisdom that is life changing is not gained however, through simply filling your head with all kinds of information. The world is filled with intellectual people who are not wise and cannot discern the things of the Spirit of God. ***"My sheep hear my voice, and I know them, and they follow me; and I give eternal life to them, and they shall never perish; and no one shall snatch them out of My hand." (John 10: 27-28)*** That is because God is the author and purveyor of truth and true wisdom. His truth, as we study it under the guiding of His Holy Spirit, makes us wise. Wisdom therefore has a distinct Spiritual dimension.

We have all known many "uneducated" people who are spiritually wise. We most likely have also met several educated people who are not wise. Our Universities and colleges employ many professors and teachers who are foolish. Godly wisdom combines the knowledge of something with its truth, context and relevance as well as the lesson to be learned or experienced in its proper application. Godly wisdom is the only wisdom that can discern between right and wrong and good or bad. Beyond that it is wisdom that applies itself in such a way as to reveal truth and to reflect what is best. It finds its foundation in the truth of Gods word and the admonition of His Spirit. In fact wisdom is most evident when it is contrast with the foolishness of the world. It manifests itself in our perspective about life and its experiences.

There are many different kinds of wisdom. For example, much wisdom will come to us when we are able to view the lessons of history from the perspective of truth. We learn from our own mistakes in light of the truth whenever we are able to exercise the discipline and moral courage to adopt and live in the knowledge of the truth.

Sustaining liberty demands a nation of people who live in the knowledge of the truth and are guided by the Spirit and wisdom of God. That, of course, means that we must live our lives perpetually under a spirit and discipline that seeks after and lives according to the truth.

Living a life of deceit is just the opposite. It hates, hides and runs from the truth. The spirit of deceit breeds fear in us because God has said all men are without excuse because He has revealed the truth to all men. Deceit and rebellion are acts of the will of man that leaves men in terrible bondage. It is like walking in a minefield. If you walk in the minefield of deceit long enough you will ultimately be destroyed by one or more of its millions of mines. Satan owns the spirit of deceit and he manages the minefield.

The majority of the social and relational problems our citizen's face cannot be solved by our government or by our people because in our spiritual blindness we have not determined, recognized, accepted or attacked the real cause. We live in denial and our attempted solutions tend to be superficial and often more destructive ultimately than the problem we are intending to solve. Deceit is a deadly disease because the deceived is not able to think and act above the level of his deceit. As someone has said, 'the problem with deceit is being deceived'.

I touched on the cause and nature of the deepest and most serious problem facing all mankind and indeed America in my previous remarks. A thread of the cause and nature of the Spiritual problem that plagues America will find its way woven throughout this book in hopes that those who read this might become awakened by God's Spirit to our plight, recognize the cause and turn to the only one who can deliver us individually or collectively.

Americans have been duped into believing perhaps the most profound lie ever perpetrated on any people. It is a lie of satanic supernatural origin. It is a lie that can only be perpetuated in an arena of Spiritual blindness or by a spirit that is satanically inspired.

The scriptures teach us that in either case natural man is blinded to ultimate truth regarding his fallen nature and he will perish unless he is awakened to his blindness and rebellion by divine intervention. The deceit that keeps man in bondage denies his sinful nature, excuses his ungodliness and justifies his selfish and foolish actions and attitudes and leads him in rebellion against God. His spirit and Gods Spirit are mortal enemies. The incredible lie leads men to systematically destroy themselves, families, friends, communities and even nations.

The same liar who presented the lie in the Garden of Eden continues to present the lie to all men today and argues its wisdom to deceived minds! Satan's lie is, *"You shall not surely die"*. The lie says that natural man is not a fallen creature and whatever he deems right for himself is right and beyond all that he is naturally good and his judgments are wise and his nature charitable without any divine influence in his life. The lie tells man he is not a sinner by nature and that given the facts most men will make the right, honorable, just and wise choices even when it is contrary to his selfish interest or even when and if it costs him dearly to make those tough choices. The lie tells man that he can do as he pleases and does not have to be accountable to God or anyone else for that matter.

Natural man has believed the lie rather than God and is trapped in the foolishness of his deceit and he is condemned by his condition. In fact every man is condemned by his sinful condition unless and until God opens his eyes and chooses to deliver him. Men act naturally according to the leading of their deceit. They are trapped in a condition in which they will do what is wrong even when they know it is wrong if it will benefit them. God has revealed to all men that His existence is proven because of what he has created and that every man is therefore without excuse.

Man is born and lives under the curse of his sin and rebellion and naturally follows after the dictates of his fallen nature through whom Satan, the God of darkness and the God of this world, works. Every man has a fallen nature and without the working of the Spirit of God all men would perish. Without God's forgiveness and grace all of mans works are worthless at best and evil at worst. The flesh of man is drawn to pride, the lust of the flesh and the lust of the eyes.

Listen carefully to these scriptures; (I John 2:15-17)*"Do not love the world, nor the things of the world. If anyone loves the world, the love of the father is not in him. For all that is in the world, the lust of the flesh and the lust of the eyes and the boastful pride of life, is not from the father, but is from the world. And the world is passing away, and also its lusts; but the one who does the will of God abides forever."*

Through His son Jesus Christ God has revealed His love for mankind and His redemptive plan and purpose. He has provided, to every man who will accept it, the way of escape from the curse of death and He delivers man from the deceit that condemns him. God opens his eyes to a perspective of truth and access to his Creator and to divine wisdom to guide him if he will humble himself before God and receive it. However, if men reject God's deliverance they are condemned and trapped in their spiritual deceit and they will perish. The consequences of deceit and rebellion obviously have profound current and eternal implications in our individual and collective lives.

The incredible lie that places man above God and the spiritual blindness that allows the lie to continue to grow and darken men's minds and hearts is a lie shared by all men that impacts every aspect of human life. Our leaders, our public education system, our government, our legal system, our Judiciary, our public policies and programs, our value systems and our national perspective are all the result of our individual and collective deceit or the lack of it.

This incredible lie we tell ourselves is typically not detectable by the deceived person. The wisdom of the secular humanist mind is a product of the fallen nature of man. The Scriptures speak of the way of deceit: *"There is a way which seems right to a man, but its end is the way of death"(Proverbs 14:12).* Therefore, mans nature confirms to him that he is worthy and his way is good and his decisions right even though there is a still small voice speaking to him, "this is the way follow after it". Mans fallen nature attempts to convince him that he does not need God because he is not a fallen creature who lives under a curse, nor will he perish. The Lord speaks of our circumstance in this way; *"Enter by the narrow gate; for the gate is wide, and the way is broad that leads to destruction, and many are those who enter by it. For the gate is small , and the way is narrow that leads to life, and few are those who find it. "* (Matt 7:13-14) Man is in a life or death circumstance and his deceit and arrogance will destroy him without God's divine intervention.

Worshipping the creature rather than the Creator is the foundational lie that has perpetuated the secularization of American Government and destroyed our public education system with the destructive slogan *"separation of Church and State".* This statement is not found in any of our founding documents. History, nor any of our founding documents, produces any authority or mandate to separate church and state in the context of removing the public demonstration of our faith as a people. This perspective regarding how we must remove God from the governing process is an act of the spirit of rebellion and a product of utter deceit.

The deceit that led the Judiciary and many of our legislators and many of our citizens in adopting this judgment came from the notion that we are indeed able to carry out faithfully, justly and righteously our constitutional and moral responsibilities without the wisdom of God or the presence and protection of His guiding Spirit. The perspective itself is self-condemning. The deceit of the foundational lie attempts to convince man that he can live in peace without the charity and Spiritual guidance of God.

Once again, the foundational premise of the lie is that we are not fallen creatures. It leads us to believe we don't really need wise and righteous leadership, Godly example, moral discipline, training in righteousness or the right incentives to guide us to live righteously and preserve liberty and justice. It teaches us that what is right is what men say it is and not what God says it is! It brings a perspective that leads men to authorize and promote through legislative act any idea, act or activity that satisfies men's fleshly appetites or otherwise pleases him. It deceives men into thinking that just because the many approve, even if it is the approval of unrighteous men, it is right and just.

Mans deceit and the satanic lie that leads natural man are so profoundly devastating in their effect and ultimate objective it is necessary and appropriate to examine what the Holy Scriptures say about our condition and its implications. Read these words prayerfully considering their implications: *"For those who are according to the flesh set their minds on the things of the flesh, but those who are according to the Spirit, the things of the Spirit. For the mind set on the flesh is death, but the mind set on the Spirit is life and peace, because the mind set on the flesh is hostile toward God; for it does not subject itself to the law of God, for it is not even able to do so; and those who are in the flesh cannot please God. However, you are not in the flesh but in the Spirit if indeed the Spirit of God dwells in you. But if anyone does not have the Spirit of Christ, he does not belong to Him…If you are living according to the flesh, you must die; but if by the Spirit you are putting to death the deeds of the body you will live. For all who are being led by the Spirit of God, these are sons of God."* (Romans 8:5-9, 13-14)

Natural man in his fallen state walks according to the flesh. His wisdom and reason serves the interests and appetites of his flesh. The Scriptures reveal this battle that rages in every man who does not walk according to the Spirit of God: *"But I say, walk by the Spirit, and you will not carry out the desire of the flesh. For the flesh sets its desire against the Spirit, and the Spirit against the flesh; for these are in opposition to one another, so that you may not do the things that your please."* (Galatians 5:16-17)

The Scriptures also tell us what we can expect of the flesh of man when it is allowed to control our attitudes and actions: *"Now the deeds of the flesh are evident, which are; immorality, impurity, sensuality, idolatry, sorcery, enmities, strife, jealousy, outbursts of anger, disputes, dissensions, factions, envying, drunkenness, carousing, and things like these, of which I forewarn you …..Those who practice such things shall not inherit the kingdom of God."* (Galatians 5:19-21) Recognize any of these? Where do you suppose they come from? Certainly not from the Spirit of God!

The notion the Supreme Court of the United States has forced upon America is that men with fallen natures can effectively lead us and live and act out their deceit and somehow still arrive at wise and just decisions that will set the best future direction of our nation. This is the deceived thinking of secularism. The premise of this foolish thinking, of course, is that mans nature is not fallen and he is not naturally deceived in his thinking. Therefore it denies the need for divine guidance. Natural man in his humanist deceit believes he can be depended upon to hold to that which is right and best for himself, his fellowman and his nation without the aid of God's Spirit to guide and influence their thinking.

The deceit of secularism is the most deadly disease facing America and the Spirit of Satan is the most formidable force at work in the minds of the secular humanist to utterly destroy him. The Scriptures teach that he *"goes about like a roaring lion to see who he can devour."* The pride of life is the foundation of secular humanism and it destroys every man unless God intervenes and rescues man from his deceit!

Deceived thinking gives man the glory for his existence, his exploits and his environment. It leads men to believe they can separate character (who we truly are) from our decisions, actions and responsibilities...It leads us to believe we can bring whatever wisdom we might need or that we can rise to any occasion and become whatever we need to be to bring about a righteous and just result whenever we are called upon to do so regardless of what we really believe.

Deceived thinking promotes the idea that man is complete within himself and teaches man that he has it within himself to overcome most anything, even his deceit, if he really needs to, without God's guiding wisdom or divine power. It teaches us that we can act impartial or even contrary to what we believe when necessary in dealing with critical issues or making critical decisions. It teaches us that even though men habitually live and act like heathens they can discern the need to act or judge righteously and can indeed judge and act rightly when necessary.

The deceit of this incredible lie allows men without a moral compass or without the guidance of the Spirit of God to rightfully claim to be Children of God and to believe they stand arrogantly in the light of his favor. It has created a culture which sees no tangible need for God and it encourages us to appoint judges and elect political leaders over us who believe they are capable of justice without the guidance of God simply because they have a diploma from a school of law or the vote of the people.

The law schools of today perpetuate the deceit of the lie because they lack the leadership and wisdom of men like Blackstone who believed that the foundation of all law and the principles of its administration must be God and come from God. The incredible lie further teaches us to trust in the justice, righteousness and wisdom of human government without the source of the wisdom of truth and righteousness or the disciplines to guide it. Last but not least humanism teaches that most people are good and are therefore heaven bound due to their own merit and that ultimate truth and goodness, heaven and hell are lies created by religion to force men to adhere to its bigotry.

The Scriptures assures us that every man, women and child is born isolated from God and by nature children of wrath: *"And you were dead in your trespasses and sins, in which you formally walked according to the course of this world, according to the prince of the power of the air, of the spirit that is now working in the sons of disobedience. Among them we too all formerly lived in the lusts of our flesh, indulging the desires of the flesh and of the mind, and were by nature children of wrath, even as the rest." (Ephesians 2: 1-3)*

These are indeed sobering scriptures! When we reject God and the influence and leading of His Spirit and Word we are obviously in great trouble and we are heading down a road that leads to death and destruction unless we somehow become awakened to our plight.

Deceived, foolish, arrogant and rebellious people have rejected the Spiritual guiding light, wisdom, power and influence of God. The relevancy of the God of the Christian bible is under question by our government, our society and even the mainline denominations of the church. God has been totally rejected by our Judiciary, by the institution of government, by public education and by many of our citizens.

However, approximately 85% of our population professes a belief in God and approximately 70% profess a Christian faith and a significant number of Americans attend church. However, the organized church, for the most part, has allowed itself to become intimidated by the world system and has surrendered to it. Many of the mainline denominational churches are in apostasy having committed adultery with the world and have become almost indistinguishable from the world it was sent to provide salt and light to.

There is a remnant church of born again Christian believers, however, it has found itself isolated from the mainline denominations and its influence limited. The mainline denominations have limited most of their activities to the mundane things of church government and a variety of introverted social activities. They have bought into the idea of separation of church and government. The guidance of the abiding Spirit of God working though the organized mainline denominations, who once considered themselves to be ambassadors for Christ to a new nation and to a dark world, has been replaced by the same spirit that guides the world. There is little difference between the guiding philosophies of the church from those of secular government, education, entertainment, media, the flourishing secular humanist social engineering institutions, human psychology, worldly social ideas that satisfy the flesh and the appetites of men and promote confidence in the wisdom of man. Unfortunately the world's wisdom, human psychology, positive confession, self-esteem and material prosperity have replaced the principal message of the Word and wisdom of God in the pulpits of many of our churches of today.

Many of the churches have decided that if they are to enjoy a large enough following to finance the construction and maintenance of large church facilities they must bend to the cultural norm of the world system and present that which tickles the ears and attracts a worldly congregation of church goers who attend weekly to attempt to justify selfish and sinful attitudes and lifestyles.

Many church goers tend to seek out those teachers who will send them away from church each week feeling good about themselves, their worldly attitudes, activities and lifestyles. Teachers and preachers have learned that it is much easier to sell self-esteem, positive confession and material success than it is to sell repentance to deceived people. So they labor over the scriptures in order to discover just the right spin to place on God's word so the congregation is not convicted, offended or challenged to true repentance.

The anti-God secular humanists have convinced our government and most of our citizens, including much of modern church leadership, that government must be completely separated from the influence or the reminders of God, Godly wisdom, Godly principle, Godly morality, or the influence of Godly leadership!

The threat against the church by our secular government is the loss of tax-exempt status. The threat is designed to intimidate the church and "keep her in her place" so to speak. The campaign to place the church under the state has captured the interest and imagination of the people and has brought the organized church to its knees in surrender of its Spiritual mandate to the political agenda of the state. The federal government threatens the potential revocation of the tax exempt status the church currently enjoys. In light of that the church has come to recognize that a majority of its adherents are not Disciples of Christ and/or ambassadors of the kingdom of God. They also recognize that most of them would withdraw their financial support in a heartbeat if the tax-exempt status of the church was to be revoked.

Their fear is well founded and would no doubt be realized if the church should actually choose to become the salt and light they are called to be. The church fears that becoming politically active would divide the church and invite the government to come against them. Certainly these are all potential ramifications of doing what is right in a wrong world. Perhaps the church and the world would then get a glimpse of who the real Christians are.

It should not surprise any Christian that a secular government bureaucracy would want and actively attempt to remove God, His purpose and His wisdom from the public agenda or arena. However, I am deeply disappointed that the church has been so easily deceived into thinking that secular is another word for neutral or objective. Folks there is no neutral ground! We either gather with Christ or we scatter against Him.

It is disgusting and disappointing to consider that the church has cowered from the intimidation of secular government and an anti-Christ world and have so easily allowed themselves to be silenced, isolated and controlled by these threats. The church has in essence tried to become more like the world with the idea that the world might like the church better if it was more worldly. How foolish it is to agree to silence our calling to be salt and light so the government will agree to continue to allow religious organizations to exist and continue to glean from the tax coffers.

When will the Church awaken to the fact that the World is its enemy? The world is the declared enemy of God and His Church! We, who consider ourselves to be the Church of Jesus Christ, are in a Spiritual battle to the death against the world. The secular humanist government bureaucracy in America would eliminate the church in a heartbeat if they dared, just as the secular socialist government did in the Soviet Union. At some point in our transition to a fully secular society the government will dare to try to do so in America.

Every time our Judiciary rules against prayer in school, or at public functions, and every time any expression of our faith is shutdown in the schools or in the public arena our government has just taken another step toward removing the influence of God in the lives of our people.

The less the influence and voice of Christian Americans is heard and felt in America the closer the time becomes when the public expression of our faith will no longer be tolerated!! In the meantime we as a people have been duped into allowing our government to limit the political activity and involvement of the church through the carrot of tax-exempt status.

There are many other more subtle ways for government to administratively restrict the activities of the church however none quite as blatant as allowing the church tax exempt status if the church agrees to stay out of the politics of electing government leaders and governing our nation. It has worked for the most part thus far and the church is bowing at the altar of mammon.

America has fallen from a society of predominantly committed Christian believers to a society of luke-warm professing Christians, secular humanists, pagans and atheists. The atheist, the evil, the heathen, the pagan and even the secular humanists were clearly perceived by early Americans as the deceived, the lost, and the personification of evil and totally out of step with the culture. They therefore were not typically considered for elected office or positions of power, influence or prominence in society unless and until they demonstrated true repentance before God and man.

The idea that a pagan or atheist or secular humanist might have a leadership position in government or in early American society was a repugnant idea and totally foreign to the thinking of our founders and to most Americans and American leaders. However in America today the exact reverse is true! Today our modern culture sees the Christian world-view and those who hold it as narrow, bigoted, destructive and negatively discriminating rather than wise and just and in consort with the truth and the purposes of God!

There has been a fundamental and profound shift in America's world view and belief system that has happened relatively unnoticed and unchallenged by an indifferent, sleepy, comfortable luke-warm church and the vast majority of our population. We have adopted the world's perspective, which has literally reversed our perception of that which is evil, perverse and foolish and our perception of that which is good and wise, righteous and just! We have come to believe the lie and now we label that which is good as bad and that which is bad as good.

These heretical and evil ideas that guide our secular judiciary and our government bureaucrats and leaders as well as much of the conventional thinking of modern America finds its origin in the world system whose king is Satan himself. This world-view is alive and well in modern American society and controls the governing process. Unfortunately it is also alive and well in much of the professing church.

The twentieth century perception of politics, elections, government, taxation and representation and most social issues of the day are perceived as distinctively secular. We deny any spiritual relativity to the governing process or to the administration of social matters or to dealing with Constitutional issues. The political process and the election of political leadership as well as the governing of our nation is perceived by our national leaders and our citizens as distinctly separate and outside the sphere of influence of God, His wisdom or any consideration of His purposes.

American's have been sold the idea that governing somehow loses its objectivity and fairness if God and His truth become the standard that guides us or even if it is allowed to enter into the process. In our utter foolishness America has elected to reject God's influence not only in the process of electing our leaders and governing our nation but also in educating our children. We have tragically come to believe that Godly influence is wrong for our people and our children and worldly influence as right and best for our children! Prayer is removed from school to make room for the unrestricted parading and promoting of sex, rebellion and the homosexual lifestyle in front of our children as good and acceptable lifestyles.

God and His wisdom has become placed in the social venue somewhere beneath abhorrent sexual activity, smoking pot and the many detestable things that go on in the private and public lives of many of our fellow citizens. The perspective of modern America is that so long as God is kept out of sight and His will does not directly influence the day-to-day lives and activities of people, or the governing process, He and His people will be tolerated. If the Church in America should ever decide to truly become the salt and light it is called to be there will be an immediate polarization of our society and a mass uprising against the church, which will result in the public persecution of Christian people just as there is in many parts of the world today.

Those who believe and practice Christian faith in America are considered by our government and our culture to be fanatics whose beliefs and faith is no longer *the way* but rather *in the way* of social justice and progress. We no longer turn to the Word of God and its proponents and teachers as the way to truth and justice and the way to find the answers to life's troubling matters. So long as the Christian perspective is kept essentially within the walls of the Church and considered irrelevant in its influence against social reform the government will allow the church to continue to exist and enjoy its tax-exempt status.

As a nation we have dug a Spiritual hole for ourselves that we cannot climb out of nor from our limited view in the hole can we see any longer what is really going on around us!

We are trapped in our deceit. As a nation we have failed to protect the faith of our fathers and instead society has foolishly chosen to embrace the many secular or pagan religious views encompassing them and adopting them as part of a national belief system we proudly and foolishly refer to as diversity.

Being of the same mind spiritually is considered by our culture as a foreign and destructive concept to America. Spiritual unity was vital to the early church and to America. The Apostle Paul admonished the worldly Corinthian Church of the danger and divisiveness of spiritual diversity. *"Now I exhort you brethren, by the name of our Lord Jesus Christ, that you all agree, and there be no divisions among you, but you be made complete in the same mind and in the same judgment. —For the world of the cross is to those who are perishing foolishness, but to us who are being saved it is the power of God." (I Cor 1:10-18)*

We have decided the constitutional principle of religious freedom is intended to be the justification for relegating the Christian faith to just another of many religious views that have come to proliferate our society. History clearly establishes that was never the intention of the founding fathers. America was founded as distinctively Christian. The principles established to guide us reflected in the founding documents and the vast majority of the founding fathers themselves were distinctively Christian.

In the context of our Christian foundation the founders did not want government to have the authority to restrict the observance of our Christian faith and they did not want government to promote a particular Christian religious denomination as the Church of the state. Their insistence upon religious freedom was clearly intended to keep government from choosing up sides an adopting one of the Christian denominations as the church accepted and/or sponsored by the state.

The considerations of our founding fathers were based upon the recognition that God has given man the right to chose whether or not he will worship God and how, when, where he worships, therefore, man must be allowed to have the same liberty in America. Government was not intended to require religious observance or dictate religious practice nor was it to prohibit its free expression.

The problem our founding fathers were dealing with was how they were going to legislate or establish the relationship between Church and State. The oppression of the religious institutions of Europe was far from the liberty they were seeking or that God had ordained for His people. Likewise, the oppression of a government that used the Church to bring about and enforce its political agenda was something they would never allow in America. At the same time they never intended that America separate its governing process from religious principle or the leadership of religious men or that the church isolate its interests to theological interests as apposed to the political interests of America. America was distinctly Christian, followers of Christ, as apposed to institutionally religious. The founding fathers recognized our Christian faith was the foundation of our nation and they were fully dedicated to the cause of promoting and maintaining our Christian faith and practice.

It is the Spirit of God that draws men to God, however, man has a choice as to whether he will listen and follow after that calling. God's love and hope cry's out to men who will not listen and who chose to rebel against His gift of life, nevertheless, God has decided it is mans choice. It was this principle that would eventually guide the legislative efforts of our founders. They recognized the Spirit of God cannot be separated from the lives or affairs of men regardless of how men might attempt to regulate it. They, therefore, recognized that what was best for America was to completely leave government out of the equation in the context of not isolating government from the church. To do that they would prohibit government interference in the church and they would trust God to do as he willed with His church. His followers, which they recognized as distinctly separate from the followers of the religious institutions that dominated Europe, were the Christians that dominated the scene in America.

Three groups are clearly apparent in the founding documents! They are the followers of Christ, the religious institutions and the institutions of government. Escaping religious oppression was escaping the heavy hand of the religious institutions of Europe as the institution of government used them and as they used government to meet their various religious ends.

However, in America we have added a fourth group, comprised of many sects, cults and world religions, secularists and atheists. As a result of opening our borders to the world, the world has come in like a flood and it has brought with it cultural religious baggage that threatens our Christian foundation. In judging between the various interests and doctrines of these religious groups we have forgotten from where we came and we are rapidly becoming a heathen nation of peoples who worship and serve any number of foreign God's. Our Judiciary has determined that each of these heathen religions should have the same protection and standing as Christian religious practice and expression.

We, as a nation, have thrown the only true God of the bible into the mix with the heathen God's proudly applauding our compromise and diversity as good progress and demanding that all these God's and their religions enjoy equal status and protection under the constitution. Sound ridiculous? It is utter deceit and foolishness and America is beginning to pay the price big time!!!

In light of our constitution how are we to deal with our diversity? Certainly a Christian perspective is tolerant and inclusive, however, its faith is not diverse. On the contrary it is single minded. Our response can only be found in the word of God and will be dictated by what resides in the hearts and minds of men. What men believe dictates what they say and do and is indeed who they are. An attempt by government to keep believers, followers of Christ, out of government and to keep the church out of the public debate and the political arena is the direction our government has taken and a direction we must vigorously fight against.

The dramatic shift away from the God of the bible in our national thinking during the last half of the twentieth century, and certainly during the past decade under the executive leadership of William Jefferson Clinton, and his equally spiritually bankrupt and politically ambitious wife Hillary along with a secular humanist Judiciary has accelerated our spiritual decline, national confusion and national disgrace.

America is in a moral freefall and the only safety net is the grace and mercy of God who we have collectively chosen to reject. The mere fact that Bill & Hillary Clinton ever made it to the highest executive office in our nation should give sincere minded American citizens a wake up call. It should reveal to us a panoramic view of our national deceit and a sobering look at the kind of people we have become.

However, Clinton is no longer our nations leader. America's bigger problem is not the legacy of the Clintons, it is the people who, despite their knowledge of the truth, continued to support him and his leadership and professed to sincerely believe he was a leader who was good for America.

The various poles reported to us that some 60% of our citizenry acknowledged President Clinton's moral degeneracy and lack of character and yet more than half could see no problem with the fact that they chose to make him as the nations chief executive!

How is it possible that America's citizens have become so deceived they are unable to see the connection between character, morality, integrity, sincerity, example and desirable leadership? The perspective of the individual who is blind to the truth or refuses to acknowledge and act accordingly indicates Spiritual deceit. It was amazing to observe the working of madness that seemed to lead our nation. The more perverse and corrupt his actions the more our citizens seemed to support him and the more popular president Clinton seemed to become.

Millions of Christian Americans were pleased to see a new political wind blowing in Washington D. C., particularly in the white house, in 2000. America elected George W Bush as President and a new Vice President Dick Cheney defeating the liberal democratic candidate Al Gore and his running mate. It was a close and bitterly fought election in which the electorate was almost evenly split. In fact the election was so close the Gore camp contested the election results in the state of Florida demanding endless recounts. Recount after recount under the scrutiny of the Supreme Court at both the state and federal levels ended in confirming George Bush, the republican candidate, as President.

What this means to the future of America remains to be seen, however, I am encouraged because George Bush professes and seems to demonstrate a strong Christian faith and does not seem to be intimidated by the world system, our secular government or its leaders or its followers! He seems to be a wise and courageous man committed to attempting to lead America back in the right direction.

His battle will be a bitter fight because the number of deceived Americans in spiritual darkness continues to increase and the deceived are not going to surrender easily to the leadership of George Bush any more than they will surrender to the leadership of Jesus Christ. The battle lines have been drawn however and the liberal secularists, the democrats and the world are clearly intimidated and frightened of Mr. Bush and his administration. They hate him and they hate God and they don't want to reintroduce God and His purposes back into American government or society and they clearly don't want the perverseness and foolishness of their thinking to be exposed. One thing is for sure; they definitely don't want to be called into accountability by biblical wisdom and truth.

The abortion activists, gay rights activists, NAACP, civil liberties union, NOW members, socialists, the NEA and our public educators, the radical environmentalists, the welfare crowd, big government bureaucrats and their employee's and supporters make up a majority of this crowd. However, when we look at cause we can find plenty of blame to go around. Satan sits on the throne of sin and evil as is its unchallenged king and ruler. Satan and his angels, the god of this world, the god of darkness and evil is continually **"going about like a roaring lion to see whom he can devour."**

From the human perspective there are two primary culprits who, I believe, are to blame for what is happening to America, and indeed the rest of the world, and should be high-lighted. God says he will expose evil and reveal the truth to every man and will hold him accountable for how he deals with it!

The *first* culprit is Satan and his disciples who act as ambassadors of his evil kingdom. The scriptures warn us that Satan's disciples often manifest themselves as messengers of light; however, they are false teachers, deceivers, and liars, who embrace the world and its wisdom and work diligently to destroy the works and people of God. They work actively to mold our culture, educate our children, destroy the church and govern our nation. Their true character and purpose is often not easily discernable and, in fact, is not discernable by those who are without Spiritual discernment.

The *second* culprit is the flesh of man through whom the god of darkness works. Men all have a fallen nature and without the working of the Spirit of God to convict and guide us our works are evil and we naturally reject God's truth, wisdom and righteousness. We are trapped in our fallen condition. The flesh of man is drawn to pride, lust of the flesh and lust of the eyes. Men find it difficult to discern good from evil and right from wrong and we readily adopt the teaching and leadership of false and evil teachers because it is satisfying to our flesh. Listen to his words: **"do not love the world, nor the things of the world. If anyone loves the world, the love of the Father is not in him. For all that is in the world, the lust of the flesh and the lust of the eyes and the boastful pride of life, is not from the Father, but is from the world. And the world is passing away, and also its lusts; but the one who does the will of God abides forever."** (I John 2:15-17)

Something I am sure you have noticed of both of these culprits is they find their source and spiritual inspiration in the evil spirit that leads the fallen nature of man. The apostle Paul said, **"For our struggle is not against flesh and blood, but against the rulers, against the powers, against the world forces of this darkness, against the spiritual forces of wickedness in the heavenly places." (Ephesians 6:12)**

The scriptures remind us of our only protection. They call it the Spiritual armor of God! That is the only armor that will deliver and sustain America as well!!

It is easy to point the finger at our fellowman. Our flesh finds it appealing to hear that all our problems are someone else's fault. Given all that it is still necessary to point out that the world hates God and is His avowed enemy. The world finds its inspiration in the avowed enemy of God. That enemy is Satan and his rebellion against God has affected the life of every human being. The enemy lives within each of our fallen natures and manifests himself to varying degrees depending upon how much of our lives we have surrendered to God.

The bible describes the culprit within as the flesh of natural man, a fallen creature, who gets his marching orders and inspiration from the father of lies. He has been taught and instilled with the fear necessary to keep him hiding from the truth in order to enjoy his own ways, which are utterly sinful.

The Scriptures also assure us there are no exceptions to be found among men other than Christ himself sent to us with a divine nature. Therefore, a fallen spiritual nature controls the flesh of man impacting his thinking, attitudes and actions. The flesh of man is very much alive in men and women in and out of the church. Carnal Christians profess belief but walk according to the dictates of the flesh. They are in rebellion against and drift away from the Spirit of God and His truth to satisfy their flesh. They soon find they do not want to hear God's word or be judged by it so they search for a church whose message from the pulpit tickles their ears. They find themselves hiding from the truth because they don't want to expose the lie they are living. So in the ever-deepening grasp of deceit they create a sort of Godliness that attempts to give dignity to their lives and justifies their attitudes and activities in the sight of men. However, the message that appeals to them discounts repentance and ignores humility before God. The deceit it brings denies the need for faith, the essential element in our access to God and His provision. The scripture captures it best by pointing out that because of the condition of the heart of natural man **"men loved the darkness rather than the light for their deeds were evil."**

America's problem is clearly not unique, however, it is nevertheless profound! We have learned to wink at our problem while it continues to destroy us. It is a problem that is beyond the deceit of the natural mind of fallen man to discern let alone fix.

However, the good news is that God has given every man a way of escape and if man will except God's redemptive gift He will give man His Spirit to remind man of, and guide him into, truth. He offers to every man a perspective of truth and the power of supernatural wisdom to guide him if he will humble himself and receive it. If men chose to reject deliverance from his sin and deceit and refuses to accept the Spirit of truth he is condemned by his deceit. His life and attitudes will ultimately bear the fruit of his deceit.

However, the core and strength of the Christian worldview finds its inspiration from the Spirit of God and it resides in those of the true church, the body of Christ. It is the perspective of those who have been delivered from the deceit of secularism through Spiritual rebirth as it is defined in the Scriptures. They are people who depend upon the Spirit of God to inspire and guide them to live, love and walk according to God's wisdom, will and way. This perspective recognizes mans ultimate accountability to the Creator and that the foundation of truth and righteousness is from God and that they are void in the flesh of man. The scriptures teach and the Spirit bears witness that it is the only perspective that offers hope for America, or any people.

The Christian worldview recognizes the value of moral character and the family unit as described biblically. It recognizes truth, righteousness and justice as pillars of any society and insists on a culture that honors these pillars and the God who is the foundation and authority of every society. It is a perspective that detests sexual perversion and profane expression because it degrades and destroys the soul of man and the dignity and value of human life. The Christian worldview detests abortion and the hypocracy that attempts to disguise the horribleness of it with the idea that the real issue is "the woman's right to choose".

The Christian worldview sees the distinctiveness and sacredness of our constitution in the unalienable God given rights and the freedoms it protects and its preamble, which acknowledges the role and sovereignty of the God of the Christian bible and the self-governing responsibilities of the people. The power of democratic government, from the perspective of the Christian worldview, is not found in the competing of evil intentions and selfish interests in hopes that something tolerable for all and agreeable to most will evolve. Rather it is the competing of good intentions and the mutual commitment to that which is right and good that must evolve in the hope that a more perfect union will come forth that is committed to God's plan and purpose for mankind.

The Christian worldview recognizes that right is not always popular and yet it is still right and must be insisted upon. It also recognizes the distinct difference between that which is right and that which is wrong and that which is good from that which is bad from a moral perspective as it is clearly delineated in the bible. It recognizes that man is a moral creature, as apposed to an amoral creature, and therefore distinct from any other creature on earth and for him to function effectively and enjoy God's blessing he must live according to God's moral law because that is how God created him.

The Christian world view believes that man is a fallen creature and unable and unwilling to live according to God's will and plan for him outside of Spiritual rebirth and the guidance of the Spirit of God. It is a perspective that recognizes the implications of mans fallen conditions and therefore the responsibilities of those who lead and teach. It realizes that man cannot deliver himself from the deceit in which he is trapped. It recognizes that the deeds of the flesh are *"immorality, impurity, sensuality, idolatry, sorcery, enmities, strife, jealousy, outbursts of anger, disputes, dissensions, factions, envying, drunkenness, carousing, and things like these…. But the fruit of the Spirit is love, joy, peace patience, kindness, goodness, faithfulness, gentleness, self-control"* (Galatians 5:19-24).

The Christian perspective also recognize that man born of the Spirit can walk according to the Spirit of God, however, he can also choose to walk according to the flesh if he chooses to ignore the leading of the Spirit. Mans best hope in this life is to choose to walk according to the Spirit of God and to actively seek out and choose men born of the Spirit of God to lead us. Christians recognize the importance of insisting upon leadership and laws that reflect God's righteous judgments, His mercy and His revealed will.

It is a perspective that recognizes the implications of secular leadership in government, business, education and in the home. Unfortunately, America has not discerned the implications of what has happened and therefore stood by and watched as our Courts ruled out Gods influence in electing our leaders, governing our nation and educating our children and in doing so made America a secular nation. America is beginning to reap the fruit of the flesh of man and suffer the consequences of secular humanist deceit. The church has not raised prophetic warning and therefore our people have been lulled to sleep while Satan is destroying us through secular humanism.

The Christian worldview is a divinely imparted perspective born out of the wisdom of God and it is the only perspective that will lead men toward purpose, hope, fulfillment and peace in this world and the only perspective that will lead men to desire to grow to become what God created him to become. It is the only perspective that offers a message of the hope of redemption and deliverance from deceit.

Simply put, America has fallen away from God and surrendered to the flesh of man that has lead us to separate the expression of our Christian faith from the governing process and from expression in public settings! Deceit has slowly overtaken us and in our deceit we have failed to recognize that deceit is not a disease that touches only the evil and ignorant. It functions most destructively in the church, in government, among our leaders and educators and among those in positions of influence in our society.

In turning control over to our fleshly ways and attitudes men naturally drift away from God and progress in their apathy and deceit. We have and continue to experience this decline in America to the place where as a nation we feel right and justified in attempting to separate God and His influence from the governing process, from education and from having any tangible influence in the day to day debate of the public issues of life in modern American society.

Simply put, America has chosen to rely on the secular humanist mind and will of fallen men who seek to lead us to abandon and ultimately prohibit the expression of our Christian faith. Secularism is an enemy of God because it is the flesh. In turning control of our lives and government over to our fleshly ways we have drifted away from God and progressed in our apathy and deceit until we, as a culture, have arrived at the place where we have judged it to be good to remove any influence of Gods wisdom and truth from the governing process, from the education process and from having any influence in the day to day public debate of the social and political issues of life.

Our deceit has allowed the development and promotion of a secular humanistic religious theology (philosophy) the bible refers to as **"a form of godliness"** that allows us to appear Christian without belief in order to give dignity and acceptance to our lives. It is hypocracy to be sure! We claim to be a Christian nation while we live as heathens and relegate God to the superstition of "a higher power"!

We seem nationally to have become comfortable with the idea that how we govern and live our public life is none of God's business. We somehow have concluded that God is not really interested in the leadership and guidance of our nation or the development of those laws and policies that lead, protect and further restrict our liberty.

We have bought into the idea that God is not interested in who becomes our President, our nations highest executive, or who we choose to become members of our congress, or who our judges and Chief Justices on the highest court in our land are to be, or what the legislation that creates the laws and policies that govern us are to be.

If it doesn't seem possible to you that such deceit could overcome a nation like the United States of America consider Israel, a nation of people chosen by God to be his people and to be a witness of his glory in the earth.

In 1948 a glimmer of light begin to shine on Israel's horizon. God word declared and it came be ordered in the affairs of men that it was time for Israel to once again become a nation in the land of promise. The bible reveals what the future holds for Israel and tells us when the full effect and penalty for their deceit and rebellion will be completed.

If it happened to Israel it can certainly happen to America should we continue to mock God! The scriptures teach us: *"Do not be deceived, God is not mocked; for whatever a man sows, this he will also reap. For the one who sows to his own flesh shall from the flesh reap corruption, but the one who sows to the Spirit shall from the Spirit reap eternal life. And let us not lose heart in doing good, for in due time we shall reap if we do not grow weary." (Galatians 6:7-9)*

The world abandoned God and crucified its deliverer when they crucified Christ on the cross at Calvary. In their rebellion and deceit they did not recognize Him then and they will not recognize him now, therefore, in our rebellion and deceit we are abandoning our only hope. The Supreme Court of our nation has chosen to destroy all witness of His being, His wisdom, His grace and his sovereignty in the affairs of men and our nation now stands in agreement with their judgment. However, the scriptures warn that this time there will not be another savior sent forth to act as atonement for our sin and rebellion. His return will not be for deliverance of the rebellious, but rather a time of judgment. Those who have not humbled themselves before God will perish!

CHAPTER NINE

THE REJECTION OF GOD

—〰—

"For even though they knew God, they did not honor Him as God, or give thanks; but they became futile in their speculations, and they're foolish hearts were darkened. Professing to be wise, they became fools.." (Romans 1:21-22)

Certainly at the very core of our political struggle and many of our current social problems is the secularization of America. I have discussed the destructive disease of secular humanism at length throughout this book because this deadly disease is systematically destroying America and it requires a clear diagnoses and a detailed analysis of its implications to be fully exposed.

Secular humanism is not an idea foreign to the history of mankind; however, it is a late and radical change in direction for America, which has historically been distinctively Christian in its origin and tradition. America's government and social structure is founded on Christian principle and Presidents who were typically men of Christian faith and character led America in the early years. Its laws and its justice system reflected values and moral principles distinctly Christian. What has been exposed in these latter days is that even though America's religious choice has been Christianity, it has proven of late to be more a cultural distinction than religious.

We have become a people comfortable philosophically with Christian religious values however most of us are not truly believers and followers of Christ. We talk the talk but we no longer walk the walk. Many have a love affair with religion but not with Christ.

There is a distinctive difference between someone who has simply been raised in a Christian environment from the one who is in fact a Christian according to the scriptural definition of Christian. True Christians, according to the scriptures, are born of the Spirit of God and are indeed followers of Christ. Christians are a distinct group of people within whom the Spirit of Christ resides, the holiness of God is glorified, the wisdom of God is apparent, the Character of God is displayed and through whom the love of God is manifest.

It is necessary to recognize that a person is not a Christian simply because he says he is or because he accepts some conservative or Christian principle or principles that represents a Christian worldview. Nor is a person a Christian because he has adopted a certain set of doctrinal beliefs or religious values. A Christian is not a Christian because he lives a good life from the world's perspective or because he has turned over a new leaf, although these are clearly signs of conversion. A Christian is a Christian when he becomes a new creation in Christ Jesus and Gods (life) Spirit resides in Him. He is a person in whom the life of Jesus Christ lives and through whom Jesus Christ works. He is an ambassador of the kingdom of God. He is no longer an ambassador of the world. As he matures in his Spiritual walk he walks according to a new Spirit delivered from the deceit of the world that has guided him previously and his life begins to produce the fruit of the Spirit.

Every society on earth tends to experience deterioration in its character and morals with each new generation unless the people pass on their faith or God brings Spiritual awakening. Spiritual awakening has happened at least twice in America's recent history. However, currently in America the awakening work of His Spirit and the judgment of God against sin seems to be more distant with each passing year. We see in each new generation less evidence of God's Spirit and Character. We see more and more evidence of men separating themselves further from God and each generation seems to more freely reflect the perverse nature of man than the preceding one.

The ability to recognize the hand and voice of God at work has become more remote. The hate the world has for God and His church is becoming more manifest and intense. The fallen nature of man and the fruit of mans character in all of its perverse glory is being revealed. The true church, the body of Christ, is beginning to be revealed causing a polarization between the Christian (Spiritual) world-view and the secular world-view.

The world is raising its ugly head and revealing its hate for God and His people. Its followers are making their eternal choices regarding whom they are going to follow. The government of America has made the choice, through a tragic and symbolic decision by our Supreme Court, to reject God.

The saints of God observe the hand of God at work but they are beginning to show strain under the load of a Church and a nation lacking in spiritual leadership. The saints of God are becoming more and more anxious to see God's ultimate judgment, however, their hearts cry out to see their fellow countrymen awaken to their desperate circumstance. In the meantime the saints continue to work feverishly to awaken the church and to help preserve our national Christian tradition. As ambassadors of the Kingdom, they attempt to encourage America to live up to her calling as a nation bringing light, salt and hope to the people groups of the world.

God reveals to us in the scriptures that he has a plan and a timetable based on His purpose. He has said that He desires that none perish. Nevertheless, come soon Lord Jesus!!

It is hard to accept but must be reiterated often that a truth and reality we all must come to grips with is that the fallen nature of man hates God! The ways of the world are the ways of the fallen nature of man. The scriptures teach us and our experience confirms that God and the world are enemies. The flesh of man is the spirit of the man without God. It is the world at work manifesting the appetites, lusts and pleasures of the flesh of man. It is man doing naturally what he has become naturally. That part of us must die. Remember these words? *"If you are living according to the flesh, you must die; but if by the Spirit you are putting to death the deeds of the body you will live" (Romans 8:13)*

The spirit of the one who goes along and follows after the ways of the world is an enemy of the Spirit of God. The world cannot discern God and has no desire to seek God without the divine intervention of God in an individual's life. The spirit of man is the spirit of the world and it is entirely comfortable with the ways of the world. It is pre-occupied with serving the desires and appetites and pleasures of the flesh. It all seems so right, however, those who follow after the ways of the world will perish!

The scriptures reveal that the church has several distinct advantages over the world beyond eternal life. The first and most profound, of course, is eternal life that began the day a person experiences Spiritual rebirth. Another distinct advantage that Christians have in this life is the capacity to discern the working of the Lord and the signs of the times. *"Now as to the times and epochs, brethren, you have no need of anything to be written to you. For you yourselves know full well that the day of the Lord will come just like a thief in the night. While they are saying, "Peace and safety!" then destruction will come upon them suddenly like birth pangs upon a woman with child; and they shall not escape. But you, brethren, are not in darkness, that the day should overtake you like a thief; for you are all sons of light and sons of day. We are not of night nor of darkness; so then let us not sleep as others do, but let us be alert and sober."*

The implications of this capacity to discern are liberating and powerful. The men and nations who discern God are able to lead men and nations out of and through critical and times. It's prophetic in its insight and a powerful tool of the church to bring light to a world that is lost without God. A man attempting to lead a nation without that prophetic insight is a blind man leading a blind people. Unfortunately many who profess to be Christian are cultural Christian and not born of the Spirit of God. Therefore they lack the capacity to bring light to the world that God has said He loved so much that He gave His only begotten Son to save from the judgment that is to come.

Folks, according the Scriptures, this is the big picture! We tend to get lost in thousands of social issues that are derivative in nature, none of which we can solve without the intervention of our Creator. We lack the wisdom, power, authority and control over the natures of men. Our cause is hopeless without God.

Unfortunately it appears that even though Americans perceive themselves as Christian many are not. Much of the institution of church lacks discernment and wisdom and therefore we follow the same destructive wisdom and course as the rest of the world. The secularization of the church is leading the secularization of America. Secularization of America is the agenda of the modern culture and it is the declared goal of our judiciary for America.

It is sad to watch the secularization of our government by the Supreme Court. It is even more discouraging to see the decision by the court welcomed by our people, many of who, lack the Spiritual discernment to recognize the implications of what has happened.

The church, for the most part, has not reacted with outrage because of the lack of Spiritual discernment and leadership. A spiritual blindness is overtaking America as if someone is pulling a curtain down over the stage of life and the people in the audience can no longer see what is happening behind the scenes.. That same blindness and deceit allows man to declare himself his god and believes that his own wisdom offers a better hope to mankind than the mind of Christ and the love of God.

Perhaps it bears repeating that the Scriptures teach **"there is a way that seems right to man, however it is the way of death."** Secular humanism is the way that seems right to man and it was and is welcomed by the rebellious, perverse and self-serving spiritual nature of man. The enemy of all of Gods creation used a spiritually blind majority on the Supreme Court to carry out this incredible act of deceit that has condemned America. It might be the crowning blow that will ultimately topple America unless as a nation we are awakened spiritually.

The Church goes its own way thinking in its religious arrogance it is above and isolated from the government and the world. They have this pious notion that God only cares for the institution of Church. They see the nation of people as a no mans land to which they have no direct Spiritual responsibility. I somehow think God sees it much differently. God does care what happens to America and to every American. He cares for those who suffer from the evil in which they are trapped. He is more concerned about those among us who are not Christians than He is with the ones who are Christians. He left the Church here on earth to serve His purposes in the earth by bringing salt and light to the world. The Apostle Paul offered a prayer that is appropriate and applicable to Americans today: *"I pray that the eyes of your heart may be enlightened, so that you may know what is the hope of His calling, what are the riches of the glory of His inheritance in the saints, and what is the surpassing greatness of His power toward us who believe. These are in accordance with the working of the strength of His might which He brought about in Christ when He raised Him from the dead, and seated Him at His right hand in the heavenly places, far above all rule and authority and power and dominion, and every name that is named, not only in this age, but also in the one to come. And He put all things in subjection under His fee, and gave Him as head over all things to the church, which is His body, the fullness of Him who fills all in all." (Ephesians 1:18-23)*

Two devastating attitudes and their accompanying code phrases exemplify and describe the lost and perverted condition of our society. The phrases are "The Women's right to chose" and "Separation of Church and State". A deceived majority on the Supreme Court and a few morally and spiritually blind attorneys opened the door to a Pandora's box of moral decadence and secularism. The Supreme Court has potentially destroyed the most politically significant Christian nation in world. America will now systematically and inevitably go down the drain morally not far behind the rest of the western world unless our people awaken Spiritually.

Our national leadership lacks spiritual perspective and leadership. It is the man who argues against perversion and moral decadence that now finds himself the criminal and in trouble with the judiciary, rather than the anti-God perverts who are at work aggressively trying to destroy the influence and foundation that supports all that is, or ever has been, good about America. These two pop phrases are now commonly used by our culture and our courts to justify attitudes and judgments that are intended to remove God, His will, His Church and the influence of His word from government, from our judicial system and from our system of education.

The Holy Scriptures reveal to us that we have condemned ourselves: Jesus said, *"And this is the judgment, that the light has come into the world, and men loved the darkness rather than the light; for their deeds were evil. For everyone who does evil hates the light, and does not come to the light, lest his deeds should be exposed. But he who practices the truth comes to the light, that his deeds may be manifested as having been wrought in God." (John 3:19-21)*

Secularism is not objective according to the scriptures. Jesus pronounced to the unbelievers of His day the sad truth about the deceitful condition of secular man. Listen to His words, *""You are doing the deeds of your father…If God were your father, you would love Me; for I proceeded forth and have come from God, for I have not even come on My own initiative, but He sent Me…….You are of your father the devil, and you want to do the desires of your father. He was a murderer from the beginning, and does not stand in the truth, because there is no truth in him. Whenever he speaks a lie, he speaks from his own nature; for he is a liar, and the father of lies. But because I speak the truth, you do not believe me……He who is of God hears the words of God; for this reason you do not hear them, because you are not of God.*

He proceeded to tell His own people, *"But you do not believe, because you are not of my sheep. My sheep hear my voice, and I know them, and they follow Me; and I give eternal life to them, and they shall never perish; and no one shall snatch them out of My hand. I and the Father are one."*

"The separation of church and state "is pointed to by many Americans who think the court has done a good thing rejecting God from the judiciary and the government of the United States.

This decision to secularize America has now become the law of the land. Its implications seem to have gone completely over the heads of the Legislative and Executive branches of our government and most of our citizens. Those of us who have given it a thought seem to accept it not recognizing its meaning and implications. We have watched the court declare prayer in school against the law. We were a little surprised but we accepted it as no big deal because it was presented to us as the politically correct and just thing to do because it is "FAIR" to the other religious peoples.

The secularists are pleased because it is another step towards their goal of secularizing America. Because prayer in public reflects the existence of a Christian national heritage we feel we must somehow apologize for. Shame on us for publicly expressing our deepest beliefs and most precious faith or our dependence upon God. We have watched religious symbols removed from public buildings and we fail to connect it with the rejection of God and therefore we do not seem to understand the significance of what is taking place. We have watched the public celebration and the public display of Christmas outlawed by our courts. We simply go along with the worldly who readily accept the idea that it is fair and politically correct to get rid of Merry Christmas and adopt the politically correct "Seasons Greetings". We have watched the "Christmas break" from school change to the politically correct words "winter break". We watch the courts struggle with the issue of "In God We Trust" on our coins. Once again, rather than confront the real issue the court has thus far decided to leave "In God We Trust" on our coins and "under God" in our pledge. However, their rationale for decent has been that these slogans don't really suggest the nation is Christian and does not establish a state endorsed church. They conclude that God is a meaningless idea that is used universally in every religious movement. We have said these symbols are no different and equally as meaningless as any other symbol we may choose to put on our coinage.

Our people should be outraged at the courts reasoning. Patronizing the Christians by throwing them a few crumbs is not what any Christian American should accept. We are a Christian nation and "In God We Trust" means just what it says. We do trust in God and honor Him with our national symbolism. "Under God" means we are a people who humble ourselves under the hand of God recognizing His sovereignty over us and declaring our desire to live according to His revealed will and way when we can discern what that is. That's the issue and therein is where we must draw the line in the sand.

We seem to be unable to make the connection between the secularization of our nation and the Supreme Courts reasoning. We are unable to discern the Spiritual implications of the nature and hypocrisy of the court. We just sit back and say, well O.K. I guess that's the only way we can really be fair. Folks, get a life, this is not about being fair it's about being a humble people before our Creator and Lord.

In the foolishness of our government they appointed secularists to our nations highest court. Secularists hate God and are determined they must remove the influence of God and His wisdom from the governing process and its institutions as well as from the public forum. Americans, for the most part, seem to be intimidated by these very foolish men.

In our secular perspective America has adopted abortion and separation as the most correct and objective application of the first amendment. These court decisions are obviously two of the most blatantly tragic examples of the outworking of men's spiritual blindness and deceit. They are obviously the direct disregard by the Supreme Court of the first amendment right to religious freedom and its public expression. It is a determined act of rejection and direct rebellion against God and His revealed purpose and will.

Secularism is having a devastating effect on our nation and its destructive impact will continue until it divides and ultimately destroys us or until our Lord has mercy upon us and awakens our people spiritually. The irony of all of this is that we watch the devastating fruit this secular idiocy bears and we not only fail to recognize the source of its deceit we ignore its destructive impact and continue to allow it to perpetuate its agenda. Indeed most of our professing Christians who ought to be able to see what is happening do not appear to recognize the signs of the times. Is it because the institution of church has lost its spiritual sight?

Secularism is a path that only fools walk down. Many of the courts decisions are almost unbelievable to our people and yet we let them go without protest because we cannot fathom this level of blindness in the highest court of a professing Christian nation.

Folks doesn't this make the court ritual and the black robes of these supposed honorable men seem a little ridiculous? Their decisions take away their right to honor and respect and make it a mockery of justice. It reminds me of a movie I watched one time where they put a tuxedo on a monkey.

The proposition is not whether the court decides justly or fairly according to the law between two combatants in court regardless of the religion of either. It is not whether the court will chose for us how we wish to live according to dictates of a religious institution. The problem is that without the Spirit of God at work in the lives of the justices their discernment and choices, if they are to be just and wise, lack justice and righteousness. They, of all men in government leadership, need the leading of the Spirit of God.

The spirit behind the deceit in these judgments should be obvious to any believer. It is not the Spirit of God but rather the spirit of the evil one whose goal is to destroy any remnant of God and Godliness and to promote the systematic secularization of American.

For evil to prevail in America a government lead by the Spirit and wisdom of God must be toppled. Secularism had to be adopted. That has happened and now its tentacles are beginning to spread and spread they have into every aspect of our existence.

The spirit of secularism has taken over public education. Secularists are actively involved in educating our children to reject God and His revealed will. Meanwhile they are openly displaying and teaching tolerance and acceptance of the abominable homosexual life style as an alternate life-style equally acceptable in America to the traditional family lifestyle and values. At the same time we have chosen to specifically prohibit teaching the fundamental truths of scripture or even prayer in school. We have removed the symbolism of

Christmas and the public Christmas greeting. It makes one wonder which part of Christmas greetings the government objects to? Is it peace on earth or goodwill towards men?

When I think about these and other tragic decisions by the courts and our government and contrast them to God's judgments as revealed in His word I am amused by the arrogance and spiritual deceit. We cannot help but smile a little over our utter foolishness. Our collective focus is so lacking in wisdom and discernment. Even though the world is destined for hell unless they are awakened from their deceit many of them are passionately focused on the environmental efforts to save the planet, the forests and the animals at the expense and sacrifice of their fellowman. They are occupied with saving the homosexuals from aids, protecting abortion rights, secularizing our schools and attempting to spiritually destroy our children so we can focus on issues like global warming!.

Many are absorbed totally with the idea they really might be able to significantly affect a change in global warming and the size of the ozone hole. They believe that through mere secular education we can change the will, lusts and appetites of men. I am amazed at the mired of secular efforts by foolish men to protect us from ourselves and force upon us government dependence when even secular history proves this to be a dead-end street.

We are little more than a spec on a huge planet whose environment is affected more by the eruption of one minor volcano than years of environmental effort can correct. I am not against protecting and providing a reasonably healthy environment to live and work in, however, I am against ridiculous schemes of disrupting the lives of millions of my fellowmen and causing no end to the sacrifice and suffering thousands of people must endure to supposedly save the owl based on the research of a hand full of secular wing-nuts from Davis or Berkley.

America's problem is not the ozone hole, or the trees or the losing of some of the species or protecting the nation from the tree cutters, the SUV drivers or the oil drillers. The problem they are having now regarding global warming is that no one is really able to determine whether there is such a thing. As far as the almost extinct Owl situation we have discovered that after the lives men and women have been disrupted and in some cases destroyed those silly owls are showing up everywhere. Where there are no owls there are lizards whose habitat also trumps the lives of men and women. What utter nonsense.

Removing God from the governing process and from public education by separating Church and State as well as making abortion legal are both evil aberrations that have been forced into our thinking by self-absorbed and very foolish and spiritually blind people during the last 50 years of our history. The incredibly disappointing thing is that we American citizens, for the most part, do not seem to be moved to outrage and action by these destructive distractions. There are things we can do to influence change. Our outrage ought to reach the heavens through prayer and we should be constantly engaged in firing politicians and Judges through impeachment and the voting booth who are out to destroy our way of life and we must begin to demand that the church begin to be the salt and light it is called to be.

A secular America is an idea created by the court and nowhere found in any of the documents associated with the creation of America or of our constitution or its amendments. Secularization of America was never an idea presented by any of our founding fathers in any of their writings or even inferred in the federalist papers nor was such a crazy idea ever introduced in the recorded proceedings or meetings of our founders while framing the declaration of independence or the constitution nor was it ever a part of American thinking or tradition prior to the Supreme Court decision.

A foolish, rebellious people have rejected the invaluable Spiritual guiding light, wisdom, power and influence of the Spirit of Almighty God. The relevancy of the revealed will of the God of the Christian bible is under question even in the church and it has been totally rejected by our government leaders and most of our citizens.

There is a remnant church, much smaller in number than the number who profess to be the church, which are in fact the true church. Much of the church has chosen to isolate itself and it's Spiritual and political influence to the mundane things of church government, the financing of a religious bureaucracy and a variety of introverted social activities. They are no longer a source of salt and light to our nation.

A phenomenon of the last 50 years of our history is the advent of huge churches primarily among the Pentecostal religious movements. There were exciting and seemingly Spiritual movements considered by many born again believers to be a distinctive move of God in America. They may well have been, however, the faith that sustained many of them waned because they recognized that if they were to continue to enjoy a large enough following to finance the construction and/or maintenance of large and lavish church facilities and bloated pastoral staff's they must become appealing to the culture and the world system. They recognized they must present a message that tickles the ears and attracts a worldly congregation of churchgoers, many of whom, attend regularly to give dignity and justify their foolish, selfish and sinful attitudes and lifestyles.

Some members of charismatic congregations seek out those teachers who are celebrity candidates who are hired more as entertainers than ambassadors of the Kingdom of God appointed to lead the flock. Our Lord seems to use them, however, their goal tends to be to send the members away from church each weekend feeling good about themselves and their worldly attitudes, activities and lifestyles so they will return next Sunday. Teachers and preachers have learned that it is much easier to sell self-esteem, positive confession and material success than it is to sell truth, repentance and eternal life. That is because the message of truth falls on the deaf ears of those who have not responded to God's call upon their lives.

Many in our church pulpits today sound like motivational speakers hired by corporations to motivate sales representatives rather than men of God who are indeed prophets of

God speaking under the anointing and counsel of the Spirit of God. Some labor over the scriptures to discover just the right scripture text they can spin so the congregation feels justified in their deceit and not convicted, offended or challenged to repentance.

The anti-God secular humanists have convinced our government leaders and most of our citizens that government must be completely separated from the influence of the Spirit of God or the reminders of God or His wisdom, principle, morality, or the influence of His leadership!

The threat against the church by our secular humanist government is designed to intimidate the church and "keep her in her place" so to speak. The government, of course, will respond to this idea with the arrogant campaign to convince you and I that everything they are doing is in our best interest. They are totally deceived. The campaign has captured the interest and imagination of the people and has brought the organized church to its knees in surrender to the state. The federal government threatens the potential revocation of the tax exempt status the church currently enjoys unless the church stays out of politics. In light of that the church recognizes that a majority of its adherents are not disciples of Christ and/or ambassadors of the kingdom of God. They also recognize that most would withdraw their financial support in a heartbeat if the tax-exempt status of the church were revoked.

The fear of the church leadership is for good reason and will no doubt become reality if the church should choose to become the salt and light they are called to be. They fear that becoming politically active would divide the church and the government would come against them. They fear that such a move would, forfeit their tax-exempt status, reduce the following and the incentive of its followers to bring donations into the church. Perhaps the church and the world would then get a glimpse of which the real Christians are. They are correct.

It should not surprise any Christian that a secular government bureaucracy would want and actively attempt to remove God, His purpose and His wisdom from the public agenda or arena. However, It is deeply disappointing to realize the church can be so easily deceived into thinking that secular is another word for neutral or objective.

Folks there is no neutral ground! We either gather with Christ or we scatter against Him. It is disgusting to watch the church cower from the intimidation and allow itself to be so easily silenced, isolated, controlled and irrelevant because of these threats. The church has in essence agreed not to insist upon being salt and light in the public arena if the government will continue to allow the church to exist and enjoy relief from the tax collectors.

When will the Church awaken to the fact that the World is its enemy? We, who consider ourselves to be the Church of Jesus Christ, are in a Spiritual battle to the death against the world. The secular humanist government bureaucracy in America would eliminate the church, as we know it, in a flash just as the secular humanist communist government did in the Soviet Union, if they dared! That time will come in America unless the church and our people are Spiritually awakened.

Every time our Judiciary rules against prayer in school, or prayer at public functions, and every time any expression of faith is shutdown in the public arena the institution of government has just taken another step toward removing the influence of God from the lives of our people and they have moved America closer to becoming a secular society.

The less the influence and voice of Christian Americans is heard and felt in America the closer the time comes when the public expression of Christian faith will no longer be tolerated!! In the meantime we as a people have been duped into allowing ourselves to become government dependent and we have therefore allowed government to limit the political activity and involvement of the church through the carrot of tax-exempt status.

There are many other more subtle ways for government to administratively restrict the activities of the church however none quite as blatant as financially. The government bribes the church with tax-exempt status to keep it in line politically. It has worked for the most part thus far and the church is bowing at the altar of mammon.

The atheist, the evil, the heathen, the pagan and the secular humanists were clearly perceived by early Americans as the deceived, the lost, the outcast, the personification of evil and were therefore not considered for positions of leadership in government, the church or society unless and until they demonstrated true repentance before God and man.

The idea that a pagan or atheist or secular humanist might have a leadership position in government or in early American society was a repugnant idea and totally foreign to the thinking of most Americans and American leaders. However today that idea of excluding them is considered bigoted and the exact reverse is true! Today Americans see the Christian world-view and those who hold it as narrow, bigoted, radical, destructive and negatively discriminating rather than wise and just and in lock step with the truth and the purposes of God!

The twentieth century perception of politics, elections, government, taxation & representation and most social issues of the day are perceived by a majority of our people as distinctively secular. We deny any spiritual relativity to the governing process or to the administration of social programs or to dealing with Constitutional issues. The political process and the election of its leadership are perceived by our government's leaders and our citizens as distinctly separate and void of the influence of God, His wisdom or any consideration of His purposes.

American's have been sold the idea that governing somehow loses its objectivity and fairness if God and His truth become the standard or even if it is allowed to enter into the process. In our utter foolishness America has elected to reject God's influence not only in the process of electing our leaders and governing our nation but also in educating our children. We have tragically come to believe that Godly influence is wrong for our people and our children and worldly influence as right and best for our children! Prayer is removed from school to make room for the unrestricted parading and promoting of sex, rebellion and the homosexual lifestyle in front of our children as good and acceptable.

Those who believe and practice Christian faith in America are considered by our government and most of society as right wing fanatics, rather than the foundation of our society whose beliefs and faith is no longer *the way* but rather *in the way* of social justice and progress.

We no longer turn to the Word of God and its proponents and teachers as the way to truth and justice and the way to find the answers to life's troubling matters. However, so long as the Christian perspective is kept essentially within the walls of the Church and considered irrelevant in its influence in society the government and the secular humanists will allow it to exist.

We have chosen to throw the only true God of the bible into the mix with the heathen God's of the world proudly applauding our compromise and diversity as good progress demanding that all these God's and their religious trappings be given equal status and protection under the constitution of a nation that was founded as distinctly Christian. Sound ridiculous? It is utter foolishness and America is beginning to pay the price big time!!!

The dramatic shift away from the God of the bible in our national thinking during the last half of the twentieth century, and certainly the last decade of the twentieth century under the executive leadership of a spiritually bankrupt administration accelerated our spiritual decline and national disgrace.

We have allowed ourselves to relegate our religious faith to little more than a badge worn by a few on Sunday morning! The typical minister preaches self-esteem and humanistic psychology to the choir and the Christian broadcast networks and station owners play their ministry tapes!

We find ourselves deeply divided philosophically, religiously and therefore politically. The line between the liberal and conservative perspective is becoming more polarized. The Christian and the secular worldviews cannot co-exist. The secular view is the liberal view and is led by the spirit of man, which is anti-Christ, and it will not tolerate the Christian view led by the Spirit of God.

Its interesting to note there are professing Christians in both the liberal (secular) and conservative camps, however it is difficult, to say the least, to hold the liberal view and the Christian view unless you happen to be deceived about what being a Christian is all about.

Clearly, the stench of political posturing to gain power and the secular humanism that has become the guiding philosophy that leads our nation and directs our public must to be flushed back into the gutter from where it arose.

Our supreme court has become a literal embarrassment to America as it relates to carrying out its constitutionally assigned responsibility. The liberal members of the court are busy usurping legislative power, removing God from the public forum, and declaring unconstitutional the legislative attempts to lead our nation back on course.

We have systematically made our government responsible for our individual welfare, our health, our security and our education. We have traded our liberty for one or another intrusive law, government benefit, or government promise to take care of us. We hate the slavery of dependence and yet we continue to give government greater and greater power over our individual and collective lives.

We, like blind and indiscriminant men following a modern pied piper, have unwisely agreed to turn our back on God and his truth and place our trust, turn over our individual rights, surrender our constitutionally guaranteed authority over our lives and relinquish our freedom and liberty to a secular humanist government bureaucracy believing that in doing so we have done a good thing. Sounds crazy doesn't it? That's because it is crazy and we must somehow become awakened to what we have done and see to it that it is reversed or we will soon find ourselves subjects of a totalitarian government.

The result of our collective deceit is indifference and dependence. We become more irresponsible and feel more secure and less bothered by what is happening to us with each new generation. We have forgotten or failed to recognize that liberty in a lost world requires Spiritual alertness and a constant readiness to fight to protect it at the least hint of infraction!

Men have forgotten the lesson that history teaches over and over again. "Power corrupts and absolute power corrupts absolutely." The federal and state governments have become secular humanist beaurocratic power seeking government nightmares that now have their tentacles into virtually every area of our lives taking resources, power and authority away from individual citizens and depositing those resources and that power into an ever-growing and oppressive government.

I find amusing but sadly true one of our past President Reagan's comments regarding our governments view toward the economy: **"The governments view toward the economy can be summed up in a few short phrases; " If it moves, tax it. If it keeps moving, regulate it. And if it stops moving, subsidize it." (Ronald Reagan, President)**

From a spiritual perspective we have been conditioned to accept and indorse the idea that our federal and state governments must become amoral institutions mandated to pass amoral legislation. We somehow have reconciled this tragic and devastating idea with the belief that you can trust an amoral government to be moral and fair and just. Sound preposterous? It is!!! How could intelligent and honorable men get hood winked into such deceit and support such hypocrisy.

We have been sold on the idea that justice must not be guided by Godly truth and principle. We have somehow decided we can trust man, however, and we, like sheep headed to the slaughter, follow cooperatively along in our collective deceit. We celebrate our debt driven prosperity, our spiritual diversity, and our government dependence. Like Alice in wonderland we march merrily, merrily down the path to our own utter individual and national destruction.

We are totally pre-occupied with our pleasures and have forgotten the meaning and purpose of life. We have rejected God our only hope!

CHAPTER TEN

CHURCH APOSTASY

—ɯ—

*"Because you are lukewarm, and neither hot nor cold,
I will spit you out of my mouth". (Rev 3:16)*

This scripture was written to a church that had become rich. They were deceived they were in need of nothing. They did not discern their wretchedness. The Lord's admonishment was to repent. He goes on to remind them, *"Those whom I love, I reprove and discipline; be zealous therefore and repent. Behold I stand at the door and knock; if anyone hears My voice and opens the door, I will come in to him, and will dine with him, and he with Me." (Rev 3:17-20)*

In the Old Testament book of Proverbs, chapter 14, verse 34 God's word says, *"Righteousness exalts a nation, But sin is a disgrace to any people."* America's current culture has rejected righteousness and therefore our nation is becoming a disgrace in the site of God and in the perspective of righteous people.. We have rejected God and have embraced the sinful ways of the world. We have rejected the hope that drew most of the world to us and now we are finding ourselves alone and despised by the world.

Sin, rebellion and selfishness are more pronounced in every aspect of today's culture. Our arrogant opulence and introspective focus is not only bringing disgrace upon us as a nation among the nations of the world, it is destroying America from within. The Scriptures teach that when a people become rebellious and depraved charity and goodness is overwhelmed by evil and God removes His protective hand and that people suffer the consequences of their unrighteousness and wrong choices. When God chooses to turn a nation over to the depravity of their deceit he has in essence brought judgment upon that nation.

The scriptural principle which condemns our rebellion and reveals God's response to rebellion and perversion is found in Romans 1: 18-32. *"For the wrath of God is revealed from heaven against all ungodliness and unrighteousness of men, who suppress the truth in unrighteousness, because that which is known about God is evident within them; for*

God made it evident to them. For since the creation of the world His invisible attributes, His eternal power and divine nature, have been clearly seen, being understood through what has been made, so that they are without excuse. For even though they knew God, they did not honor Him as God, or give thanks; but they became futile in their specula-tions, and their foolish heart was darkened. Professing to be wise, they became fools, and exchanged the glory of the incorruptible God for an image in the form of corrupt-ible man and of birds and four-footed creatures. Therefore, God gave them over in the lusts of their hearts to impurity, that their bodies might be dishonored among them. For they exchanged the truth of God for a lie, and worshiped and served the creature rather than the Creator, who is blessed forever, Amen. For this reason God gave them over to degraded passions; for their women exchanged the natural function for that which is unnatural, and in the same way also the men abandoned the natural function of the woman and burned in their desire toward one another, men with men committing inde-cent acts and receiving in their own persons the due penalty of their error. And just as they did not see fit to acknowledge God any longer, God gave them over to a depraved mind, to do those things which are not proper, being filled with all unrighteousness, wickedness, greed, evil; full of envy, murder, strife, deceit, malice; they are gossips, slanderers, haters of God, insolent, arrogant, boastful, inventors of evil, disobedient to parents, without understanding, untrustworthy, unloving, unmerciful; and although they know the ordi-nance of God, that those who practice such things are worthy of death, they not only do the same, but also give hearty approval to those who practice them.."

America was unique from its inception in that its calling was distinctive. It was born for the purpose of living and demonstrating a divine vision and purpose to its citizens and to a lost world. Because of this divine vision and the hope that accompanies liberty America became a nation of ambassadors to the Kingdom of God. There has never been a nation before or since that was as distinctively Christian as the United States of America. Our heritage is one of faith, hope, liberty and justice for all men. It is true that we have not always lived up to that vision but our purpose was never out of focus by a majority of our leaders and citizens from the inception up through the first half of the twentieth century.

Clearly we were a nation of sinners, since all men (and women) are sinners, and some of our people did many sinful and disgraceful things during our development as a nation and so it shall be until our Lord delivers us. However, a majority of our citizens were humble before the Lord and a Spirit of love, hope and charity abounded in America. Our foundation, our hope, our liberty and the guiding light to a majority of our people and to a majority of our leaders of national government during the first 150 years of our existence were clearly the bible and the Church.

We find incontrovertible historical evidence that even before the advent of the declara-tion of independence, the constitution, the debate surrounding the issue of separation of church and state, even before the existence of the supreme court, a national government our national dependence upon biblical wisdom and truth was evidenced in the laws of the colonies and the lifestyles of the people, the writings of our founders and the decisions that lead the government of the colonies.

Biblical truth and moral character provided the foundational source of guidance in the development of this society and was the center- piece of the development of the central government and the governing process. The government and the people looked to the bible not only for direction but also for authority in the establishment of the laws of the land. Biblical truth and law provided the wisdom and authority and guided the development of our legal system. The bible provided the foundation and wisdom that established and guided our education system. It also established the foundational principles of jurisprudence and guided the education of our lawyers. The laws of the land and the judgments of the courts found their wisdom and authority in the Christian bible. God's truth, wisdom and charity guided the lives of the vast majority of the people of America.

The issues of life were interpreted by, centered around and directed by the Word of God and the wisdom it presents. Life, character, values and the social order was defined by biblical truth. We were a Christian nation of Christian people. The propriety and dignity of life in America was defined by Christian principle. Not one nation in the world considered that America was anything other than a nation whose very essence was Christian. This distinctive Christian tradition and its implications has been set aside by the Supreme Court in its "Separation of Church and State" decision.

The preponderance of history reveals that men and women of this budding nation turned to the preachers, prophets, biblical teachers and the Word of God to help them interpret where they must stand on the issues of the day and how they were to measure the qualifications and character of the political leaders they chose to lead them. Out of this kind of wisdom and leadership was born a nation and a national tradition dedicated to the glory and purposes of God.

This heritage and tradition is indeed a precious and priceless tradition and legacy in which Christ's glory, character and purpose was lived out through the lives of sincere believers and patriots. God, His redemptive hope, His incredible grace, His abounding mercy, His incorruptible wisdom and His endless provision was the hope that led our nation and remains today the only hope for our national survival.

The truth and righteousness of God's grace does not justify the sinfulness of men, it simply points out the powerlessness of the fallen nature of man to reach down and pull himself up by his bootstraps regardless of his good intentions and/or of his attempt to follow the perfect law of God by itself. Regarding the perfect Law that condemns the man who sins Jesus said, ***"Do not think that I came to abolish the law or the Prophets; I did not come to abolish, but to fulfill. For truly I say to you, until heaven and earth pass away, not the smallest letter or stroke shall pass away from the Law, until all is accomplished. Whoever then annuls one of the least of these commandments, and so teaches*** *others, shall be called least in the kingdom of heaven, but whoever keeps and teaches them, he shall be called great in the kingdom of heaven." (Matthew 5:17-19)*

The scriptures ask the question for us to consider, *"Is the law then contrary to the promises (and mercy) of God? May it never be! For if the law had been given which was able to impart life, then righteousness would indeed have been based on law. But the Scripture has shut up all men under sin, that the promise by faith in Jesus Christ might be given to those who believe…..before faith came, we were kept in custody under the law, being shut up to the faith which was later to be revealed. Therefore, the law became our tutor to lead us to Christ that we may be justified by faith. But now that faith has come, we are no longer under a tutor. For you are all sons (those who believe and become born of His Spirit) of God through faith in Christ Jesus. For all of you who were baptized into Christ have clothed yourselves with Christ." (Galatians 4:23-27)*

"It was for freedom that Christ set us free; therefore keep standing firm and do not be subject again to the yoke of slavery. (Galatians 5:1) "…the one who looks intently at the perfect law, the law of liberty, and abides by it, not having become a forgetful hearer but an effectual doer, this man shall be blessed in what he does." , "This is pure and undefiled religion in the sight of God…to keep oneself unstained by the world" (James 1:25,27)

Religious men (and women), in the context of the above scriptures, regardless of where they exist in the religious or political hierarchy, who have not repented of their sin and accepted God's redeeming grace do not inherit His Spirit and do not become new creatures in Christ and will not see the Kingdom of God. Those who live by the law will be judged by the law and will perish with the rest of the world unless they likewise repent and call upon God's saving grace and mercy.

Our works without God are not adequate to attain to God's demand for holiness.

The scriptures say our religious attempts to become acceptable to God are as filthy rags in the sight of God. God is perfect and men's works will not meet his standard. Man cannot redeem himself from the curse of death through his works. However, religion tends to take God's standard of holiness and arrogantly works to create a doctrine that will allow men to think they can somehow pull themselves up by their bootstraps, so to speak, and "will" themselves to live up to that doctrinal standard and in doing so live a sinless life and earn Gods favor and their redemption.

Mans attempt to live righteously or to save himself by his works is a foolish and hope-less cause. Our acceptance is not dependent upon our efforts or acts. We are made accept-able by our trust in the atoning death of Christ. Our acceptance has to do with life rather than works! God declares that He is eternal life and He shares that life with the redeemed. God is eternal and the life that He has and gives is eternal. Spiritual life is found in the Spirit of God, who says He is Spirit, and without his Spirit there is no life. Man has been separated from the Spirit of God because of His sin and must be re-born of the Spirit to see God. Since God is eternal the life we inherit is eternal when we become born of His Spirit. Man cannot please God without the Spirit of God to awaken, inspire, guide, deliver, forgive and empower. Man cannot live up to God's perfection of holiness. It is a religious notion that fails to recognize that *"by grace you have been saved through faith; and that not of yourselves, it is the gift of God; not as a result of works, that no one should boast."* **(Ephesians 2:8-9)**

The scriptures teach us, and our experience bears testimony to the fact, that natural man cannot see beyond his own deceit unless his spiritual eyes are opened to his problem. If he repents of his sinfulness, seeks God's forgiveness and allows God to deliver him, God will receive him and he will begin a Spiritual walk towards sanctification.

It is a false and condemning doctrine that teaches man can somehow make himself holy and that he must do so if he is to be acceptable to God. The idea is absurd and an incredibly arrogant attitude to say the least. This does not mean obedience to the revealed will of God is unimportant to God. Attempting to walk in obedience to God is profitable and God does bless those who obey His will. However, our redemption is not based on our ability to obey God, it is based on His grace manifest in the atoning death of His son Jesus Christ.

God has said through the scriptures quoted above that, *"all men have sinned and come short of the glory of God".* Since man is a sinner by nature he soon finds in his attempts to practice his religious doctrine that he cannot meet the standard of God's holiness. However, in his deceit, he attempts to live in hypocracy rather than humble himself. He lives in a state of denial of his need of forgiveness or of the redeemer's deliverance. His fallen nature and *"the spirit of the prince of the power of the air that is now working in the sons of disobedience"* leads him to believe in his own righteousness and to reject the atoning sacrifice of Christ for his sin blinding his eyes to his utter sinful nature. Every man, woman and child is condemned because they are sinners. Their sin and rebellion demands the penalty of death. That penalty was paid by Christ that you and I might be delivered from spiritual death through the atoning death of Christ and the grace of almighty God. The Scriptures are clear, Jesus said, *"I am the way the truth and the life and no one comes to the Father but by Me"*

Many false teachers who profess to be prophets of God have arisen within the covering of the institution of church over the centuries. Spiritually deceived men have gathered and created many religious movements that deceive many. The scriptures warn us that *"not everyone who says, to me, Lord', Lord', will enter the Kingdom of Heaven; but he who does the will of my Father who is in heaven. Many will say to me on that day, Lord, Lord, did we not prophesy in Your name, and in Your name cast out demons, and in Your name perform many miracles? And then I will declare to them, "I never knew you; depart from me, you who practice lawlessness."(Matthew 7:21-23)*

The scriptures tell us we will know them by their fruit! They often tend to demand holiness and sinless lives which they fail to live. Clearly holiness is God's will for us, however,

He is our holiness and He enables us to fulfill His purpose in our lives if we live by faith and trust in Him. There is no hope for even the brightest and most just man to deliver himself or meet God's Standard! Men become justified when he humbles himself before the Creator and accepts the atoning death of Jesus Christ for his sin and rebellion.

Within many religious movements men take one or more of God's attributes which best suites them and they create a religious movement that places that attribute out of context with the fullness of the character and purpose of God. Therefore, denominational divisions occur. These various divisions tend to pick and chose which portion of God's word best fits the way they would like to interpret it and the way they want their followers to believe and live there lives. The point, of course, is that sometimes well intended men in their deceit decide what they want to believe and then attempt to build a religion, denomination, sect, or cult around it.

Unfortunately, these divisions are creations of the reason of the minds of men who are not walking according to the Spirit of God. The problem is immature believers often chose to walk according to the flesh and not according the leading of the Spirit, which leads to confusion within the church.

The problem is not that these sects or religious movements are completely wrong in all their doctrine or activities or that they have nothing good to contribute from a social perspective. On the contrary, some of them subscribe to some, perhaps most, of the same Christian ideals of charity and humility before God. They often subscribe too much of what the true body of Christ subscribes to. They usually teach that we ought to live obedient and disciplined lives, which give life dignity and purpose and gives good works and faithful service honor and gives God glory. These are all things that are part and parcel to Christian orthodoxy. However, the Lord characterizes the works of secular minded men who work good works for the purpose of gaining Gods favor as "filthy rags" because, even as good as they may seem to natural man, they arise out of the flesh of man and fall short of the perfection God demands. Mans attempt to keep the Ten Commandments cannot save him; nevertheless his efforts are honorable and profitable for Him and the Kingdom of God.

The various world religions contain many noteworthy doctrines. The world, which does not hear or listen to the Spirit of God, therefore has a difficult time sorting out the differences between Christianity and the various world religions and cults.

The great divide between the bible and the world's religions always leads us back to how a religious movement views the role of Jesus Christ in God's plan of redemption and how His life and death relates to God's redeeming grace, and how man avails himself of God's redeeming grace.

The thing that most distinguishes Christianity from all the world's religions is the incredible grace of Almighty God! Except for Christianity most world religions believe we must somehow make ourselves worthy of Gods grace before He will accept us through a variety of activities, rituals, sacrifices, deliverances, or even through many reincarnated lifetimes.

Religion is mans effort to find a path to God and walk that path. A path is something man walks on to get to a destination. However, there is no path to God! That path has been severed because of mans sin. The penalty for sin is death, therefore, every man is condemned to death. Man cannot reach God by his own efforts no matter how hard he tries. The world Religions are mans various attempts to find a path to God and walk that path so he can reach God.

God has made a way to Himself for mankind, however there is only one-way according to the scriptures. Jesus calls it a narrow way. The way to enter the kingdom of God is limited to the acceptance of the death of Christ as the adequate atonement for your sin. Christ's life in you becomes your holiness. Man, in his most perfect efforts, cannot live up to the perfection of God's demand for holiness because man is a sinner by nature. It is the height of arrogance for a person to think that in his or her fallen state he or she can somehow pull themselves up by their bootstraps and attain to a sinless holy life that meets the admonition of the Lord to "be holy as I am holy". The only way we can attain to the holiness of God is through the life of Christ. Once we are born again of His Spirit we become holy because the Spiritual life that resides in us is holy and eternal!

Some cults and religions worship man, priests, false prophets, cows, statues, the sun, the moon, the stars, the earth, the king, the government, Mary, Satan and some worship religion itself. No matter how inspiring and well intentioned the religious movement, without God's Spirit it becomes bondage and places a burden on the people they cannot possibly lift. Their religious life becomes like the world with all of its unattainable expectations, political efforts, worldly ways and attitudes. It is a way that seems right to man but the Lord says that it leads only to death.

The role of the Church, according to the scriptures, is to bring the message of Gods redeeming grace, to reveal to the church the nature, character and the revealed will of God, to minister to the needs of the needy and to provide salt and light to a confused and lost world. Bringing Salt and light has to do with preserving goodness and revealing truth.

Unfortunately, The institution in America recognized as the Church finds itself having become so like the world its attempts to bring salt and light that the salt and light it brings has become indistinguishable from the ways of the world. The culture and the secular thinking of the world has taken over much of the Church.

It is necessary to distinguish the body of Christ, which the scriptures refer to as the church, from the institutions we call the church. The institutions we call church are religious institutions created by man to represent the purpose and character of God in the earth and to help lead men to righteousness. The Church spoken of in the Scriptures as the true church is the body of Christ. It was and is created by the Spirit of God. It has very little to do with buildings or religious meetings. The scriptures refers to the body of Christ this way: *"I pray that the eyes of your heart may be enlightened, so that you may know what is the hope of His calling, what are the riches of the glory of His inheritance in the saints, and what is the surpassing greatness of His power toward us who believe. These are in accordance with the working of the strength of His might which He brought about in Christ when He raised Him from the dead, and seated Him at His right hand in the heavenly places, far above all rule and authority and power an dominion, and every name that is named, not only in this age, but also in the one to come. And He put all things in subjection under His feet, and gave Him as head over all things to the church, which is His body, the fullness of Him who fills all in all." (Ephesians 1:18-23)* Members of the body of Christ can be found both in and out of the institution of church.

The more worldly the institution of church the least likely you will find members of the true church among its congregation. Ideally the body of Christ and the institution of church would be synonymous. However, the institution no longer functions spiritually at the cutting edge of God's will nor typically does it see the hand of God or hear the voice of God and it does not always follows after His Spirit. Therefore it has lost the power and authority of prophetic ministry because it is not lead by the Holy Spirit. Some of the institution of church is being lead by false prophets and teachers who come in sheep's clothing but inwardly are ravenous wolves. Some of the church is being lead by those who tickle the ears of carnal Christians.

Many, perhaps the majority, according to the polls, of those who attend the main-line denominational churches are not "born again" believers in the biblical context according to the recent Barna report. If that is true the institution that calls itself church is not the true church even though it might contain part of the true Church.

The institution of church has become a cultural institution rather than Spiritual. Therefore it tends to change and become conformed to the culture it serves. A poll recently revealed that more than 50% of those aspiring ministers who went to seminary as born again believers graduate saying they do not believe Jesus Christ is the Son of God nor do they believe He is the only way of redemption. If that is true the implications are devastating. The implications are, of course, that the majority of those who lead and attend church in America do not believe the bible is the inspired word of God and they are not born of His Spirit and therefore they are not God's ambassadors nor are they led by God's Spirit. Such a church cannot bring salt and light to a nation or to the world.

Many are secularists or agnostics or theists who believe there is a God but they are not sure about Jesus redemptive death or the role of His Spirit in the life of the church and they live as religionists. Their wisdom is the wisdom of the secular mind of fallen man. That wisdom concerns itself with the appetites, pleasures and things of spirit of man. The scriptures explain it this way: *"For those who are according to the flesh, set their minds on the things of the flesh, but those who are according to the Spirit, the things of the Spirit. For the mind set on the flesh is death, but the mind set on the Spirit is life and peace, because the mind set on the flesh is hostile toward God, for it is not eve able to do so; and those who are in the flesh cannot please God. However, you are not in the flesh but in the Spirit, if indeed the Spirit of God dwells in you. But if anyone does not have the Spirit of Christ, he does not belong to Him. And if Christ is in you, through the body is dead because of sin, yet the spirit is alive because of righteousness. But if the Spirit of Him who raised Jesus from the dead dwells in you, He who raised Christ Jesus from the dead will also give life to your mortal bodies through His Spirit who indwells you. So then, brethren, we are under no obligation, not to the flesh, to live according to the flesh—for if you are living according to the flesh you must die; but if by the Spirit you are putting to death the deeds of the body you will live. For all who are being led by the Spirit of God, these are the sons of God." (Romans 8:5-14)*

Some, perhaps many who attend church regularly are cultural Christians. Many are agnostics who have not read or do not believe the bible or don't know God from personal experience. They are unable to discern the existence of God from observation of God's creation and cannot discern the fruit of His Spirit working through the lives of His people. They therefore cannot determine whether, indeed, there is truly an intelligent superintending God. These men cannot find God because that which is begun by the Spirit cannot be discerned or completed by the flesh. Human intellect cannot reach God and will never find Him. The spirit of the world has been severed from the life of Christ.

Many secularists and agnostics believe we ought to do good works according to the biblical admonition and that we ought to help our fellowman and indeed we should. They consider that kind of effort and commitment to be significant enough proof they are good people and worthy of mercy because they see their goodness as meeting God's standard of holiness. They consider themselves to be orthodox Christian. Unfortunately they are foolish men and women. Only the Lord Himself knows how many who go to church fit in this category, however, He tells us that many attend the worlds church who are not Christian. He says it this way: *"Not everyone who says to me "Lord, Lord" did we not prophesy in Your name, and in Your name cast out demons, and in Your name perform many miracles? And then I will declare to them, "I never knew you; Depart from me, you who practice lawlessness." (Matthew 7:21-23)*

Some denominations within the Christian faith see no evidence of the working of the Spiritual gifts so they have concluded the Spiritual gifts arc really not for the church in this age. They offer a bunch of theories, which are nothing more than speculation, that make them comfortable with their lack of Spiritual power or Spiritual fruit that comes forth from the church.

God warns us of a tragic reality. Listen to His admonition: *"Enter by the narrow gate; for the gate is wide, and the way is broad that leads to destruction, and many are those who enter by it. For the gate is small, and the way is narrow that leads to life, and few are those who find it." (Matthew 7:13-14)*

Some who are aware of the Scriptural declaration that the manifestation of Gods power, authority and charity will follow those who believe attempt to create the working and power of the Holy Spirit through emotion, music and the conjured up public display of a Spiritual gift. Such men are deceived and their activities little more than show business.

In their deceit many who have attended a Seminary or bible school and are therefore chosen to lead in the church see themselves as spiritual and often they are not. Many of us fail to see the many expressions of the Spirit in the church. Religionists of every sort exist somewhere in between these various extremes. Some do not believe the bible is the inspired word of God because they see no evidence, acceptable to secular mind, of God literally performing what He promises in the bible.

The Lord says this regarding those who profess to be His followers; *"My sheep hear my voice, and I know them, and they follow me; and I give eternal life to them, and they shall never perish; and no one shall snatch them out of my hand. My father, who has given them to me, is greater than all; and no one is able to snatch them out of the father's hand. I and the father are one."* **(John 10:26-30)**

He says that His followers can be detected by the fruit their lives produce, by the wisdom with which they live their lives and by their confession. Listen carefully to His Words, *" You will know them by their fruits. Grapes are not gathered from thorn bushes, nor figs from thistles, are they? Even so, every good tree bears good fruit; but the bad tree bears bad fruit. A good tree cannot bear bad fruit, nor can a bad tree produce good fruit."* **(Matthew 7:16-18)**

In the context of Scriptural truth it appears that most of the mainline denominations of the organized church are indeed religionists and many of them have fallen into apostasy. They lack the leading of God's Spirit and have become so like the world they no longer have the light to lead those who are lost or the salt to sustain truth. Unfortunately, much of the organized church no longer represents or declares God's grace, will or purpose. They no longer manifest the working of God's Spirit and are not able to give a prophetic voice to times and circumstances of the world that confront mankind. They have become religious movements organized around various humanistic social ideologies or fleshly appetites.

The scriptures declare that the body of Christ is the only church God recognizes as His Church. His Church is given the role of ambassadorship ordained with the responsibility to bring salt and light into a fallen world. Regardless of the vastness of the apostasy of the Church, the Scriptures declare that Satan will not destroy the true church and their will always be a remnant of believers scattered throughout the world, who are still salty. Wherever they are, they are the true church, the body of Christ, and without there presence America, and indeed the rest of the world, would have long since perished.

The scriptures teach that a time will come when the world will perish and all its followers with it. The church is the only group of people on earth who will spend eternity with the Lord according to the scriptures. It is the only people on earth who has God's message of deliverance, has access to His wisdom and has hope for mankind. At some point God will remove His church, His Spirit and His message of grace and begin to reveal His wrath against a rebellious and evil world.

It is not simply disappointing, but it is heartbreaking to consider because it has devastating implications for millions of Americans and for people of all nations. The church, created to be the ambassadors of the kingdom of God, has a religious counterpart in the world born out of religious zeal.

Its beginning was divine and its power and fruit dynamic and real. The fullness of our Savior was apparent in the gathering of the early church. The church was the gathering of the Saints of God who comprised the body of Christ in the earth. As the church became worldly it's Spiritual power and authority became less and its testimony became confusing and less appealing. As it begin to lose its Spiritual power and authority its attempts to resemble the working of the Spirit of God in its religious rituals became little more than hypocrisy.

Today, in the minds and hearts of most Americans, the church with its many denominations represents organized religion, which scattered among its membership there can be found some members of the true church. However, for the most part the organized church is lacking in Spiritual life and it no longer discerns, communicates or communes with God. In far too many cases these religious institutions have become a stumbling block to many Christians and have lost the vision and zeal for God. Religious observance in much of the mainline denominations of the church has surrendered to the ways of the flesh of man led by the spirit of the world. Its capitulation with the world has caused its message to go unheeded by the world it is ordained to minister to.

The tragedy is that much of the church in America has cowered under the intimidation of the state system rather than ministering light to it. It has allowed itself to become isolated and controlled by the threats and bankrupt philosophies of deceived men who interpret the constitution to satisfy the world's agenda. The government legislates its secular influence upon our national existence limiting the ability of Christianity to influence the election of political leaders and our national policy.

The church has in essence agreed to put its light under a peck measure rather than place it on the hill where it's light could be seen by all. Unfortunately, in many instances the church no longer has a light to set on a hill. Much of the church has surrendered to the world and to the state. It has agreed with the state that it will not insist upon functioning as salt and light, particularly as it relates to electing government political leaders or to issues involving our national policies, if the state will allow the church to exist and enjoy exemption from taxation. The church has also removed itself from attempting to influence the content of the curriculum or the moral standards taught and maintained by our public education system. The secular thinking world and much of the church says "that seems fair" and Satan finds it all very amusing!

The church has lost its ability, and desire, to distinguish between our Christian faith and the various religious cults that permeate our society under the banner of Christianity. Our society is no longer a people of faith; rather, we are becoming a nation of fools led by the spirit of man whose deceit is destroying us. We were once a people who proudly proclaimed that we were "One Nation Under God".

One of the basic admonishments of our Savior to every believer is to be salt and light in the earth which implies the need to confront and contrast the ways of the world with truth and reveal prophetically the will of God in the circumstances and issues that face us individually and collectively. The modern church in America has not been publicly active in either of these roles in the past half century and therefore we see the American society set adrift in an ocean of secular and evil influence without any beacons of light by which to navigate. The ship of state is being guided toward a storm that will destroy us.

Meanwhile many of the people who attend some of the relatively powerless and irrelevant "churches" of our mainline denominations have slowly drifted off to sleep and now slumber in a spiritual "la, la " land indifferent to what is happening on a national level and unwilling and unable to offer guidance toward solving the real spiritual, social, economic or political problems of our day or to impact positively the lives of Americans.

Most Christians seem comfortable to set on the sidelines marveling at the spectacle of the culture passing by but never entering the parade. They do not seem to discern the spiritual battle going on around us. The scriptures warn of the danger of not staying alert and on the cutting edge of the will of God. Listen to the words of the apostle Paul to the church at Ephesus; **"Awake, sleeper, and arise from the dead, and Christ will shine on you. Therefore be careful how you walk, not as unwise men, but as wise, making the most of your time, because the days are evil. So then do not be foolish, but understand what the will of the lord is."** (Ephesians 5:14-17)

We, the church, have not always been faithful or loyal ambassadors of God's kingdom. We have been given the light and the truth to be the purveyors of it to the world lost in its sin and deceit. We have failed to recognize the profoundness and implications of our calling as children of God and we are not aware or not concerned with our national circumstance.

We have preached the gospel from the pulpits of the church and through our missionaries in far away lands but we have not believed the truth we have preached nor practiced the faith we profess. Therefore, our culture and the new generations of Americans are rejecting our message and ignoring the cause of Christ.

We, the church, are losing the spiritual war, in part, because we have failed to recognize we are in a spiritual battle to the death. We have somehow concluded that secular means fair and therefore we overlook its evil nature. In our utter deceit we refuse to accept the notion that there is a clever supernatural enemy actively at work among us and dead set on destroying us. There are those in the church who think foolishly they are clever enough to perceive his evil schemes and are powerful enough to fight off his spiritual attack. The

Scriptures teach us; *"Humble yourselves, therefore, under the mighty hand of God, that He may exalt you at the proper time, casing all you anxiety upon Him, because He cares for you. Be of sober spirit, be on the alert. Your adversary, the devil, prowls about like a roaring lion, seeking someone to devour..." (I Peter 5:7-9)*

Only the Spirit of God can battle victoriously against Satan and his angels. Satan has leveled his attack against the institution of church because he cannot defeat the true church. God protects His Church and promises it's members are eternally secure and *"the gates of Hades shall not overpower it" (Matthew 16:18)* The people in many of the mainline denominational churches who profess to be followers of Christ, but are not, are not able to discern the difference between the secular church and the true church. Satan has come in as a minister of light and we, like lemmings, follow along in our blindness not recognizing what is happening to us.

As a society we find ourselves embroiled in tragedy, failure, perversion and utter confusion. We are so preoccupied with pleasure, lust and fleshly entertainment we scarcely have time nor do we have the inspiration to consider our circumstance or its eternal implications.

The Church has allowed it's witness and ministry to become measured by and subject to the world's standard of measure rather than the standard revealed in the word of God and confirmed in our hearts by His Spirit. It has abandoned its role to be salt and light in the critical area's of our collective and individual lives and has willingly accepted the role the world system has assigned it.

There are few areas in the public arena that has more impact on the lives of Americans and needs to be impacted by light and truth than the election process. This process is vital to our nation because through it we select our national leaders. However the church has failed to effectively influence the process and/or challenge the destructive rulings of the judiciary that prohibit the church from entering the public debate over issues and candidates for public office. To justify its intimidation by the state and the world the church pretends to rise above the process as if it is beneath the dignity of Christ and His church to insure we have wise, good and competent government leadership.

The reaction of the church to the world has been to isolate ourselves from the reality of the environment and circumstance in which we live and preach the message over and over again to ourselves. We have, for the most part, failed to recognize how good citizenship and walking the walk of faith affects the issues that impacts the lives of our fellow citizen and impacts the growth of our individual and national character. God left the church on earth to be a dynamic force actively and aggressively working to redeem the world God said He loved so much that He gave His only begotten Son that whosoever believeth in Him shall not perish but have everlasting life.

Deceit from false teaching and the pervasive desires and appetites of our flesh have worked to lead many believers astray and caused others to become lazy, sleepy and indifferent. The church has not effectively challenged the deceit and evil within nor has it adequately warned the followers of the nature of the battle and the critical role of discipline and repentance. We have not believed and walked in the most precious faith we profess, therefore, worldliness and deceit has come in like a flood.

When I travel and observe the great cathedrals in Europe that speaks of a time of religious passion and fervor and recognize they are little more than historical reminders of the past and therefore tourist attractions I see the church in America following the same path. These monuments do not deliver hope and passion for the Savior of the world and they do not significantly impact the day-to-day lives of their members.

We must fight to insure the church and its people in America do not suffer the same destiny. We must not be another unsinkable titanic in which we fail to see our vulnerability. The indestructible titanic now rests at the bottom of the ocean. We also have arrogantly thumbed our nose at the dangers we face thinking that we don't have to be alert nor do we have to stand firm in the cause of Christ. We have turned "it" over to God thinking we no longer have to worry about it or contend for it. We think we are unsinkable as a church and a nation, however, we find ourselves badly damaged and destined to sink in a cold sea of deceit, evil and spiritual darkness.

The church has decided that we are to simply pray and watch God work! We surely need to pray, however, we must also act wisely, firmly, decisively, aggressively and promptly against the evil and deceit that works to distract and destroy us.

The church has used the following scriptures out of context to justify its do-nothing position: *Finally, be strong in the Lord, and in the strength of His might. Put on the full armor of God, that you may be able to stand firm against the schemes of the devil. For our struggle is not against flesh and blood, but against the rulers, against the powers, against the world forces of this darkness, against the spiritual forces of wickedness in the heavenly places. Therefore, take up the full armor of God, that you may be able to resist in the evil day, and having done everything, to stand firm. Stand firm therefore, having girded your loins with the truth, and having put on the breastplate of righteousness, and having shod your feet with the preparation of the gospel of peace; in addition to all, taking up the shield of faith with which you will be able to extinguish all the flaming missiles of the evil one. And take up the helmet of salvation, and the sword of the Sprit, which is the word of God. " (Ephesians 6:10-17)*

It adorns itself with spiritual ritual thinking it has done what it is called to do. Perhaps the church needs to be reminded the reason for armor is war! The church has been preoccupied with saving itself and promoting its programs. Meanwhile it has set its followers and the nation adrift in a sea of deceit, evil and darkness with precious few lifeboats and without the ability to see the rescue boats in the darkness that surrounds us. The prophets have not come forth from the church to give context to current events or interpret the times for the people or the nation and the church has not entered into the public debate of the issues that impact the lives of Americans. The strategy we need to employ is not to put on the armor so we can hide, but rather, so we are prepared to enter the battle.

Our beacon of light allowing those adrift in a sea of confusion and evil to spot a rescue boat is dieing out. Even when a few struggling to save their lives spots a lifeboat, they find the boats occupants preoccupied with religion and their own circumstances and over-whelmed with the battle. They find little Spiritual power, room or interest in helping their fellowman in his time of desperate need!

The problem in the religious institutions is spiritual just like the problem in our culture and our national government. We have a spiritually blind church, for the most part, attempting to provide light and guidance to a spiritually blind people who have turned the governing of the nation over to a spiritually blind government.

The Apostle Paul admonishes a church that has become worldly and has lost not only the power of the Spirit to bring deliverance to the lost through the Gospel message, it is lost itself because of its compromise with sin and has therefore lost its power to be salt and light into the darkness of the world. He said to the church, *"Therefore be imitators of God, as beloved children and walk in love, just as Christ also loved you, and gave Himself up for us, an offering and a sacrifice to God as a fragrant aroma. But do not let immorality or any impurity or greed even be named among you, as is proper among saints; and there must be no filthiness and silly talk, or coarse jesting, which are not fitting, but rather given of thanks. For this you know with certainty, that no immoral or impure person or covetous man, who is an idolater, has an inheritance in the kingdom of Christ and God. Let no one deceive you with empty words, for because of these things the wrath of God comes upon the sons of disobedience. Therefore, do not be partakers with them; for you were formerly darkness, but now you are light in the Lord; walk as children of light for the fruit of the light consists in all goodness and righteousness and truth, trying to learn what is pleasing to the Lord. And do not participate in the unfruitful deeds of darkness, but instead expose them; for it is disgraceful even to speak of the things, which are done by them in secret. But all things become visible when they are exposed by the light, ...for this reason it says, Awake sleeper, and arise from the dead, and Christ will shine on you. Therefore be careful how you walk, not as unwise men, but as wise, making the most of your time, because the days are evil. So then do not be foolish, but understand what the will of the Lord is." (Ephesians 5:1-17)*

America needs salt and light from a vibrant Spiritually alive church that is alert and morally strong. We need spiritual leadership that has a prophetic voice that is functioning on the cutting edge of the will, plan and purposes of God. The Church has lost its prophetic voice and its Spiritual power; therefore, it has lost its distinctive witness because it has become like the world. It is considered by the world to be ineffective and therefore irrel-evant. America has therefore turned to secularism and placed our hope and destiny on the futility of the minds of natural man.

Church, it is maddening to hear supposed Spiritual leaders predict that when the real America stands up we will find that America is still the greatest nation on earth, as if that is the standard, and that we will find our people are still deeply rooted in Christian heritage and tradition. It is not prophetic reassurance it is wishful thinking at best.

Sticking our heads in the sand and accepting the idea that this current amoral and/or immoral liberal culture that follows blind guides and promotes destructive ideas and life styles, are simply part of a spiritually dead minority lunatic fringe who will simply go away and everything will return America to her Christian worldview and her conservative moral values is a foolish and tragic perspective. Unfortunately, such talk is exciting and encouraging to hear, but sadly it is a pipe dream presented to disguise the problem and help us enjoy the trip to our complete destruction!

The truth is simply that America, as a nation, has rejected God, His wisdom and moral standard and the church sent to guide and sustain America has failed to provide salt and light and now finds itself in apostasy. America will not get better unless divine intervention inspires the church and the church inspires America toward goodness, righteousness, justice and humility before God.

The historic influence of the true church in America and the historic response of the people is the reason God has allowed America to survive as a nation as long as it has. The true church is the only instrument of God's purpose on earth about which the apostle Paul said, **"He put all things in subjection under his feet, and gave him (Jesus Christ) as head over all things to the church, which is His body, the fullness of Him who fills all in all."** (Ephesians 1:22-23) If God chooses to restore America it will be accomplished through the witness of the remnant of believers who comprise his true church. However, it is very unlikely that it will be accomplished through the apostate institutions that claim to be the church.

The world will not find the light of truth through organized religion or through the secular education we are imparting to our children. These misguided children will grow up to be not only America's political leaders but also leaders in the Church and society and teachers in our schools. Some will become business leaders, political leaders, ministers, priest and even pastor's educated through apostate seminaries and universities or through secular educational institutions or through the influence of a secular humanist government and the deceived scientific community that is dedicated to studying the delicate and marvelous creation and yet fails to recognize the Creator.

We can't seem to grasp the idea that these secular institutions are anti-Christ and have rejected God and His role in the lives of men. They will impart their anti-Christ bias to our children and our people. They have no choice because their deceit controls who they are and what they believe.

Many of our citizens are naïve and lacking in their understanding of how far American culture has deteriorated from its Spiritual foundation through the passing of generations and therefore they fail to recognize the profound implications of our downward Spiritual and moral spiral.

Many who are truly seeking God have walked away from the organized church because they have trusted and have been misguided by deceived spiritual leaders who they have looked to for moral courage, spiritual truth, direction, encouragement and inspiration in confused and critical times only to find more of the thinking of the world they were trying to escape.

Unless one is brain dead he has to be aware that we are all being lead astray by perversion in our arts and entertainment and by a secular humanist liberal media which, for the most part, is in the hands of men who have no regard for God or his people. They are void of spiritual discernment and they therefore refuse to seek wisdom, truth and/or to give glory to God.

Media is money driven and Christian media is no exception. Since that is true the Christian radio and television media is tempted and unfortunately inclined to air anything that has the religious label attached so long as someone is willing and able to pay for the airtime.

As brutal as this may sound, it is nonetheless true. Adequate financing and broadcasters with Spiritual vision are desperately needed in Christian media if they ever hope to awaken the prophetic voice of the church and become salt and light that will awaken the nation to our utter need and dependence upon the grace of Almighty God.

Seldom do those in the Christian media call the church to repentance or expose the deceit of government leaders or the foolishness of government policy or the lack of character of potential political leaders in an attempt to call them into accountability nor does it typically confront the foundational lies and deceit of some of the decisions of the judiciary or the decisions of our government and/or our nations leaders.

Many of us flock to churches to watch charismatic celebrities prance back and forth in front of huge audiences and television camera's attempting to entertain us and tickle our ears. These men typically demonstrate a Spirit of arrogance and present an image that is out of context with the Spirit of God as revealed in His Word. Many of them would have you believe it's easy to be whatever you want to be if you just know the right "Christian" formula, which they offer exclusively. They want us to recognize they have found the formula and won the battle between the flesh and the Spirit within and if you listen to them, follow the steps they have laid out for you and send money to support the ministry you will participate in their special faith and Jesus will remove all problems He may have put in your life to mature you spiritually.

The confidence they exude is an arrogance that attracts the flesh but it is not consistent with the humility of the Spirit of God, the soberness of repentance or the working of faith. However, they draw a big crowd and a big crowd means big money!

Some of them have become so deluded they believe their brilliant arrogance attracts special Spiritual power. God's Spirit simply cannot resist them. They are so anointed with spiritual power that it overwhelms Satan who is therefore no match for them. The implications are that if we would all simply follow after their message and example and adhere to the formula they offer and support their incredulous ministry we wouldn't have spiritual or material or relationship problems. Yet some of them have been married two or three times and they justify their circumstance by God's grace and they imply that your problem is that you are not following the correct prayer methodology or you are not casting out the devil often enough or that you are not pretending to put on the armor of God each morning or that if you are not speaking other than victory you can never hope to be victorious. They place great emphasis on the gifts of the Spirit and tend to ignore the fruit of the Spirit, which the Scriptures tell us is the sign we are to look for in the character of the one who professes to be Christian.

The point, of course, is that these ministries have huge audiences that finance big churches and Christian media. These ministries spend millions of dollars on airtime on Christian television and radio. Certainly, it is unfair to paint all large radio and television ministries with the same brush because there are many good and credible ministries involved in Christian broadcasting. However, there are only a very few Spirit led prophetic ministries that are on the salt and light cutting edge of what God is doing among His people in the church and what he is speaking to the nation and the world.

Unfortunately, for the church to teach the truth it has to come to some understanding of what the truth is. The church has existed since the death of Christ and yet religious teachers, leaders and the institutions they represent are still debating foundational doctrinal issues. Instead of resolving them we have chosen to create our own little doctrinal cliques (denominations) and declare our diversity a blessing. We have had to do that because much of what we call the church is not the church at all!!

All of us want to see the word, and particularly the message of God's atoning sacrifice and willing deliverance from death and deceit, broadcast around the world. However, when the word goes out it needs to be true, relevant and prophetic and the only way that can happen is if somebody accepts the responsibility for organizing and screening "Christian" programming.

On the social scene in America we find Sunday; the Lord's Day, one of the largest shopping days in America. The church nor the Christian media challenges the world's cultural influence, priorities or lifestyles or attempt to call it to be accountable to our Creator.

Many station owners, under the guise of attempting to draw the world in continue to play the worlds music with Christian words. They call it Christian music and entertainment and they justify it by trying to sell the idea that it attracts the world. Much of it appeals to the flesh of carnal Christians and our modern culture tends to ignore it because they are much better at it than we are. We, the Church and the Christian media, are becoming so like the world that our message and example is no longer distinctive or powerful.

If we do not wake up and "smell the coffee" so to speak, the time will come when the courts will determine that the radio and television broadcaster who use the public airways, in light of the need to separate the church and state, can no longer broadcast Christian messages, prayer, or music with religious themes over public airways unless that station gives equal time to atheists, pagans, cultists and heathens.

America will lose the battle unless, while the church still has the platform to speak from, uses that platform to awaken and challenge the church to become salt and light and the nation to become worthy of their calling. The airways will become secular and the mention of God's name or glory or the promotion of biblical principles will be against the laws of the land.

Christian broadcasting will become something like values clarification or social objectivity or politically correct discourse, or the value and grace of religious diversity. God, His son Jesus and the Holy Spirit and biblical teaching will slowly disappear from the airways of America.

The secular courts will once again become convinced this is the course determined for us by our constitution. First will come censorship under the banner of separation of church and state soon to be followed by radical politically correct censorship and finally we will not be able to mention God or His son Jesus Christ on the public airways.

The government currently allows Christian broadcasters to continue because their audience is primarily Christian and most of these ministries are not seen as a significant threat to the government or to anyone else for that matter. The movers and shakers in Christian ministry are feeling the heat of the devil and his disciples!! That heat will increase as the impact of church influence among the people diminishes.

Christianity has to become a voice that must be reckoned with in the social and political issues of our day. Christianity has to begin to present a power, distinctiveness, wisdom and practical application that makes a difference in peoples lives in practical ways. Christian prophetic wisdom and leadership needs to begin to occupy the pulpits of the churches and the airways while there is still time.

The instrument of radio and television Christian media must lead the way with an apostolic and prophetic voice to America. It is distinctively positioned to challenge, inspire and rally believers to become alert and involved and to show the lost world the power and distinctiveness of the Christian faith. It must challenge the church to become relevant once again in helping to shape the American culture.

Surely the calling and vision of providing salt and light must include informing the people and giving a spiritual, biblically perspective to the issues that affect the lives and concerns of Americans? Doesn't it include speaking out on the issues that are central to America's survival such as its leadership in our Judiciary? Church, in case you don't get it, God did not appoint a secular Supreme court in America to decide His will and direction for His people. He appointed the church to do that. God knows exactly where He is going and what He is trying to do. What we must do if we ever hope to follow after Him is somehow begin to learn to hear His voice and see His hand at work.

Are we Christians fresh out of vision? Have we grasp the world's vision and at best are wasting the leadership opportunity to be salt and light squandering the opportunity?

The obvious thinking of the church can be likened to someone who is given a gun to protect himself and instead of preparing himself to use it at the appropriate time for the purpose it was given; he shoots himself in the foot playing with it and finds himself unwilling, unprepared and unable to use it when he was called upon to do so.

If we want to continue to enjoy liberty and religious freedom in America we better join in the battle against the forces of evil that wish to blot out every trace of the God and of the bible from American life, government and culture. Our only hope is to repent and beg God to somehow return the dominant thinking of Americans to the hope and truth of His word.

My hope is to awaken and inspire those who have the opportunity to speak the truth and distribute the prophetic voice of the Spirit of God and its practical application to a lost and disintegrating society. We need to grab the opportunity and run with it!!

You can bet your life God is speaking to America and to His Church! The problem is that very few are listening and many of those who are listening are having a hard time interpreting what they are hearing because they have allowed the world to fill their hearts and minds.

His call to those who have heard His voice and responded is a call of service, good works and ambassadorship first and last. It is not this modern introspective Christian sanctuary away from all danger and worldly reality. That's more like Disneyland than Christianity. Besides that, Disneyland is much better at fantasy than the church. However, I must say, we are getting better!!

A nation of people who honor God's will reflect his love, wisdom, justice, righteousness and charity toward him and each other in their lives. The fruit of the Spirit of God as reflected in the attitudes and through the actions of any people group is clearly the measure of the character and spiritual health of that people!

If a nation is spiritually healthy and growing in their spiritual health He blesses their efforts and sustains them as a nation. He historically blesses them with great resources and places them in positions of honor, authority and leadership among the nations in order to bring hope, help, encouragement, wisdom and deliverance to the rest of the world.

If a nation rejects Him and His will and mocks His glory their sin is perhaps the most grievous of sins. He honors our choice to reject him and His Spirits leading. He removes His Spirit and His vision and turns them over to their reprobate minds to live and do as they please. The choice is a self-condemning choice because as the people become blinded by their deceit they inevitably become a degenerate and confused people lead by their deceit and their appetites and their intent becomes continually evil.

Historically God ultimately removes that nations Spiritual leadership mantel and the nation squanders its wealth and allows the deceit of the people to destroy the moral foundation of their society. He allows their deceit, lust and pride to lead them into division among themselves, which leads to wars and ultimately the destruction and/or scattering of the people.

The scripture teaches us that the rain falls on the just and the unjust! Therefore when a nation of people is being destroyed everyone suffers, even the Christians. The way America goes here on earth is the way we go! What America is destined to suffer, we will suffer. As someone has said, "you can run but you cannot hide" so you just as well get involved. Maybe you can help make the Church and the nation a better place to live and minister God's truth and light.

Who is God's voice to the lost of the world? Who has God given to the world to distinguish Him and His wisdom from the world system? Who does God depend upon in the world to protect His will, present His message of hope and faith, and demonstrate His truth, love, justice and righteousness? Who has He given the mantel of ambassadorship for Him and His kingdom to the world? His word tells us it is His Spirit at work through His church born of His spirit!! The destiny and survival of the nation is dependent upon the cry and testimony of the righteous and the response of the nation. The scriptures teach us that which is condemned on earth by the church is condemned in heaven.

If God judged His chosen people, the nation of Israel, because of their sin and rebellion causing them to wonder aimlessly throughout the world without identity or a national existence for almost 1500 years before he restored them once again as a nation what do you think God has in store for America if we choose to reject Him and Spiritual awakening?

It is in this sense that the dominant thinking of our nations people is a vital issue to Christian Americans. Our nation in that sense is either secular or God fearing! Our people have an identity as a society of people with a vision and a role in God's governing of things just as Israel was a people with a collective identity before God even though each person also had an identity, a role and accountability before God.

If you are a professing believer and you don't believe that God's revealed will is best for America you have good reason to examine your belief? The bible speaks of many who simply profess but do not truly believe. It is therefore healthy for us to examine ourselves and asks the question, "who am I and what do I believe and how does my belief manifest itself in and through my life? Do you believe that God, love, honor, dignity, justice, and the value of human life, morality, honesty, integrity, truth, loyalty and humility are essential to human life? Well the source of all these things is our Creator and Lord.

Do you believe that Christianity is not simply what we do but who we are? Do you believe we can separate ourselves from what we believe? Do you believe that we must live this faith and stand firm in its hope, power and truth for the sake of liberty, righteousness, justice, truth and charity for the Glory of God? Do you believe the most loving thing anyone can do for his fellowman is be a beacon of light and hope to the one who is lost and confused?

Unfortunately, there is a large group of professing Christians who have bought into the lie and deceit having adopted the philosophy that "what is best for America is to proclaim peace when there is no peace and celebrate spiritual diversity as if it is something to be proud of"! This is a foolish idea and those who hold it are fools mocking God and the sacrifice of His son as they proclaim the utter nonsense that there is more than one way to God and His kingdom.

The religious inclusive crowd has found acceptance by the world and secular humanism, which should not surprise us. However what should alarm us is that this foolishness has found acceptance by much of the church. Much of the Church has adopted the politically correct way of simply denying the fact of scripture, which declares that Christ is indeed the only way to truth and eternal life.

They have also adopted the perverted idea that peace is the absence of war and confrontation to preserve truth and righteousness is wrong. They mistakenly believe that this hypocritical unity will bring about religious tolerance and ultimately all religious men will come together and walk hand and hand in some sort of secular fairyland down a path of greater religious tolerance thinking it will lead to an inclusive church more acceptable to more men, forgetting the truth and the will and Spirit of a sovereign God, and therefore bring about a more untied America. This is a kind of insanity.

What do we do with the statement of Jesus who said, **"I am the way, the truth and the life; no one comes unto the father but through me."**

In their utter deceit the world and much of the church fails to recognize their unbelief or its implications. There are secular humanist religionists who consider religion as religion. Therefore they consider Christianity, Islam, Buddhism, atheism, and every other "ism" as religions we must embrace as if they are all equal in the sight of God. That kind of thinking borders on at best insanity and at worst satanic. The scriptures condemn it outright.

If you are a lazy, indifferent, carnal Christian or not a professing Christian American this book will either awaken you or it will rain on your parade. It will not tickle your ears! On the contrary if you read it I promise that the truth expressed herein will challenge your thinking and perhaps even change your life. Its message will be in your face every place you turn for some time to come.

The message of *"perspective"* is not original with this writer. It began with the old testament prophets and continues to be proclaimed by many others who have been awakened to our nations and our churches declining spiritual condition and authority.

Like the message of the prophets of old, and of our Lord Jesus Himself, the world didn't want to hear it! They hated the truth so much and were so intimidated by it they killed the messenger. For the same reason they didn't want to hear it then the world doesn't want to hear it today. When the message can no longer be ignored they will also kill today's messengers! It is inevitable that the time will come when the church can no longer be tolerated by the world.

No matter how unpopular the message it is an essential one and still no less on point and clearly for the ears of much of the church in America in our time. It needs to be echoed from the housetops at every opportunity because unless there is a complete reversal in the direction America is going in virtually every area of our national life as well as our individual lifestyles the prognosis for America's national survival is grim indeed!

Our national conscience has become so seared we are no longer sensitive to the truth nor are we inspired by it when it is presented to us and we no longer seek it. The deceit that is steering our nation toward the proverbial cliff is overtaking us collectively like a dark cloud that precedes the storm that is sure to encompass us soon!

A bright and encouraging spot in our immediate future that awakens us to recognize that God is still at work attempting to lead us back to Him self is that our people chose to elect George W. Bush, a born again Christian believer, to his second term as President of the United States. His faith seems to have had a marked impact on many Americans. However, it has exposed the hate and deceit of the secular humanists and liberals. This is a sign to many of us that God's Spirit is indeed still working in the hearts and minds of many American Christians.

The church has forgotten that the enemy of God is the enemy of his church and that enemy is out to destroy the church and any memory of God or His will and its impact for good in the world.

The world does not want God, His church or His wisdom to be actively involved and publicly engaged in the process of governing the lives of men or nations. The world has been victorious in America by isolating and discouraging the church from any organized effort at selecting and choosing the nations leaders who will set the course for the nations future.

Without Godly leadership what kind of leadership do you suppose we ought to expect? What kind of legislation do you suppose will come forth from secular humanists, atheists, homosexuals, pagans and fools? What kind of judges will be appointed and approved by blind guides of the world and what kind of justice do you suppose these judges will dispense? What kind of administrative governing bureaucracy do you suppose will evolve from the ungodly process we have chosen to guide and manage governing programs established by unprincipled men? Who is it that will administer the business of the nation and set the agenda for America's future?

Maybe its time that you ask yourself these tough questions America! For we who profess to be believers it is time to reassess our calling and mandate as a Christian believer and an American citizen to be salt and light among a deceived and lost nation of people.

We have been deceived into thinking that our government and the world loves the people and is committed to an agenda that will always insist upon and protect what is good, honorable, just, righteous and best for the American people. That is the same kind of lie Eve fell for in the Garden of Eden.

We have been educated by the world to place our trust and our resources in a secular humanist, atheistic, materialistic government to provide the wisdom and guidance and protection of the best interests of our nations citizens! You would seemingly have to be brain dead to believe it. There has never been a government capable or willing to do that unless its loyalties, laws, justice and its leaders find their mandate, authority and guidance from the God of the Holy Scriptures! America is headed in the opposite direction currently.

When is the last time you heard in the halls of congress the cry by its members to insist on doing what is right because it is the revealed will of God? When have you heard from any government leader that the overriding mandate of government is to uphold, protect, and exemplify the will and ways of God in all matters because God is the author of liberty and He insures the liberty and ultimate good for the people individually and collectively and His will is the most compassionate and just way to govern.

Let me suggest to the church that it just as well get in the worlds face because the world is its eternal enemy and is actively involved in the process of limiting the influence of God and His church in the world. If you reach out your hand to a secular humanist government you will pull back a bloody stump. If and when the public influence and spiritual authority of the church is weakened to the point of little consequence, the world will aggressively move to destroy it.

When the influence of Christian ideal's and values no longer impact public opinion in America sufficiently to hold the world and the secular humanist government it has chosen to lead it at bay it will begin to actively persecute the Christian church. Men will not only be fired from their jobs because of their faith and be arrested for public prayer and for leading public worship services, evangelism will be considered against the law and evangelists and ministers of the gospel will be executed for presenting the gospel and expressing their faith publicly! And it will all be done constitutionally!! The government will appoint priests and the church will become just as the Russian Orthodox Church became in the Soviet Union.

Most of the evangelical church limits itself to preaching to the choir and singing a few hymns on Sunday morning. They seem to think that somehow staying out of the fray of politics and out of the face of a secular government and world is the godly way. They feel justified in their isolation and deceit because they can point to sending a few dollars to a few missions somewhere and perhaps even sponsoring a few local outreach ministries. The church is also called to be salt and light and to be wise as serpents while being gentle as doves.

The Christian believer should be the wise and morally courageous man in the community in which he lives. I am not suggesting that every Christian is an intellectual genius, nor a David ready to slew Goliath, however, he is called to be a man of moral courage whose principles, witness and example are distinctive and his actions wise.

Men who walk according to the Spirit of God are men who can discern between truth and falsehood and can distinguish between good and evil and insist upon doing what is right. They should be known in their circle of friends and acquaintances as men of honor and integrity who can be trusted to act responsibly and in the best interest of others. They are men other men can look to for truth and wise counsel. A Christian believer should be a leader and a servant in a community working aggressively to glorify God and expose evil wherever it might be found and to promote good in every circumstance. Christian believers should be politically active and alert always guarding against and exposing wolves in sheep's clothing.

God doesn't suggest anywhere in his word that his people set back and watch the world select and elect atheistic and pagan political leaders who deny Christ and work to diminish any example or witness of his presence and influence in society. The separation of Church and State is not God's idea!!

Nor does God distinguish between church organizations and the state except to state to Peter that he should give to the pagan emperor Caesar what is his and give to God what is his. The only distinction God makes is between His church and the world. If we are in fact Christian people who govern a Christian nation then God would have us live and govern as Christians. Christians cannot separate ourselves from who we are when we are in public or private or when we are or when we govern or when we are in church. A Christian nation is not a secular nation.

The church seems to busy' itself by trying to put their fingers in the many holes in the dike while the water is pouring over the dam. Is the church ignorant of the impact of government and social leaders? Has the church forgotten the destructive effect of oppressive government and oppressive laws put in place by foolish, unwise, or evil men? Has the church forgotten it's calling to be salt and light? Is the church saying that being salt and light does not include influencing national and local direction and leadership?

Don't the leaders of our cities, states and our national leaders impact the life and direction of the people and the nation? Don't our political leaders carry the mantel of leadership, which levies upon them the responsibility to lead? Isn't selecting and following Godly leaders encompassed within the vale of being salt and light to the people of the nation in which we live?

The government created by the constitution we purport to follow is dedicated to the glory of God and the furtherance of the gospel of Jesus Christ in America. The government once guided by the Spirit and the intent of the constitution has become the spiritual enemy of Jesus Christ and his church.

God's watchman at the gate of the nation and the world, his church, has lost its vision and inspiration. It has become the proverbial fox guarding the hen house rather than the watchmen who is the bold protector of righteousness, justice and holiness. The watchman has allowed the enemy to enter the camp because it has lost its ability to distinguish between good and evil and/or its friends and its enemies.

The role of the church to preserve righteousness, justice and holiness in our culture and to provide the light that leads men to his only hope has become defused, distracted and confused with the philosophies, attitudes, lifestyles and idea's of the world. The church finds itself often attempting to undo what God is trying to do in the lives of people. It finds itself having been politically neutered by a secular and pagan culture that sees the church as a psychological crutch for a few followers, rather than the purveyor of the salt and light that will preserve and guide the nation in the wisdom of God.

When I read of the stoning of the Apostle Paul and of Steven and others I often wonder why we have no stoning and persecution of any of our Pastors and church leaders? Is it because America is not plagued with evil and worldly people who hate God or is it because our Pastors and their churches present little or no threat to the state or the world.

Americans looking for help in choosing political leadership and voting direction on political issues find the church leadership looking the other way. The church leadership attempts to justify their "hands-off" attitude and actions by explaining that the church would be overstepping its mandate and breaking the law if it was to actively engage in the political matters of state. The church has bought into the idea that God is subservient to the state, not interested in the state and decided it is God's will for the church to stay out of the governing philosophy or process and has no business in confronting the state on those issues involving the public expression of our faith.

It has not always been that way. The modern church has been put in its place by the world and it has accepted its subservient role carved out for it by blind guides and deceived legal minds under the guise of constitutional authority.

God ordered the rising up of this nation and then clearly intervened in the development of the documents that became the founding documents that would guide a new nation in a new way according to the words and spirit of the founders of our nation. Doesn't it seem ridiculous that God would carve himself out of the formula for building and maintaining the republic once he has put it in place?

The role of the church in American society today has limited itself to prayer and presenting the gospel of Jesus Christ in religious settings. Even that role is now limited by our government to other than organized public events and prohibits religious witness on public property or in our schools or on our university campuses. When we are ask what within us gives us the hope and faith to persevere we must be careful to respond, "the government has mandated that I must not tell you on public property"! Prayer and or presenting the gospel of Jesus Christ are against the law at graduation ceremonies or any other school ceremony in any public school.

How is it possible that we find community leaders and a community of people who see the swearing of allegiance to God as wrong and choose to prohibit it? Its amazing since it is the role of the church to reveal to the lost the only way man can be delivered from the curse he lives under and can thereby be empowered to live a life whose entire purpose and focus is allegiance to God.

Christian believers will soon begin to experience some of the suffering Christian believers have experienced throughout the centuries and most recently in the soviet socialist republic.

Christians will be arrested and publicly tried much like American authorities arrested and prosecuted card caring communists in the fifties! Only this time it will be American socialists, communists, secular humanists and atheists who are running our government who will be doing the arresting and prosecuting of Christians.

The idea that the church should be separated from the political matters, activities and the governing of the nation is utter insanity born in the pit of hell and sold to America by deceived men in government and in the courts and even in the pulpits of some of our churches. It is the height of spiritual deceit!

The irony is there is clearly no authority in our constitution to suggest the church should keep its nose out of politics or that the government has any authority to prohibit or in any way limit the churches involvement in politics. The only prohibition the constitution places regarding religious activity is against the government and not the church. That prohibition placed upon the government is from establishing any given Christian church or Church denomination as a state sponsored or state controlled church whose dogma establishes the religious practice and observance of the nation.

The church, in the context of a body of Christian believers who join together for the distinct purpose of insisting that there voices be heard, should be actively involved and in the middle of every political debate, political action, or political decision that impacts our individual and collective lifestyles, our God given and constitutional guaranteed freedoms, our family structure and safety, our schools, our churches and the free public expression and exercise of our Christian faith.

The church must be actively and aggressively involved in the establishment and maintenance of a Godly and moral environment in which to live, play, worship and work. It must become pro-active in the selection of candidates for national, state or local public offices of leadership in government and education. The church must organize itself to challenge and rebuild the entire public education system and restate its purpose, focus and vision and replace its leadership and many of its teachers.

Christian's believers should see their involvement as key participants in the election of any and every political leader as a mandate from God!! God has declared to us that he expects us to be salt and light and God ordained ambassadors who are to be witnesses, examples and protectors of His will and ways in a lost and evil world.

Christian involvement in the political process must be recognized by Christians as a vital part of God's will for their lives. The opportunity for Christian involvement is slipping away and we must awaken and act so long as we have opportunity in a nation that still enjoys representative government and rule by law.

The church of Jesus Christ is the only recognized group of people in America who finds themselves considered at odds with the law when they collectively attempt to promote and put into place national or local Christian political leadership. Our government protects the rights of any other special interest group to organize themselves for political reasons except the church. The church must wake-up and begin to confront the world's agenda.

The only religious threat our government seems to recognize is Jesus Christ and his followers. For believers and bible readers this should come as no surprise, however, it should point directly to the culprit behind the deceit.

The consistency of the worlds response to Christ and Christianity should encourage believers because its defiance reveals beyond any doubt that the world is evil and without excuse because they, each one, knows there is a God of all creation and there is absolute divine truth and they hate it because it judges them and their attitudes and lifestyles.

What has to happen in the church to alert it to the fact that it has drifted away from a significant element of its ordained role in the earth? The publicly visible church is busy celebrating and promoting its own glory, building self-esteem and big buildings while tickling the ears of those who chose teachers who say to them what they want to hear.

Our lord explained the tragic condition of fallen man; **"for God so loved the world, that he gave His only begotten son, that whoever believes in Him should not perish, but have eternal life. For God did not send the son into the world to judge the world, but that the world should be saved through Him. He who believes in Him is not judged; he who does not believe has been judged already, because he has not believed in the name of the only begotten Son of God. And <u>this is the judgment, that the light is come into the world, and men loved the darkness rather than the light; for their deeds were evil.</u> <u>For everyone who does evil hates the light, and does not come to the light, lest his</u> deeds should be exposed. But he who practices the truth goes to the light, that his deeds may be manifested as having been wrought in God."**

I have searched the Scriptures through over many years of study and prayer and I find no middle ground. God has no tolerance for sin and rebellion. The penalty is death and all mankind is guilty and lives under the curse of death trapped by his own deceit. There is only forgiveness and deliverance for any who will repent of their rebellion and receive the gift offered through the atoning sacrifice of God's only begotten son Jesus Christ.

The "so-called" great world religions who find their foundation in the life of various prophets all have aspects of their religious doctrine that are good in the sense that they have a moral code that encourages men toward performing good deeds and they typically recognize there is a God or prophet or some higher power they are ultimately accountable to. However, they all require man through his own efforts and discipline to pull himself up by his bootstraps, so to speak, and attain to the standard set by God. They do not recognize the fallen nature of man and the hopeless state of living in his deceit.

America was born a Christian Nation and it was clearly the intention of the founders that its institutions of government, education, justice and its laws, and certainly its citizens, be and remain distinctly Christian. The thought that America's greatness and liberty in the practice of religious freedom would be construed to mean that its glory was to be found in the diversity of all the world religions be recognized under the umbrella of constitutional protection. These are matters of profound importance and they have been totally misinterpreted by the Judiciary whose foolish decisions in this regard are systematically destroying our society.

How do we know the intentions of the framers of the constitution? We still have direct access to the writings of our founding fathers and to the debates they had. They were prolific writers and we can easily determine from reading their individual writings and public testimonies and the strength of their faith in God and how they viewed these governing documents in light of their Christian faith and how they viewed our nations Constitution and its government with and/or without God as the ultimate head of all government.

It is also clear that the framers of the constitution limited the authority of the federal government specifically to those areas authorized by the constitution. (Amendment #9) *"The powers not delegated to the United States by the constitution, nor prohibited by it to the states, are reserved to the states respectively, or to the people."*

Perspective is written as another voice crying out to our people to humble themselves before our creator and only redeemer. I pray that God will awaken a church and a nation that have lost their way and inspire them to become the light and salt they were called to be.

At any rate, every religious cult, pagan, new age, secular humanist, homosexual, racist, or satanic group who organizes and leads public political action, marches, or political activities designed to support the election of political leaders who support their special interests, or discourage the election of those who they consider to be their political enemies go virtually unnoticed and unabated by the federal government. **The only religious threat our government seems to recognize is Jesus Christ and his followers.** For believers and bible readers this should come as no surprise, however, it should point directly to the culprit behind the deceit.

The messages we hear from the pulpits of the churches on Sunday are rarely on point as it relates to what Americans need to hear and deal with if they are to truly act as lovers of their fellowman by being the salt and light we are called to be!!

We don't want to hear it because we American Christians are simply not willing to pay the price! Jesus said, **"if the world hates you, you know that it has hated me before it hated you. If you were of the world, the world would love its own; but because you are not of the world, but I chose you out of the world, therefore the world hates you... if they persecuted me, they will also persecute you;"** (john 15:18-20)

Every time our Judiciary rules against prayer in school, or prayer at public functions, and every time any expression of our faith is shutdown in the public arena our government has just taken another step toward removing the influence of God from the lives of our people. The less the influence and voice of Christian Americans is heard and felt in America the closer the time becomes when the public expression of our faith will no longer be tolerated!!

There are many other more subtle ways for government to administratively restrict the activities of the church, however, none quite as blatant as financially to a materialistic church. The government bribes the church with tax-exempt status to keep it in line politically. It has worked for the most part thus far and the church is bowing at the altar of mammon.

It should not surprise any Christian that a secular government bureaucracy would want and actively attempt to remove God, His purpose and His wisdom from the public agenda or arena. However, I am deeply disappointed that the church has been so easily deceived into thinking that secular is another word for neutral or objective. There is no neutral ground in the battle against evil and injustice! Either we gather with Christ or we scatter against Him!

The twentieth and twenty first century perception of politics, elections, government, taxation & representation and most social issues of the day are perceived by a majority of our people as distinctively secular. We have denied any spiritual relativity to the governing process or to the administration of social matters or in dealing with Constitutional issues.

God and His wisdom and righteousness and His Church has become placed in the social category somewhere beneath the many detestable activities engaged in by detestable people that go on in the private and public lives of many Americans of today's culture.

The perspective of the modern American culture is that so long as God is kept out of sight and does not directly influence the day-to-day lives or activities of people or the governing process He and His people will continue to be tolerated. If the Church should become the salt and light it is called to be it will bring about the mass persecution of Christian people and the public expression of Christian faith will become against the law. We are nearing that point in our culture as I write these words.

Those who believe and practice the Christian faith will be considered fanatics whose beliefs and faith is no longer *the way* but rather *in the way* of social progress. We have long since rejected the Word of God as the ultimate truth and we ignore its proponents and teachers as the ambassadors of God who possess many of the answers to life's troubling matters. However, so long as the Christian perspective is kept essentially within the walls of the Church and considered irrelevant in its influence in society it will be allowed to exist.

If you are thinking to yourself "the direction America is heading is total insanity"! Why would we chose to trade the liberties envisioned and established by our founders for the tyranny of an all powerful central government to whom we are becoming more and more dependent? Historically it has been governments that have been the biggest threat to nations and have ravished the people it was intended to serve!

CHAPTER ELEVEN

LOSS OF OUR SPIRITUAL VISION AND OUR MORAL COMPASS

—◊◊◊—

"Where there is no vision, the people are unrestrained"
(Proverbs 29:18)

America is a nation blessed more than any nation in the historical record. However, we have taken God's abundant blessing for granted and have forgotten to express our thanks to our Creator. In fact, we want more and more to lavish more luxury and leisure upon ourselves trying to satisfy our fleshly appetites and pleasures. The world has come to hate America not so much because God has given us so much but because we think we deserve so much more.

We have come to think the ideal America is one in which people are guaranteed financial security by the government whether or not they work or produce anything. We have adopted an entitlement mentality that insists that financing our medical care and our welfare is someone else's responsibility. We are being led to believe the true humanitarian economic and political system is socialism and that capitalism and free enterprise is an oppressive economic system that is bad for the poor. Those who have never managed a business that employ's workers and must be profitable in order to stay in business and provide jobs have been taught to detest the word profit more than the most profane words we can think of.

Without business there is no jobs and even though the taxes from business finances much of the medical care and welfare that millions enjoy in America, the government dependent Americans who receive the care and welfare financed by business consider business as greedy and taking advantage of our citizens.

In this philosophical insanity of entitlement we have come to think that attempting to hold men and women responsible for themselves and accountable for their words and their deeds is cruel and insensitive and therefore bad.

We have decided parents must not hold their children accountable for their rebellion because it impacts their self-image. The idea of discipline as an important tool in raising children is considered a bad idea. The scriptures speak a lot about the necessity and benefits of discipline. In fact it teaches us that the parent who does not discipline the child destroys the child. *"Those whom the Lord loves He disciplines"(Hebrews 12:6)*

We have come to believe that attempts to keep America a sovereign independent nation in which we protect our borders, govern ourselves and live our lives according to the values we consider important is a bad idea. We have been lead to believe that if we establish borders to define the boundaries of our nation and enforce the laws to protect our borders we are cruel and wrong. Protecting American security and our distinct way of life from the intrusion of illegal immigrants is not considered politically correct in much of our culture. They see nothing wrong with immigrants coming into our nation illegally and then attempting to change America to conform to their culture, speak their language and adopt their way of life rather than assimilating into our way of life. Our liberal friends see that diversity as good for America. We who recognize the price that was and continues to be paid by those American patriots who protect this treasure of liberty and abundance don't see it that way; therefore they are characterized as selfish and insensitive people.

The productive men and women in our society are held in contempt by many of the very people who depend upon them for their survival. According to the poles, the average American citizen doesn't seem to understand or appreciate what it takes to provide the jobs and protect the liberties they enjoy and in some cases demand as though a job and personal security are a civil right. Many do not seem recognize or appreciate the value of the liberty and opportunity they enjoy in America nor does the average American understand the basic principles or recognize the value of the economic system that creates the wealth that finances our standard of living and way of life.

In their ignorance many think America ought to adopt a global perspective and open the borders and allow anybody and everybody to come and live in America. They fail to recognize that within five years that mentality, if allowed to become policy, will destroy America. America will be just as bankrupt and destitute economically and morally as the rest of the world.

We tend to forget that when people come to America they bring all their home countries bankrupt political and social philosophies, false religious baggage and political agendas. This thrills the diversity wing nuts but it is destroying America. Spiritually dead intellectual morons in education have taught us and government to believe that diversity is our national glory.

Far to many of our citizens fail to give thanks for what we have in America because they fail to value our liberty and wealth. Many of them haven't had to pick up the tab for what it takes to sustain and secure it. They foolishly have adopted the notion that physical and economic security is a right along with medical, education, welfare etc, etc, etc,

236

however, they are completely oblivious to what it takes to protect and finance those so called "rights". Many of us are so into ourselves and our own agenda's we fail to recognize the incredible gift we have been given and tend not to value America, therefore, we tend to naively think we ought to give it away to anyone who wants it. They don't recognize that if we do America will become something else and will soon cease to exist as a land of liberty and prosperity.

I have traveled virtually all over the world and I know from experience there is no place on this earth that compares with the America of our founding fathers. It is heart breaking to see America lose her faith, integrity, honor, dignity and liberty. We are abandoning our Creator and Sustainer and adopting the bankrupt spirit of the world. Very few Americans in this generation have any idea of the poverty and slavery much of the world lives in or what causes much of it.

We have lost our vision and to get America back on track we must re-gain it! Where there is any vision at all it is not the vision of an America wherein our people are humble before our Creator. We are no longer a nation dedicated to the glory of God and to the manifestation of His charity and wisdom to a lost world.

The vision of an ideal America according to our culture has become one of an America where everyone does and says whatever he pleases and no one has to work, sacrifice or suffer any hardship and everyone lives in luxury. Our vision is of living in an expensive house and owning an expensive car or perhaps two or three cars and having a pool in the back yard. For some in our culture the vision includes an environment where perverts are free to publicly express their vulgarity and have indiscriminant sex freely with anyone without consequence. For some their vision is a higher debt limit on their credit cards, a morning after pill, bigger welfare checks, free day care for their children so they don't have to raise them, free medical care, a right to work law no matter our demeanor, laziness or incompetence, more free vacation and for some the ability to eat more fattening foods without getting fatter.

Our vision has become an existence where we can do whatever we want financed by someone else and without accountability for our welfare, words, deeds or indolence. We are a nation becoming FAT, DUMB, PERVERTED & LAZY and we want more and more of it. Unfortunately many of our morally bankrupt politicians are trying desperately to somehow provide more of it for us if we will promise to vote for them.

We carefully seek out political candidates without moral character or integrity because we are without moral character and integrity and we are seeking those who are willing to respond favorably to our demands for more of those things that are in fact destroying us.

The Spiritual vision that has historically led America is no longer leading our government or our people. We have failed to protect the faith of our fathers. We have rejected God and he is removing His Spiritual guidance. In the spiritual void our society is foolishly embracing secularism and pagan religious views. Our judiciary is attempting to unite us all as part of a national nondescript secular humanist system our people can foolishly and proudly adopt and refer to as diversity.

We boldly and foolishly proclaim spiritual diversity to be one of our great strengths. We confuse Spiritual diversity with religious tolerance. We like to perceive ourselves as a tolerant people whose great strength as a society is found in embracing any and all life styles, philosophy's, religious views and political perspectives.

We are becoming a people so nondescript that we have difficulty in determining who we are or what we believe and if or when we ever discover what we believe we will lack the moral courage to proudly declare it publicly. We are so confused we no longer communicate truth because it is not considered politically correct. We reject truth for concession in order not to offend liars, liberals, the ignorant and the evil in order to maintain this great example of tolerant diversity that supposedly is so liberating. It is utter nonsense and very destructive! Our strength and greatness as a nation is found in our Creator working His will and way through the lives of believers and it is not found in Spiritual diversity.

We have used the constitutional principle of religious freedom to justify relegating our Christian faith, which is the distinctive corner stone and the foundation upon which our nation was built and sits, as just another religious belief system among the many other world religions and cults that have come to proliferate our society.

According to the poles some 86% of Americans believe in God, however, Christianity has come to be no more or no less distinctive in this culture than a piece in the quilt work of religious diversity. We have rejected the God of Israel and His Son, our redeemer, and there is every evidence that God has begun to remove the guidance of His Spirit from us! To the atheist and the evil this social change is what they are seeking. God's Spirit and life appears to be leaving America to our self-destructive ways and attitudes. This is evidenced in the fact that we, collectively, are losing our Spiritual vision and moral compass. Our judiciary has determined that our diversity demands that our government abandon our Christian faith and embrace secular humanism. The Supreme Court has determined this was the plan of our founders and considers secularism to be a more objective way to govern the nation and interface with each other. Secularism presents an "I'm all right – Your' all right" perspective without moral standard or direction. Secularism is a lie and it is clearly not from the Lord. As God's Spirit abandons us we will become a nation of peoples divided Spiritually who worship and serve any number of foreign God's.

Perhaps we need to be reminded that our religious faith, our value system, our moral compass and the uniting Spirit that has guided us through the first 200 years of our national existence and established a way of life, a system of government and an economic system that has historically been the envy of the entire world, even with some of its faults.

That is until the Vietnam War! Until the 1960's era we Americans historically marched to the same drummer when it came to patriotic loyalty and the security of America even though a few of us were a little out of step from time to time. We shared the same vision, and the uniting spirit of our collective being. There was no confusion about who we were as a people or about what was right and wrong, good or bad. Life had spiritual guidance in which there was truth and purpose that went beyond satisfying the appetites of our flesh. That purpose was found and fulfilled in the greater good we were unanimously committed to.

When our neighbor was in need his need was more important than our surplus. Christian believers had a passion for God and the driving purpose in the Christian life was "His will be done". America was in word and deeds a Christian nation. We were sinners for sure, as is every man and women, but we were a God fearing nation of people growing and maturing Spiritually until the sixties. We changed direction and charged off in the wrong direction in the sixties and as a nation we have never looked back

The spiritual diversity of our people divides us presenting diverse visions and purposes that separate us as a people. Our perception of reality varies with the various visions our people follow. We fail to recognize this diversity polarizes rather than unites. We have divided loyalties and therefore different social agenda's and we march to different drummers. The scriptures teach us that if we desire to live in peace we are headed the wrong direction as a nation. *"Finally, brethren, rejoice, be made complete, be comforted, be like-minded, live in peace and the God of peace shall be with you. (II Corinthians 13:11)* The scriptures are clear regarding the hostility of the mind that is not set on God. The utter futility of Spiritual diversity is obvious to any who recognize the battle between the spirit of man that continually wages war against the Spirit of God.

Spiritually, America's government has chosen to throw the only true God, the God of the bible, into the mix of heathen god's proudly demanding that we give them all equal status and protection under the law. This is necessary in order to support the cause of secularism and the perverted notion of religious fairness. Sound ridiculous? It is utter insanity. We, as a people and a nation, are beginning to pay the price big time!!!

The church began its spiritual slumber in America sometime before the Second World War. It lost its vision and became prophetically out to lunch by 1960! The church in America slumbered in the thirties and forties while the church in Germany allowed Germany to be "sucked in" by a politically ambitious and evil pervert, Adolph Hitler.

While Hitler took over Germany and ravaged Europe the church remained quiet. AS Hitler began murdering millions of Jews the church remained relatively silent in America and the world cowered in fear of Germany. The Church failed to shine the light of truth on the evil nature of this man and his deeds. History is full of such examples. The church completely ignored the fundamental problem with Nazism and Socialism from the biblical perspective. The church would not publicly renounce Hitler even when it became apparent he was murdering millions of Jews in death camps and enslaving Europe.

How could the church in Germany allow the German people to be swallowed up by Hitler's evil? The same way the Church in America is allowing America to be swallowed up in secularism. It refused to be salt and light. Finally, God used Winston Churchill to awaken our conscience until we became so convicted we began to recognize we must accept our responsibility to our fellowman and defeat and rid the world of this cancer that was destroying Europe. There was no other people group in the world that God could raise up to do it. The United States had a moral obligation to fulfill and we did it!

That era is passed and the church is once again standing by Spiritually and watching while America is choosing to place the state above God. We have chosen to establish a secular government to negotiate between God and man in order to attempt to insure that God gives all men a fair shake. The Supreme Court has decided that God has no say in the governing process, in the education of our children or in the public affairs of our government or our nation.

Some of us lived to witness the ushering in of the end of the America of our founders by Franklin D. Roosevelt through his "new deal" philosophy of government.

The "new deal" idea began to mesmerize America because it was a government entitlement and dependence program in which government created a giant give away system that began to change how Americans viewed government as the ultimate provider and the final arbitrator of men's needs. Thus an era of government dependency and big government was born wherein men would look to the state for its health and welfare!

Indeed it was a "new deal" but it was the beginning of a bad deal for America because it would ultimately begin to enslave our people to dependence on government. There were several factors that inspired Roosevelt's "new deal" government give-away program. The late twenties had brought a crash of the stock market causing the layoff of more than 10% of America's workers. A major drought caused by five years without rain had destroyed much of the farmland of mid America. Many of our people had no way to provide for themselves or their families.

The "New Deal" was "A Chicken In Every Pot" deal provided by government. It was a blessing to millions of Americans and gave America hope during a very difficult time for America. However, it also began to teach people to look to government for anything and everything. It forever changed the people's perception of the role of central government and the church in America. The state began to become God and America began a downward spiral of greater and greater dependence upon government and less dependence upon themselves or upon God.

Unfortunately, when the national emergency was over our political leaders did not have the political courage to revert America back to responsible economic policy or force government back to its constitutional role. The people had discovered they could vote whatever resources they wanted from the public coffers and the government would simply take the resources away from those who possessed them and give them to those who wanted them.

The politicians soon discovered they could get the votes of the people if they could discover what the people wanted and then promise it to them. America would never be the same again! What has evolved is a government dependency perspective that sets as its ideal standard for America as physical and economic security virtually cradle to grave.

What had to evolve to publicly finance the give away programs was a confiscatory tax system that taxes income, consumption, services of productive Americans and then gives the fruit of productive effort to the unproductive or lesser productive through various entitlement programs. The government took over the responsibility God assigned to men and the role of God in the affairs of men.

The problem that has evolved is that for government to function under its new mantel as our keeper requires the government to systematically take more and more of our resources and liberty. With each new or increased dependency on government came the loss of a little bit more liberty, individual resources and independence. We soon forgot the individual freedom and collective liberty our constitution guarantee's requires a citizenry that is accountable and responsible for their actions or inactions.

Americans began to expect government to bail them out of every evil and human tragedy even if and when the action or circumstance causing the tragedy was the result of our own foolish or irresponsible decisions or acts. Americans, and our institution of government as well, have long since ignored the fact that public money was someone else's money before it was public money. Somebody had to sacrifice and earn it before government took it away so someone else could enjoy the provision.

Once we decided it was the right of every man to expect the government to provide for his welfare and his health care cradle to grave no matter how lazy or irresponsibly he chooses to live a government dependent society was inevitable. The perspective of far to many Americans has become that since it is government's responsibility to take care of me it is government's responsibility when I am not being cared for as I feel I ought to be.

What would be the price of entitlement? It would cost the productive men in our society approximately 50% of his gross income plus the sales, service, property and various consumption taxes he must pay to finance this huge government welfare bureaucracy. The indolent would no longer have to be responsible for their own welfare or that of their families nor would they have to become accountable for their unproductive and wasted lives!

It was never intended by our founding fathers that America would become a socialistic state wherein central government would become the re-distributor of wealth and administrator of a huge national welfare system.

The era of personal accountability, self- reliance and small government experienced the beginning of the end with the advent of the "New Deal". The American dream became the "New Deal". The national perspective changed and America began the systematic trade-off of freedom and opportunity for what they thought would be a utopia of government entitlement. .

Government must and will continue to increases the taxes on productive Americans to finance welfare and socialism until working Americans and American business cannot earn enough to pay the tax bill and still have the necessary resources to sustain themselves, their businesses and their families. As it makes less sense to work to pay taxes men will turn to the government to take care of them. The taxes will have to be increased further on the productive American wage earners and American business to finance the bureaucracy and the various government welfare programs. The ultimate end of this will be tighter regulation and higher taxes until we ultimately nationalize industry and services and follow the disastrous economic and government model that destroyed the atheistic communist Soviet Union.

This is the direction America is headed! America is turning to the Godless social ideas of secularism, socialism and/or communism, which incidentally if you haven't noticed, seem to dovetail into the liberal worldview held by much of our modern American culture.

At any rate if we do not reverse our dependence on government and stop our moral free fall America will become another Godless society serving a totalitarian government bureaucracy, rather than it serving us. Most of our people have lost the vision and have become totally deceived about what is happening to them and our nation. The American dream will become a nightmare if we do not reduce the size and scope of government.

If you are thinking to yourself "this direction is total insanity" you are right! – Why would we chose to trade democracy and the liberties envisioned and established by our founders in the constitution for a secular oppressive government that will ultimately destroy America, bankrupt our economy and ravish the peoples under its rule? The culprits destroying us are unprincipled leadership and our own ignorance, indolence, deceit, and evil.

This degeneration of a society is not a new process just created by America. Throughout the history of the world we can see the process repeat itself! Very few take the trouble to remember, notice or recognize the devastating lie at work as it overcomes a nation. Secularism is a deceit that keeps us from hearing the truth let alone declaring it with enough passion and consistency to warn the people of America in order to change the direction we are headed before it is too late.

In the 1992 Presidential election our President, George Bush (senior), was floundering on the rocks of defeat to Bill Clinton the governor of Arkansas, a relatively unknown challenger. Just a few short months before the election President Bush held some of the highest popularity in the media poles ever recorded for any President in American history. How could a man so admired and seemingly trusted by the America people lose the election as our national leader to a politically dubious and unknown contender from Arkansas, Bill Clinton?

Bill Clinton's character and political record was exemplary of everything contrary to what a suitable America Presidential candidate would be expected to possess. He was reportedly a draft dodger, a sexual pervert and a drug user. How could a people be so blind and mesmerized by such a man? President Bush, like many in America, could not believe there was enough Americans so deceived and out of touch with the America of our founders to elect someone like Bill Clinton to become their chief executive.

Bill Clinton was a smart man, not necessarily a wise man, and a good communicator. Unfortunately, he would say anything that came to his mind and continue to say it until the people began to believe it even though it may or may not be true. He presented himself as a man of conviction and vision even though he sometimes had little knowledge of what he was saying or where he was going.

Unfortunately, the vision President Bush had to offer America was to keep on keeping on. That was exactly the discipline that America needed however, America refused to respond to it. President Bush could not believe America had become a fickle, drive thru fast food what have you done for me lately society. He knows now!

President Bush forgot the history lesson of how Americans at home had abandoned the troops and the war efforts in both Korea and Vietnam. Americans are a people who will not even tolerate a long book or movie and definitely will not tolerate long complex wars or long church services.

Our Presidents popularity rating reached beyond any Presidential rating ever recorded and he was pleased to have administered a successful campaign in the Middle East. The troops, for the most part, were coming home. The economy was slowly getting back on track and the interest rates were receding. However, he failed to communicate a vision for the future of America to inspire and guide America's economic recovery and enforce our national pride. His perspective was that we just needed to keep on –keeping on!!

George Bush Senior was a good President and a wise man with many great leadership qualities, however, he lacked a critical gift and quality essential to a leader if you expect people to stay engaged and follow. He did not understand the necessity of articulating vision to our people or the role vision plays in leading people who are without vision them selves.

The problem was not with George Bush alone, it was with the American people who needed someone to promise them the moon and present a plan to get them there with little or no effort on their part. Bill Clinton was promising the moon even though he had never been there and had no idea what he was promising.

On a positive note God created us a people whose life was to have meaning, direction and purpose. Americans have long since abandoned the notion that direction is up to them and purpose and meaning is intended to come from the Creator. Americans have been taught during the last half of the twentieth century that it is up to government to give their lives direction and meaning. The mundanness of life and the discipline of endurance did not satisfy the appetites and pleasures of most Americans. Americans needed to be heading somewhere! It really didn't seem to make much difference where or whether it was the right way so long as they were on the way to some sort of change. Every mid-term election demonstrates my point.

The press kept asking President Bush during the campaign what his vision was for the future of America. President Bush couldn't imagine that the biggest issue facing America at this point was one of vision. He didn't get it. He kept telling America everything was good and getting better and we just needed to keep on "keeping on".

He didn't understand this ***"vision thing",*** as he put it, and he didn't understand the American peoples need for a national vision to inspire them. We are a people who need to be going somewhere and we constantly demand something more. From his perspective the economy was turning around, the war with Iraq was overwhelmingly victorious. The boys were coming home from the Middle East and the unemployment figures were not bad and they were improving. Interest rates were coming down and individual pay was increasing. He couldn't believe the people were so short sighted and ungrateful.

The war in the Middle East was short, victorious and exciting to watch on the evening television, however, it was behind them and now they wanted something more. The President didn't seem to recognize the necessity of communicating vision to give the people confidence there was a direction for America and we were headed in the right direction and were in good hands.

I personally found his attitude far more reassuring than the irresponsible blathering of a day dreaming wind bag from Arkansas who just wanted to be President and whose idea's were so heavenly they were of no earthly good. However, it is also true that most people wish to follow someone who they feel is headed somewhere. Unfortunately, many were a not so concerned with where he was headed as they were with the fact that he was headed somewhere new and different and promised more government give away programs.

For those of you who are leaders or have had some formal leadership training you will recognize there is a vital difference between a leader and a manager. George Bush Senior was a good man and a good manager; however, he simply did not understand and/or appreciate the difference between the dynamics of leadership and management. The Lord tells us in the scriptures that people are like sheep and they must have a leader with vision and without vision the people are scattered and confused. Our nations President could not understand what it was the people were demanding of him or why they were demanding it.

Clearly vision is the primary prerequisite of leadership! George Bush Senior was a good manager but lacked the vision necessary to inspire the hopes and dreams that would lead the nation into the future. God created us to either follow visionary leadership or to provide it! Americans, for the most part, are a people on the go and they demand leaders on the go who have an idea of where they are going and what we are doing to get there. When our leaders don't know the way or the answer or fail to articulate a vision for us to follow most of us tend to panic at the thought that we might have to be responsible for our own future.

Visionaries founded America. Their collective vision was liberty and free enterprise for a people of faith in a merciful and sovereign God. This is a combination that historically produces results like no other combination. These were exciting and inspirational times. The new constitution declared the unalienable rights of men given by the Creator, which created a republic of free people who would be governed by a government of, for and by the people. The potential of a new nation was exciting to consider and on top of it all the mandate of the government they established was to protect individual liberty and free enterprise.

The provisions of the constitution demonstrated beyond a doubt the presence and essence of the divine vision that led the founding fathers. America's evolution came out of a divine vision implanted by God in the hearts of our founders and the dream inspired many to come to these shores. Without that vision America, as defined by the constitution and the bill of rights, would never have come into existence.

The American people, who weeks earlier thought George Bush was right next to God in popularity and approval ratings, abandoned his leadership for the leadership of someone more charismatic, more liberal and more articulate and more exciting to listen to on television. It was a fascinating thing to observe. It confirmed to me that in lieu of Godly vision men will tend to follow most any vision that seems to give their life new exciting direction, meaning and purpose and promises them the moon! Not a very good commentary on our culture.

A leader without vision and the capacity to articulate that vision is, in fact, a contradiction in terms. A leader by definition is a man of vision. Positive change in nations, communities, and businesses or in individual lives is not possible without visionary leaders to guide and inspire that change and visionary followers to implement the vision. Vision is not an option. A nation of people must have a vision to follow to give their existence purpose, focus, inspiration and a sense of meaning and destiny.

Biblical vision has to do with understanding the purpose of God and seeing the hand of God at work. For a leader to have biblical vision he must be a man with a pure heart who knows and walks with God. The scriptures say; *"Blessed are the pure in heart, for they shall see God." (Matt 5:8)* The context of the word heart as it is used in scripture is the essence of a person. It is the spirit of the man. The man with a pure heart is the man who knows and walks in the Spirit of the Lord. This is the man who will see the works of God.

The Psalmist speaks of the nature and character of the man who is able to see God as the man with *"clean hands and a pure heart"*. It is the man who *"shall love the Lord your God with all your heart, and with all your soul, and with all your mind."(Matthew 22:37)* This kind of man is a man who does not have mixed motives. He is not a man of deceit that is one kind of man in public and another kind of man in his heart. He is also a man that has a singleness of purpose. There is a single mindedness about him that always leads him. The context is perhaps best explained in I Kings 21: *"And Elijah came near to all the people and said, 'How long will you hesitate between two opinions? If the Lord is God, follow Him; but if Baal, follow him."*

Matthew speaks of the problem double minded men have. *"No one can serve two masters; for either he will hate the one and love the other, or he will hold to one and despise the other. You cannot serve God and mammon. (Matthew 6:24)* James speaks of the problem God has with the double minded man; *"Let not that man expect that he will receive anything from the Lord, being a double-minded man, unstable in all his ways" (James 1:7-8)* He describes such a man as without faith and he describes the character of such a man as *" like the surf of the sea driven and tossed by the wind." (* James 1:5-6)

A man of vision implanted by God is a man with a pure heart and clean hands who can interpret the times and see the hands of God at work and is committed to follow the will of the Lord when he is able to discern it. People look to men of vision to lead them. Such men are single-minded men. There are many other important character traits that make a leader desirable, **but the one he cannot be without is vision.**

Vision is a mental portrait that exists in the minds eye and in the heart. George Barna, a polling expert, said wisely, **"to some the concept of vision may seem mystical and "out there", but to those who possess it, vision is as tangible as your tax bill. Vision focuses on what does not yet exist, but should exist...a preferable future.!"** And, I might add, it points the way and provides the inspiration to head in that direction.

Divine vision is a full-orbed view of the kind of life God would have us to live and the kind of world he would have us to live in. It is firmly attached to a faith or firm belief that we can experience or achieve it and that we are proceeding according to God's will and plan and that God is actively involved in its fulfillment. Godly vision has a Spiritually inspired passion attached that drives Satan and his disciples crazy because it touches the basic instinct in man to seek men of vision to follow.

Most wise men will allow themselves to be lead by a leader of vision, but they will not voluntarily follow someone who is without vision. They deem the visionless leader unworthy of their support. They are right. Men refuse to place their trust and future in the hands of a leader who lacks a compelling picture of a better tomorrow and lacks the passion and commitment to move the nation in that direction. To put it in perspective, who wants to be devoted to a leader who is pursuing nothing of consequence? **I can think of nothing less exciting than following the leadership of someone who isn't going anywhere.**

Vision believes, hopes and inspires and true vision for good comes from the Spirit of God. It comes to men as part of the package when men desire a better and more purposeful life and they repent and believe and become born again as a new creation in Christ Jesus. Visionaries become ambassadors of God's kingdom. It does not imply that such men are perfect, however, it does imply that God has chosen to use them to bring about change for the better among His people.

Men of vision often have a low tolerance for men who are attempting to lead without vision. Many of our greatest military leaders were great leaders because they were men of vision. The loyalty, commitment and single mindedness of these men was a testimony to their leadership. George Patton was one of the world's great military leaders because he was a man of vision. Men would follow the "GI" General anywhere under any conditions because he made them believe their efforts had a high and important purpose. His confidence inspired them to recognize they were following someone who knew where he was taking them, what they were going to do when they got there and why they were going there in the first place.

There were some things George Patton may not have been, however, in spite of those things he was perhaps one of America's most successful military leaders. Without his leadership world WWII in Europe would have turned out different. The record is clear; during WWII whenever America or our allies were in trouble on the battlefield and they needed a leader to rescue them our President and his staff, even though most of them were intimidated by his leadership, knew George Patton was the leader in Europe above all others who had the vision to inspire his men to get the job done. He knew the way to fight and win a war and to inspire his men to fight and win as well.

In all my years working along side men in various walks of life and commanding men in military combat situations I have never met the person who is inspired by the idea of losing. Leadership has to do with reaching goals. Winning requires leadership. Losing doesn't require leadership. The entire notion of politically shutting down a military effort that has been deployed to win and can win is a demoralizing experience because it is contrary to the very purpose and reason for leadership. The fundamental reason for leadership is victory.

Leaders who are losers are diametrically opposed ideals impossible to reconcile. The way to destroy a good leader is to place him in a position to lead and then deny him the opportunity to be victorious. The bible reveals the same thought, listen to the Apostle Paul speak about his Christian walk; ***"Do you not know that those who run in a race all run, but only one receives the prize? Run in such a way that you may win." (I Corinthians 9:24)*** Paul is giving the Corinthians a vision to guide and inspire how they were to live their lives as believers.

What leaders recognize as vision, lesser men often discount as nonsense. That is the difference between leaders and followers. General Patton perceived and believed that what he and his men were doing was important and honorable and vital to the war effort. He instilled honor, dignity, purpose, discipline and pride in his men and most importantly he never lost the vision, which led in large part to victory in Europe.

Unfortunately, a lesser man albeit a good man, General Eisenhower, a diplomat who ultimately became a mediocre President, was chosen by President Roosevelt to be the supreme allied commander in Europe because of his diplomatic and managerial skills rather than his military leadership ability.

General Eisenhower was a politician who desperately needed but was intimidated and often frustrated by General Patton's wisdom and competence and forthright aggressiveness. He ultimately relieved Patton of command near the end of the war. The managers, administrators and housekeepers and the politicians were and will always be intimidated by men like Patton. The Patton's of this world are leaders who have vision, confidence and an uncompromising attitude and focus toward the goal. They are not socialites who need the crowd to give their life meaning and purpose. They are men who give others lives meaning and purpose and vision and have little time for leaders who do not. Without leaders like Patton the Second World War and every war before and since or in the future will end like the war in Korea and Vietnam ended. Simply put we lacked the political and military leadership in Vietnam to get the job done. I am fearful of the need for aggressive leadership in the clean-up action in Iraq.

Douglas Macarthur was another great military leader of vision who led the war effort in the Pacific. He was a great leader because he too was a man of vision. He understood the value and role of vision among any people. He knew that without vision there is no hope. His promise to the people of the Philippine Islands that 'I SHALL RETURN' instilled the vision of hope and deliverance that sustained thousands of Island people and kept them loyal to America even as they were under siege by the Japanese for more than a year awaiting his return.

Many criticized General Macarthur for staging the walk up the beach for the cameras when he returned to re-take the Philippine Islands calling him a hypocrite and a coward. Douglas may have been a little dramatic but he was not a coward nor was he a hypocrite. He knew exactly what he was doing! The walk up the beach and the slogan "I SHALL RETURN" on every pack of camels inspired our government, our soldiers and all America to meet their moral obligations to the people of the Philippine Islands. A lesser leader would never have lead America to achieve victory in the pacific. He and his forces did return and when he did he delivered the Philippine people from Japanese control. Thanks to his leadership and vision the Philippine Islands are still our allies. If it had been left to Roosevelt, the President, the Philippine Islands would be controlled by Japan this very day.

McArthur knew the necessity of the vision that accompanies the inspiring ideas that drive men have to do with God, Duty, Honor and Country. America is in bad need of that kind of leadership in government and in Iraq today!

Beyond that McArthur's leadership in the occupation of Japan returned that nation to a productive economy and to national pride faster than the occupation of any nation in the history of the world! Years faster than Germany! People follow leaders of vision.

On the European front our President and our Supreme Allied commander Gen Eisenhower lacked the vision to do what had to be done. His failure at leadership was directly responsible for enslaving the people of East Germany and much of the rest of the world for four decades because he and his political leaders did not have the vision and moral courage to confront communism. Another leader on another front at a different time had to confront communism at the Berlin wall.

I have never seen one instance when the involvement of politicians in the theatre of operations or in their attempts to up-stage the Commander in Chief ever did anything to help us win any war. In Vietnam and Korea they were directly responsible for the loss of more lives than the enemy. The same is true for Iraq. The most efficient way to fight a war after congress has sent us to war is to unite America behind the effort and allow the Commander in Chief to administer it. Congressional oversight does not mean competing with the President.

Unfortunately, we have had to go back again to complete the job in the Middle East. The visionless among us, hippies left over from the Vietnam era are some of the leaders today and they are throwing rocks from the sidelines. However, honorable men of vision recognize we must finish the job because the people of Iraq depend upon it and the soul of America needs it because it is the right thing to do and our national honor and international respect demands it! Beyond that a true leader cannot tolerate any less!

The only justifiable reason to accept the privilege and responsibility to lead is to help people bring to fruition in their nation, community and in their own lives greater liberty, purpose, opportunity, fulfillment and a better more productive and meaningful life. Vision is essential although by itself incomplete without its soul mate moral character. If the people are going to be lead toward the fulfillment of God's purpose or calling upon their lives they will have to have leaders of vision.

There are many visions that lead men toward a variety of objectives. All of them are not of God. However, the bible teaches us that all men are in training to be disciples of God led by the vision and the calling to bear His image, speak His message and demonstrate His truth, wisdom and glory in our actions, attitudes, wisdom and words.

A Christian leader by definition, has a clear mental portrait communicated by God of God's will and God's purpose in His creation and His will in current circumstances based upon an accurate understanding of the nature and the purpose of God and the nature of Man.

America has lost the vision of her divine appointment. The time and inspiration when the Senate or the Congress is moved to do something because it is the right, just and timely thing to do has long since passed. Truth, honor, integrity and righteousness go over the head of most of our elected representatives. Most of these men are moved by the potential for political power, money and self-interest. They typically react rather than act.

America has several major problems that beg for congressional action. They each require leadership. Unfortunately our government operates without vision. We have no particular direction we are headed except where circumstances and the press or the special interest groups that finance the lobbyist efforts lead us. As a people we are becoming a nation of government dependent entitlement minded people dedicated to the cause of satisfying our own interests and appetites with greater ease and more luxury at someone else's expense. Our leaders respond and are lead by those interests

The vision of a strong, righteous and just America has been traded for a vision of more comfort, more lustful fulfillment and less effort expended to produce it. The principle goal of education today is to teach our children how to work less and make more money rather than to teach them to be people of faith, character and charity.

In 2000 America elected a man with spiritual vision and strong moral character. His name was also George Bush; the son of George Bush Sr. His vision is not welcome or appreciated by the secular government leaders in Washington D. C. or by the liberal press and the liberal members of our society. He has tried desperately to raise the expectations and re-instill the spiritual vision of traditional America. The world hates him because of his spiritual vision for America and because of his strong moral character.

The spiritual blindness that is falling over America has kept many Americans from recognizing and appreciating his vision. He has tried to elevate the level of the moral character of the men who serve in the executive branch of government. His leadership during the 9-11 attack brought him great popularity. However, when the disciplines necessary to live life, protect our security and confront evil returned the focus of our people on the day to day issues that impact our lives, the people became restless and returned to criticizing his leadership. The liberal, inspired by a liberal press, continues their quest to use the war on terror and Iraq to destroy his credibility in the eyes of America, however thus far he has been up to the task of defending himself. He won re-election in 2004 and it remains to be seen whether he will be able to unite a fragmented and fickle America into people to honor, integrity and national purpose who will carry out the work that must be done in Iraq.

There is no question that our President is the man God has sent to us. The question is whether America will be able to grasp the vision and chose to follow his leadership. If indeed 85% of America really believes in God President Bush should have overwhelming support in the poles. Unfortunately, he does not. At this point in the war in Iraq the people of American are looking for another exciting roller-coaster ride. The towers have been replaced with a park and the families of the victims who were given millions have want more and our people are all bored with evening news about the struggle to save Iraq from itself and instill a functioning democratic government.

The most popular cry and theme of the detractors is that we have soldiers being killed in Iraq. However, after four years we have lost less than 3000 soldiers in the battle against terrorism and evil. We lose more people than that every month to drunk driving on the highways in America. Where are all the protesters? We have historically lost many times that in previous wars for lesser causes. Wars are indeed costly and lives are lost. The only way to get a return on this incredible investment is to achieve victory!

The vision for Iraq is liberty and the right of self - determination for over 25,000,000 people. Is it worth the investment of resources and a few lives and a few dollars and a few years to deliver 25,000,000 million people from tyranny? Those who appreciate the value and understand the price of liberty would say that it is. That is the vision we in America need to be instilling in the hearts and minds of our citizens and in those who are fighting the war in Iraq. Our people here in America need that vision. We need leaders of vision in our government who have vision and are able to impart it.

We have lost the Spiritual vision that gives us a moral like-mindedness and the singleness of purpose to unite us as a people. Many of the elected and appointed members of our government are desperately lacking in vision and they fail to see the necessity and power of vision.

These same liberal minded people lost the war in Vietnam and they are mudding the water in the Middle East confusing and dividing the American people who are looking to leaders to present a united vision to follow.

I remember the war correspondents during WWII who kept us informed about the war and in keeping us informed inspired us with their leadership. Every movie in every theatre in America began the evening with a 3 to 5 minute patriotic film segment of what was happening at the front. We learned of the triumphs and the defeats but we were assured that our leaders were good leaders and they would lead us to victory —and they did. The reporters and the national media were cheerleaders to the folks at home and they provided the leadership and inspiration to keep America united and committed to the war effort. They helped America and her allies prepare for and win the wars in Europe and the Pacific.

PERSPECTIVE

A
Book
By
Charles D. Gaines

"Do not be deceived, God is not mocked;
for whatever a man sows, this he will also reap.
For the one who sows to his own flesh shall from the flesh reap corruption,
but the one who sows to the Spirit shall from the Spirit reap eternal life.
And let us not lose heart in doing good, for in due time
we shall reap if we do not grow weary."

SECTION IV

EFFECT

—ɰ—

"See to it that no one takes you captive through philosophy and empty deception, according to the tradition of men, according to the elementary principles of the world, rather than according to Christ." (Colossians 2:8)

CHAPTER TWELVE

A DECEIVED JUDICIARY
&
CONSTITUTIONAL CHAOS

—⁓—

"For many deceivers have gone out into the world,
those who do not acknowledge Jesus Christ as coming in the flesh. This is the deceiver
and the antichrist" (2 John 7)

Unfortunately, the Supreme Court, in its anti-God deceit, has created more pain and injustice for America than all the wars we have fought. It is a secular institution that sees its mantel and judgments above the will and purpose of God. The court functions in a secular "kingdom" of there own making where they feel they must consider issues so complex they reach beyond the justice, charity and wisdom of God! This is obviously the height of deceit! There is no such thing as justice without righteousness and there is no such thing as righteousness without God!

As a society we see the destruction, perversion and deceit working its evil among us like a cancer. We see this deceit and foolishness impact our government, our own lives and the lives of friends and family members. However we seem unable or unwilling to connect the devastating impact of the courts secular decisions.

This disease of secular deceit that seems to control the lives of some on the court is lethal. It is one of the most destructive diseases known to effect mankind. It is even more destructive when it is manifest in the judicial leadership of a society. Its impact on our perception of things is profound and subtle because it presents a perspective that often appears to be objective and seems good and reasonable to the secular mind. We therefore readily adopt the secular perspective of the Court. It is like a deadly virus that works slowly and deliberately until it ultimately brings forth death. It is the way that seems right to the minds of men but it is a lie and the bible teaches us that its end is death!

Unless our leaders and our culture become awakened the secular government and the secular court that rules this republic will have totally destroyed the America of our founding fathers.

Those who walk according to the spirit of the world are deceived and condemned. Those who walk according to the Spirit of God are delivered from the condemnation that accompanies deceit and rebellion. Deliverance is not a gift awarded by God for achievement! It is not given to those who have won an election or gained a certain popularity or to those who have amassed a material fortune or to those who have great power over others in this world. Deliverance is a gift given by God and it can only be accessed through faith.

Those traveling on the wrong road are a much larger group than those who travel the right road. The wrong road includes men and women from every level of human existence and every walk of life. It includes Congressmen, Senators, Supreme Court Justices, teachers, college professors, industrial giants, doctors, laborers, pastors, church members, and members of every profession who have placed their trust in secularism rather than in Christ and have looked to each other for glory rather than humbling themselves and seeking after God.

Mans fallen nature and the implications of the condemnation natural man is under was not a new revelation to the founding fathers. They knew the fallen nature of man causes him to march to an evil drummer that continually attempts to lead man down the path of lust and deceit. The founding fathers were therefore very careful to construct our founding documents with checks and balances necessary to protect us from ourselves and from the deceit and selfish interests of misguided leaders. They recognized the limitations on governments to govern a people whose interest is centered on themselves and their pleasures and appetites even at the expense of the their fellowman. They also recognized how impossible it would be if our nations leaders were men of selfish interests who walked in spiritual deceit.

Our founders recognized full well that power in the hands of men with fallen natures leads to corruption, evil, injustice and ultimately slavery. They therefore divided the governing power between three equal and independent branches of government to act as a check and balance against the deceit and special interests of each other. Beyond that, the founding fathers were dedicated to the proposition of limiting the power of government by limiting its scope and authority.

Contrary to the interpretation of the Supreme Court, and most of the judiciary, the founding fathers never dreamed the Chief Executive of the United States or the Justices who would set on the highest court of the land or the Legislators who make the laws that govern us would be anything other than followers of Christ

They were far more concerned about out of control government creating a nation of dependent servant citizens. They warned the people to not forget they had the ultimate responsibility for governing themselves and they must insure that government remains subservient to that cause and the collective will of the people.

They boldly declared that if government, or any of the three separate and independent divisions of government, became to powerful and no longer dedicated to serving or protecting the rights and interests of the people it was the responsibility of the people to remove that institution of government from power and start all over again with a new leadership, new people and a new government that would function according to the scope of the constitution and the intent of the founding fathers.

The role and scope of each branch and its limited power was spelled out clearly. The Legislative and Executive branches would enact the laws of the land in context with the limits and the spirit and intent of the constitution. The Executive branch would provide the governing leadership of the nation according to and within the framework of the law and the constitution and would manage the military. The Supreme Court would interpret the application of the law under various circumstances according to the spirit and intent under which it is written and according to the constitution. The principle scope of the Supreme Court was to be the protection of the constitutional rights of the people under the law of the land. They were also responsible to insure a law is indeed constitutional according to the original construction of the constitution filtered through the spirit and intent of the founders. They would administer justice under the law.

Unfortunately, the Supreme Court that has evolved does as it pleases which has created constitutional chaos, legislative confusion and a legal disaster for America. The Supreme Court through several critical decisions has done more to destroy the America of our founding fathers than any other enemy, internal or external, America has ever faced.

America was to be a self-governing nation ruled by the law. The laws that govern any society of people are a public statement of their deepest held beliefs and their social philosophy and values. Laws are established to protect us from the dangers of the unrestrained flesh of fallen man and they reflect the way of life of the people of that society. The laws of the land reflect those issues, ideas, lifestyles and attitudes which a society of people will or will not tolerate. The law would be the final arbiter and the court would apply the law and define justice for our society based on the Judeo Christian ethic. In the perspective of our founders the Lord stood as the authority that underpins our constitution and sets the principle and standard of the law.

The Constitution and Bill of Rights, much like the Ten Commandments of the bible, reflect the social and political stand on the major issues that effect our lives. For us to apply these constitutional rules and protections to our society they must be interpreted and applied in the context they were written and their application appropriately determined in a particular circumstance. This is an enormous responsibility and requires great wisdom and character to meet the challenge and perform justly. The decisions made by the Supreme Court have incredible consequences. These are not decisions that should be left to spiritually deceived minds.

As discussed earlier, deceit is a disease of the mind and heart inherited by every man. Many factors contribute to deceit, however, the significant contributor is spiritual and it affects the will of man. It creates a perspective that controls man's reason and will cause him to rebel against righteousness and blinds him to truth. Simply put, he is blinded to the source of power and the truth that guides his perspective and will.

The path of deceit leads to death and destruction. It is a trap that makes us think we can rescue ourselves from this devastating human dilemma. We cannot escape by ourselves or by our efforts! The spirit of the world leads our will and blinds us in our foolish and destructive thinking and ways even if by chance we may be reminded from time to time that we may be headed in the wrong direction. Deceit leads us in rebellion against God and therefore against truth.

Francis Schaefer, and several others, warned America in his many writings and by his lectures and teaching at Universities throughout Europe and America during the 1970's and 80's regarding the wrong direction in which we were heading. His writings were indeed prophetic. The conclusions and forecasts he made regarding the systematic and inevitable degeneration of America's people without God and the devastating results of the misguided leadership of Spiritually blind leaders have unfortunately proved to be right on target. I recommend further study of his writings to anyone who is not yet satisfied or convinced by my arguments.

He warned that despite the polls declaring that almost 85% of Americans believe in God that faith and its partner liberty are rapidly becoming a ghost of the past. He suggested we were appointing leaders who simply did not have access to the wisdom of God and therefore were destroying our liberty and morality.

He warned passionately of the forthcoming of a secularized government and a secular society that would become lead by sociological law. Sociological law is secular and it therefore has no fixed base. It is law in which a group of people decides what is sociologically good for society at any given moment in time. What the group in power decide is law in fact becomes the law of the land.

Oliver Wendell Holmes (1841-1935) fully supported the sociological law perspective. Frederick Moore Vinson served as Chief Justice of the United States Supreme Court from 1890 –1953. He totally supported the Sociological (secular) law perspective as a foundational principle of governing America. Listen to his remarks regarding constitutional law, *"Nothing is more certain in modern society than the principle that there are no absolutes."* He was a fool! There are absolutes and he simply was not aware of them.

Dr Schaefer warned that a time would come when we would no longer value human life. We would not only abort the birth of children we would eventually murder the elderly and infirmed because of the cost to care for them and the need of people to service their needs. He spoke of the time when the debate over life or death for the infirmed would be a serious debate. He spoke of secularization of America and the discarding of our constitutional protections. He spoke of the self-destruction of our nation and society.

Sociological, secular, law has moved the United States of America away from the foundation of belief in a sovereign Creator and His law and the unalienable rights that are the foundation of all liberty. Sociological law has also moved us away from the constitution. William Bentley Ball, Chairman of the Federal Bar Association on Constitutional law from 1970-1974, wrote a paper entitled, "Religious Liberty: The Constitutional Frontier". He wrote, *"secularism militates against religious liberty, and indeed against personal freedoms generally, for two reasons: first, the familiar fact that secularism does not recognize the existence of the "higher Law"; second, because, that being so, secularism tends toward decisions based on the pragmatic public policy of the moment and inevitably tends to resist submitting of those polices to the "higher(law) criteria of a constitution."*

Clearly America has moved away from the Constitution in several critical court rulings that have lead the way toward secularism. In point of fact the First Amendment rulings of the court have proved to remove or reverse the protections and the declared purpose and intent of the First Amendment. The historical record reveals that the First Amendment was established for two distinct purposes. The first was to make sure there would be no established national Church, or sect, by the federal union. There would be no "Church of the United States" according to James Madison (1751-1836). He clearly articulated the concept of separation. His concerns were in the context of protecting the rights of every Christian to worship freely. The context of Religious liberty as established in the constitution had to do with the recognition of the various <u>Christian denominations</u> as equal before the state.

The First Amendment established the rights of the various Christian denominations to worship according to the Christian doctrine they believed and practiced. Madison stated that his concern was **"the people feared one sect might obtain a preeminence, or that two Christian denominations might join together and establish religious doctrine to which the others would be compelled to conform."** His idea of separation was to protect religious freedom and not limit or destroy it.

It needs to be stated that the idea of separation was never intended to consider the protection of the rights of the various world religions or religious cults. In the eyes of the founders the Christian religion was the religion of America. Since America was a Christian nation their concern was specifically addressed at protecting the various expressions of the Christian Church. They clearly wanted to keep the government from establishing one or the other denominations of the Christian Church as the Church of America.

The second purpose of the First Amendment was the very opposite from the interpretation of today's Supreme Court. The Amendment expressly states that government should not impede or interfere with the free practice or exercise of religion. Listen to what Justice Douglas wrote for the majority opinion of the Supreme Court in the United States v. Ballard in 1944: *"The First Amendment has a dual aspect. It not only "forestalls compulsion by law of the acceptance of any creed for the practice of any form of worship" but it also "safeguards the free exercise of the chosen form of religion."*

The Supreme Court today has determined that religious practice and worship in public is prohibited because it would tend to establish a state religion. This is a judgment that defies the intention and plain meaning of the first amendment. The clear intention of the court today through the concept of separation is one of silencing the church and the believer rather than protecting the free exercise of religious practice.

The current interpretation by the Supreme Court is that there is a separation to be maintained by Court edict that establishes totally a secular state that will prohibit religious practice in public. It potentially prohibits religious practice or observance from any institution or forum controlled by the state. Thus far the Supreme Court has opened the door for other lesser courts to require the prohibition of prayer, worship or the display of Christian symbols in the public forum. Special interest atheist and secular humanist groups are working actively to expand the impact of this ruling to include the airways, television, telephones etc. This is truly ironic because the only reason for the constitutional protection of religious freedom was to insure that people could observe religious practice and worship **in public**!

The consequence, of course, of the "Separation" decision has lead to the removal of religion as an influence in civil government, in the public forum or in the education of our children. It was a devastating ruling by the Court!

John W. Whitehead in his book entitled, "The Second Revolution" states, *"separation is a false dictum used to restrict the influence of Christian or biblical ideas".* He is obviously correct! The perspective of separation is totally out of context with the intentions of our founding fathers and the notion would have appalled them.. Expressing our mutual reliance upon God was this nations foundation and it was as natural as breathing to the founding fathers and the citizens of the colonies.

The federal government recognized that adopting a particular denomination of the Christian religion as the federally sponsored church would alienate rather than unite the colonies of the offended sects. Beyond that, many of the settlers were not religionists however they were followers of Christ and they all taught that mans best hope was to follow the teaching of Jesus Christ. Therefore, they did not consider the relatively minor doctrinal differences between the denominations as significant so long as it was clear they were followers of Christ and a people whose motto was "In God We Trust"!

"In God We Trust" declared the foundational truth and principle on which this nation was founded. William Penn (1644-1718) expressed the truth clearly, *"If we are not governed by God, then we will be ruled by tyrants".* The simple truth is whose wisdom do you think we should follow to govern us? Should we follow Satan and the mind and heart of the fallen nature of man or should we follow the wisdom of God?

It is a matter of historical fact that the founding fathers firmly believed and publicly declared that the public interest was best served by the promotion of religious practice and observance. The Northwest Ordinance of 1787 set aside federal property in the territories for schools. It was passed by congress in 1789. It states *"Religion, morality, and knowledge being necessary to good government and the happiness of mankind…etc, etc, etc."* In 1811 the court of New York upheld an indictment for blasphemous utterances against Christ. In it's ruling, written by Chief Justice Kent, the court said, *"We are Christian people, and the morality of the country is deeply engrafted upon Christianity"*. Some fifty years later the (1861) court declared *"Christianity may be conceded to be the established religion"* of the United States of America.

The Pennsylvania state court affirmed the conviction of a man on charges of blasphemy against the Holy Scriptures. The court said, *"Christianity, general Christianity, is and always has been, a part of the common law…….not Christianity founded on any particular religious tenets; nor Christianity with an established church and tithes and spiritual courts; but Christianity with liberty of conscience to all men"*

Sir William Blackstone (1723-1780) was an English Jurist who wrote (in the 1760's) a very famous work called *"Commentaries on the Law of England"*. At the time of the Declaration of Independence there were perhaps more copies of his commentaries in America than in England. These commentaries shaped the perspective of American Law and established for the judiciary, and for The United States of America , the foundations of law. He declared there were only two foundations for law. They were *nature* and *revelation, the Holy Scriptures*. Until 1970 to have not been a student and master of the Blackstone Commentaries would have kept you from graduating from law school.

There were many other noted jurists and professors who confirm our foundation. Joseph Story in his 1829 inaugural address as Dane Professor of Law at Harvard University stated, *"There never has been a period in which Common Law did not recognize Christianity as laying its foundation."*

John Adams (1735 –1826) declared that our *law was rooted in a common moral and religious tradition, one that stretched back to the time Moses went up on Mount Sinai*. Similarly almost everyone agreed that the foundation of our liberties were God-given and should be exercised responsibly. He went on to declare the distinction between liberty and license.

Only a fool or a person with a rebellious spirit or evil intent would challenge the reality that Protestant Christianity was the foundation of law and the American culture. It was the foundation of an America system of morality and values, which would go essentially unchallenged until the 1920's when Protestant custom and morality began to be challenged.

What has changed in America? Surely God has not changed! His word says: *"Jesus Christ is the same yesterday and today, yes and forever." (Hebrews 13:8)* The Constitution has not changed! The copy of the constitution displayed in our nations capitol reads exactly as it read when it was signed. The wording of the Amendments has not changed since they were adopted. The founding fathers have not changed their minds. They have all been dead for almost 200 years! Truth has not changed. Truth has always been the facts presented in context. The Holy Scriptures have not changed!

So what has changed? It is we who have changed! We have determined that modern liberal interpretation of the truth by twenty first century Americans is a wiser perspective and therefore more responsive to the way of life that exists in the twenty first century.

Therefore we consider a modern interpretation (spin) of our constitutional rights as more accurate because it makes more sense to the mind of the man of the twenty-first century. Whether it is closer to the intent of the founders and the will of God is not as important to us as whether it better meets the introspective needs, appetites, pleasures and lusts on display during the twenty first century.

We have somehow determined that a wiser modern interpretation is much closer to the will and purpose of God than the declarations and judgments of the men who authored the founding documents. Sound a little arrogant and stupid? That's because it is!

The court justifies this nonsense with another slogan the liberal contingency has adopted; "The Constitution is a living document". Which is code that says we can interpret it any way we want because it is a work in progress. Ultimately it means that America does not have a definitive distinction or standard regarding foundational truth, or who we are as a people, or what we believe, or what our purpose for existence is, or what moral code we live by.

The significant advances of America during the past half- century have not been in character, but rather technical and economical. During this time the Supreme Court has made some unfortunate decisions that have created an America contrary to the America of our founding fathers. They have explained and justified their decisions with pompous words that build upon a foundation of other misguided and out of context court judgments than the truth. They have made some disastrous judgments that have caused the murder of millions of unborn babies and given sanction and protection to the porn industry and they finally made America a secular nation. They established our government as a secular government, which took prayer out of school and prohibited the public expression of our faith. They have judged as if the people who established the constitution were to simple minded to really determine what is right and wrong and what they meant or did not mean.

Deceit is not a disease that only effects the ignorant and downtrodden. It equally affects the intellectual, the rich, the educated and the powerful including Supreme Court Justices. It also impacts the minds and hearts of professors of law schools and teachers throughout academia. In point of fact, there are more liberal college professors working in academia teaching our children, as expressed as a percentage of our citizens, than the liberal contingency found in any other sector of our citizenry.

Most of them shutter at the thought of a Christian nation of people because truth will reveal who and what they are. Truth is the last thing they are interested in! They have been taught to despise God and our free enterprise and capitalistic system. Profit is an evil concept to them because they have been taught to philosophically endorse socialism. They have been taught the secular notion that men are inherently good without God. They have been taught that responsible thought and actions are bigoted and bad. False teachers have led them and now they are false teachers leading others. Many of them really believe they are the ones who ought to be in control because they are the ones who really know what is right for America. They have adopted the liberal (secular) worldview of virtually everything. They have been taught and they live a lie and want to force the rest of us to adopt it. They have been actively involved in changing history to support their liberal agenda. They are winning the battle because they have the attention of the minds of our children.

What boggles the mind is that American parents, including Christian parents, often scramble financially to insure their children have the opportunity to get into these secular institutions. Our institutions of higher learning are the spawning grounds of the secular perspective. They are destroying the minds and hearts of our children and we are allowing them to do it. They fill the young minds of students with philosophical nonsense and they rob students of the only hope they have. A majority of these teachers are without faith. *"They pay attention to deceitful spirits and doctrines of demons, by means of the hypocrisy of liars seared in their own conscience as with a branding iron." (I Timothy: 1-2)* Unfortunately naïve Students eager to learn and inflated with the notion of the importance of what they are learning and intimidated by the prestige the world gives to these supposed great secular institutions of learning have their minds filled with the same hypocrisy of liars. They come to these institutions to be received by fools and false teachers perceived as wise men and women. They are like lambs brought to a slaughter.

America needs to wake up! Justice and righteousness lose their identity and nothing is further from the truth than the foolishness our children are being taught in the public education system and in many of our nations colleges and universities.

The Supreme Court is a prime example of the danger and destructive impact of deceived men who are products of this perverted system and appointed to high office that requires them to make critical decisions that impact the soul of America.

The Court has arrogantly disregarded or twisted the Constitutional protections in several critical decisions. Beyond this, they have taken it upon themselves to usurp the authority of the Executive branch of government and through the unconstitutional invention of a process called **"judicial review"** they have usurped legislative authority denied them by the constitution. They have become the fox guarding the hen house and they continue on their destructive path unchecked by the other two branches of government or by the people.

The historic evidence is overwhelming and incontrovertible that God inspired a hand full of men to found this republic and create the foundational documents that would inspire and guide her. These documents sought and found their authority and governing principles in the word and wisdom of God as revealed in the Christian bible. These inspired ideas, if they are to properly guide us, must be interpreted in their clear meaning and the clear intent of the founding fathers.

The declaration of independence and the constitution with its amendments are documents distinctively unique in annals of history because their thrust and principal focus was humility before and honor to a superintending and righteous God. Their overriding purpose was to create human government that would reflect and extend God's love, righteousness, justice, grace and liberty to a people through a government of His people, by His people and for His people.

America would be a people and a government guided by law and the laws that were to guide us would be biblically inspired, righteous and just laws. They would be executed the same for every citizen! The laws of this nation would be the road map that would guide us socially. They would define our character as a nation of people. The values that would guide our nation and the foundation of the laws that would govern us were taken directly from the word of God. They reflected the will, the justice and the grace of God as best they understood it. They, when properly administered, would make the United States of America an ambassador for God in the world.

For the United States to be given birth it had to separate its ties with Europe and become a new creation. The declaration of independence is the document that separated this people from an oppressive government whose tentacles had reached from Great Britain to the shores of this new land bringing a new vision and a new government. The essence of the declaration is included in these remarks:" **we hold these truths to be self-evident, that all <u>men are created</u> equal; that they are <u>endowed by their Creator</u> with certain unalienable rights; that among these are life, liberty, and the pursuit of happiness. That to secure these rights, governments are instituted among men, deriving their just powers from the consent of the governed; that, whenever any form of government becomes destructive of these ends, it is the right of the people to alter or abolish it, and to institute a new government, <u>laying its foundation on such principles,</u> <u>and organizing its power in such form</u>, as to them shall seem most likely to effect their safety and happiness."**

This new government would recognize certain rights as divine in origin, which cannot be separated from man by men or governments. They are rights established under God's authority and stated to be fundamental to human existence. The founding fathers considered these rights to be held supreme and go beyond the purview or authority of human government to limit, regulate or in any way to infringe upon. These unalienable rights have to do with mans life and liberty and they are foundational to what distinguishes America and Americans from the rest of the nations of the world.

These fundamental God given rights would become the distinctive foundational principles of our existence. They would be the essence of the character of our national existence and it would become the purview of our national government to protect these principles from encroachment from either outside our inside infringement..

Upon the heels of this declaration would come the constitution whose overriding theme and purpose would be to create a central government to secure and guarantee individual liberty and freedom from the intervention of the institution of government itself or from the intervention of foreign governments or people groups. Listen carefully to the introductory paragraph of the constitution, **"we the people of the united states, in order to form a more perfect union, establish justice, insure domestic tranquility, provide for the common defense, promote the general welfare, and secure the blessings of liberty to ourselves and our posterity, do ordain and establish this constitution for the United States of America."**

The constitution itself would spell out our national purpose and in its articles (of which their were seven) would establish the type of government, its method of formation, its authority and responsibilities, and how its leaders were to be chosen and/or removed from office.

On the heal's of these articles came 10 amendments which would spell out more specifically the rights that would protect citizens against government encroachment. This document, referred to as the bill of rights, would outline more specifically those primary individual rights considered vital to the founders to sustain a free society. They were rights to publicly expressed religious freedom, the right to speak out for the cause of truth and justice without fear of reprisal by government, the right to protect yourself by bearing arms from any who would attempt to steal your property or dignity of person, the guarantee of justice supported by the right to a speedy trial by a jury of peers and the prohibition and/or limited authority of government to infringe in these specific areas.

The bill of rights would first and foremost, as part of its guarantee to protect our personal liberty from government intervention in some very special areas, establishes for all the world to see those values and liberties that defined liberty and freedom for Americans.

One thing very clear is they wanted to carefully protect these freedoms from erosion for the generations to follow! When governments infringed upon these freedoms the society, by constitutional definition, would no longer be considered, by our founding fathers, to be free!

The first amendment spells out the essence of freedom. It deals with the freedoms of **religion, speech, press, assembly and petition for redress of grievances.** These were obviously matters of highest priority in the minds and hearts of our founding fathers. These are all matters that are designed to limit government and protect citizens! Listen carefully to these words with your mind and heart as you read them. **"Congress shall make no law respecting an establishment of religion, or prohibiting the free exercise thereof; or abridging the freedom of speech, or of the press, or the right of the people peaceably to assemble, and to petition the government for a redress of grievances."**

This is certainly a mouthful. These notions emerge from the will and heart of our Creator who has decided that man must have the right to choose for himself the direction his life will take and his right to choose must be protected. Virtually every special interest group in America has had to face the reality and authority of these constitutional guarantees.

The judiciary has usurped authority having, either through ignorance or agenda, ignored and/or deliberately set aside certain constitutionally guaranteed freedoms and protections to justify their decisions. First, in order to mold or completely disregard the essence of our foundational documents, it became necessary for the Supreme Court to define the constitution of the United States as a living document. Living, in this context, means that the constitution as originally constructed according to the spirit and intention of the founders is no longer the foundation of our national existence and character as it was written. A living document is one that can be revised and/or its original meaning changed. Changed by whom and to what? Changed through misguided interpretation by the Supreme Court to embrace whatever appeals to the court. Therefore the constitution and its amendments are no longer the final authority that protects our freedom, defines our character as a nation, determines how we are to live and be governed or what we hold to be true and of supreme importance to our society and nation. Who is the final authority then? Bingo!! It has become the Supreme Court!!

The Supreme Court and the living document crowd have placed America on quicksand, which is as unstable as the fickleness of the secular mind. It is destroying the essence of American tradition by interpreting the constitution and the associated founding documents as a work in progress rather than a firm foundation.

For the Judiciary to promote its liberal agenda it had to take the next step and establish itself as the body of government who had authority over all other branches of government to disregard the Spirit and intent of the law and in point of fact legislate their point of view into the law of the land.

Unfortunately, the Supreme Court has provided activist support for the active anti-American liberal fringe group of elitists working within our nation to destroy the America of our founding fathers through the court system. Liberalism has created a culture that is *"destructive, disobedient, irresponsible, haters of good, filled with unrighteousness, wickedness, greed, full of envy, strife, deceit and malice; they are gossips, slanderers, haters of God, insolent, arrogant, boastful, inventers of evil, untrustworthy, unloving, unmerciful, without understanding."* They are systematically, with the help and support of the Supreme Court, setting a course to destroy America.

Since 1803 in a Supreme Court case called "Marbury versus Madison" the court was called upon to rule on the scope of its authority. A new term came forth from this case that would over the years become the common understanding and language that would remove the constitutional boundary of the scope of the authority of the Supreme Court. The term and the legal process of *"Judicial Review"* was born. It became a foundational operating premise of the court blindly accepted by both the Congressional and Executive branches of government. Allowing the courts decision in this case to stand established the

Supreme Court to be the final authority in deciding the constitutionality of Congressional or Executive decisions and actions. The sovereignty of the Executive and Legislative bodies ended. Never again would we have three separate and independent branches of government that had separate responsibilities and authority. Whenever the court concludes, for whatever reason, that acts of the other two supposedly, "separate but equal" branches of government somehow violated the constitution (as they interpreted it) they usurp the power to overturn their decisions or actions.

This judgment and perspective was a devastating and bold power grab by the Court that opened the door to a governing system in which the Supreme Court, not the representatives of the will of the people or the elected officials of the government would ultimately rule America. Thomas Jefferson warned of the consequences of letting the Supreme Court decision go unchallenged. Listen to what Jefferson wrote to his friend William C. Jarvis in 1820. *"To consider the judges as the ultimate arbiters of all constitutional questions is a very dangerous doctrine indeed, and one which would place us under the despotism of an oligarchy. Our judges are as honest as other men and more so. They have, with others, the same passions for party, for power, and the privilege of their corps. Their power is more dangerous as they are in office for life and not responsible, as the other functionaries are, to the elective control. The Constitution was erected so such single tribunal, knowing that to whatever hands confided, with the corruptions of time and party, its members would become despots. It was more wisely made all the departments co-equal and co-sovereign within themselves."*

This decision of "Marbury vs Madison" started us down a slippery slope. We are reaping what we have sowed. After 200 years we have landed at a plateau at which we can access the devastation of the decision. What we can clearly see is that a terrible mistake was made that will be very difficult, perhaps impossible, to correct. We must correct it or it will destroy America.

We should have listened to the words of warning from Thomas Jefferson and collectively confronted the court! We did not and over the past two centuries the court has chosen to ignore the expressed will of the founding fathers and the American people.

We find ourselves being governed today and our values determined by the will of a five-man majority on the Supreme Court. For 200 years the elected branches of government have acquiesced to judicial watch tyranny. This tyranny has become more and more apparent and aggressive.

If you don't think this is important consider this! The Supreme Court alone decides when and whether the constitution is relevant, when and if the laws passed by representative government meet the challenge of a constitution the court feels justified to interpret as they please. They have determined they are the interpreters of the constitution and decided they have the power to change the meaning and context of the Constitution at will. They have decided they have the power to rule against the declared intentions or original construction of the constitution by the founders. They totally discount and reject the Christian value system that is our national heritage and tradition and gives the constitution its power and authority and gave the people the right of liberty.

The court has decided on its own that it is in the best interest of the nation to establish government as secular. They have decided the constitution is whatever they say it is as it relates to any issue or matter they chose to look at. They have decided they are the final authority in everything. Judicial review is where the buck stops. In essence our liberty, rights, value system and way of life are in the hands of a secular humanist court system that hates God and disregards the sovereignty of the other two branches of government. They have usurped authority outside the scope of their constitutionally assigned by the founding fathers.

Ronald Reagan warned of the deceit and usurpation of power by the Court! He said, "The constitution was never meant to prevent people from praying; its declared purpose was to protect their freedom to pray"

It is frightening to realize that the court system we traditionally looked upon to protect our liberty, our justice, our values and our rights has become revealed as "wolves in sheep's clothing" who are destroying the very essence of who we are and how we choose to live.

Since our founding documents declare our liberty is from God the judiciary had to remove God and His moral judgment from the public arena so the basis upon which they could define freedom would be secular thought and perspective. This they did with little interference by the Legislature, the Executive branch of government or by our citizens. This move, "the separation of church and state" began a slide for America down a slippery slope toward the death of our nation, as it was constituted by our founding fathers.

The judiciary has seen fit to interpret the "freedom of Speech" amendment to include protection of the profane, the perverted, the slanderer, and the liar. The freedom of speech amendment was clearly written to provide protection for the one who would speak the truth when the truth was unpopular politically or unacceptable to powerful men and governments. It was intended to protect the truth and not the lie. It was not intended to protect the profane and the liar or the destructive.

We get all choked up when we listen to these political speeches about how essential it is to protect the rights of perverts, liars, slanderers and deceivers because it is the American way. It is not the American way! It is the blathering of misguided and unprincipled men attempting to make their perversion a civil right. It is utter nonsense! The speech that must be protected is the truth even when it is not popular.

The Supreme Court has become masters at misapplication of the letter of the law. The First Amendment is crystal clear in its intention. It states that congress is prohibited from enacting any law that infringes upon those freedoms described in the first amendment!!!! The judiciary has interpreted this to mean that the only constitutional prohibition from enacting laws, regulations, policies that infringe upon freedom of religion, press, assembly, the carrying of firearms etc., applies only to the Legislature. The Court has decided the prohibition is not against them. The court ignores the fact that the intention of the founding fathers was to prohibit any branch of government from infringing upon these rights. They see themselves above the constitutional prohibition.

The founding fathers never concerned themselves with having to restrict the Supreme Court from establishing laws that restrict or limit constitutional rights because legislation was outside the scope of their role or authority. Since any limitation against the Supreme Court is not stated in the constitution the court has assumed that the constitution does not therefore limit or prohibit the judicial branch of government from infringing upon constitutional rights.

It would appear from this kind of assessment that the Executive branch of government can also consider itself also free to infringe upon these rights since it is not specifically prohibited from doing so constitutionally.

The constitution authorizes three branches of government: the executive, the legislative, and the judicial. Article I, section I of the constitution states: **"all legislative powers herein granted shall be vested in a congress of the united states, which shall consist of a senate and house of representatives."** "Article III section I states, **"the judicial power of the united states shall be vested in one supreme court, and in such inferior courts as the congress may from time to time ordain and establish."** Article III, section 2 states, **"the judicial power shall extend to all cases, in law and equity, arising under this constitution."**

The judicial branch has no authority to alter the plain meaning of the constitution or interject itself in the governing process accept to protect the people from government infringement upon these freedoms protected by the constitution. Their mandate has to do with protecting the constitutional freedoms and administering justice and equity under the law in the context of these constitutional freedoms.

The incredible usurpation of power, lapse of moral courage and/or lack of the Supreme Courts understanding of its sacred mantel to protect freedom found a beginning in the nineteenth century with the **Dread-Scott decision**. The Supreme Court ruled for the slave owners and against the slaves when the constitution clearly prohibits slavery.

The Supreme Court should have expressed outrage at the idea of slavery and should have ordered the arrest and detention of every slaveholder and every slave trader and slave owner in America. The problem was, of course, that some of our astute politicians were themselves slave owners or friends of slaveholders.

This failure of the court to protect the people against slavery was just the beginning of many such failures to adhere to the protections promised in the fragile constitutional guarantees. The court ignored the fact that they were pledged to protect the people and administer justice through their rulings on critical constitutional issues. These rulings would come to define the character and core values of America.

With God and the constitutional guarantees removed the court now has ultimate power to change the face and character of America. The power of the courts goes unchallenged by an intimidated Executive and Legislative branch of government and an indifferent and deceived citizenry leaving the Supreme Court free to twist or reject the constitutional protections and limits.

Perhaps the most blatant current examples of judicial arrogance are the courts rulings on abortion and religious freedom. More recent decisions include a 6-3 ruling against a Texas school district policy that allows, but does not require, students to pray at football games construing the policy to be somehow unconstitutional. Even the most elementary intellectually honest thinking would force anyone who reads the first amendment to conclude that the first amendment prohibits the federal government from taking any action to prohibit the free exercise of religious expression in public or private. Neither the executive or legislative branches of government confronted the court.

Our judiciary, instead of dismissing these cases that challenge religious freedom and its public expression on the grounds that such limitation is clearly prohibited by the constitution, has decided contrary to the constitutional prohibition acting arrogantly and illegally in concert with the secular humanist agenda to remove God from the public arena.

They have ruled that the public expression of faith is prohibited in certain public settings because it would suggest government establishment of that particular religious expression as the religion of the state and would therefore be tantamount to the government establishing a religion and the government is prohibited by the constitution from establishing a state religion.

Obviously that kind of reason is radically out of context with constitutional construction since it totally ignores the constitutional prohibition against infringement by government upon the free public expression of religious faith.

We have a judiciary that is out of control and a Congress so dedicated to their own individual survival in an environment of corrupt politics they are unwilling to take any steps to begin to rein in the Supreme Court by taking positive and aggressive action to reverse these judgments or move those justices whose bizarre judgments are clearly constitutionally unacceptable.

We seem to have forgotten or fail to recognize that freedom and justice must be diligently pursued and aggressively protected against encroachment from without or within. Our people have been lulled to sleep and fail to see the incredible problem facing them. Therefore they see no need and feel no sense of urgency to hold their government representatives in congress accountable nor do they express publicly their outrage at the blatant infringement and erosion by government of our constitutional rights and protections or the systematic removal of traditional religious values from the public arena.

They have blindly trusted a judiciary who has proven to be controlled by blind guides who do not judge according to the law. They have blatantly rejected the biblical foundation of righteous judgment as the standard by which all judgment is to be made. Lesser courts have blindly followed along.

Who is looking out for the unalienable rights of Americans? Not the legislature, not the citizens and certainly not the judiciary! America is being lead by blind guides. Men and women who are Spiritually lost. We, the citizens, have allowed the creation of a secular humanist government through activist judges on the Supreme Court and the various circuit courts.

One of the most profound examples is the rejection of the core biblical and constitutional value of individual life and liberty. The Supreme Court has subordinated traditional values and biblical truth to endorse the idiocy of the feminist abortion rights special interest group agenda. Even a moron recognizes that agenda is evil and devastating to America and her people. There is nothing in the constitution that supports it and everything traditionally and biblically abhors it.

To clean up this abominable act so it is digestible and to distract us from the central issue abortion activists have attempted to disguise its horrible reality with the slogan, "the right to chose." Our glorious Supreme Court has chosen to support a women's right to kill her unborn baby indiscriminately for whatever reason. Murder has somehow become a lesser concern than the right for a woman to choose!

Our constitution does not give us the right to choose to murder! No one has the right to choose to murder even in our compromised society. Therefore, the abortion rights group had to devise some way of reinterpreting and redefining the killing of babies so it is not called murder. They had to even go beyond that definition in order to disarm any law that might otherwise bring upon them manslaughter or even a lesser charge.

Liberal politicians and judges did the identical thing when they used the establishment clause completely out of context to justify running God out of the governing process, out of education and out of American public life.

Since God and His bible are no longer the guide and standard used we are free to interpret anything and everything anyway that fits the morays of the culture or the agenda of the Court. Therefore the solution to unwanted pregnancy is now simple! All they have to do is sell to the majority the idea that life does not begin at conception and a fetus is not human life, therefore, there should be no stigma attached to abortion and no basis for prohibiting it by public law. It's an easy sell to a sex crazed society.

Today in America you can be arrested and thrown in jail for killing a nuisance animal without the sanction of government, however, you can kill an unborn baby at will. In fact if you are a teenage girl you can have an abortion without even getting your parents permission. Sound ridiculous! That's because it is!!

That same Court that protects abortion on demand protects the graduating high-school and college students who act defiantly, dress atrociously, display satanic symbols all over their clothing or skin, fill the air with profanity, disregard the discipline of their teachers, waste thousands of tax-payer dollars in school, strip naked in front of the graduating class, read aloud in public profane and/or virtually any kind of secular humanist garbage he or she might fancy. The Court gives this stupidity and rebellion the full protection of the freedom of speech guarantee of the constitution. Meanwhile they deny the constitutional protection of freedom of religious expression. It doesn't take much reason or research to recognize that this is not what the freedom of speech amendment was intended to protect!

The student who has a message of hope, encouragement, and respect for life cannot quote from the bible, or pray, or give glory or even thanks to God or express his or her faith in any way because this kind of expression, if tolerated, would somehow violate the establishment clause! Stupid is a horrible word but it applies here!

How do these honorable and all wise Supreme Court judges look to you now fellow Americans? Don't those priestly robes and the "honorable" hype seem a little silly when it adorns fools? Some of these leaders of the judiciary must either be awakened or removed from office and replaced by principled men. They get glory and wisdom from each other and not from the God of all wisdom. The examples are endless of our Supreme Court acting illegally and arrogantly. Their decisions, in many instances, have been socially devastating; they dishonor God, contradict the constitution and smear the character of our national identity.

The only way the state can separate itself from the church in a democratic society is if the government only includes those people who reject God and live in rebellion against his will. Unfortunately that is the kind of government our Supreme Court is attempting to force upon America.

Once God and His word ceases to be the foundation of the national ethic and the laws of the land the government is then free through deceived, perverted, confused and arrogant secular humanist leaders who hate God and God's people, to systematically remove God, His people, principle and His influence. In doing so moral value, restraint, individual rights and freedom will soon disappear placing this once great nation of freedom loving people into the terrible bondage of secularism and unrestrained evil.

When life is no longer protected by a moral people of faith and good conscience concerned for their fellowman then enslaving, isolating or even murdering people who will not cooperate with a secular governments foolish and destructive agenda is easy to justify.

When there is no longer a divinely defined objective system of justice then freedom and justice is whatever suits the interests of the courts, the government and the nations leadership. Justice is no longer what God has said it is and the constitution defines it as but rather what the state says it is or what a court decides it is!

When there is no longer value found in good character the character of men soon changes so as to conform to the selfish interests and value system that satisfies our appetites and justifies taking what you want and destroying whatever gets in your way. The people then find power and value in material success, in getting to the top. The people become driven by selfish interest, greed, pride, lust for power and their lives and life styles become characterized by" **immorality, impurity, sensuality, idolatry, sorcery, enmities, strife, jealousy, outbursts of anger, disputes, dissensions, factions, envying, drunkenness, carousing, and things like these..."(Gal 5:19-21)** Their God becomes their appetites. Hate, greed and lust replace love and commitment and men steal from each other, destroy and murder each other to get what they want.

Where as, the fruit of the Spirit of God working through men and women of God reflect these character traits according the scriptures: **"but the fruit of the spirit is love, joy, peace, patience, kindness, goodness, faithfulness, gentleness, self-control, against such there is no law." (Gal 5:22-23).**

Our courts have relegated the battle to defend freedom of speech into arenas that serve to distract them from dealing with the core issue as it relates to constitutional protection of freedom of speech. The courts find themselves occupied with attempting to defend constitutionally "no-brainer" issues, most of which should have been thrown out of the lower courts.

Often the courts set for days listening to special interest group attorneys raise cocka-mamie freedom of speech arguments that most elementary students could see through in a moment. The justices find themselves listening to arguments in defense of things such as the public display of vulgarity and nudity in the gay parades in cities such as San Francisco, whether we can hand out needles to dope addicts or whether these parades can be comprised of nude and vulgar acting men riding on floats and marching in the streets. The same streets that would be denied use by the church or the boy scouts.

Lets ask our selves some simple but straightforward questions. What do you suppose the freedom of speech amendment was framed to protect from censure? We can be sure that when our founding fathers framed the First Amendment they didn't look at each other and boldly declare, "well one thing for sure we want protected is the right of anyone to use profanity, print and publish pornography, the right to public nudity, the right to public homo-sexual expression, the right to pervert the minds of children in our public schools with homo-sexual nonsense, the right to incite people to riot or the right to engage in destructive actions and activities or the right to tell deliberate lies or bring false testimony no matter how offensive, disruptive, destructive and degrading they might be."

Likewise I am reasonably sure they were not debating the right of an individual to publish and distribute pornography and literary filth when they established the principal of "freedom of the press."

From a study of the writings of the founders it becomes crystal clear that what they were hoping to protect was the right of a citizen to freely express the truth without the threat of censorship by government or by the law or by any other group. History as reflected in the writings of the delegates to the constitutional convention regarding those issues being resolved when the national government was being created teach us the context and the spirit and intent of the freedoms the founding fathers were attempting to protect. They wanted to protect the right of individuals to speak out on substantive matters of individual rights and public policy even when it may be critical of government or not popular without the fear of government harassment or any attempt to incriminate or stop them from expressing their point of view.

Freedom of Speech does not protect the right to destroy the good name of another or to speak or act profanely in the presence of others, or to disturb the peace or destroy the dignity of an environment or person or to scream fire when there is no fire without suffering the just punishment for such intrusions. We don't need the Supreme Court to interpret such straightforward issues for us. Common sense dictates the judgment and existing law, if enforced, can resolve these matters.

The Court has determined the word "religion" in the First Amendment to be a broader term that includes all religious expression. The court has been faced with having to determine what is to be included in religion. However, it is important to note that even the most casual observer of history, if he is intellectually honest and sincerely seeking the truth, will recognize that the word religion as it appears in the constitution and the idea of religious preference dealt exclusively with Christian religious expression as it was expressed in its several different denominations.

It is unmistakably clear that the glory and religious expression our founding fathers wanted protected from government was the glory of the God of the bible. The legacy that was theirs to protect was freedom, opportunity, justice and the message of redemption, which gave the people hope. Our forefathers recognized that it was the God breathed word that defined truth and morality and held out the best hope of men living peaceably together. The Christian bible was the foundation and final authority of morality and law in America!

They were concerned with prohibiting the government from taking over the church and establishing a particular denomination, one that best suited its politics, its secular interests and doctrinal interpretations, and establishing it as the only true church.

In addition most of the founders recognized a deeper truth regarding the church, and that is, that the church is the body of Christ and it doesn't recognize any particular denomination as representative of "thee church", the body of Christ.

Another travesty of miss-interpretation of constitutional protections has to do with today's Coot's interpretation of second amendment, which deals with providing the authority for men to protect the security of our nation, of our communities, our homes and our person. The second amendment gives us the right to bear arms to protect our families and properties from illegal incursion, search or seizure.

If we read the second amendment we find provision, authority and responsibility to develop and maintain a military sufficient to keep America and her vital interests secure. We also find the right for men to bear arms and the prohibition against the governments infringement upon this right. Listen to its words, **"a well regulated militia, being neces-**

sary to the security of a free state, the right of the people to keep and bear arms, shall not be infringed."

It doesn't take a brain surgeon to figure out that America and her vital interests have to be protected from the encroachment of other national interests. That often requires force. Nations must be alert to the problem and committed to security from the encroachment of aggressor nations and/or people groups. We must not only be prepared as a nation to protect our collective interests and our homeland we must individually accept the responsibility of protecting our communities and our homes from domestic incursions. Since that is reality our founders saw fit to insure that every man had the right to bear arms to protect himself, his family, his property and his vital interests. Citizens were guaranteed for posterity by the constitution that this right would not and could not be infringed upon.

It's fundamental to our common understanding of reality that most people tend not to pick a fight with the biggest, toughest and/or the best prepared and most willing to defend himself! Likewise the nation that is the best prepared to fight and demonstrates its will to fight is the safest from encroachment.

The founding fathers recognized that providing for our national security was essential in an evil and fallen world and that since the federal governments scope was national, as apposed to local, the responsibility for national defense and security would best fit into the arena of the national government.

They also recognized it would bankrupt the nation and the local communities if government was to attempt to protect every citizen from evil encroachment. The citizen had a responsibility to look out for himself and his family. What is true regarding nations is also true regarding individuals. The man who is best equipped to protect his family and his belongings is the least likely to have to protect them or to have them harmed.

Our founders recognized the individuals right and responsibility to care for himself and his family therefore they included provision for his family's protection. They also recognized that an armed citizenry would have the means to protect itself from slavery by the state. The state and the community was given a law enforcement arm to provide some help, however, we were and remain to this very day primarily responsible for our own protection.

Once again many foolish people have reasoned that since guns in the wrong hands are dangerous and that since we are a people prone toward violence that our government must take away the guns, the clubs, the knives, etc from all the people. The attitude seems to be that in doing so the criminals will somehow stop robbing and killing. However, just the opposite is true. The man who breaks into private property with full understanding that if he is caught by the owner he will most likely be shot will think twice before breaking into a home or place of business. In response to that argument some will suggest that if we take guns away from the people that gun accidents will be less likely to occur. That argument is valid, however, there are relatively very few accidents involving firearms. There are far more frequent accidents with cars, with vacuum sweepers, with scissors and with just about every other tool or piece of equipment or machinery we use. However, the benefit far outweighs the risk. The protection of this constitutional right far outweighs the risk of allowing firearms in the hands of the people. That determination was made in 1776!

Obviously, the issue is not guns it's the hands that hold the gun. Robbing and killing was happening long before there were firearms. Besides that, taking away mans ability to protect himself is clearly not the way to discourage the criminal. The problem with children and guns is a parenting problem and not a gun problem. Making the parents libel will reduce this problem. If a child took their parents car and ran over someone the parents would be held responsible and would be sued by the victim in civil court. Why would it be different for children who injure someone with a gun?

Beyond all the debate there is a foundational problem that is seldom considered It has to do with the capacity of government to protect you! The police and the military can never keep the guns away from the criminals nor can they prohibit the criminal's use of them. They physically cannot be everywhere. The social reformers who refuse to face up to the issue tells us the way to handle it is to give the criminals whatever they want! Sound stupid! That's because it is stupid. If you want to invite crime let the criminals know that you won't or can't fight back they will look out for you. The government doesn't want citizens to take the law into their own hands and accept any responsibility for their own welfare because protecting yourself is dangerous business. So it is, but it is nevertheless essential if we ever hope to limit crime and remain free in America. The more secular our society the larger the criminal element within our society will become. The biggest problem and greatest enemy facing every American today is ourselves and the second largest is a secular humanist government.

Men grow up to recognize what is acceptable and what is not acceptable by the value system imparted by parents and confirmed during the education process, exemplified in the society, reflected in the laws of the land, enforced by government and demonstrated in the character of those chosen by the society to lead and govern them.

The bible teaches us that men with fallen natures, under the right circumstance, will do anything, even kill, to get what he wants. He will deliberately destroy what he hates and he will hide what he does not wish to have revealed. That is the world we live in and it is getting worse, not better. Once again, wake up and smell the coffee!

The men who framed this constitution recognized that for this government to work successfully Americans would have to be predominately a Christian people who loved his neighbor and his freedom and was willing to sacrifice when necessary for his fellowman and would be willing to protect his liberty. For this new government to work we would have to be a people of vision and principle pledged to live honorably and peacefully together willing to fight to the death for our liberty, our faith, our families, our property and our nation.

Therefore, for our form of government and our freedom to survive and to govern and administer justice it must have wise, Spiritually alive and morally courageous leaders who are principled men committed to upholding and protecting the spirit and intent of the law.

Unless we are awakened I predict that by 2010 the right to utilize the public airways to express your Christian faith will be outlawed by the court. The broadcasting of Christian programming over public airways will be outlawed, carrying a bible in public will be against the law; bibles will not be allowed in public libraries and any reference to God or His commandments in public will be prohibited and considered inciting a riot and any display of the cross or the commandments in public or at the monuments in our nations or state capitols or public institutions will be considered unconstitutional.

Those Christian emblems and symbols that currently exist on public buildings will have been removed just as prayer has been outlawed in public schools and public gatherings even though our constitution clearly prohibits the government from interfering with the free public expression of our faith. Christians who worship or give God glory publicly will be arrested for publicly expressing their Christian faith or for witnessing to others of their faith. It will be construed to violate the "separation of Church and State" judgment of the Supreme Court. Any public expression of loyalty to God will be considered bigoted or unpatriotic and religious private schools will not be allowed to credential students. They will be legislated out of existence and forced underground because their existence will be construed to be unpatriotic and in direct violation of separation of church and state.

The First amendment that guarantee's protection from the federal governments effort to limit or interfere with the public expression of our Christian faith will continue to be ignored by the Court. A spin will be put on the Courts judgment much like the spin used to justify the rejection of God or Godly activities and principles in the public schools today.

That myth and spin finds its foundation in the implantation of the idea of "separation of church and state". This term does not exist in our constitution. It is a distortion diametrically apposed to the context of the First Amendment. It is another slogan like "the woman's right to chose". Our courts and much of our society have adopted this myth to support the secularization of America and in particular the institution of government.

Without a spiritual awakening of the people the United States of America is doomed by its rebellion against God and the deceit of secularism. This nation will ultimately be added to the pile of forgotten nations piled on the ash heap of history.

John Quincy Adams, one of our founding fathers, **wrote "The highest glory of the American Revolution was this: it connected, in one indissoluble bond the principles of civil government with the principles of Christianity."**

Patrick Henry declared**; "It cannot be emphasized too strongly or too often that this great nation was founded, not by religionists, but by Christians; not on religions, but on the gospel of Jesus Christ!"**

John Jay, the first Chief Justice of the United States Supreme Court declared, **"Providence has give to our people the choice of their rulers, and it is the duty...of our Christian nation to select and prefer Christians for their rulers."**

Even the court itself in 1826 stated boldly, **"No free government now exists in the world unless where Christianity is acknowledged, and is the religion of the country. Its foundations are broad and strong, and deep. It is the purest system of morality, the firmest auxiliary, and only stable support of all human laws. Christianity is part of the common law."** (Updegraph v. Commonwealth, 1826)

For a more exhaustive study of America's religious heritage I recommend Peter Marshal and David Manuel's "The Light and The Glory", "Sounding Forth the Trumpet" and David Barton's "The Myth of Separation".

The evidence is so overwhelming of our dependence upon our Creator and the indissoluble bonds between America and Christianity that one would have to be blind or committed to a predisposed evil purpose to deny them inseparable.

George Washington, at the conclusion of the War in 1773 addressed the governors of all the states with this declaration: **"I now make it my earnest prayer, that God would have you, and the State over which you preside, in His holy protection, that he would most graciously be pleased to dispose us all to do justice, to love mercy, and to demean ourselves with that charity, humility, and pacific temper of mind, which were the characteristics of the Divine author of our blessed religion, and with an humble imitation of whose example in these things, we can never hope to be a happy nation."**

Washington, the Father of our country, and a vast majority of our founding fathers, could not have successfully led the nation, according to their declarations, had the nation not concurred with the beliefs of their Christian faith. The Spirit that guided them and their Christian beliefs was typical of the Spirit of the entire nation, as confirmed by a pamphlet written by Benjamin Franklin while he was serving as emissary in France. It was written to those who were considering a move to America! **"Bad examples to youth are more rare in America, which must be a comfortable consideration to parents. To this may be truly added, that serious religion, under its various denominations, is not only tolerated, but respected and practiced. Atheism is unknown there; infidelity re and secret; so that person may live to a great age in that country without having their piety shocked by meeting with either an Atheist or an Infidel."**

Court decisions throughout our nations existence up to the middle of the twentieth century reveal the courts understanding that the political system under which we chose to live was the political expression of Christian idea's and ideals.

The 1892 Supreme Court declared:*"This is a religious people. This is historically true. From the discovery of this continent to the present hour, there is a single voice making this affirmation. These are not individual sayings, declarations of private persons; they are utterances that speak the voice of the entire people. These, and many other matters which might be noted, add a volume of unofficial declarations to the mass of organic utterances that this is a Christian nation."*

There can be drawn no other conclusion after a serious and honest study of the historical record. America was as Christian as the Church in the perspective of the founders and in the hearts of the people.

What ought to be troubling is that an honest person could arrive at any other conclusion. Only ignorance or deceit or a predisposed anti-God agenda would allow any other conclusion.

When the intent and the intended application for which the law was framed is ignored, that law can be separated from its meaning, purpose and context and twisted assigning it new meaning, purpose, context and application. The Supreme Court has done that in critical issues.

The early courts diligently strived to do the necessary research to ensure that the people were protected from the results of rulings that occurred which were based on absurd interpretations and/or applications of a law. For example, in 1887 the Church of the Holy Trinity in New York employed a clergyman from England as their Pastor. The Church had technically violated the letter of the law, which stated, **"It shall be unlawful for any corporation, in any manner whatsoever to in any way assist or encourage the importation of any alien or foreigners, into the United States to perform labor or service of any kind"**.

The Church argued they had not broken the law because the law was never intended to impact or effect the hiring of ministers. The prosecution contended that the church had violated the written, black and white, wording of the statute. The court did its homework. It researched the law's intent and context and discovered, from the congressional record, that the law was enacted only to correct a specific abuse in the domestic railway labor market by prohibiting the importation of slave-type labor.

Although the church's actions fell within the literal and technical wording of the law, they did not fall within the intent of that law. Therefore the court ruled that a prosecution of the church under that law would be an "absurd" application and gross misuse of the law. The Court ruled for the church and commented on the principle which guided their decision; **"It is a familiar rule that a thing may be within the letter of the statue and yet not within the statute, because does not fall within the spirit of the law, nor within the intentions of its makers. Frequently words of general meaning are used in a statute, words broad enough to include an act in question, and yet a consideration of the whole context of the legislation, or of the circumstances surrounding its enactment, or of the absurd results which follow from giving such broad meaning to the words, make it unreasonable to believe that the legislator intended to include the particular act."**

Thus the Holy Trinity court determined that to settle a dispute arising from under a law it must first determine the spirit of that law by examining; **"The evil which was intended to be remedied, the circumstances surrounding the appeal to the Congress, the reports of the committee of each house and the intent of Congress."**

There are numerous examples throughout history that drive this point home. In the case of the State V. Clark (1860) the court ruled, "**The language of the act, if construed literally, leads to an absurd result. If a literal construction of the words of a statute is absurd, the act must be so construed as to avoid the absurdity.**" In this case the first count against Clark was that he "maliciously and willfully broke down the panels of rail fence belonging to and in the possession of George Arnwine. The Section of the Statute upon which this indictment was found provides that if any person or persons shall willfully break down or destroy any fences belonging to any other person they shall be deemed guilty of a misdemeanor.

On the surface it appears that this is a very clear and concise description of the law and of its violation by the defendant Mr. Clark. Investigation revealed that Clark had clearly destroyed George Arnwine's fence and he was guilty as charged because he had violated the law.

However, Clark showed by way of defense that when he broke down the fence, he had title to the land on which Mr. Arnwine insisted on building his fence. The fence he broke down was erected upon Clark's land. Despite Clarks many discussions with his neighbor, Arnwine persisted In deliberately building his fence on Clark's property.

The court found that Arnwine was the real abuser of the law. The court decided that even though this case was a violation of the letter of the law it was not in violation of the spirit of the law and the charge was dismissed.

In the case of **The United States v. Kirby** the court ruled; "**All laws should receive a sensible construction. General terms should be so limited in their application as not to lead to injustice, oppression or an absurd consequence. It will always, therefore, be presumed that the legislature intended exceptions to its language, which would avoid such absurd results. The reason of the law in such cases should prevail over its letter. The common sense of man approves the judgment that the law which enacted, "that whoever drew blood in the streets should be punished with utmost severity," did not extend to the surgeon who opened the vein of a person that fell in the street requiring the surgeon to draw blood. The same common sense accepts the ruling which enacts that a prisoner who breads from prison shall be guilty of felony does not extend to the prisoner who brakes out of prison when the prison was on fire, "for he is not to be hanged because he would not stay and be burnt." A like common sense will sanction the ruling we make, that the act of Congress which punishes the obstruction or retarding of the passage of the mail, or of its carrier, does not apply to a case of temporary detention of the mail caused by the arrest of the carrier upon an indictment for murder.**"

In this case the defendants were indicted for willfully obstructing the passage of the mail and of a mail carrier. **The congressional act provides "that, if any person shall knowingly and willfully obstruct or retard the passage of mail, or of any driver or**

carrier he shall, upon conviction, for every such offence, pay a fine not exceeding one hundred dollars."

The indictment contained four counts and charged the defendants with knowingly and willfully obstructing the passage of the mail of the United States and with willingly and knowingly obstructing the mail carrier, Farris, while he was engaged the performance of his duty; and with willingly and knowingly retarding the steamboat General Buell, who was contracted to carry the mail of the United States from the city of Louisville, Kentucky to the city of Cincinnati Ohio.

Clearly the law was passed to insure that the mail would go through and that there would be no interference with those whose duty it was to make mail deliveries. Kirby, who by the way was the Sheriff of the county, and three of his deputies were clearly guilty. However, the grand jury had commanded Kirby and his deputies to Arrest Farris on two counts of murder. Kirby and his posse of deputies were engaged in lawfully arresting Farris.. To do so they were forced to enter the Steamboat to detain him and they used only such force as was necessary to detain him.

They did indeed interfere with the delivery of the mail by arresting the mail carrier, thus causing a delay for the Steamboat. The court recognized this as a violation of the "letter" of the law, but not of its "spirit".

Early courts were not confused by the common sense approach to the administration of justice. They recognized that the court must be wary of absurd applications, which result in incorrect judgments and devastating results. However, it required hard work by honest men on the court who loved justice

However, the Supreme Court lost its zealousness for justice and its common sense. In doing so it dealt a deathblow to America. It removed Christianity from the foundation of law, its influence from the public education system and its justice from the court system. It did so by applying the letter of the law out of context with its revealed intent. This is perhaps the most devastating act ever brought against our nation and the constitution in the entire history of our nation.

When our Founding Fathers enacted the First Amendment, the abuse they intended to avoid was establishing one specific denomination of Christian expression over another to be selected, adopted, protected or promoted by the federal government as the only Christian denomination recognized by the government. The problem was not which "world religion" the government might adopt. It was clearly intended to be limited to Christian expression since America was a distinctively Christian nation.

The founders and the nation were followers of Christ and they did not wish to experience the same evil religious oppression in America they had been subjected to through the Anglican Church of England or the Catholic Church of Europe.

The founders clearly established Christianity as the basis of government and of all public institutions, yet they wished to protect freedom of conscience to all individuals within the confines of the foundational biblical principles of the Christian faith.

However, the fluke of absurdity that is a part of everything deceived and fallen man touches is no longer a fluke. It has become the business as usual standard of the judiciary. This switch from basing Court rulings on the Spirit and intent of the law to the often out of context application of the letter of the law became firmly in place by the Court in the middle of the twentieth century.

Court rulings since 1947 have moved predominately from Spirit and Intent to the letter of the law placing our nation under the absurd result which previous courts warned us of. America became a nation who was being lead by a Supreme Court majority of secular humanists who had an agenda to secularize America and particularly government.

My heartaches for our nation every time I watch deceived anti-American and anti-Christ liberal democrats on the Judiciary committee in the Legislature begin their political battle to discredit a Presidential appointment to the Court who professes or demonstrates faith in God or biblical conservative values in his attitudes or actions or in previous court decisions. These secular minded liberals hate Spiritual wisdom and are almost deathly afraid of conservative ideas. They have good reason to be because they obviously march to a different drummer and they cannot tolerate a court that recognizes our dependence upon God or who recognizes that justice demands knowledge of the Spirit and intent of the law rather than the letter. This destructive appointment process is a blatant example of the condemned running away from the light as Jesus predicted in the Scriptures. **"For everyone who does evil hates the light, and does not come to the light, lest his deeds should be exposed. But he who practices the truth comes to the light, that his deeds may be manifested as having been wrought in God."** (John 3:20-21)

Men afraid of the truth don't want anyone on the court who is going to expose their foolishness or limit the spread of their deceit. They are in rebellion against God and truth and they hate righteousness and everyone who is righteous or seeks justice.

This new government would recognize certain rights as unalienable, divine in origin, meaning they cannot be separated from man by men or governments. These are rights established under God's authority and stated to be fundamental to human existence. The founding fathers considered these rights to extend far beyond the purview or authority of human government to limit, regulate or in any way infringe upon. Obviously, that limitation includes our Supreme Court and any or all the subordinate courts of our land.

These unalienable rights have to do with rights inherent in God's creative plan for mankind. Life and liberty are God's intended order for human life. These rights are the uniqueness that distinguishes America and Americans from the governments and social orders of the rest of the nations of the world. These fundamental God given rights became the foundational principles that authorized Americas independence and gave our national government authority, direction and purpose. The founding fathers considered protection of these unalienable rights as the paramount mantle of national government. The Constitution and the Bill of Rights were written to define and protect the application of these foundational rights.

Our form of government and our national existence have no special significance short of the mandate of these God given unalienable rights. These rights give our national identity a distinctive character and purpose by establishing the underlying theme and mantel of government to guarantee individual liberty and freedom under the guiding hand of our Creator who gave men certain divine and unalienable rights among which were life, liberty, and the pursuit of happiness.

The overriding theme and purpose of the constitution and its government would be to secure and guarantee individual liberty, religious freedom and a representative form of government. **The government must consider any intervention or subversion of these rights or any attempts to erode the constitutional protections to be acts of treason against America.** These are very serious matters and these acts of treason cannot be tolerated if America is to survive. The promoters and perpetrators of these acts are enemies of America whether they should come from within or without the government or the nation. Contrary to our Courts interpretation, treasoness acts or expressions are not protected by our Constitution. Listen carefully to the introductory paragraph of the constitution, **"we the people of the united states, in order to form a more perfect union, establish justice, insure domestic tranquility, provide for the common defense, promote the general welfare, and secure the blessings of liberty to ourselves and our posterity, do ordain and establish this constitution for the United States of America."**

The beginning of movement away from the Spirit and intention of the First Amendment began within a few years after the end of WWII. The atheists and the disciples of the devil began to work hard to get America away from the God who had guided the United States and its allies successfully through the war. The historical record shows their thrust begin to show some success after the courts 1947 rulings on the First Amendment. Prior to this time the court could be counted on to almost universally make its rulings based on the Spirit and intent rather than on the letter of the law when the application of the letter would set itself against the Spirit, intent or context of the law.

David Barton reviews some 200 First Amendment case citations among first amendment cases since 1947. The record shows that 178 of those cases held against the spirit and intent and for the letter of the law. Previous to this the court ruled virtually universally against the letter of the law when it did not support the Spirit and intent of the law. This date appears to be the great watershed of American Justice and constitutional protection.

The first major case in which the Supreme Court misapplied separation to overturn the longstanding tradition of school prayer was the case of **"Engel v. Vitale, 1962."** At issue was whether it was constitutional for New York students to offer this prayer: **"Almighty**

God, we acknowledge our dependence upon Thee, and we beg Thy blessings upon us, our parents, our teachers and our Country."

The Supreme Court declared the use of this prayer in school as unconstitutional. They said, in essence, that this prayer and the forum in which it was prayed were against the will and intention of the Founders as embodied in the constitution. They said our founders would have opposed it because it was damaging and destructive. This is not only very unlikely history proves it an absurd conclusion.

Even under the most absurd examination this particular prayer would have passed constitutional muster because it was voluntary and non-denominational which was the only concern raised by the Founders as it related to the First Amendment. On the contrary, the First Amendment specifically protected religious expression. I believe prayer qualifies as religious expression. At any rate, the First Amendment was not established to discourage prayer by any public servant in any public institution.

The Supreme Court's declaration regarding prayer was as follows: '**Neither the fact that the prayer may be denominationally neutral nor the fact that its observance on the part of the students is voluntary can serve to free it from the limitations of the First Amendment. It ignores the essential nature of the program's constitutional defects. Prayer in its public school system breaches the constitutional wall of separation between Church and State."** The court went on to explain, **"A union of government and religion tends to destroy government and to degrade religion."**

This, of course, is absurd! The founders would totally disagree with this Supreme Court! **"True religion affords to government its surest support". (George Washington)**

"Religion and virtue are the only foundations of republicanism and of all free government". (John Adams)

"Religion is the basis and foundation of Government." (James Madison)

"God grant that in America true religion and civil liberty may be inseparable and that the unjust attempts to destroy the one, may in the issue tend to the support and establishment of both." (Dr John Witherspoon)

"Our constitution was made only for a moral and religious people. It is wholly inadequate to the government of any other. (John Adams)

The Supreme Court went on in the ruling to express contempt for the religious views of the founding fathers. Listen to this incredible revelation of the Courts predisposition against any religious expression in the public arena. **"It is true that New York's prayer does not amount to a total establishment of one particular religious sect to the exclusion of all others. That prayer seems relatively insignificant when compared to the governmental encroachments upon religion which were commonplace 200 years ago."**

The attitude expressed by this court is obviously preposterous and arrogant! It clearly reflects a predisposition by the court to remove any evidence of God or our religious heritage from government and the public arena. By this accusation against the Founders practice of violating the principles of the Constitution they are setting their understanding of the constitution above the expressed intent of the men who wrote it

The Court always cites previous cases as precedents. It is the means used to give credibility to current decisions and it is the foundation upon which current decisions are justified. However, not one legal precedent was cited by the Court to support its decision to remove prayer from our public schools! In this bizarre decision the court overturned 350 years of tradition and educational history in America without citing one single legal precedent.

The Court was obviously proud of itself, because in a later case, " **Abington V. Schempp**" they declared, "**In Engle V. Vitale, only last year (1962), these principles were so universally recognized by the court without the citation of a single case reaffirmed them.**"

Of course the reason they did not site any precedent was that there was none to cite that would support its absurd conclusion! They refused to cite the opinions of the Founders, the Congress and the previous courts because those opinions differed radically with the position of the 1962 Supreme Court. The Engle decision was an unveiling of the Supreme Courts new interpretation of the First Amendment.

What is incredible about all of this is, despite the oath the Justices took when they entered the office to uphold the Constitution they did not intend to educate themselves or follow the original intent. In 1962 an official survey of the nation indicated that 64% of our people were church members while less than 3% professed no religion. That fact is important because the Court, in an effort to justify its decision, declared, **"Attempts to enforce acts obnoxious to so great a proportion of Citizens tend to enervate the laws in general and to slacken the bands of society."** Obviously an even more absurd declaration!

In 1963 another Supreme Court case **"School District of Abington Township v. Schempp"** the court was able to spread its absurdity even further by prohibiting bible reading in school. At issue was the school policy, which stated: "**Each school shall be opened by the reading, without comment, of a chapter in the Holy Bible. Participation in the opening exercises is voluntary. The student reading the verses from the Bible may select the passages and read from any version he chooses. There are no prefatory statements, no questions asked or solicited, no comments or explanations made and no interpretations given at or during the exercises. The students and the parents are advised that the student may absent himself from the classroom or, should he elect to remain, not participate in the exercises.**"

Dr. Solomon Grayzel testified that if portions of the New Testament were read without explanation, they could be, and had been, psychologically harmful to the child. The Supreme Court used this ridiculous testimony from someone who was neither a historical figure or a former Justice as foundation to prohibit bible reading in school.

Again, here is what some of our founding fathers had to say about the bible;

"I have always said, and always will say, that the studious perusal of the sacred volume will make us better citizens" (Thomas Jefferson)

"It is impossible to rightly govern without God and the Bible." (George Washington)

"The bible is a book worth more than all the other books that were ever printed." (Patrick Henry)

"Suppose a nation in some distant region, should take the Bible for their only law book, and every member should regulate his conduct by the precepts there exhibited, what a utopia, what a paradise would this region be. (John Adams)

"The moral principles and precepts contained in the Scriptures ought to form the basis of all our civil constitutions and laws. All the miseries and evils, which men suffer from vice, crime, ambition, injustice, oppression, slavery, and war, proceed from their despising or neglecting the precepts contained in the Bible. (Noah Webster)

The court stated; "The First Amendment's purpose was not to strike merely at the official establishment of a single sect. It was to create a complete and permanent separation of the spheres of religious activity and civil authority."

In contrast to the Supreme Courts statement listen to the statements of the founders and early congress:

"The highest glory of the American Revolution was this; It connected, in one indissoluble bond, the principles of civil government with the principles of Christianity. (John Quincy Adams)

"Whoever shall introduce into public affairs the principles of primitive Christianity will change the face of the world." (Benjamin Franklin)

"Had the people, during the Revolution, had a suspicion of any attempt to war against Christianity, that Revolution would have been strangled in its cradle. At the time of adoption of the Constitution and the amendments, the universal sentiment was that Christianity should be encouraged, not any one sect. In this age there can be no substitute for Christianity; That, in is general principles, is the great conservative element on which we must rely for the purity and permanence of free institutions. (House Judiciary Committee, 1854)

The court's statement was not only historically inaccurate, the Founders would have universally rejected it. The Court's declaration is acceptable only to those who reject outright America's Christian heritage and the Spirit and Intent of the founders.

The Court in this case stated, "**Almost 20 years ago in Everson (1947) the court said neither a state not the Federal Government can pass laws which aid one religion, aid all religions, or prefer one religion over another.**" This presumption is absurd. The early courts established the opposite, "**By our form of government, the Christian religion is the established religion; and all sects and denominations of Christians are placed upon the same equal footing. By our form of Government, the Christian religion is the** established religion; and all sects and denominations of Christians are placed upon the same equal footing. " (Runkel V. Winemill, 1799)

"Christianity, general Christianity, is and always has been part of the common law. The laws and institutions are built upon the foundation of reverence for Christianity. (Updegraph v. Commonwealth, 1826)

"Providence has given to our people the choice of their rulers, and it is the duty, as well as the privilege and interest of our Christian nation to select and prefer Christians for their rulers." (John Jay, First Chief Justice of the Supreme Court.)

A Supreme Court case **"Stone v. Graham, 1980"**, brought 17 years after Bible reading was banned in public schools by the Supreme Court is but another of a long list of cases brought to completely separate America from the Creator and to remove any evidence that America was ever a Christian Nation.

The Ten Commandments was hanging in the hallways of Kentucky schools. At issue was whether it is against the constitution for students to see a copy of the Ten Commandments displayed at a public school. The Commandments were not required reading and were not displayed in the classrooms.

This case raises the height of the Courts deceit to new levels of absurdity. The very foundation of the civil laws of the western world is the Ten Commandments! It is amazing and unbelievable that the Court could possibly conclude that viewing the Ten Commandments was a violation of the Constitution. What makes it even more ridiculous is the fact that James Madison, the chief architect of the Constitution believed that obeying the Ten Commandments was at the very core of the Constitution.

The Supreme Court found for the secularists. These deceived Jurists have led the evil battle for secularism in government and society. They're deception and its accompanying evil web now permeates the entire judiciary, our government, and our public education system and is positioning its ugly tentacles in every aspect of our culture. Their perspective is secular humanist, which by definition is anti-Christ and therefore it is anti-American.

Justice and righteousness in constitutional matters is impossible for the Court because their perspective is contrary to the Spirit and intent of the law. Justice has everything to do with Spirit and intent and less to do with word alone. Words can be manipulated to mean whatever we want them to mean. Secular humanists are lead by a different spirit and they march to the beat of a different drummer than did our founding fathers.

Christ and Christianity are Spiritually and historically inseparable from freedom and the Constitution created to protect freedom and free enterprise. Therefore they are inseparable from the laws by which our society is governed or from the law making and administering process. Justice, or judging the application of the laws and the provisions of the Founding documents must necessarily be Christian.

The Supreme Court has become the enemy within during the past half-century because it has embarked upon a deliberate secular course ignoring the historic record and the Spirit and intent of our constitutional protections and its associated laws. It is rapidly and systematically destroying America's Spiritual heritage. Unfortunately we have all followed and obeyed the leadership of this deceit and insanity like a bunch of brain dead lemmings. Collectively we have acted indifferently to the implications of these momentous and disastrous court decisions. Our governments Legislative and Executive political leaders have spent their energies swatting at knats while swallowing camels. They have ignored, overlooked or failed to recognize this gross miscarriage of truth and justice and/or its implications.

The cases in which the courts have come forward with absurd judgments never seem to end. In 1970 the **"State Board of Education v. Board of Education of Netcong"** the Supreme Court of New Jersey following the lead of the United States Supreme Court held that the free exercise of religion as guaranteed by the constitution could not be tolerated. At issue was the Policy of the Netcong school board which was as follows: **"On each school day before class instruction begins, a period of not more than five minutes shall be available to those teachers and students who wish to participate voluntarily in the free exercise of religion as guaranteed by the United States Constitution. This freedom of religion shall not be expressed in any way, which will interfere with another's rights. Participation may be total or partial, regular or occasional, or not at all. Non-participation shall not be considered evidence of non-religion, nor shall participation be considered evidence of or recognition of an establishment of a religion. The purpose of this motion is not to favor one religion over another nor to favor religion over non-religion but rather to promote love of neighbor, brotherhood, respect for the dignity of the individual, moral consciousness and civic responsibility, to contribute to the general welfare of the community and to preserve the values that constitute our American Heritage."**

The New Jersey Supreme Court declared the act unconstitutional based on the states ownership of the children. **"It is hereby declared to be a principle governing the law of this state that children under the jurisdiction of said court are wards of the state which may intervene to safeguard them from neglect or injury.**

The court did not want its children exposed to religion and therefore it must intervene to protect them from the neglect or injury that might be caused by allowing them to hear or offer voluntarily prayer.

It was argued that the United States government has Chaplin's who lead congress in prayer; surely it can do no harm for students to hear the same prayer our Congressmen hear The court declared, **"Public schools, unlike the halls of Congress, present a special case. This audience is without the maturity to express independence. What may be wholly permissible for adults therefore may not be so for Children."**

It was argued that the students could read the Congressional record published by the United States Government and available to any person, which contains the remarks and the prayers of the Chaplain. The Court declared, **"It is a religious exercise to read from the Congressional Record the remarks of the Chaplain. Reading from the Congressional record may be an unconstitutional infringement upon the First Amendment.**

This is about as absurd as it gets! How long do we, as a nation, set back and allow the court to continue to lead us down this destructive path? This happened in 1970 and we have done nothing in protest nor have we demanded action by our elected officials. Looking out for the interests of the American people clearly involves protecting our Spiritual heritage and the administration of justice.

Any heat brought against the Judiciary for their Anti-Christian agenda has caused them to run for cover under the idea of religious plurality. They began this thrust to promote the idea of a pluralistic society in 1970 in a United States Supreme Court case known as **"Waltz v. Tax Commission of the City of New York."** A pluralistic society is one, which acknowledges no one religion above any other.

It must be stressed over and over again that America was not founded as or never intended to become a pluralistic society. The evidence is overwhelming against such lunacy! Our Founders were not pluralistic and their writings confront the idea of pluralism with clear, distinct and "in your face" declarations:

"It cannot be emphasized too strongly or too often that this great nation was founded, not by religionists (Pluralism), but by Christians; not on religions, but on the gospel of Jesus Christ!" (Patrick Henry)

"Let statesmen and patriots, unite their endeavors to renovate the age by educating their little boys and girls leading them in the study and practice of the exalted virtues of the Christian system. " (Samuel Adams)

"You do well to wish to learn our arts and ways of life, and above all, the religion of Jesus Christ. Congress will do every thing they can to assist you in this wise intention." (George Washington – 1779)

"The religion that has introduced civil liberty is the religion of Christ and His apostles. This is genuine Christianity, and to the we owe our free constitutions of government." (Noah Webster)

"In this age there can be no substitute for Christianity. That was the religion of the founders of the republic, and they expected it to remain the religion of their descendants." (House Judiciary Committee, 1854)

You cannot help but wonder what the Supreme Court could not grasp regarding these statements and the hundreds of other statements made in this regard by our founding fathers. The only conclusion reasonable men can come to is they are unaware of the truth. The other conclusion requires acknowledging that we have a powerful and destructive enemy within that is either incompetent or are deliberately and systematically destroying us.

Whatever the reason for the absurdity, the court does not grasp it and, in fact, they took great pride in their absurd declaration in this case: **"We (the Court) have been able to**

chart a course that preserved the autonomy and freedom of religious bodies avoiding any semblance of established religion. This is a "tight rope" and one we have successfully traversed. The line we must draw between the permissible and the impermissible is one which accords with history and faithfully reflects the understanding of the Founding Fathers."

What an incredible declaration of pride in their obvious deceit. The absurd declaration they made believing they faithfully reflected in that declaration the Spirit and intent of the Founding Fathers who framed the First Amendment. They ignorantly continued on with one foot firmly entranced in their collective mouth's: Listen to the absurdity; **"One of the mandates of the First Amendment is to promote a viable, pluralistic society and to keep government neutral, not only between sects, but also between believers and non-believers."**

The promotion of a religiously pluralistic society (all religions seen as equal in the sight of the state) was clearly the courts intention and it was also clearly contrary to the intentions of the founding fathers. The most elementary examination of the record would reveal the absurdity of this courts decision.

The constitution, much like the outreach encouraged by the bible, allows men and women of other religions to come visit and even live in America and to worship according to their own custom, except for the destructive rituals that destroy life like those of the satanic cults. However, the focus was not to change the nature and character of America by absorbing the world religions or the wacky philosophies of a lost world into one guiding faith and truth that set the course for American justice and direction.

It was clear to any who are interested enough to investigate, that the state recognized the principles of Christianity and the foundation of its government and its faith was and is the gospel of Jesus Christ in its various expressions (denominations). The foundation and sustaining faith of America, over any and all other religions, was Christianity. America was created as and intended by the founders to forever be a Christian nation with charity for all but not encompassing all the diversity and evil of world religions and cults in the fundamental guiding principles of our government or of our social character or ethic.

One of the confronting issues of the courts move toward pluralism was centered around the constitutionality of tax exemptions for the various movements that declared themselves religions and of the various recognized world religions.

The principle guiding the court was there interpretation that the constitution guaranteed any religious expression no matter how contrary to Christianity or America to be treated equally in the site of the state.

The Court made God politically correct. He became whatever we wanted him to be. He began to become a " higher power" figure (or nature itself) in American society. God became He, or she, or it who could be anything from an animal to a rock, even Satan, or the sun, the moon, the stars or a planet or a person or an idea.

The Court boldly declared that the intent of the framers of the First Amendment was protection of religious expression in all its cultic, satanic, pagan and secular diversity. Our culture adopted the idiotic attitude that the great thing about America was no longer the blessing, guidance and protection of the Creator and Lord but rather religious diversity! The "I'm all right – your all right" mantra.

This devastating ignorance and the declaration of it as fact by the Court are light-years away from the Spirit and intent of religious expression in America.

Somehow, the American Spirit still sought a way to honor God and to consider His goodness by establishing a brief period of meditation and silent prayer in the Alabama Public Schools. The devil and his Atheistic and secularist disciples soon brought a case **"Wallace v. Jaffree, 1984)"** before the United States Supreme Court. The Court declared the silent meditation and silent prayer in school to be unconstitutional. Interestingly they found the silent prayer and meditation unconstitutional on the basis of the purpose of the silent prayer and meditation in school: **"It is not the activity itself that concerns us; it is the purpose of the activity that we shall scrutinize. The prime sponsor of the bill is promoting an effort to return voluntary prayer to our public schools. He (the sponsor) intended to provide children the opportunity of sharing in their spiritual heritage of Alabama and of this country."**

This is really wild! The court established the legislator's intent when he authored the bill, and the intent of the people of Alabama and the legislator in voting for the bill, however, the court declared the bill **"Invalid because the sole purpose was "an effort on the part of the State of Alabama to encourage a religious activity."**

The court declared it unconstitutional because they determined the sponsor's motive to be wrong!

In 1967, a few years earlier, a kindergarten teacher had her students recite the following poem in school: **"We thank you for the flowers so sweet; We thank you for the food we eat; We thank you for the birds that sin: We thank you for everything"** Amen!

Atheists, paranoid about exposing their children to anything that smacks of religious observance, brought the case **"DeSpain v. DeKIalb County Community School Dist. 1967"** which declared the poem to be unconstitutional. The appeal was heard by the 2nd Federal Court of Appeals and allowed to stand by the United States Supreme Court.

The teacher did not use the word "God" in the poem. She testified that she used the poem to encourage the Children toward thankfulness. The Court ruled that it was unconstitutional for the children to be allowed to recite it. **"Despite the elimination of the word "God" from the children's recital of thanks, ..the word is still there in the minds of the children. Thus we are asked as a court to prohibit, not only what these children are saying, but also what the children are thinking. "**

The Court now feels a mandate to guess what the children who hear the poem are thinking and declare that poem unconstitutional on the basis of that thinking. How far do you suppose this absurdity could or can be taken by the court? Could it include even having a bible or a scripture verse on your desk at school? Yes it could and eventually it did!

Earlier, in 1948, an atheist brought a case **"McCollum v. Board of Education, United States Supreme Court".** The thing of issue was religious the constitutionality of classes being offered as school electives. The Council on Religious Education, which included Jewish, Roman Catholic and a few Protestant faiths, obtained permission in 1940 to offer classes in religious instruction to public school pupils in grades four to nine inclusively. The classes were made up of students whose parents signed printed cards expressing their child's desire to attend and authorizing their children's attendance. The school did not pay the teachers of these classes and the classes were voluntary.

The court declared these classes to be unconstitutional!

"As we said in the Everson Case, the First Amendment has erected a wall between the Church and the State which must be kept high and impregnable. Separation means separation, not something less. It is the court's duty to enforce this principle in its full integrity. Illinois has here authorized the commingling of sectarian with secular instruction in the public schools. The Constitution of the United States forbids this.

Mrs. McCollum was an atheist who, according to a dissenting judge, was attempting to force the school board to **"adopt and enforce rules and regulations prohibiting all instruction in and teaching of religious education in all public schools in said district. The plaintiff, as she has every right to be, is an avowed atheist. What she has asked of the courts is that they not only end the "released time" plan but also ban every form of teaching, which suggests or recognizes that there is a God. She would ban all teaching of the Scriptures. She especially mentions, as an example of invasion of her rights: "having pupils learn and recite such statements as, "The Lord is my Shepherd, I shall not want" and she objects to teaching that the King James version of the Bible "is called the Christian's Guide Book, The Holy writ and the Word of God," and many other similar matters."**

The Court ruled in favor of this single atheist who was not involved in any of the voluntarily attended classes in question. She brought suit against the school district because Christianity personally offended her. She, with the help of a secular humanist court, was able to **"prohibit the free exercise of religion"** in every school district in the nation! Where was our President? Where was our Legislature? Where was the church? Where were our Christian citizens? They were either sleeping soundly or they were moral cowards.

How is our society to respond to such absurdity? Surely we must respond promptly and aggressively or we are just as guilty as the culprits who have forced this evil deceit upon America. Court rulings completely contrary to anything our founders could have ever imagined have become the standard for the Courts of America and acceptance and silence has become the response of our government, the church and our citizens.

David Barton in his book "The Myth of Separation" reveals five defenses the court uses to justify its decisions in its attempts to protect itself from legal criticism in its misapplications of the First Amendment.

1. They misapply the Fourteenth Amendment;
2. The courts total misrepresentation and out of context appropriation of James Madison's, and other of our founders, names and statements regarding the relationship between the Constitution and Christianity;
3. The mischaracterization of Thomas Jefferson's faith, name and his statements regarding Christianity and the Constitution by the Courts.
4. The Courts intentional omission and/or mischaracterization of historical fact;
5. Its omission of the public statements made by the founding fathers relative to the Spiritual nature of our nation and their declarations regarding the vital need to sustain the Spiritual nature and Christian character in the governing process.

Literally hundreds of court cases in virtually every state have been defeated because they were confronted with misapplied and absurd court precedent. One of the most recent cases (2003) was the display of the Ten Commandments at the entrance to a Court House in Alabama. The presiding Justice of the Alabama Court refused to have the Ten Commandments removed, however, he was over-ruled and removed from the Court.

'The bill of rights was intended to be a restriction on the national government, not the states". Chief Justice John Marshall in the 1833 decision of **"Barron v. Baltimore"** emphasized that the bill of rights restricted only the national government. But since the 1940"s the Supreme Court has interpreted Section I of the Fourteenth Amendment as incorporating the entire bill of rights making it applicable to all the states (in every decision whether applicable in Spirit or not) The Supreme Court has thus achieved precisely the opposite of what was intended by the framers of the Bill of Rights; instead of being solely a restriction on the national government, the Bill of Rights is now a restriction on the states."

The significant point is that prior to the Courts use of the Fourteenth Amendment as a precedent in First Amendment cases, the First Amendment "separation" decision had not been applied as a restraint against the states. For more than 70 years following the ratification of the Fourteenth Amendment in numerous First Amendment cases no Court saw fit to couple the Fourteenth Amendment provisions to the First Amendment or any other Amendment for that matter.

Second, the Courts attempt to give itself credibility by attempting to invoke, totally out of context, James Madison and Thomas Jefferson's lack of involvement in framing the First Amendment construction has created a similar myth to the myth of separation of church and state.

The court decided that Jefferson was not a proponent of the First Amendment since Jefferson did not play a leading role in the First Amendment construction. However, they completely overlook the fact that he did not play a role in its construction not because he was not interested but, because he was in Paris, France during the framing process. As a matter of historic fact it was Fisher Ames of Massachusetts who proposed the wording of the First Amendment.

Even though Jefferson did not participate in the framing of the First amendment he spoke and wrote much about its intent. What is strange is that the Court refuses to use this evidence. Could it be because of the predisposition of the Court toward secularism? **Kentucky Resolutions of 1798 (Thomas Jefferson), "No power over the freedom of religion is decreed to the United States by the Constitution."**

Second Inaugural Address, 1805 (Thomas Jefferson); "In matters of religion I have considered that its free exercise is placed by the Constitution independent of the powers of the general (federal) government."

Letter to Samuel Miller, 1808, (Thomas Jefferson), "I consider the government of the United States as interdicted (prohibited) by the Constitution from intermeddling with religious institutions, their doctrines, discipline, or exercises. This results not only from the provision that no law shall be made respecting the establishment or free exercise of religion, but from that also which reserves to the States the powers not delegated to the United States (10th Amendment). Certainly, no power to prescribe any religious exercise, or to assume authority in religious discipline, has been delegated to the General Government. It must then rest with the States, as far as it can be in any human authority."

Not only does the court omit the precedents set in cases prior to 1947, conspicuously absent from the debate and decisions are the public statements made by George Washington, Benjamin Franklin, John Adams, John Jay, Samuel Adams, Patrick Henry, John Hancock, Roger Sherman and many other prominent founding fathers.

Why would the court omit the statements of these prominent founders? Dr Paul Vitz, who conducted research on the treatment of religion in student textbooks offered the following observation: **"Over and over, we have seen that liberal and secular bias is primarily accomplished by exclusion, by leaving out the opposing position. Such a bias is much harder to observe than a positive vilification or direct criticism, but it is the essence of censorship. It is effective not only because it is hard to observe, it isn't there and therefore hard to counteract, but also because it makes only the liberal, secular positions familiar and plausible."**

The Court to this day portrays Madison and Jefferson as being opposed to permitting any religious influence on government or public affairs. This is a false and misleading representation; the record shows that **"while serving in the Virginia General Assembly Jefferson personally introduced a resolution for a Day of fasting and prayer in 1774. When he established the University of Virginia, he encouraged the teaching of reli-**

gion and set apart space in the Rotunda for chapel services and encouraged the use of the local courthouse for religious services"

While Jefferson was President of the United States he also served as the first president of the Washington D. C. school board he authorized the use of the Bible as classroom reading text. This was a period well after the adoption of the First Amendment. Jefferson stated: **"I have always said, and always will say, that the studious perusal of the sacred volume will make us better citizens."**

The record also shows Madison's passion against the Judiciary becoming lawmakers: **"The preservation of a free Government requires not merely, that the metes and bounds which separate each department of power (in the federal government) be invariably maintained; but more especially that neither of them be suffered to over-leap the great barrier which defends the rights of the people. The rulers who are guilty of such an encroachment, exceed the commission from which they derive their authority, and are Tyrants. The People who submit to it are governed by laws made neither by themselves nor by an authority derived from them, they are slaves."**

In 1788 Madison warned of the weakness of our system to guard against the tyranny of a court of unprincipled men: **"As the courts are generally the last in making the decision (regarding the constitutionality of laws) it results to them, by refusing or not refusing to execute a law, to stamp it with its final character. This makes the Judiciary dept paramount in fact to the Legislature, which was never intended, and can never be proper."**

James Madison's warning went unheeded and we find ourselves now governed by laws neither made by the people nor by the authority derived from them. We find our courts filled with atheists, fools and secular humanists, our schools have become the devils playgrounds and our society overrun with perverts protected by our Courts. The devil has drawn a line in the sand at the place of appointment of justices to the courts.

The Courts have discarded the revealed beliefs and intents of the founders and have also set aside the historic court rulings that supported their intentions. The rulings of the contemporary Courts are diametrically opposed to those of the earlier Courts.

The problem goes beyond First Amendment issue of separation. It extends to every aspect of Constitutional law. The Courts are at war with the Spirit and intent of the founding documents and the dignity of life. For instance the Court has elected to uphold public profanity as a freedom of speech right. In the case **"Cohen v. California, 1971"** the court declared; **"The appellant was wearing a jacket bearing the words "F— — the draft in a corridor of the Los Angeles Courthouse. The state cannot make the simple display of this four-letter word an offense. The California law prohibiting such use of the word infringed upon his rights to freedom of expression guaranteed by the First and Fourteenth Amendments of the Constitution. This is not an obscenity case. That the air may at times seem filled with verbal cacophony is, in this sense not a sign of weakness but of strength."**

Listen to this absurdity.

In a different case, **"The People v. Ruggles, 1811"** declared, **"Nothing could be more offensive to the virtuous part of the community, or more injurious to the tender morals of the young, than to declare such profanity lawful nor shall we form an exception in these particulars to the rest of the civilized world."**

The contemporary Court ruling says tolerating public profanity is a sign of our strength while the historic court ruled that profanity is injurious to the morals of a people and a demonstration of their perversion.

In another cases dealing with Lewdness and indecency, blasphemy, the equality of all religions, on atheism, on Sunday laws, on invocations, on Christmas and Nativity Scenes, on personal appearance, on the ownership of children, on the protection of children etc, all the historic rulings and founders intentions have been utterly discarded by the court of the last half century. What do you suppose the next half-century holds for American Juris-Prudence?

We have, as a society, concluded in our twisted deceit that we must have a court that is "fair and balanced" between good and evil as if there is something right and just about not letting truth, good and righteousness lead the parade of justice. In our stupidity and deceit we have concluded that evil is not our enemy; in fact it is simply another perspective that must be protected and given equal consideration.

The Courts have declared rights guaranteed by the Bill of Rights as unconstitutional and/or void while they have overlooked the historical record, which reflects the Spirit and intent of the law, and have decided to march forward in the darkness of deceit to lead America into the future under the banner of what they consider "a more perfect union."

If we are looking for a culprit to blame for our cultural decline at the national leadership level we would have to be brain dead to not place the mantel of blame for the secularization of America, the almost total destruction of public education and the out of control cultural rebellion on the myth of **"Separation between Church and State"**, which is the exclusive creation of a secular humanist Supreme Court.

It must be pointed out, of course, that the Court Justices responsible for this devastating decision were all appointed by the Nations Chief Executive and approved by the Legislature. The problem with the court is the Justices and their secularist interpretation of our Constitution and the law.

Our current President George W. Bush has appointed several honorable and principled men to the high court. The majority of these appointments were wise men that honor God and recognize the vital need to hold fast to our nations Spiritual heritage. Unfortunately, foolish liberal Democratic Legislators who support secularism have risen up consistently in a concerted effort to defeat every attempt to place principled men on the Court.

This destructive group of political hacks are deathly afraid of restoring Justice, honor, wisdom, dignity and righteousness to our nation and its highest Court. President Bush is clearly the most dedicated and Spiritually discerning leaders our nation has had in the Whitehouse for decades. Everyone, even his political enemies recognize his Spiritual strength and wisdom. They hate it and desperately fight against him because of it; nevertheless they cannot escape its truth or its national and international impact.

Our President recognizes that we must bring this current activist Court back in line with its constitutional mandate. The Court must be manned by principled men who recognize the rule of true justice is based on the proper understanding of the Spirit and intent of the Constitution as our founding fathers constructed it as well as the Spirit and intent of the laws that guides the way for Americans.

The dictionary defines treason as a **"violation by a subject of his allegiance to the state, the betrayal of a trust or confidence; breach of faith, treachery, or any attempt to overthrow the government or the well being of the state, through speech, writing, actions etc"**. Allegiance to the state fundamentally entails allegiance to the Spirit and intent of the vital foundational principles upon which it was created as spelled out in the founding documents and in any duly authorized amendments to the founding document.

A misdemeanor is defined by the dictionary as any misbehavior or misdeed considered under the law to be less serious than a felony. The point, of course, is that congress has broad latitude in choosing whom to impeach and for what! The reasons can be anywhere between treason and a misdemeanor, therefore, they have incredible responsibility to stay alert and to act swiftly and decisively when a breach is committed.

From my experience and knowledge of government operations and its political activities it is abundantly clear that the everyday conduct of many of our elected politicians makes them candidates for impeachment if congress had the moral courage to do its job. Unfortunately the internal political, economic and social corruption is so intertwined it is virtually impossible to carry out the mandate. We watched this corruption at work when Congress attempted to impeach a President who lacked the moral character and integrity to remain our nations Chief Executive.

The Democrats aligned themselves behind the President and against truth and justice blocking the impeachment. They didn't care about doing what was right. They were concerned about their political careers.

We would have a much less corrupt and far more effective government operation if congress would have remained alert and conducted several impeachment procedures throughout our history. Our Courts and much of congress needs to have the fear of God placed directly on their doorstep through the reality of the impeachment and recall processes.

There is nowhere that I know of that provides us a more clear application of mans deceit as presented in the Scriptural warning which states, **"There is a way that seems right unto man, but its way is the way of death"**, than the collective absurdity of the liberal agenda as reflected through the highest court in our land.

American's have naively surrendered the faith that gave America meaning, purpose and hope as well as their constitutional rights to a deceived judiciary. We have been sold the idea that the law is what a judge wants it to be and pronounces it to be regardless of what the constitution guarantees and what the spirit of the law intends!

The Lord has given us a Christian President, who is hated by the devil and his disciples and by the totally deceived atheists and secular humanists, who are trying to lead us back to a faith based foundation for our society, our government and our public institutions.

Unfortunately we have government leaders who lack the moral courage to stand for what is right and we have an indifferent, deceived and intellectually lazy citizenry who have long since let their Spiritual guard down accepting as just and righteous anything government or the courts throw at them.. They have lost the sacred since of the value of freedom and justice that is inherent in the constitutional protections placed there by our forefathers.

We seem to have forgotten or fail to recognize that freedom must be diligently pursued and aggressively protected. Our people have been lulled to sleep and fail to see the need to go to the trouble of holding their government representatives in congress accountable nor do they express publicly their outrage at the blatant infringement and erosion by government or the courts of constitutional rights and protections as well as traditional religious values.

What our founders envisioned was a court system that was a lean and effective service agency dedicated to protecting the people and their freedoms from injustice. They envisioned a society founded and grounded in religious principle and perspective. They recognized and declared throughout our historical documents that our freedoms had a divine foundation. They recognized the need for a federal institution of government that received its authority and marching orders from the people it was hired to govern.

Our government and our legal system have failed us because we have elected and appointed foolish and unprincipled men and despots to positions of leadership. We have no one to blame but ourselves!

Instead of working together in a spirit of common purpose we have divided ourselves up in to hundreds of special interest groups for the purpose of promoting and insuring our interests and desires at the expense of the other special interests that are in conflict with our own. We want to increase our share of the pie even if it destroys the needs and interests of the other group.

In order to govern this divided and selfish people we have had to pass millions of laws. The problem is that another precious liberty is stolen away every time a new law is passed. Besides the loss of freedom we are creating an enormous, inefficient, expensive bureaucracy that is slowly and deliberately stealing more of our liberty and consuming more of our resources and taking more of the constitutional guarantees away from us.

In return for government dependence we get to enjoy the presumption and illusion that we are secure because our special interests are being protected. However, hundreds of special interests groups are actively engaged in getting their agenda recognized or their

PERSPECTIVE*

interests and desires satisfied at someone else's expense! The most powerful and persuasive special interest wins the day and America loses!!

America is currently in the throws of examining once again whether "under God" in our pledge of allegiance is constitutional. The Supreme Court is going to hear the case and make their pronouncement soon. An atheist in northern California brought the case on behalf of his daughter on the basis of his belief that the words "Under God" in our pledge is unconstitutional because of the establishment clause.

Every American will now have to choose on which side of the battle line they will stand. We cannot profess Christian faith and stand with those who are in rebellion against God. Will we insist that our government and our Judiciary remain humble and subservient servants of God and America, a government of, for and by the people or will we accept the secularism as our god and allow the Supreme Court to continue its inclination as its enforcement instrument? The idea of separation between church and state and all the baggage it carries with it, is not found anywhere in the constitution and clearly not in the first amendment which reads;" *congress shall make no law respecting an establishment of religion, or prohibiting the free expression thereof; or abridging the freedom of speech, or of the press; or the right of the people to peaceably assemble, and to petition the government for a redress of grievances.* " (Article I – constitutional amendments – ratified by three fourths of the states December 15, 1791 along with amendments 2-10)

John jay, the first chief justice of our nations supreme court wrote regarding the religious make up of our collective population, **"I have as often taken notice that providence has been pleased to give this one connected country to one united people descended from the same ancestors, speaking the same language, professing the same religion...."** (John Jay in a letter (a part of the federalist papers) to the people of the state of New York regarding the forming of a national union uniting the various states that comprised the nation of America)

Tolerance is a great word, however, its application is limited to behavior and not principle! If the length of a timber needed to build a house according to the plan was twelve feet the carpenter would not tell his helper to cut a timber somewhere between eleven and thirteen feet. He would insist that the timber be cut at precisely twelve feet. It is not a matter of tolerance it is a matter of truth and the discipline required to build the house according to the plan.

So it is with our lives. The principle upon which our society rests is the truth expressed in the scriptures of the Christian bible. Tolerance in regard to the feelings of those who are not Christian is certainly in order, however, the principle upon which this house is built and rests is distinctly Christian. Others can enter the house but the discipline of the construction must stay in tact or the house will not stand. Truth is like gravity! You may not like it, however, whether you like it or not you will still fall to your death if you chose to ignore it and step off a cliff in defiance.

CHAPTER THIRTEEN

BLIND LEADERS

—ɱ—

"This people honors Me with their lips, but their heart is far away from Me. But in vain do they worship Me, teaching as doctrines the precepts of men" (Matt 15: 8-9)

In our deceit a majority of Americans have deliberately chosen to overlook the vital need to elect or appoint government leaders of character, vision, moral courage, integrity, spiritual discernment and a strong moral compass. Somehow we have rejected these values in favor of other secular values we somehow deem to be more important. In fact, as a society, we have decided we prefer secular humanists political leaders to men of faith and Spiritual discernment.

Our government has blindly endorsed the secular humanist notion of "separation of church and state". Separation is not found anywhere in our constitution or in the founding documents. We have broadened the application of the separation notion to include even the display of the Ten Commandments in public institutions or the practice of prayer in our schools.

Most Americans may not understand the implications of the choice the Supreme Court has made, nevertheless we (America) have made that choice. This choice suggests that, as a professing Christian people, we have somehow seen fit to reject the need for moral character, spiritual wisdom, self discipline, righteousness, integrity and charity as essential qualities in those we elect as political leaders and/or appoint to serve as judges in our judiciary system. Perhaps this says more about our true character than our profession. I prefer to think that America has been hoodwinked by the shouting and out of context spin of the proponents of secularism who hate God. This moral blindness surprises many of us because it really isn't that difficult to figure out!! Nevertheless we don't seem to be able to figure it out.

Leaders by the very definition of the title "leader" are people who lead. Government leaders are either elected by the people or appointed by other leaders according to our constitutional system, however, true leaders in any society are defined by their character, wisdom, integrity, charity and vision. When we elect or appoint leaders who are not leaders they cannot lead effectively and they will always ultimately lead us in the wrong direction. Leaders are no different than the rest of us in that their vision and discernment is limited by their wisdom or deceit. They cannot see beyond what they do not have eyes to see and they will not make righteous judgments unless they are righteous; they will not make sound moral judgments if they do not have moral courage and a moral compass.

In America we are victims of our own choices and the choices of our political leaders. When we elect a leader on the basis of what cause he promises to champion or on what welfare program or special interest he supports we are foolish indeed! A true leader is one who supports what is right and good as best he can determine it regardless of the political consequences for himself or for those he leads. A good leader is a trustworthy person of character who we can depend upon to always respond according to what is right and just. He is a person of vision, moral purpose, integrity, charity and Spiritual wisdom. Electing leaders must be far more about character and far less about politics!

Most of our Judges are appointed by a political leader or assigned to a position in the judiciary by other Judges. In a few states and local communities Judges are elected. However, all federal Judges are appointed by a political leader or appointed by other federal Judges. Therefore, the ramifications of whom we elect as our government leaders are dramatic and can be tragic. Voting for or against a potential political leader is a profound choice that can have eternal implications. Who we chose to lead our government is but a reflection of who we are and what we believe as an individual and as a people. The standard of character we demand in the leaders we elect is but a reflection of our individual and collective moral character and value system.

When America decided that we are better served by a secular government that governs and makes its critical decisions on a secular basis we made a very foolish and devastating judgment. We chose to ignore who we are as a people and the historical heritage and tradition that lead the United States of America to become the greatest nation on earth from any perspective you might want to compare it. The basis upon which we chose secularism was totally out of context with our constitution as it was written by our founding fathers. Perhaps you are not sure about that? You need to become sure about it because it has eternal implications for America.

Secularism, according to the American College Dictionary, is defined as **"a system of political or social philosophy which rejects all forms of religious faith and worship".** Secularism is a view that **"public education and other matters of civil policy should be conducted without the introduction of a religious element; to exclude religious instruction as in education".** To Secularize means, according to the same dictionary, **"to separate from religious or spiritual connection or influences; to make worldly or unspiritual".** If you support secularism these definitions defines the choice you have made.

We profess to be a Christian nation. Various polls tell us that 85 to 90% of Americans believe in the God of the Christian bible. The belief of many Americans is obviously limited in its scope and power to profoundly effect their lives and decisions, nevertheless, 85% of us profess that we recognize there is a Creator even though many are not sure about His role in their lives or in the governing of our Nation. A much smaller percentage of Americans attend church regularly. However, as a nation, we are not atheists or Satanists by choice, however, we make choices on every Election Day that do not support our profession.

If we are to adopt a secular view we must consider the source of such thinking and what we have done or are doing. We must determine the foundation on which secular thought stands. We must get real and become engaged in an attempt to determine from where such thought typically originates and the agenda of those who promote it.

In that context, consider what gives secular thought its power and authority! What does a government, and therefore a nation, destitute of Spiritual truth look like? Perhaps the most prominent recent example we can look to was the Soviet Union. What does a nation of people and a government dedicated to serving the will, wisdom and charity of God look like? The only example of such a nation in recent history has been the growth and development of the United States of America. If you compare the history and heritage of the Soviet Union and the history and heritage of the United States the contrast speaks for itself. Which of the two would you chose to live in? The choice is obvious. A person would have to be brain-dead or stupid to choose the atheistic Soviet Government system and the devastation, death and suffering its spiritually bankrupt system of secular government caused its people and the world around it.

The choice the world seems to have made regarding where they want to live and the system of government they want to live under is the United States because we cannot keep people from all over the world out of our nation. Unfortunately the United States has set aside the foundation that made it strong and has adopted the premise of secularism that was foundational to the Soviet system. That premise is that government must be secular and atheistic. Our choice to reject God and adopt secular humanism as our state religion will ultimately lead us in precisely the same direction the Soviet Union followed and we will end in a similar way to the way Soviet Union ended.

We seem to fail to recognize that secularism is not another word for objectivism? Do we not recognize that the foundational belief system that supports secularism is atheism? From where does the spirit of atheism come? Creation itself leads us to conclude there is a Creator. Once again the dictionary defines Atheism as **"the doctrine that there is no God; or the disbelief in the existence of God or an attitude of Godlessness"**. Atheism is anti-God and anti-Christ. There are many questions about God that we do not understand and will not understand until we stand in His presence, however, one of them is not whether or not He exists.

Secularism is a philosophy that finds its authority in the Spirit of Atheism. God has never suggested anywhere in the bible that we are free to chose without having to suffer the consequences of our choices. In fact the bible declares, ***"He who is not with Me is against Me; and he who does not gather with Me scatters. (against me). Matt 12:30)*** His admonition to all of us is ***"Choose this day who you will follow". "There is a way that seems right to man, but its way leads to death".*** Secularism ignores the revealed will of God because it denies the existence of God. It is absent of the Spirit, character, moral purpose or charity of God. It is not an objective way to govern that somehow rises above God's way.

Beyond allowing the foolish choice of the court to stand making our government a secularist government, America has chosen to ignore the constitutional principle of democratic representative government and the concept of self- rule presented in our constitution. We have deliberately chosen to take the perverted value system of atheism, supposedly held by approximately 10% or our nation, and force that destructive system upon the rest of America. In doing so the government has established a form of religion and is actively forcing that belief system on our people and on our children through our judiciary, our colleges, universities and public education system.

I have heard many ridiculous attempts to argue that our government must govern all our people as if governing all our people means that we must govern America according to various secular and distorted views and interests of people or according to some sort of secular anti-God spirit that inspires and leads the thinking of a small percentage of our people. The secularism that has been mandated by the highest court of our land is a tragic thing for America. It must be changed or America will perish as a home of the free and the brave.

Government has a mandate to govern through representative government according to the constitution as it was constructed by our founders and according to the expressed will of a majority of the people of America. The constitution finds its authority and wisdom in the revealed will of Almighty God. Government has no other legal or moral authority outside the will of God and the people. When government acts outside its constitutional authority its actions are unconstitutional. Secular Humanism is the state religion that has been chosen and is being established and mandated by the Supreme Court. This is contrary to constitutional government and contrary to the Government's principle mandate to secure and protect the God given rights associated with the principle of individual liberty and collective freedom.

Secularism is not a friend of America. It has no place in the governing of America. We as a people have been hoodwinked by a hand full of atheistic misguided attorneys who have sold the Supreme Court on the idea that we as a nation are a people of diverse religious values in danger of having our government taken over by Christian religious zealots. In over 230 years our government has never been in danger of being taken over by the church nor has there ever been any attempt to do so. The focus of the Church is ambassadorship for our Creator. Christian scriptures require that its adherents submit to those chosen to govern because they are instruments of God used to serve and guide the people. The Governments of Europe attempted to establish a religion and manipulate the people through the use of that man-made religion. We have been asleep or lazy while the enemy of liberty works overtime.

Has the enemy won? Have we truly lost our way? As a nation supposedly "Under God" we seem to have lost the fundamental vision of a nation of people maturing Spiritually and ever growing in the knowledge of God walking in His will and acting more like his revealed character defined in the bible as a character of love, joy, peace, patience, kindness, goodness, faithfulness, gentleness, self-control and a passion for righteousness, justice, integrity, wisdom and a will guided by mercy and grace. The Scriptures tell us that "*against such things there is no law*" and they remind us that "*those who belong to Christ Jesus have crucified the flesh with its passions and desires*" and the scriptures admonishes us that since we profess to "*live by the Spirit, let us also walk by the Spirit*". (*Galatians 5-22-26*)

We no longer see our greatness, purpose and fulfillment as walking as an example of God's character and revealed purpose in a lost and evil world. We find ourselves apologizing for the very strengths, faith and value system that made our nation a great and prosperous nation setting us apart in every aspect of life on earth as the example every nation would like to emulate.

We as a people have become fascinated and mesmerized by another term that defines America. That term is "diversity"! We have been lead to accept the idea that our true strength as a nation is really found in the political and religious baggage that comes from the combined input of the political and belief systems that emanate out of every cultural and religious view found among our citizens and/or immigrants. We actually have people that promote the idea that our greatness must be attributed to our contrasting beliefs rather than the single mindedness of a Christian faith.

The bible attributes unity to the fact that "*There is one body and one Spirit, just as also you are called in one hope of your calling; one lord, one faith, one baptism, one God and Father of all who is over all and through all and in all*". We are admonished to " *be diligent to preserve the unity of the Spirit…*". We are not to be "*tossed here and there by waves, and carried about by every wind of doctrine, by the trickery of men, by craftiness in deceitful scheming; but speaking the truth in love, we are to grow up in all aspects into Him, who is the head, even Christ; "* (*Ephesians 4:3-6, 14-15*)

The scriptures warn us about walking "*in the futility of our minds, darkened in our understanding, excluded from the life of God, because of the ignorance that is in them, because of the hardness of their heart; and they, having become callous, have given themselves over to sensuality, for the practice of every kind of impurity, with greediness.*"(*Eph 4:3-6. 14-15, 18-19*)

In rejecting the Spirit of God we have lost our ability to discern the negative and destructive impact of secular humanism or religious plurality. We have become so deceived we cannot understand why electing or appointing atheists, secularists or even perverts to our highest courts or to our highest political offices is tragically wrong and will bring destructive results. Mans appetites, lusts, greed and pleasures determine the value system of the secularist and atheist.

We are rapidly losing our moral perspective and we are beginning to reap what, in our deceit, we are sowing. The culture we have allowed to arise is betraying our youth and leading them in a lie that will ultimately consume them. Modern Culture has bought into the great lie that secularism is the dream of the founding fathers because it translates in our thinking as objective thinking which we have somehow decided soars above the truth, will and wisdom of God. We have decided that issues of running a complex government are too great for God so man must take them into his own hands and govern according to his own wisdom. Therefore, Spiritual wisdom and Godly principle are considered to be bigoted and wrong for America.

You are perhaps wondering how we arrived at this place? Surely you are wondering how a nation that has become the greatest nation on earth by trusting in God and being lead by his wisdom and truth could ever chose to reject His wisdom and will?

The word that best describes our insanity is deceit! It is part and parcel to Spiritual blindness, which is the curse of separation from God inherited by every man because of sin. It is such a blinding force that those who come under its spell cannot even discern they are under its spell. It is a disease that cannot be diagnosed by those who have it and it is a disease that all who reject the grace of God and hate the Spirit of God share. It is a disease worse than aids because all who share in it will perish unless they are somehow delivered from its grasp. Deceit and secularism worship the same God. That God is Satan the master deceiver whose spirit is the spirit of the world. *"Just as through one man sin entered into the world, and death through sin, and so death spread to all men, because all sinned… through one transgression there resulted condemnation to all men, even so through one act of righteousness there resulted justification of life to all men." (Romans 12,18)*

It is deceit that leads us to believe the lie that we are not condemned and that man is fundamentally good without the influence and guidance of the Spirit of God and therefore does not need to be redeemed. That lie is foundational to the destructive perspective held by many of our people that has lead us to adopt many of the destructive and foolish public policies and much of the destructive legislation that becomes public law and guides our way of life.

Deceit has lead us to fail to recognize the need for our institution of government to make governing decisions, create public policy, pass legislation and enforce laws that reflect our values and deepest beliefs. Our laws, to be effective, and the incentives they provide must be the right incentives that express our values given the fallen nature of man and where that nature will lead us without divine intervention.

The bible speaks of the nature of the flesh of the man who rejects the guidance of the Spirit of God. Listen carefully as you read this and I guarantee you that your entire being will be crying "YES" that is what my experience and my instincts tell me about our natural condition as fallen creatures and members of a secular culture. In our fallen condition we are pre-determined to be anti-God. Read carefully, *(Walk by the Spirit, and you will not carry out the desire of the flesh. For the flesh sets its desire against the Spirit, and the Spirit against the flesh; for these are in opposition to one another, so that you may not do the things that you please.....Now the deeds of the flesh are evident, which are: immorality, impurity, sensuality, idolatry, sorcery, enmities, strife, jealousy, outbursts of anger, disputes, dissentions, factions, envying, drunkenness, carousing and things such as these...." (Galatians 5:16-21)* Our foolishness and destructive perspective is reflected in the laws, policies and programs we are now enacting to guide, govern and protect us.

Sin is a word we reject as a society. We underestimate the condemnation it brings upon us individually and collectively. We joke about its condemning nature and pretend it is not a relevant consideration. We do so because we are all by nature "sinners". We do not confront sin because we do not walk according to the Spirit of God. The scriptures speak of the evidence that is reflected in the character of those who do walk according to the Spirit of God. Once again I ask you to read slowly and consider the implications; "*But the fruit of the Spirit is love, joy, peace, patience, kindness, goodness, faithfulness, gentleness, self-control" (Galatians 5:22-26) The* typical American refuses to face the profound implications of the contrast between the fallen nature of man and the character of the one who walks according to the Spirit of God. Since we don't face it we fail to recognize the implications of the contrasts in governing a people who have two distinctly different natures.

Since we overlook the sin inherent in the fallen nature of man we therefore have bought into the lie that man is essentially good with or without the guidance of God's wisdom and will. The result of our deceit is that we fail to recognize the need to elect or appoint leaders who are men of faith and character.

In our utter deceit many have been lead to consider secularism as another word for objectivity and we have concluded that morality and the public expression of our faith is bigotry and offensive. In fact, we have decided that depending on biblical principle as the standard to guide society and governing is bad and therefore religious expression and faith expressed in public no longer gives us reason to rejoice but rather it is considered politically incorrect and even illegal in some settings.

We, as a society, have degenerated spiritually to the point that we do not consider the will and wisdom of God a foundational part of education and we are actively engaged in legal action to remove "under God" from our pledge of Allegiance and to remove "In God we trust" from our money. We have removed prayer from our public schools and from school sponsored activities. Our courts are filled with activist judges who are involved in the evil agenda to remove the "Ten Commandments" from the walls and hallways of our public institutions. Anti God atheists and special interest legal groups are attempting to have the broadcasting of Word of God removed from the public airways based upon what has become known as the establishment clause of the constitution.

It should not surprise us that there are evil men and women who would pursue such things, however, what should surprise and appall us is that far too many Americans have gone along with these deceivers. Are the majority of Americans so deceived, so ungrateful or so ignorant and isolated from the truth of the Word of God they do not hear the Spirit of God in His attempt to lead us out of this utter deceit.

While writing this book our President George W. Bush has made stunning appointments to the Supreme Court and one of the appointments, Justice Roberts, has become the Chief Justice. The liberal democrats in the senate tried every way to destroy Justice Roberts because he is a just and righteous man.

Unfortunately, our people see our glory and greatness in our diversity without thinking about the implications and application of their thinking. Certainly God has created many different peoples, however, that does not imply we have many different Gods. The strength of our diversity is not found in molding together the different religious beliefs, attitudes, cultures and evil baggage of all the worlds cults into one big cultural stew that we serve up to our people thinking it will somehow make us a better society.

The truth is not diverse it is specific and absolute. It is the attitudes and ideas that flow from various levels of ignorance and rebellion that are diverse. It is the blending of evil and selfish attitudes, appetites and agenda's that mold a rebellious and dead-end perspective.

If there was perfection in our knowledge and understanding and our hearts were pure our thinking would not be diverse at all. Our strength as a nation is found in our like-mindedness as it relates to our religious faith and Spiritual life. Diverse thinking in our foundational belief system is not glorious and strengthening at all, in fact, it is a testimony to our incredible need for the wisdom and love of God.

A heart searching for the truth will soon find him or herself moving away from diverse thinking not toward it. Our eyes become opened and we begin to see the truth and our hope and strength becomes founded on the nature, character, power and grace of God. Our strength and hope is in the sovereignty of one God and Creator who, as the bible teaches and our founding fathers recognized, takes notice of every sparrow that hits the ground, knew you and I before the foundation of the earth, knows every hair on your head and loves you and I and uses all things for good for those who love God. This nation, nor any person, was or is born or lives without His notice and in fact His direct involvement.

Unless we are total dunces we must ask ourselves the question, where does rebellion and destructive attitudes come from? History, our personal experience and our conscience, teaches us that all that is good and wholesome in our society can be traced back to biblical truth and principle of the bible, the character of God and the guidance of His Holy Spirit. It is the rebellious will of man inspired by the deceiver that adopts and promotes these foolish ideas and attitudes that, unfortunately, are but a reflection of the emerging lack of our national character.

A nation of people who chooses to honor God and His will and earnestly attempts to discern and walk according to His will and way are indeed a courageous people of high moral character. They are typically industrious, honest, loving, trustworthy, fruitful and kind people. They typically obey the laws of the land and submit themselves to those leaders elected to guide and lead our nation. The United States of America emerged out of the hearts and minds of that kind of people. Everything good about America is found in the goodness and grace of the God we serve!!

Our current President George Bush is clearly a gift of God. He is attempting to lead a rebellious people by using principles that are right and just and biblically based. Unfortunately the majority of Americans who profess to be Christian are proving not to be Christian at all. Many are deceived and fail to recognize or appreciate his leadership. He depends on God to go before and prepare the way. He is morally strong and does not appear to be intimidated by the devil or his disciples or by his evil schemes. He has learned that he is called to believe and obey and the rest is up to the Creator. I pray that he will stay the course!!

Because of his faith many hate our President and do everything destructive they can think of or promote to discredit him and to ultimately destroy him, destroy his ability to lead and destroy his political popularity among the people of America. The secularists and the liberals hate him because he professes to be a man of faith and they hate God and His people and certainly His guiding truth's and principles because they know they will ultimately be judged by these truths and principles.

We must therefore ask another question; " why would anyone want to fight against what is right and good?" The battle our President has is to produce goodness, justice, liberty and fruitfulness out of the lives of all Americans, including those Americans who are spiritually lost in the confusion of evil worldly ways and walking in active rebellion against God. He recognizes he is the President of all our citizens, even those who are no longer able to discern or love the truth. These are very difficult times and President Bush has a tiger by the tail because he is face to face with the deceiver, the spirit of Satan, who God declared to be the king of this world. The world hates God and hates every Christian believer because the world is evil.

It's really not very complicated. The bible declares, and history confirms, that a nation is blessed whose God is the Lord. The bible also teaches us and history also confirms that a people who rejects God and His revealed will are a foolish people without vision or moral character since they have rejected the author of morality and the foundational truth and principles on which courage, character and morality stands and by which life is defined and lived. The Word of God defines the essence of moral character. Without God's wisdom and the biblical moral code outlined in the Ten Commandments there is no such thing as moral character.

Wise leadership is impossible without the discipline of moral truth and the character it produces in the hearts and minds of those who are not in rebellion against God. Spiritual leadership and inspiration are as indispensable to good national leadership, courage and moral character as Spiritual vision, which is vital to leadership. Vision establishes purpose and inspiration. These qualities, wisdom, moral truth, Spiritual vision and inspiration are all indispensable qualities in the character of Godly leadership.

We reap what we sow according to our Creator! History allows us to look back at the impact of past leadership. Its results cannot be hidden. *"You will know them by their fruits, grapes are not gathered from thorn bushes, nor figs from thistles, are they? Even so, every good tree bears good fruit; but the bad tree bears bad fruit. A good tree cannot produce bad fruit, nor can a bad tree produce good fruit. (Matthew 7:16-18)*

The direction a nation chooses and the culture it produces are impacted vitally by the character and the fruits of the efforts of their leaders. Unfortunately what often seems good to man at the moment is not good. The Lord warns us **"there is a way that seems good to man, but its way leads to death."** What we often settle for seems good, however, it is simply not always what is best or wisest. Our decisions and focus without God's wisdom and guidance tends to be short sighted and the short-cut solution which often makes the problem worse.

The scriptures teach us that *"those who are according to the flesh set their minds on the things of the flesh, but those who are according to the Spirit, the things of the Spirit. For the mind set on the flesh is death, but the mind set on the Spirit is life and peace, because the mind set on the flesh is hostile toward God; for it does not subject itself to the law of God, for it is not eve able to do so; and those who are in the flesh cannot please God." (Romans 8:5-11)* The contrast between the perspective of the man of God and the man of the world is profound and it likewise has profound implications.

The women's liberation movement in America has introduced almost irrecoverable damage to the cause of the family not to mention the social, moral, economic and political implications. Society and the church has surrendered to this rebellion and the movement has advanced to the point of total rebellion even to the extent of women's groups promoting attempts at re-writing the bible to change the identity of God from the masculine to the neutral gender in which God can be a he or a she depending on whether you prefer to think of Him as male or female.

The church because of its intimidation and its capitulation thinking somehow the need to hide from the repercussions of such foolishness now finds itself involved in endless secular debates over the issue of women priests and pastors. The Word of God gives clear direction to the church in that it rejects the idea outright. God has clearly given the role of leadership in His creation the responsibility of man. Man has not always accepted his responsibility and men have abused it. Since God is our Creator we will ultimately have to decide his purposes are good enough for us!. If we chose not to we will reap what we have sown.

This women's equal opportunity social revolution has opened the door to promiscuous sexual activity, divorce, live-in relationship arrangements, and homosexual marriage arrangements and has devastated the family unit, which God created as the foundation of society.

Love has become an emotional, physical and political thing of mutual accommodation often tied to physical attraction and racing hormones rather than a spiritual and moral relationship in which a man and women are committed to that which is best for each of them and for their relationship from a biblical perspective and to serving the interests and needs of the other and the family.

We have allowed the politically correct gender equal opportunity nonsense to prevail in our public discourse to the extent that all government and politically correct social correspondence and public discourse must avoid the words he, him, his, man, men, male etc when referring to employees. The term now must be "person" or it is considered to be discriminatory and politically incorrect.

Women have declared themselves to be a minority because in doing so they can use discrimination to get special treatment by the court and benefits not otherwise available to them. In the workplace discrimination is the common cry of many women who are denied employment or promotion because the employer feels a man is better suited for the job! How dare the employer who pays the salary and benefits for his employee's be so bold as to define the sex of the person he desires to be his employee or employee's!

In the social realm every institution created by and for the exclusive fellowship of men is finding its right to exclude women from membership is being challenged on the basis of discrimination by amoral attorneys in liberal secular courts, such as the infamous liberal 9th circuit court in San Francisco, California.

There is an active feminist movement of a few rebellious women who are constantly engaged in a deceitful move to encourage rebellious young women who refuse to grow up to carry the banner for the women's liberation cause in America by attempting to enter one or the other of the traditionally all male military academies. This move is designed to challenge the role of men and the right of the nation and its military institutions to limit and establish the role of women in the military to those jobs they are best suited to fulfill.

The courts seem to have overlooked the constitution, which places the operation of the military under the jurisdiction of the Commander and Chief. They have decided they must take it upon them selves to determine what is best for the military.

We, the American people, expect our Commander in Chief and the commanders he in turn selects to command, train, prepare, and employ the military. The military is an instrument of our national policy. Its mission, size and use are determined by that policy. Our

313

President and the congress set our national policy. However, the people do not elect our President to be a puppet of the Supreme Court or the Congress.

The cost, economic and militarily of the court imposed placement of females in our military academes and in combat roles must be counted in lives lost, troop morale, force effectiveness and in the foolish and needless expenditure of billions of dollars.

The brain dead arguments that support this sexual neutral move in the military is obviously recognized as foolish to anyone who has served in combat in the military. The general confusion, inefficiency and division this idiocy has caused affect virtually every aspect of the military and its cost is astronomical. And its effect has negative moral and Spiritual consequences. It has needlessly cost the loss of lives in combat situations. Beyond that, out of wedlock pregnancy in the military has gone off the charts. I wonder why?

The military complex has been devastated and emasculated by the foolish decisions of liberal Judges and foolish political leaders, who, under political pressures have endorsed the foolish and destructive idea of forcing upon the nation and the military the placement of women in inappropriate roles and places in the military.

Certainly an even more destructive and foolish decision in regard to military personnel policy was the decision to allow gay men and women to serve in the military in virtually any role. The crazy idea of "don't ask – don't tell" is a brain dead idea. If anyone has to explain to you the many problems associated with this move, then there is no explanation simple enough for you to understand.

At any rate, serving in the military is not a right! You must be qualified. Millions are turned away from military service because they don't pass physical, mental, psychological and a mired of other qualifying tests. The military also discriminates against age, disabled, freaks of nature and convicted criminals. Why? Because the nature of the mission of the military discriminates against the use of many groups of people. That is the way it should be. Americans don't want a military that is some sort of social experiment where every nut case attempts to advance his psychological bent or his or her liberal agenda.

The point is, we elect and appoint leaders to make decisions for us and we expect them to do just that. We also give them the authority to make those decisions and carry them out. Attempting to micro-manage the military is not the way to create an effective military. When the court and every other Senator attempts to play the role of Commander in Chief it devastates and confuses our soldiers, undermines the authority of the Commander and Chief encourages our enemies and demoralizes our military leaders.

Someone needs to wake up and realize that politicians without the wisdom and moral courage to lead have lost every war we have been engaged in since the end of WWII until the war to liberate Kuwait.

Since that time we can look to the recent war in Iraq as a textbook example of military success. However, we are now slowly but surely allowing the liberal contingency of the legislative branch of our government to destroy the effectiveness of the mission in Iraq by misguided and sometimes treasonous acts, attitudes and public declarations.

I got distracted for a moment. Before we get away from the role of women in our society I should point out that I believe women should be allowed to work for the government in limited military roles at primarily domestic locations and only when they are in fact qualified and the environment is appropriate. Consider the following reasons that guide my reasoning:

> First, military service offers career training and opportunities to those who serve on active duty that would otherwise be denied to women not allowed to serve.
>
> Second, women can serve effectively in administrative, medical, logistic and support roles in the military that can free-up men for combat and combat training roles.
>
> Third, when women graduate from high school and cannot afford college, or are otherwise unable to go on to college, they face the need for employment to sustain themselves and training to prepare themselves just as the men do unless they get married and begin raising a family. The military offers an opportunity to extend their training and serve the country at the same time.
>
> Fourth, military training and discipline tends to accelerate the maturing process while serving our nation in important and appropriate roles.
>
> Fifth, Military service also helps provide financial help with college tuition after the tour of military duty is completed. This opportunity would otherwise only be extended to men.
>
> Sixth, Women can make a significant, important and needed impact on the efficiency and effectiveness of the military if properly trained and assigned.

The military is not a social club or a public equal opportunity welfare program. The training results and the associated operational problems the military is experiencing in implementing this equal opportunity policy in the military exposes the foolishness of the idea. It destroys the morale of the men who have to meet the standard. They see the hypocracy of the game and wonder why meeting the standard is important for them and not important for the women. Unfortunately, there does not appear to be anybody in a leadership position who has the moral or political courage to challenge this utter nonsense.

The assignment of women in the military is part of a much bigger problem in our society where the radical feminists in rebellion against God's defined roles for women and men in the family and in society have promoted the idea and in our deceit many Americans have bought it!

The scriptures teach us that women are to submit to their husbands and that husbands are supposed to love and protect their wives. **"Wives, be subject to your own husbands,** as to the lord. **For the husband is head of the wife, as Christ also is the head of the church. He himself being the savior of the body. But as the church is subject to Christ, so also the wives ought to be to their husbands in everything.''** (Ephesians 55:22-24)

Certainly it is out of context to quote the above scripture without also quoting the admonition of the lord to men and husbands: **''husbands, love your wives, just as Christ also loved the church and gave himself up for her;''** (ephod 5:25)

The context of both of these scriptures is key here. Listen: (**Ephesians 5:17**), **''so then, do not be foolish, but understand what the will of the lord is.''**

These scriptures cause much pain to many because they expose rebellion against God's call upon our lives.

We can argue all we want; however, the wisest advice is to save the words and frustration because the argument is not with me! It is our Creator you are going to have to convince because we will all be judged by His words and will. Millions, even billions, have rebelled against him before you and I came along and they have all perished in their sin and rebellion. I don't think we will be able to change His mind nor do I think it is profitable to try. His Word is clear

If you are a women's liberation person who claims to be a Christian you are obviously deceived about life's purpose and who you are created to be in Christ and you are in direct rebellion against Gods will for you. Your frustration is the product of your rebellion!

Many women are busy attempting to convince, or force, others to appreciate or conform to their agenda. If you tend to think that way you are perhaps thinking, ''I went to college four years just like my husband; I also went to law school, or perhaps medical school and graduated and even passed the bar exam. Sure, I have a family and they are being provided for. I sacrificed and made all this preparation so I could make my own way or place my mark on society, establish my own identity and independence and make up my own mind about what I want to do with my life. I am a women necessarily trying to prove that women are just as capable as men in business or as an attorney or a doctor or a pilot or perhaps even an engineer or teacher etc''.

If that is your attitude perhaps the Lord may be attempting to remind you that the greatest and most significant mark you will ever make while in this world is to become a child of God and to raise up the children he has given you in the nurture and admonition of the Lord and to work along side your husband on his team so both of you might become everything God would have you to be. Your education will help you no matter the arena you decide to live in, however, it can be best spent in the arena God has called you to live in, at least while you are raising your children. The obvious problem is that if you are planning to commit your life to worldly ambitions and/or a career outside the home then raising a family is not the direction you should go.

A decision to sacrifice the needs of the family for a second paycheck is sometimes necessary, however, it is often the wrong decision. Sometimes, for single parent families, it cannot be avoided. If you have been a Christian very long perhaps you have noticed that many of life's critical decisions usually have to be made under challenging circumstances where making the right decision requires some level of sacrifice.

Unfortunately we live in an evil world where good is not the easy or the applauded path. The right decision often requires the discernment of what is better or best. It is not that another way is necessarily evil it is just not the wise decision because it produces what it sows. Good decisions for we men and women with fallen natures require the help of God and His wisdom.

The German people during the mid – 1930's and 1940's are an example of the deceit and indifference of a society to the impact of tragic government decisions and leadership. The history of the world is filled with examples of deceived leaders who have influenced deceived followers in destructive causes that seemed like a good idea at the time!!!

Jesus refers to us in the scriptures as sheep, and so we are!! He also warns those who seek leadership positions of their responsibility because of the nature and vulnerability of those who must serve and follow.

For example, any candidate for the court or for national public office must be willing to support abortion if he hopes to get the women s vote. It, in fact, ought to be just the opposite. Abortion is a horror that makes the Jewish holocaust look like a Sunday school picnic. Those members of the Supreme Court who began this atrocity will surely have to answer for what they have done. They, much like those social reformers during the Second World War, who created and promoted "Rosie the Riveter" proceeded foolishly not understanding the potential destructiveness and heartache they were introducing for future generations of Americans. The pulpits in the churches in Europe sat silent, for the most part, as Hitler murdered millions of Jews.

Many readers will not be able to see the connection. Others will see Rosie as the heroic symbol of the liberation of women from the control and leadership of their husbands and of men in general. Others will see and understand immediately. Only those who have ears to hear and eyes to see will recognize the truth and its implications.

The purpose of the church is to reveal God's plan and offer it to those who understand, believe and receive it. The Scriptures clearly reveal that deliverance demands Spiritual rebirth. Men and women must repent of their worldly ways and accept God's wonderful plan to liberate each of us. The Scriptures teach us that we must become new creations in Christ Jesus to be delivered. One of the indications of that rebirth is obedience to God's revealed will. Spiritual rebirth re-orients our conscience and changes our nature making it possible to love God and our fellowman and to live in a family and community of committed relationships with others who are living to obey God's will and express through our lives and in our rhetoric the glory and purposes of our Lord. It is a little silly to claim to be a Christian and live in utter rebellion against the revealed will of our Lord. *"The one the one says, 'I have come to know Him, and does not keep His commandments, is a liar, and the truth is not in him; but whoever keeps His word, in him the love of God has truly been perfected. By this we know that we are in Him.." (1 John 2:4-6)* The born again believer's testimony is *"I have been crucified with Christ; and it is no longer I who live, but Christ lives in me; and the life which I now live in the flesh I live by faith in the Son of God, who love me, and delivered Himself up for me." (Galatians 2:20)*

As someone has said, "hindsight is 20-20". That doesn't imply that we ought not to study history and learn from it! It does imply that we as a society consider the use of "hindsight" as somehow unfair to engage in! Life is not a game we are playing! It is not a matter of fairness it's a matter of righteousness! It is not a matter of judgment, it is a matter of discernment. Wisdom is good and it implies a keen ability to discern good from bad and right from wrong. History reveals the works of the Creator.

Regardless, we must ask ourselves what else we might have done and why so we might not repeat the same mistakes? One thing that stands out is that we must elect wise and good political leaders and appoint leaders and Judges who have a clear biblical perspective of the "big" picture and a clear set of priorities that are aligned with biblical principle and the will of God. Man is hopelessly lost without God and the decisions he makes tend to reflect his deceit, blindness and his sinful nature.

Our people, our church leaders and our elected and appointed leaders must come to recognize they will ultimately be held accountable for their leadership at whatever level they are placed. Our government can either enact, enforce, ignore or repeal those laws that work to reflect the will of God, encourage Godly behavior and protect our best interests. Therefore, we as a society have chosen to either change or ignore those laws that interfere with our desires and appetites, lusts and lifestyles.

We as a society must be spiritually awakened because we have rejected the revealed will of God because it limits our appetites, pleasures and lusts.

A large part of the social tailspin, which has encompassed the last two generations of Americans, can easily be traced back to the failure of Church to provide salt and light to the election of our political leaders and appointment of Church leaders.

Many have drifted so far away from the light of truth that its value and wisdom is no longer visible to them. Our deceit has blinded us to the extent that we are unable and/or unwilling to associate homes without full time mothers with many of the family and social problems facing us today! We are unable to generate the wisdom to associate the cause with the solution. We have become fools!!!

It is no secret to anyone able to see the truth that the deceived world is actively engaged in the process of removing the biblical and historically fact of the great value of the properly ordered family unit to any society. Our modern culture must destroy the family and our religious heritage to be victorious in their evil secular agenda. The gay liberation movement, many of the racist legal and social organizations and the women liberation movements are working frantically to destroy the biblically established and historically recognized family unit functioning in the roles assigned by the Creator.

Unfortunately in metropolitan America the family unit that made America stable and strong is rapidly becoming a rare specimen indeed either inside or outside the church. In 2003 one out of every three children born to Caucasians in America was born out of wedlock. 2 out of three children born to African Americans were born out of wedlock. Approximately 45,000,000 abortions have occurred since Roe v Wade in 1973. 4000 abortions occur every day or one abortion every 22 seconds. (Source: Focus on the Family) Our Church and political leaders find abortion controversial so they are silent about abortion and the general moral degradation of our society that allows our society to accept abortion.

We are supported in our wrong choices because we live in a world and a culture that is no longer able to discern between good and bad and therefore does not see choices like abortion as wrong choices. We have been lead by deceived leaders with fallen natures and by deceived parents and a deceived society that accepts and promotes destructive secular idea's simply because they have been accepted by and promoted by a majority of those in society as the norm.

The bible calls it the blind leading the blind! It is indeed a matter of deceit. Once we lose our sense of purpose, our vision, our spiritual wisdom and the biblical principles and priorities that lead to life, every choice becomes little more than choosing between a variety of options each of which appear to us to have equal value depending on what you personally value. We then have no foundation upon which our choices stand nor any standard by which we can measure one choice against another.

America has become materialistic and naturalistic in our social attitudes and the philosophies that guide our thinking have become secular humanist! The naturalist sees the world as a closed system, which cannot be penetrated by an outside overseeing and overruling God that can reach down into that system and change the rules. In a collective blindness that has crept over us we have lost our moral compass. Therefore, the world's answer has to be, get rid of the family unit and its value system as we know it. The foundation block of society and community must be replaced with a secular humanist idea of man's concoction that justifies his sin and fulfills his pleasures, appetites and lusts.

Unfortunately, an indifferent citizenry, a sleepy church, deceived political leaders and a deceived judiciary has allowed liberal secular humanist ideas and men to gain leadership positions in politics, education, industry and even religion and to make their secular Godless agenda the law of the land and the culturally acceptable way of life. Liberty and freedom are certainly a gift from God, however, they are gifts reserved for those who will protect them. America is reaping the destruction it has sowed!!

When only a small minority of a society is deceived and has a destructive agenda their wrong choices have a small impact that is not particularly devastating to society. In that circumstance the wrong choices of a foolish, misguided minority are seen in strong contrast to the right choices by a majority of society. However, if foolish and destructive choices are ignored and they are allowed to grow and influence the direction of the nation and the lives of the majority the moral direction of the majority begins to erode and soon society begins to accept the wrong choices as the right choices and society increases the frequency and intensity of the same wrong choices.

The impact of wrong, deceived or evil choices reverse the traditional moral social structure and erodes away the very foundational righteous principles that were put in place to sustain it. The wrong choices in society begin to change the perspective of the people until they begin to see wrong as right and that which is right as wrong or they simply become indifferent to the effect of either choice and evil flourishes because of their bad choices. Jesus said it this way, *"Therefore, everyone who hears these words of Mine, and acts upon them, may be compared to a wise man, who built his house upon the rock. And the rain descended, and the floods came, and the winds blew, and burst against that house; and yet it did not fall, for it had been founded upon the rock. And everyone who hears these words of Mine, and does not act upon them, will be like a foolish man, who built his house upon the sand. And the rain descended, and the floods came, and the winds blew and burst against the house; and it fell and great was its fall." (Matthew 7:24-27)*

And so it is for the family built upon the bedrock of biblical principal and lead by the Spirit of God.

We have all been trained up to believe the lie that the community can replace a full time mother and now we have adopted the lie as the truth. The mother who works diligently at home and finds her purpose and identity in raising a family that honors God and parents and keeps a home that honors her family and recognizes the value of the family unit is the woman considered out of touch and out of step with the American way.

Besides each person choosing for himself or herself to deny the truth and trust the raising of the children to the world, the issue of forcing the responsibility to care for the children of working mothers upon the public through tax incentives and/or upon the employers must be confronted with the light of truth and discouraged as a social expectation.

Meanwhile the debate that seemingly never ends in America today is whether women or men are equally capable in the work place? Obviously that is the diversion and not the question we need to be focused on. Some women are better qualified for some jobs and some men are better qualified for some jobs. It doesn't take a special investigation to determine which jobs are generally performed best by which gender! However, the critical question is; what role has God ordered for men and for women in the family and in society and what are the implications and ramifications of disregarding His order? The second question that must be answered is simply what is the proper role of government leadership, education, the church and society in this regard?

Many will argue that women have done brilliant and great things in the workplace. In fact they would point to the generally accepted idea that because of women in the workplace we were able to win World War II and become a prosperous nation. They will argue that much has been and continues to be accomplished to advance America industrially, technically and economically because of women in the workplace.

They will go on to point out that women in the work place has dramatically increased the gross national product and is in large part responsible for the continued expansion of the United States economy has enjoyed since the depression years. They will argue that much of our two or three cars per family prosperity is due to the contributions of women in the workplace.

I must concede that much of their argument may very well be correct from the materialistic perspective. However, it misses the point in the larger scheme of things. Life is a Spiritual matter rather than an economic or material matter..

Unfortunately, the argument of modern culture is secular and spiritually blind. It ignores, rejects and/or refuses to acknowledge God's will and purpose nor will their deceit allow them to accept the responsibility for the destruction caused in America by taking the mother out of the home. This movement has devastated the family unit and the suffering it has brought to children and the family unit has suffered spiritual and moral devastation.

Once again the real issues we need to deal with in our society is "what is America's perspective regarding God's revealed will and what does God's revealed will have to do with the governing of America?" If the objective of life is meaningful life, strong families, children raised in the nurture and admonition of the lord and raising up children to value character and seek after righteousness, justice, peace with God and their fellowman and the development of a strong, moral and stable citizenry living in the context of the liberty God has ordered for men then we had better seek God and His will for our lives, repent and begin to turn this train around.

If the goal and only measure of true success is to make more and more money so we can continue to lavish more pleasure and luxury upon ourselves and upon our children and to train up our children to further perpetuate this goal then we would have to say we have succeeded.

Perhaps God has given America a new leader who will act as His ambassador. Perhaps he has given us another voice to awaken us to our spiritual condition and another opportunity to respond to His bidding. As a nation I encourage you to work hand and hand with our Christian President George Bush and to pray for him and encourage him to stand firm and continue to be a strong voice helping to re-establish our national direction back to dependence upon God and the biblical principles that birthed and sustained us as a people and a nation to this point.

Unfortunately it is not simple even for Godly men to discern God's voice in crises situations and it is impossible for ungodly men. God placed the church and his word in the earth to bring salt and light into the world, however, when the church becomes compromised and blinded by its deceit it is no longer bringing salt and light. It begins to become transformed into the ways of the world it was sent to help transform. In its deceit it sometimes declares God's blessings on leaders and events that do not warrant His blessing at all but rather are clearly against His will and/or provision! God's enemies are often declared to be his friends and the perspective of what is good and what is bad becomes reversed.

Looking back and comparing the past to our current social direction it seems obvious that we made and continue to make the same bad choices. We don't seem to be able to grasp the truth the evidence reveals.

Someone has suggested that one of the first things a person should do who find himself straddling a dead horse is to dismount. Liberals and secularists in our society are attempting to remove God from Government, from our education system and from the public arena when even a casual observance of the facts and our own experience reveals that everything good, just, righteous and fulfilling comes from God and much of what is bad, profane, evil, unjust, corrupt and hopeless comes from man without God.

In America today we need courageous and honorable, Spirit lead leaders! Our senate and congress needs to be flushed out along with the "behind the scene" evil power system that forces freshmen senators and congressmen to fall in line and compromise themselves and their constituents. They soon find they must join the rest of congress or the senate in the political sewer. Their compromise ultimately renders them harmless and helpless to bring any true change to the system.

We overlook the fact that the majority of our government's leaders today are secular humanists lacking spiritual wisdom and courage. In their deceit they see themselves as the repository of wisdom and right, a law unto themselves, without the need to strictly adhere to the constitutional guarantees or to follow the source of all true wisdom. They can do as they please and spend millions attempting to convince a deceived citizenry that whatever they are promoting is good for America.

Government bureaucracy and much of the political leadership of our nation is unfortunately a national disgrace. The political leadership of America has become so compromised, corrupt and self focused they are almost totally ineffective at bringing about much needed change in America. For the most part they are Spiritually blind men. The scriptures refer to such leaders as "blind guides".

Certainly there are honest and hard working government servants trying to make a difference who recognize the problem and truly want to increase government efficiency and decrease its size and scope. Unfortunately they are exceptions overshadowed by far to many politically correct, self-serving, incompetent and overpaid bureaucrats who have found a ticket to ride and they are milking it for all they can get out of it while producing as little as possible.

The exposure of the base animal nature of fallen man is becoming more acceptable to our culture and more apparent in the activities of our people as we reject the disciplines of moral restraint and as government attempts to navigate the social demand for political correctness.

Human dignity, discipline, restraint, self and mutual respect are considered bad and unduly burdensome because they fly in the face of natural lustful appetites. Our ignorance betrays us as we arrogantly measure the righteousness of our judgments with the yardstick of material prosperity and the comfort and satisfaction of the flesh!

Character, faith, sacrifice, courage, integrity, responsibility, accountability, wisdom and charity are foundational values that have been rejected by most of our government leaders and their associated bureaucracy. These value's have been replaced by a foreign value system which promotes and justifies ideas such as doing what comes naturally, lying when you need to protect yourself, keeping up appearances, deceit, arrogance, pride, if it feels good do it, and last but not least give the people what they want to hear and promise them anything to get their support.

One lesson President Clinton taught us was the fickleness and the short memory and deceit of our deluded culture. He taught us that if we just tell people what they want to hear over and over again they begin to think they are getting what they have been promised and soon they forget what they wanted in the first place.

Our political leaders seem almost universally to hold the attitude that it is not necessary to deliver what you promise the people when you are running for election because the people will soon forget what you promised. If the people should happen to remember and insist on performance the strategy becomes to just deny it and the people will think they misunderstood. '

Our people fail to see this shift in perspective as a spiritual shift away from truth and God to a new system committed to dependence upon the base fallen nature of man.

We boast and congratulate each other for our historical national greatness and criticize anyone who would dare remind us that except for the grace of God we would be desolate! Foreign policy decisions during the Clinton administration diluted our national defense capability and exposed the folly of our leadership in their attempts at international leadership. Our domestic leadership is being exposed and despised for its folly and its self-serving political motivations as we fight terrorism in the Middle East.

The American dream has become a mid-night train on a fast track toward a head-on collision with truth and reality fueled by a debt driven economic system and run by secular humanist social philosophers. The stability of the life style much of America lives today is dependent upon delusion and deceit. The biggest and hardest task national government has today is developing the spin to put on information so the truth can be hidden.

It should be no mystery to anyone that our political system is driven by a system of strong special interest groups battling each other for a bigger share of the money and power. They are all attempting to protect the many special interests of our diversity at the taxpayer's expense. Our government spends its energies and resources attempting to navigate this minefield of special interests, which brings any potential for positive progress to a virtual standstill.

The idea of truth in government or of responsive, responsible and accountable government servants is considered a radical idea in today's culture. It has long since been discarded, except in the publicity stunts and the cleverly engineered photo ops created to promote some politician and hide the truth.

Neither government nor consumer spending is controlled by the standard of affordability. That is a foreign idea considered negative and disruptive in our culture. The volunteer, so to speak, income tax system is an administrative nightmare and simply to costly and inefficient to administer. It must be changed and will be changed. The question is to what will it be changed and how will the change be administered.

The church must find the courage to act as a conscience to our nation encouraging government to establish programs which truly meet the needs of needy people, however, it must also find the courage and wisdom to respond correctly so as to inspire, encourage, guide and train people to provide for themselves and their families!

Somehow the church has interpreted its role so as to leave that responsibility to secular government programs that often tend to create a bigger problem rather than solving the original problem. If we really love our fellowman we must provide him with the leadership and inspiration to provide for himself and for his family. We cannot and ought not help the one who refuses to help himself.

The Clinton administration attempted to solve the poverty problem through a never-ending list of social hand-out welfare programs designed to redistribute wealth thinking that poverty can be solved by simply taking money from those who have some and giving it to those who do not.

Unfortunately the nature of much of America's poverty problem cannot be solved through government handouts because handout programs tend to act as an incentive toward indolence for those to lazy to work. They also tend to enslave the poor into government dependency.

Even if there was enough tax money to temporarily deliver everyone from poverty and provide them free medical care, and for the record there is not, those who are not willing to earn their way or refuse to exercise the disciplines of accountability or refuse to learn the way out of their poverty would soon be back in poverty looking for someone to bail them out again.

Prolonged give-away programs to those able to care for themselves are a serious mistake. Unless carefully administered the programs designed to re-distribute wealth will eventually destroy the incentives that drive our economic system. They will eventually bankrupt our nation and destroy the inspiration and courage of an industrious people.

The liberal thinking crowd in America has forgotten or never understood that the fallen nature of all men tends to lead him away from accepting responsibility for himself or accountability for his actions. The nature of man will tend to lead him into the dependence traps inherent in long-term handout programs. Men tend to do those things that give him the greatest return with the least amount of effort. His deceit does not allow him to see that if allowed to follow that course he will destroy himself.

As someone said, there are just too many who want to ride in the wagon and not enough willing to help pull it!! Between our government welfare system and our big government bureaucracy, which itself has become a welfare employer, the working man in the private sector who is paying his taxes and pulling the welfare wagon is overwhelmed with the ever increasing tax bill necessary to finance this bankrupt liberal agenda.

I don't want to imply that we are to ignore the needy of our society. Clearly any moral and humane people must see their responsibility to provide tangible help to the legitimate needy and disenfranchised. However, taking care of those to lazy to provide for themselves is sending the wrong signal. I might add so is an oversized government bureaucracy whose members feed at the public trough with public provided cradle to grave health care, generous retirement benefits and protection from the working world reality of the private sector is out of control at every level of government

Our political leaders simply don't have the courage or wisdom to tell America that just because someone exists in America doesn't mean he deserves to be or ought to be guaranteed cradle to grave security by the rest of us. Not only that, simply because some politician is supposedly "sacrificing" his otherwise abundant career opportunity in order to serve in civil government doesn't mean that working Americans are obligated to insure him or her cradle to grave security.

The politicians themselves unfortunately have feathered their own bed to where it is an embarrassment to men of good conscience. Congressmen and senators who serve one term and are taken care of the rest of their lives is the result of wrong public policy. They are the ones who offer these handouts and they are so compromised themselves they lack the moral courage to do what must be done to truly attack poverty, or for that matter, most any social problem in America.

Attacking the poverty problem in a way that truly reduces poverty requires wise and strong leadership. It demands disciplined courageous leaders who are able and willing to make tough decisions which will clearly impact their re-elect ability. Those citizens on public welfare of one kind or another make up one of the largest single voting special interest groups in America! Political leaders who want to move people off the welfare roles would lose support among those who see their lives as dependent upon those handout programs.

The vast majority of the electorate is brainwashed and focused on self-interest. They vote into office anyone who will offer them more than the next candidate regardless of the price, who will have to pay it, or how much individual freedom will have to be sacrificed to get it!

We no longer elect men because they are men of character and courage. We elect those who promise us the most and make noises as though they will be somehow able to deliver!

We are a nation prime for a national leader who will lead us to destruction. Thank God we do not currently have such a leader. If we choose the wrong leader all that is needed is a national emergency that requires and authorizes the President to place America under marshal law and nationalize our resources and people to adequately respond to the supposed or real emergency. That will open the door to a beginning of a totalitarian dictatorship beginning to form its root in America. Can't happen in America? Why do you think it can't? In a secular world such a move could be easily justified.

Hitler was able to mobilize Germany and inspire pride and patriotism that brought Germany out of virtual economic and social collapse. He became a hero and his intentions were to provide and protect what he considered, and what most of Germany considered, was good for Germany. He was misguided and the more power he was given the more he took. The more power he had the more corrupt and perverted his original intention became. His deceit fed his ambition and expanded his vision and Germany was trapped because they had given him the power to destroy them. He was indeed a blind guide, however, for him to be any kind of guide required a blind people to bring him to power and follow after his leadership.

An important fact we must never overlook is that clearly an overwhelming majority of the German people favored Hitler and his programs even though the defensive cry of the German people after the war was, " But we didn't know"! If there were Germans who didn't know it was because they didn't want to take the trouble to find out or they chose to ignore what was going on because life seemed good and Hitler's regime seemed to be feathering their economic nests. Hitler became what the German people allowed him to become!

Had Hitler won the Second World War, rather than having lost it, he would have become the leader of virtually all of Europe and Russia. He would have been hailed by a majority of the people of the world as one of the greatest leaders the world had ever known to that time. Another Alexander the great! It would have indeed been a tragedy! The world owes America and England and many veterans for their delivery from Hitler's tyranny.

The lesson of course is that America is becoming mesmerized with the same altruistic ideas. It is a recipe for disaster and we don't seem to be able to get enough of it fast enough. Many of our national leaders are blind and foolish leading a blind, indifferent and foolish people who will go along with almost anything so long as it feeds their appetites and satisfies their desires.

Roosevelt had good intentions and provided inspirational and practical leadership in a critical time in American history. He did many great things for America and is no doubt considered one of America's greatest presidents. His leadership brought America out of one of the greatest economic downturns and depressions America had known since the war of independence.

However, the program he labeled the "new deal" which seemed so good at the time began the movement of America toward big government and socialism. It should have been at best a temporary emergency relief program to meet humanitarian needs during a time of crisis much like we mobilize physical and economic aid in times of devastating national disasters caused by hurricanes and earthquakes etc.

The "new deal" program was a give-away program that should have ended with the advent of America's economic recovery. Political leaders became drunk with the power they discovered they have to influence the people when they simply promise the people what they want. Roosevelt was trying to help Americans who were in desperate need and, of course, he was trying to win a political election. He saw what the people wanted and needed and he gave it to them and they loved him for it and elected him four times to the office of the president

Unfortunately, Theodore Roosevelt simply didn't understand, or he chooses to ignore, the long-term implications of his programs. The political leadership of our nation saw the favor they would have with the citizens by implementing this short-term solution to America's economic depression. The problem is, they failed to recognize the long-term implications of such a program if it was to be retained and expanded as a new way to big government, government dependence and the redistribution of wealth.

As a result altruism replaced an essential ingredient in the free enterprise economic system. The necessary incentive to be productive to survive and prosper and the distinctive American philosophy of liberty and its essential counterparts free enterprise and individual accountability were on their way out. In addition constantly growing government in size and scope, out of control government spending, unimagined taxation, more and greater social programs and therefore less and less freedom was to be in America's future.

When any government promises to guarantee the financial security of its citizens and takes over the individual social responsibilities and no longer holds men accountable our way of life and our freedoms begin to be lost. Men become lulled to sleep in their security and they lose their incentive to be productive. The author, Ian Kershaw, stated, "the road to Auschwitz was built by hate, but paved with indifference."

Leadership is important and good national leadership is vital!

Unless a majority of our citizenry is awakened to the tragedy that has and continues to unfold before us this same indifference will pave the road to totalitarianism for America. Government will continue to grow and grab more power and greater control over the nations wealth and of private enterprise. Our mounting dept will absorb more of our resources until it consumes us. We will lose more of our liberty and the free enterprise will become a memory.

Should we continue on this road of spiritual blindness it will ultimately lead to the imprisonment of those who object and voice their objections to government programs and controls! Men who object to the loss of liberty, onerous taxes, and unchecked government beaurocracy that makes men slaves of government, rather than a government will not be tolerated. The government of, for and by the people intended to serve men in those specific constitutionally limited area's spelled out by our founders will no longer be the governing authority of our land. Dissenters will be considered unpatriotic and enemies of the state and therefore enemies of the people! The value of the individual and his liberty will not be the overriding doctrine that guides the government.

My views are obviously conservative, however, I don't hold conservative views in a "cultic" context as though conservatism is a synonym for Godliness since that is certainly not the case! Conservative values can only be related as Christian when they can be defined biblically and are applied out of an attitude of love for people and the desire to see justice and righteousness and the common good prevail. Otherwise conservative views are just as bankrupt as any other worldview.

My commentary is intended to alert sleepy Christians Americans, encourage change, (sometimes-dramatic change), from some firmly established ways and attitudes that currently guide our government and our way of life in America.

Those on whom God has placed the mantel of leadership are clearly targeted in this writing! It is important to note that the bible declares that they will be the most harshly judged.

"Perspective" is presented to bring light that will perhaps influence and ultimately change the current perspective of those who read it toward a more biblical view of truth and justice and help Americans reflect on why and how we arrived where we are and how we are instructed to proceed from a biblical perspective!

I fully expect "perspective" to draw criticism and controversy! I will be very disappointed if it doesn't! In some ways criticism might well be a testimony to its effectiveness!

There will come criticism from those in and out of the church who are not convinced that the bible is the word of God! They are more comfortable being able to pick and chose which scriptures they wish to adopt as truth. They are foolish and their faith will be found lacking. They will find the proposition that men who are not born of the Spirit of God are slaves of the deceit that drives the world's wisdom.

Criticism is a necessary and inevitable result of any bold proclamation of God's truth in a world that hates God and his truth. The bible teaches us that every man, even the most foolish of men, recognizes deep inside the foolishness of arguing with God's word and therefore he must find a way to discredit it in order to justify his hate lest he be proven the fool that he is! The defensiveness and hate that spews out of natural man when confronted with the truth is a testimony to his deceit or to the knowledge of the folly to which he has committed his life.

Sincere men of faith seek the knowledge of the truth that they might benefit from its power. The world runs and hides from the truth because it exposes their deceit and folly.

Criticism will surely come from those in organized religion who have enlisted in the religious unity movement. They are fools who actively promote the idea of a utopian environment in which all religion is regarded as truth for someone and therefore we ought to embrace all religion and join together with them walking hand in hand in some sort of tolerant religious peace down a path of mutual deceit to ultimate mutual destruction in an eternal since! God to this crowd has become religious unity. This deceit is an attempt by Satan to join the institution of church together with the enemies of God in an effort of accommodation having planted the foolish idea that men can hold on to the truth by walking in a lie. This kind of thinking is total nonsense! It is like committing suicide to avoid being killed in the battle! It is surrendering in a battle you can win just because you don't want to fight the battle! Clearly, that is the ideological direction America has chosen to follow in its moral and ethical battles when confronted with the seemingly overwhelming power of evil and deceit.

We have forgotten, or chose to ignore, the lessons history and the bible teach regarding how much harm can be done by the accommodation of evil compromise. We see this unwise compromise in virtually every area of American life. Deceived leaders lead us to that kind of compromise!

Jean-François revel, author of "how democracies perish" and "the totalitarian temptation" wrote, **"during the geopolitical face-off that preceded world war II, they thought they could bribe Hitler to be moderate by granting him concessions that, in fact, gave him the time to rearm and then, suddenly, to overrun the continent."**

The struggle for peace leads us to adopt less than ideal and less than truth in order to avoid the struggle. Our intentions are often that we will choose to fight another day. We justify our accommodation of evil by saying that we will pick the hills we will fight on. Certainly there is an element of wisdom in fighting those battles where truth and principle are at stake as apposed to fighting battles in an attempt to simply force our agenda on someone else that has chosen a different agenda.

Clearly, there is a level of compromise in every area of human relationship. Love and mutual respect force some compromise upon us, at least in our expression. We don't destroy a relationship because we don't agree with someone in every area of thought or activity. A recent commercial heard on radio proclaimed an old Chinese proverb, which says, **"never remove a fly from a friends forehead with an hatchet."**

I don't know whose proverb it is but it captures the thought here. We recognize the battle lines and draw those lines where the real battle is. We don't go to the mat simply because we disagree on something in which there is room for disagreement or in area's that do not threaten principle, relationship or in those things that are not spiritually destructive. However, neither do we compromise by encouraging or engaging in evil and sin simply because we don't wish to offend the one who wants to engage us in the thought or activity or because the battle is dangerous.

Americans need to be awakened to the fact that democracies demand Spiritual leadership and a level of spiritual and political alertness. They also demand a tenacious non-compromising grasp on those foundational principles of the bible and our constitution if we are to survive. It is necessary to understand that is not required in totalitarian lead nations.

Socialists and communists and evil men can work openly in democracies under the protection of the system they are at work to destroy. However, democratic leaders cannot work openly in totalitarian nations. America has been given an incredible gift of unparalleled freedom but through our indifference and deceit we have not discerned and have therefore abandoned the responsibility and the level of alertness necessary to protect it.

America has enjoyed a rather delicate system of government that is poorly suited to lead other than men of good will toward others. It requires the guidance of the Spirit of God in the minds and hearts of its leaders and a people who are filled with the spirit and wisdom of his word. It is delicate, in part, because we have the only system of government that invites the enemy into its midst and protects him while he destroys the system that embraces him.

Our sleepiness and desire for peace has allowed us to adopt the idea of the pacifist who ultimately sees himself as the only real potential aggressor. He therefore concludes that by ostentatiously laying down his own arms he will avoid all danger of war. How can we help anyone else if we allow ourselves to be destroyed by our own deceit?

We have been lured down the path toward a sort of peace to the place where socialistic philosophies are considered synonymous with "peace". We have come to think that socialistic principle is in essence peaceful. We have almost adopted it as Godly since it asks nothing better than to advance peacefully and undressed. It is not until it meets resistance for which, of course, it is never responsible is that peace imperiled. Thus far, since the mid 1950'S, America has chosen not to confront socialism and its "live-in friend" communism with the solid wall of truth that has the power to utterly destroy it.

We need to wake up to the reality that all the campaigns of the world are aimed at disarming democracy, Christian faith and the Christian way of life.

The invaluable Spiritual truth, power and influence has been lost to the public arena in America by the acts of foolish leaders who have responded to foolish, indifferent and rebellious interests and by those citizens who have rejected the Spirit and wisdom of God and/or they consider it as either irrelevant or destructive.

We have arrived at a place in America and in the church where the blind is leading the blind. Most of the main line denominations of the Church have become intimidated by, and subservient to, worldly wisdom and the world system. The church has abandoned its calling and lost its capacity to provide wisdom, direction and leadership to our people and to our system of government and its leaders. It has lost the capacity to hear or respond to the leading of the Holy Spirit because it no longer views the bible as the word of God therefore the word is no longer instructive. The church called to be the fullness of Christ in the earth has surrendered to the world and chosen to abandon its calling to be salt and light to our nation. It has isolated itself and its Spiritual influence to the mundane things of church government and a variety of typically introverted religious programs and social activities. It no longer reflects the cutting edge of what God is saying and doing on earth.

There are exceptions of course! We should all thank God for these exceptions because they are the only witness of God's love, mercy and grace and they are the only true salt and light. The body of Christ, wherever it is found, is the fullness of Christ in the earth. His church is lead by His Spirit and His people exemplify His character and wisdom. However, it is a rare find in the religious community.

The influence of the abiding Spirit of God working though much of the organized church, whose membership once considered themselves to be ambassadors for Christ to a new nation and to a dark world, has been replaced by a spirit of human psychology and secular humanism. It is the same spirit that guides most of the world. It is the spirit that guides the mind of natural man, the government, the church, music, television, computer games and virtually all forms of public entertainment. It guides the secular humanist social engineers and virtually every public institution. It permeates human psychology, social attitudes and ideals designed to satisfy the flesh and place greater confidence in the wisdom of man. Unfortunately striving for the world's wisdom, human psychology and self-esteem have replaced striving for the knowledge and character of God in our lives and the glory and wisdom of God in our society and in the pulpits of many of our churches.

It is no secret to any true bible believer that most of the mainline denominational churches are in apostasy. They have decided that if they are to enjoy a large enough following to finance their operations and the construction of large church facilities they must be willing to bend to the cultural norm of the world system and present that which tickles the ears and attracts a worldly congregation of churchgoers who look weekly to find justification for continuing their selfish and sinful lifestyles. It has created a church of hearers but not doers who live little different from the secular world around them.

The people seek out those teachers who will send them away from church each week feeling good about themselves, their worldly attitudes, activities and lifestyles. Therefore, the church pulpit tends to sell what the people are buying. At the top of the list of pop-culture teaching from the pulpit are self-esteem, positive confession and material success. Preachers labor over the scriptures in order to develop just the right spin so none are really convicted offended or challenged to true repentance.

The idea of repentance has been replaced with "come just as you are" and it is a subject avoided like the plague. Redemption is sold as the latest and greatest "good deal" which requires nothing from us if we will perform some sort of ritual and it solves all our problems. The recognition of our sinful nature and the necessity to turn from its deeds are described out of context by a buzz word called "works" which men are told plays no part in God's plan of redemption. Therefore, striving for holiness of character is considered by the modern church to be a negative religious concept.

The anti-God secular humanists have convinced our government, our supreme court and most of our citizens, including much of the organized church, that government must be completely separated from the influence or the reminders of God, Godly wisdom, Godly principle, Godly morality, or the influence of Godly leadership as if the calling to govern is a far too important cause to become encumbered with God's purpose and guidance. We have indeed lost our way!

The secularist hates the church because he has contempt for God. When secularism takes complete control of our society and our government the church will be forced underground. The threat against the church this very day by our secular humanist government is alive and well and increasing. It is clearly designed to intimidate the church and distract it from its calling to have a salt and light influence in the affairs of men. This threat is evil and it has been successful at bringing organized religion to its knees in compromise or outright surrender. The federal government threatens the potential revocation of the tax-exempt status religious institutions currently enjoy if they should refuse to become subservient to the state and its agenda or if it attempts to influence the states agenda.. The leadership of organized religion recognizes that a majority of its adherents are not true disciples of Christ or ambassadors for the kingdom of God; therefore they fear that many would withdraw their financial support if the tax-exempt status was revoked.

Unfortunately their fear is well founded and their worst nightmare would most likely come to pass if the church should choose to become the salt and light they are called to be and in doing so they decide to become politically active. They fear that such a move would reduce the incentive of its followers to bring donations into the church, which would dramatically reduce its financial base. Perhaps the church and the world would then get a glimpse of who the real Christians are.

Our elected leadership is but a reflection of our national character. The dramatic shift away from the God of the bible and away from His influence in our government and our national thinking has accelerated our spiritual decline and national disgrace.

The various media poles reported to us during the Clinton administration that the vast majority of our citizenry acknowledged our President's moral degeneracy and yet could see no problem with the fact that they chose to make him the nations chief executive! How is it possible that America's citizens could be so deceived they are unable to see the connection between character, morality, integrity, sincerity, example and desirable leadership?

The perspective of the individual who is blind to the truth or refuses to acknowledge and act accordingly has at its root a strange form of insanity that works to allow him to justify his own sin and selfishness by rejecting the truth or its significance. It was amazing to observe that the more perversion revealed regarding our Presidents life the more popular President Clinton seemed to become.

Leadership is a vital ingredient for any people. Leaders must be men of vision and conviction. Today America has been blessed with a President that is a leader who seeks after and listens to the counsel of God. He is indeed a sign of hope for America. The world will try to destroy him because the world hates God and therefore they hate God's people. They will not tolerate a Godly leader. The Lord promised that if they hated Him they will hate his followers. We see that our Lord was right

CHAPTER FOURTEEN

GROWING GOVERNMENT DEPENDENCE

—⚏—

President Woodrow Wilson warned America about the extreme danger of the concentration of powers in this or any government. I repeat this quotation from my remarks in Chapter two because it is true and vitally important for every American to think about. How we think about the process and functioning of the institution of government and how Americans citizens view and act on their responsibility to be engaged in the self-governing process are critical considerations for every citizen. Voting is not a privilege it is a right and it is our patriotic duty. If we want liberty and self-government to survive every American must be alert and sensitive to what our government leaders are doing or not doing. It's important because our direct involvement will determine whether freedom and free enterprise survives.

Government is indeed a necessary institution and when it acts subservient to the will of its people and the Creator it is acting in the way the founders and authors of our constitution intended for it to act. However, when it acts within itself to reject God and ignore the religious faith of the people it governs it must be removed from the power to govern. Unless the institution of government is strictly controlled in its size and scope it will inevitably become the bitter enemy of the society it governs.

We are heading rapidly in the opposite direction making our citizens more and more dependent upon government and less and less dependent upon themselves. President Wilson's remarks sets the stage for considering the dangers of our insatiable appetite for government dependence and the ever expanding size, scope and power of government. **"The history of liberty is a history of limitations of governmental power, not the increase of it. When we resist, therefore, the concentration of power, we are resisting the powers of death, because concentration of power is what always precedes the destruction of human liberties." Woodrow Wilson**

America has yet to learn the lesson that liberty and the freedom to self-determination are much more valuable than a ticket to ride or any temporary sense of security that might seem to come from dependence on government. We don't seem to recognize that a government that is not accountable to the people is able to set its own limits as to its size, power, scope and/or its ability to remove or to grant liberty and freedom. Since government has the ability to do as it pleases history teaches us it will inevitably do so.

What would possibly make us think that a secular government will act to protect and preserve our values and deepest beliefs and preserve our way of life? When will Americans begin to wake up to the fact that a secular humanist government cannot discern what is best and right and therefore it cannot do what is best and right for you and I or indeed for America? It ignores the most fundamental and foundational aspects of who we are as a people and what we believe.

We have institutionalized government as some sort of holy bureaucracy that rises above our Creator and His revealed will. Our founders assigned government a mandate to preserve our way of life, our religious expression, and our value systems and to administer the principles and rights declared in our founding documents. We have this warped idea that a secular humanist government can be depended upon to carry out this mandate and to look out for our people and preserve our precious heritage.

This bureaucratic anti-God institution of government is lead by far to many secularist social misfits and incompetents and it considers itself, right, just, trusted, believed and it is depended upon by more and more Americans every year. We somehow naively believe it will respond fiscally responsible and take from its citizenry only the revenue essential to govern according to the scope established by our people and the constitution.

Americans seem to ignore the fact that government has made itself all-powerful and above the constitution that gives it its mandate and authority to function. Government is free to extract money and or take property from its citizens to finance its insatiable appetite for money and power to finance its political interests. America has dropped its guard against the encroachments of government and the increasing success and constant barrage of destructive liberal special interest groups who are using our judiciary to legislate their agenda. They are constantly promoting some cause that increases dependence on government as well as the cost, size and scope of government.

In our collective deceit we seem to have overlooked the fact that whatever power we give to the institution of government we take from the individual, which limits our freedom, restricts free enter-prize and restricts individual liberty?

The framers of the constitution had experienced the tragic result of unbridled power centralized in the institution of government. They did not want to be dependent upon or controlled by another tyrannical bureaucratic government. They were a people inspired by the notion of liberty and the right to self-determination. America became an independent nation in which individual liberty and the right to self-determination was foundational to the cause. Therefore they carefully crafted a constitution that was designed to recognize our humility before our Creator and it was limited in its scope to avoid the trap of a bureaucratic and oppressive institution of government.

However, we have ignored the warnings and wisdom of our founders. We arrogantly think we are too bright, clever and sophisticated to fall into the trap of creating an institution of government in America like the governments that destroyed much of Europe. We have been fools and our foolishness is apparent to any who might be watching America continue head long into the same trap overlooking or forgetting that the money and power we give to this enormous inefficient secular humanist government bureaucracy further restrains our liberty, limits self government and negatively impacts our economy. Government is clearly the worst investment of our nations resources. The larger it becomes the worse its ineptness, incompetence and its bureaucratic inefficiency.

The thing we ignore is that every elected official who does not share our spiritual values is an enemy of the governing mandate we as a people have given government. Oh, I know the arrogant arguments that talk about the objectivity of secularism, and atheism and all the other ism's. These arguments are utter foolishness. The Lord has said it best in His word; **"You either gather with me or you scatter against me"**. Certainly there are levels of objectivity in the character of various individuals, however, turning over the sacred trust of the governing process to men and/or women who do not accept the foundational spiritual values that make us who we are and have historically established the foundational principles that govern how we live, is a huge error in judgment that will ultimately destroy the America Created by our founders and the American way of life.

There is no end to this or any governments grab for money and power because there is no mechanism in place to limit it. Our choices as a people, so long as we chose to continue to feed this devastating economic cancer, is to continually increase our individual and collective productive effort and/or increase the tax burden to meet whatever appetite the government has for increased revenue.

There is another choice! We can limit the scope of government and begin the process of removing people from elected office, through the impeachment process and the election processes, which are either unwilling or unable to carry out the mandate of the people.

Unfortunately, we must first have citizens who are informed and inclined enough to make the hard choices that must be made when they go to the ballot box. Our government is but a reflection of who we have become as a people. We have become a culture that cannot discern right from wrong and have abandoned any standard of good moral character or conscience in our life style

What is morally right, based on the foundational Christian moral code, is totally rejected by our society. Character, in our elected officials, is not a standard the American voters hold candidates for public office to. Outright fraud, theft, power brokering and money laundering is standard operating practice among our nations legislators. Steeling through government welfare programs has become epidemic among our nations minorities. In light of this moral deterioration we somehow find it an outrage when we learn that corporate CEO's have been steeling from the stockholders.

We accept the billions taken from our citizens every year to finance excesses in every branch of government and we do not insist that our legislators approve a balanced budget amendment to our constitution and begin to aggressively investigate government excess and prosecute those in fiduciary positions where such excess and fraud is found. I was amused a few years ago when our government and the press made such a big deal out of the Watergate affair. It was a break-in by a few political activists of one political party into the headquarters of another political party to learn about the dirty tricks one political party was planning in the game of lying, steeling and cheating. The government was not concerned about the lying, steeling, cheating and delusion they were planning to use to mislead the people, only about the break-in.

The problem was that someone broke the rules in the con game of attempting to destroy each other. The exposure of the lack of moral guidance at the highest office in our land was exposed. The democratic leaders, who pretended to be outraged, played this to the hilt and eventually forced the resignation of the President while most any Senator from either political party could have been prosecuted for worse offenses. The evil of common theft as contrasted to the white-collar theft that goes on in our nations capitol could be compared to steeling candy out of the bowl on mother's kitchen cabinet. The point, of course, is that the citizens among us that provide the resources and the backbone of our nation must be awakened to the reality of what is going on in government and become outraged enough to do something about it.

The welfare crowd will never be of any help in the struggle because they have become government dependent. Their battle is not with government, but with you and I who must call upon government to act fiscally responsible. Like every battle in our nations history, **"the battle belongs to the Lord, however, it must be waged by those who will humble themselves before a Sovereign Creator."**!

Clearly America needs a spiritual shower bath beginning with her political leaders, her judges and government bureaucrats and, last but not least, her people. The stench of political posturing by political leaders to gain power and the secular humanism that has become the guiding philosophy that leads the judiciary and our nation needs to be flushed back into the gutter from where it arose.

We are reaping what we have sown! Today in America virtually every department of government at the federal and state levels have become secular humanist, atheistic bureaucratic jungles. The bureaucrats who work in government, for the most part, are clearly not servants of our people and therefore not servants of God. Therefore, government (outside our military institutions) has become a word, which brings to the mind of every adult American the notion of gross inefficiency and incompetence.

Secular humanist judges and legislators continue to add to the weight of this secular bureaucracy every year with literally hundreds of new laws, acts, regulations and policy's that add more layers of bureaucracy which take away individual liberty and adds more confusion to the social problems in America..

I shudder when I consider that during the past 50 years the federal government has quadrupled in size and has passed thousands of legislative acts regulating virtually every aspect of life and commerce. In doing so it has increased the size, scope and power of government over the affairs of Americans and created a government dependence that is bankrupting our nation.

The Judiciary and in particular our Supreme Court has become a literal embarrassment to America as it relates to carrying out its constitutionally mandated responsibility. The mandate of the high court is justice and protection of our constitutional rights. The liberal members of the court are busy usurping legislative power, removing God from the public forum, and declaring unconstitutional legislation, which attempts to lead our nation back on course.

In our governments grasp for power it has systematically interjected itself into virtually every aspect of our lives and has made itself responsible for our individual welfare. We have traded our liberty for one or another intrusive law, government benefit, or promise to take care of us. We continue to give government greater and greater power over our individual and collective lives.

We, like blind and indiscriminant men following a modern pied piper, have unwisely agreed to turn our back on God and his truth and place our trust, turn over our individual rights, surrender our constitutionally guaranteed authority over our lives and relinquish our freedom and liberty, to a secular humanist government bureaucracy believing that in doing so we have done a good thing.

Sounds crazy doesn't it? That's because it is crazy and we must somehow become awakened to what we have done and continue to do and see to it that it is reversed or we will soon find ourselves subjects of a totalitarian secular humanist government. Religious expression and morality will be removed from the character of our nation and our social expression.

Men have forgotten the lesson that history teaches over and over again. **"Power corrupts and absolute power corrupts absolutely.** From a spiritual perspective we have been conditioned to accept and indorse the idea that our federal and state governments must become secular institutions and must insist upon amoral legislative efforts and amoral decisions, judgments and public expression. We somehow have become reconciled to the idea that you can somehow trust government to be moral and fair and just while all the time insisting that government be amoral. Sound preposterous? It is!!! How could intelligent honorable men get hood winked into such deceit? American secular government is no better or no worse than any other secular government. Just because we are Americans doesn't protect us from oppressive government. Our only hope is the hand of God working through the lives of people who will humble themselves before Him.

Unfortunately, there are no restraints, fiscal or otherwise, on government. Every bureaucracy has as its primary function and goal the expansion of its scope to justify its existence and increase its role in the governing process. It constantly needs more people and more money than is reflected in its current budget. Unless something outside itself limits its scope, size and spending it will continue to grow. It will never limit itself unless forced to do so by competent management and leadership.

Perspective is not written to present a detailed economic plan for America; however, it suffices to say that there must come an economic revolution in America. Our citizens must wake up and rise up against an out of control secular government that no longer represents our people nor does it function for, of and by the people. Its spending is out of control and the congress has become ineffective at doing any thing about our circumstance. It is imperative that we move immediately to begin to reduce the size, power and scope and our dependence on government if we hope to preserve our liberty and our nation economically.

We must begin by completely rejecting the concept that the freedoms we enjoy are privileges given to us by our government. In fact just the opposite is true. The liberty we enjoy is a gift from God and it is man who has allowed the institution of Government to evolve as the greatest enemy of our liberty. It is systematically taking away those inalienable God given rights guaranteed by the constitution.

President Clinton depended upon the fickleness and distracted minds and the short memories of deluded citizens. He taught us that if we just tell people what they want to hear over and over again they begin to think they are getting what they have been promised and soon they forget what they wanted in the first place.

Our political leaders seem almost universally to hold the attitude that it is not necessary to deliver what you promise the people when you are running for election because the people will soon forget what you promised. If the people should happen to remember and insist on performance the strategy becomes to just deny it and the people will think they misunderstood. '

Some of the problem is that we have set up programs that fail to provide the right incentives. We have taught our people they can do just as well on welfare as they can at entry-level jobs. They don't have to work because the government will care for them, therefore, it is hard to find candidates among the poverty level intercity minorities to volunteer to enter the school of hard knocks or any other school for that matter. He or she often does not want to learn how to provide for him or herself. The cruel truth is that for man to change his mind he must suffer the consequences of his choices.

The church must somehow seek the courage to act as a conscience to our nation and it needs to involve itself in the efforts to inspire, encourage, guide and train people to provide for themselves and their families! Somehow the church has given that responsibility over to secular government programs that simply are not solving the problem. If we really love our fellowman we must provide him with the leadership and inspiration to provide for himself and for his fellowman.

Unfortunately the nature of much of America's poverty problem cannot be solved through government handouts because handout programs tend to further enslave the poor to government dependency. Even if there was enough money to temporarily deliver everyone from poverty those who are not willing to earn their way or accept the disciplines to learn the way out of their poverty will soon be back in poverty looking for someone to bail them out again. Give-away programs unless short term and very focused in nature and carefully administered will establish government dependency and eventually bankrupt our nation, destroy our economic system and destroy the inspiration and courage of an industrious people.

The liberal thinking crowd in America has forgotten or never understood that the fallen nature of all men tends to lead him away from accepting responsibility for himself or accountability for his actions. He looks toward government to take care of him, which causes the increase in government dependence to. Men tend to do those things that give him the greatest return with the least amount of effort.

Clearly a moral and humane people must see their responsibility to provide tangible help to the legitimate needy and disenfranchised. However for those who feed at a public trough provided cradle to grave health care, generous retirement benefits and protection from have to compete in the working world reality of the private sector is out of control in America at every level of government. Reducing the size of government, its employee benefits and its intrusive power over the lives of working and productive Americans is one of the great political and economic challenges of our day!

Our political leaders simply don't have the moral or political courage to tell America that just because someone exists in America doesn't mean he deserves to be or ought to be guaranteed cradle to grave security by the rest of us. That does not mean that a single life is not important. It does mean that the rest of us are not responsible to take care of the needs of a person perfectly capable of taking care of him or herself. That message must be sent loud and clear and received by America.

Out culture considers placing strict limits on welfare support to those who are capable of making a living a lack of Christian compassion. In fact it is more often the case that just the opposite is true. Making someone dependent on government who is able to be dependent upon himself is not an act of compassion.

Attacking the poverty problem in a way that truly reduces poverty requires wise and strong leadership. It demands disciplined courageous leaders who are able and willing to make tough decisions which will clearly impact their re-elect-ability because those citizens on public welfare of one kind or another makes up one of the largest voting special interest groups in America! Political leaders who want to move people off the welfare roles would lose support among those who see their lives as historically dependent upon those handout programs.

The welfare and poverty problem in America is caused by many factors; however, it is exacerbated because our government has essentially turned its back on the issue of illegal immigration particularly across our southern border. Politically ignoring illegal immigration accommodates the large fruit and vegetable growers in Texas and California as well as the fast food industry and the construction industry. Our political leaders have looked the other way to accommodate the interests of these industries. In all fairness, it is not only the fault of the businesses that employ illegal immigrants and politicians that depend on the minority vote. We American citizens look the other way while our borders are violated daily justifying our indifference to the problem we have caused by our constant pressure to experience lower prices for services and commodities. It is true that the service industry's in southwest America are manned in large part by illegal immigrants because they are willing to work for minimum wages and in the meantime the entitlement crowd in America doesn't have to work to live.

The scope of the problem is enormous. The Los Angeles times recently reported that 40% of all workers in L. A. County (The population of L. A. County is reportedly 10,000,000 people) are working for cash and not paying taxes because they are predominantly illegal immigrants working without a green card. In addition it reported that 95% of warrants for murder in Los Angeles are for illegal aliens. It went on to report that 75% of those people on the most wanted list in Los Angeles are illegal aliens. Over 2/3rds of all births in Los Angeles County are to illegal alien Mexicans on Medi-Cal whose births are paid for by taxpayers. They reported that nearly 25% of all inmates in California detention centers are Mexican nationals here illegally. More than 300,000 illegal aliens in Los Angeles County are living in garages. The FBI reported that half of all gang members in Los Angeles are illegal aliens from Mexico. The Times reported that nearly 60% of the occupants of HUD properties are illegal aliens. There are 21 Spanish-speaking radio stations in Los Angeles to inform and entertain a growing presence of Mexicans, most of whom are illegal aliens who do not speak or understand English. 29% of the illegal aliens are on welfare. The times reported that 70% of the United States annual population growth (over 90% of California, Florida, and New York) results from immigration much of which is illegal. The cost of immigration to the American taxpayer in 1997 was a net $70,000,000,000.00 dollars a year (after subtracting all the taxes immigrants pay) according to professor Donald Huddle of Rice University.

The implications of these numbers are staggering and the long-term impact on America is potentially devastating. The entire Southwestern part of the United States is becoming an extension of the nation of Mexico. At the current birth rate the populations of the Southwestern States and California will be predominantly Mexican by 2015 most of which will be families of illegal immigrants. The children of these immigrants born in America will be American citizens. The character, culture, economy and political perspective of this entire region will be dictated by Mexican illegal immigrants. Beyond that, the things that caused the poverty that overwhelms Mexico are being transferred to America through illegal immigration.

Beyond the moral issue of the human enslavement aspects of illegal immigration our government, rather than taking the necessary steps to protect our borders, has decided to force the rest of America to finance the welfare, education and health care of more millions every year. The liberal's are outraged when we speak of forcing men to provide for themselves and their families and when the border patrol has the audacity to arrest and attempts to deport an illegal immigrant.

The illegal immigrants from Mexico, for the most part, appear to be hard working people. They often find themselves trapped in a system that demands slave like long hours six and sometimes seven days a week by employers who hold the threat of arrest and deportation over their heads. They are often forced to live in squalor and work as slaves for poverty wages. Their circumstances at home in Mexico are so bad they are willing to do whatever it takes to survive and provide for their families and themselves. The thing that must be shut down is the opportunity and the penalty for illegal immigration must be quick, severe and consistently applied.

They have proven to be productive workers whose priorities and perspective does not allow them to be concerned with the illegal aspect of their activities. They recognize their chances of escaping capture is good and they also recognize that we have a large group of liberal minded people in our society who take up their cause and bring more and more pressure against the strict enforcement of immigration laws. Beyond that our public schools are literally over-run with thousands of illegal immigrants in attendance particularly in the Border States such as California, Texas and Arizona.

California is so overwhelmed by the influx of these immigrants from Mexico that government has found it necessary to publish public notices in Spanish as well as English. I applaud the voters in California who have attempted to remove the burden on the schools in California by voting recently to begin to phase out multi language teaching over a period of years. There is a large group fighting this in the courts. No doubt at some point they will find some liberal judge who will issue an injunction against it pending some never ending period of investigation and litigation.

I salute the efforts of the volunteer border patrol. Its amazing and heart warming to watch some of our citizens rise up and take the law into their own hands as our liberal legal organizations and our government seems to be focused on removing these patrols from the border rather than thanking them for their volunteer service to our country. Our government and our people owe them a debt of gratitude. We should be encouraging them and encouraging others to join them. They are taking the correct action and sending the right message.

Finally it is "brain dead" obvious and totally ridiculous to spend billions on internal security and ignore the need to close our borders to illegal immigration. It's ironic that those political leaders who suggest securing our borders are ridiculed.

Our government must do at least three things to solve the border problem. First they must secure our national borders; second they must demand that our neighbors actively participate in the border closing effort. Failure to do so must automatically bring economic sanctions against that neighbor. Third we must complete the task of seeking out and deporting illegal immigrants as they are found regardless from whence they come.

The dependence and poverty problem in America cannot be ignored. It must be addressed because it is cruel and destroys individuals, families and our national economy. It will unfortunately continue to expand until it eventually destroys our productivity, our economy, our inspiration and our traditional work ethic. Besides destroying our character as a nation it will bankrupt America unless we take steps to put in place the right programs and incentives to help change the attitude of Americans away from entitlement and begin to get American democracy and the free enterprise idea and system back on tract.

Unfortunately when the needy and the seeking turn to the church they find much of the mainline church in apostasy and indifferent and much of the so-called "charismatic" church indistinguishable from the world it is attempting to minister to. Therefore, the church appears to them to have little to offer them in so far as salt and light, hope and comfort and true Spiritual leadership. The churches insistence upon truth, integrity, justice and forth-rightness in public leadership and in government decisions has been conspicuously absent during the latter half of the twentieth century.

Therefore, our government leaders and most of our people have long since rejected faith and trust in God, his love, his wisdom and His character as our inspiration and guide. Indeed we have rejected God and looked to each other for vision, purpose, hope and deliverance. In our deceit we are no longer able to give the leadership, hope and inspiration necessary to bring spiritual or economic deliverance to the multitudes of needy people.

The beginning of deliverance requires a new perspective that is divinely imparted to a humble, believing, God fearing people. Spiritual discernment is the only route to escape from the kind of deceit America is suffering under and it is only available to those who will humble themselves and become born of God's Spirit through an act of repentance and the acknowledgement and confession of rebellion and sin to God!

The exciting truth, which can be conveyed to any who have ears to hear, is the promise of the Lord that it is his desire that none perish and all come to knowledge of the truth and be delivered from this terminal disease of deceit. His word says, ""**if my people who are called by my name humble themselves and pray, and seek my face and turn from their**

wicked ways, then I will hear from heaven, will forgive their sin, and will heal their land." (2 Chron 7 13-14)

Bible students will recognize this message from the Lord as one recorded in the Old Testament scriptures to the apostate nation of Israel who had turned their backs in rebellion against God. However, despite the warnings Israel refused to humble themselves. God tried for many years to awaken them to the tragic end of their current direction including crying out to them in warning through prophets such as Jeremiah, Ezekiel and several others.

However, Israel would not listen and the Lord removed their national identity from the face of the earth until an appointed time almost 2000 years later when Israel became a nation once again in 1948. The tragic result was that all of Israel, of the generation in the wilderness under Moses leadership, perished because of their rebellion. The struggle will not end for Israel until the end of this age according to the scriptures.

We Americans are indeed arrogant to think that God will not allow the same judgment to come upon the United States of America that He brought against Israel if we continue to refuse to humble ourselves and seek Him, His will and His wisdom to deliver and guide us once again.

We have slowly traded liberty and freedom for government dependence, legal protection from almost everything and everyone along with quasi-guaranteed physical and financial security. The price of this bloated and inefficient bureaucracy will continue to escalate and the destruction of individual freedom, the advent of more taxation, and the ultimate oppression that comes from the concentration of power and wealth in this single out of control institution will destroy our nation unless Americans wake-up, decentralize much of government, reduce its scope, power and size significantly and limit its role to its constitutional authority.

CHAPTER 15

SOCIAL DIVISION
&
AND MORAL CONFUSION

—⚏—

*"Any Kingdom divided against itself is laid waste;
and a house divided against itself falls.") Luke 11:17)*

The greatest heritage of America has historically been humility before God. If America refuses to accept God's provision we can expect to suffer the penalty. On April 30, 1863 our president, Abraham Lincoln, ask our nation to begin to observe a national day of fasting, humiliation and prayer. His words were not only true and powerful for his time they were prophetic. Listen to the clear ring of relevant truth for America today: *"we have been the recipients of the choicest bounties of heaven. We have been preserved, these many years, in peace and prosperity. We have grown in numbers, wealth and power, as no other nation has ever grown. But we have forgotten god. We have forgotten the gracious hand, which preserved us in peace, and multiplied and enriched and strengthened us; and we have vainly imagined, in the deceitfulness of our hearts, that all these blessings were produced by some superior wisdom and virtue of our own. Intoxicated with unbroken success, we have become too self-sufficient to feel the necessity of redeeming and preserving grace, too proud to pray to the god that made us! It behooves us, then to humble ourselves before the offended power, to confess our national sins, and to pray for clemency and forgiveness."*

Thomas Jefferson once wrote; *"indeed, I tremble for my country when I reflect that God is just, and that His justice cannot sleep forever."*

The good news is that the pain, agony, deceit and evil our nation now suffers does not have to be the pain that precedes death. It can become the pain of discipline that awakens us and re-directs us to the way of truth and opens our eyes and hearts to those ideas and attitudes that bring forth true life and restores true peace, true justice, holy purpose and righteousness to our land.

As someone has said before, it will require the spiritual rebirth of America. God has said in his word, and it is certainly true for American's today, **"behold, I stand at the door and knock; if anyone hears my voice and opens the door, I will come in to him, and will dine with him, and he with me." (Rev 3:20)**

Jesus also said, **"truly, truly, I say to you, unless one is born again, he cannot see the kingdom of god...that which is born of the flesh is flesh, and that which is born of the spirit is spirit.... truly, truly, I say to you, we speak that which we know, and bear witness of that which we have seen; and you do not receive our witness. If I tell you earthly things an you do not believe, how shall you believe if I tell you heavenly things?" (John 3:3,6,11-12)**

Jesus ask the question of the men of his day that it is appropriate to ask every American today; **"how can you believe, when you receive glory from one another, and you do not seek the glory that is from the one and only god?" (John 5:44)**

If Jesus words are true— for America to survive as a nation requires the humbling of ourselves before our creator. It also requires a dramatic reduction in the size, power and role of our federal government in the lives of the people. It requires that we return government to its constitutional role.

We Americans must constantly guard against any and every effort of politicians and the government itself to take power out of the hands of the citizens and turn it over to the institution of government. Government's role is clearly spelled out by our constitution and every effort should be made to limit it to that role. The founding principle is government of, for and by the people and the goal is liberty, freedom, and faith in God.

The love of a gracious and merciful God and the wisdom and truth of his ways compels me to expose the lie we are living and bring to the remembrance of any who will listen that there is another better way for us that was given us in the beginning and will restore us to serving the will of our creator whose wisdom is all knowing and will not fail and will restore to Americans those liberties and freedoms (along with the responsibilities) in which our faith can grow and flourish.

A moral darkness has fallen over the land and America continues to suffer from divisions of class, race and gender that feed on deceit, bitterness and hate. Poor leadership, spiritual blindness, foolish government welfare policies and ill conceived economic incentives tend to polarize the divisions and increase the hate and government dependency.

Dependency on a secular humanist government isolates people from society rather than making them productive members who are united in spirit and involved earning their way and making a contribution to their community. Government programs and deceived leadership have contributed to a rise in poverty and greater government dependency particularly within the minority races. The result is the creation of generations within some of the minorities who feel they are the victims of a cruel system. They have concluded the majority owes them something. They have made a life style and profession of learning how to milk the system. They live on welfare and feed on bitterness and hate! America continues to suffer from divisions of class, race and gender in part because of ignorance, spiritual blindness, wrong leadership examples, foolish government policies and ill-conceived economic incentives.

As a society we find ourselves divided spiritually between the Christian and the secular humanist worldviews. The polarity between these worldviews continues to divide us.

The polarization of these two worldviews increasingly manifests itself in every social issue we face and particularly in the political arena. The distinctive and contrasting principles that guide each of these two worldviews are becoming more exposed through public debate. The testimony of the lives of those who hold to one or the other of the two spiritually driven worldviews that divide us tend to produce fruit of its kind.

There are many religious movements in the world. One of the things common to all the world religions and cults is they typically hate Christianity, the God of Christianity and Christian people. The exception we find is the softening of the view of the people of Israel toward Christianity. At any rate, the world religions are all aligned with the same hate for Christianity. This should reveal something very profound to any of us who are paying attention. Could it be the focus of their hate is Christ?

What inspires that hate? What is it about Christianity they hate? It's not rational to hate peace, patience, kindness, gentleness, self-control, justice, righteousness, charity, and dignity of human life, honor and integrity? What is there to hate about charity, peace on earth – good will toward men, or accountability, productiveness, responsibility, discipline, love, honor, dignity, deliverance, eternal life and reward?

America is divided spiritually, which in large part divides us philosophically and therefore politically. That division manifests itself most commonly between the liberal and conservative political perspectives driven by apposing worldviews and motivated by different Spirits.

The liberal movement tends to be secular (atheistic or at least antagonistic toward God and His followers) and liberals tend to hold a secular worldview. The conservatives tend to be traditionally religious and most professing Christians tend to be conservative philosophically and economically. Conservatives tend to hold the Christian worldview. There are professing Christians in both the liberal and conservative camps, however, it amazes me that anyone could be Christian and hold on to a liberal social philosophy.

The conservative perspective tends to be longer term and it tends to hold to biblical truth, principle and discipline. It tends to be strong on wisdom but sometimes a little short on charity. The liberal perspective tends to view itself holding to the biblical principle of charity, however, it is often short on truth and wisdom.

These two perspectives march to different drummers spiritually and therefore philosophically and politically. The liberal perspective has captured the leadership of the democratic political party. It is destroying the Democratic Party and its usefulness in the political leadership of America. The conservative perspective is aligned generally with the political views of the Republican party. Most independents tend to be either moderate or conservative in their philosophy.

Unfortunately, many self-serving secular focus groups tend to jump on both the liberal and/or the conservative bandwagons, depending on which party is winning or is the most popular, in order to promote their agenda even though they might not be loyal to either perspective or cause. This confuses voters, which of course, is its intention!

The principles of the liberal point of view tend to be secular humanist. Liberals are typically secularists who are either atheists or agnostics even though they may not perceive themselves as such or intend to be associated with either of these camps. Their worldview tends to be destructive to the traditional American worldview and in that context it tends to be anti- American.

Liberalism tends to be rooted in the philosophies of socialism, secular humanism and materialism. Liberals tend to be government dependent in their thinking and their views tend to be fundamentally anti-free enterprise, anti-capitalism and anti-limited government. Liberals tend to promote the entitlement perspective. This seems ironic because they typically hate the government they make themselves dependent upon.

The thought of having to survive in a social environment of rugged individualism would clearly strike fear in the heart of most liberals. The liberal finds his life and sustenance by gleaning from the hard work, investment, sacrifice and risks taken by others. They tend to be socialistic in their economic thinking so long as what is being confiscated to support their socialistic programs comes from someone else. In fact, liberals typically feel entitled!!

Conservatives tend to recognize the need for strong government but they also recognize the need for a limited government role in society for a healthy and productive society to exist. Conservatives tend to want government out of the peoples lives and they tend to want all the people to pull their fair share of the load. They tend to be the most industrious people, the most generous people, the most honest, the most productive and the most trustworthy.

There are people of both camps who claim the favor of God and some even claim they are led by the Holy Spirit even though the perspectives the liberals typically promote are diametrically apposed to the wisdom of God and the fruit of the Spirit as it is expressed in His Scriptures.

The liberal attitude is prevalent in our education system and therefore the system is foundationally flawed because it tends to be secular, materialistic and philosophically socialistic. It sees the essential answer to solving most social problems is simply the transfer of money, opportunity, status, jobs, resources or materials through government programs from those who have them to those who don't. Common sense and history teaches us that such thinking and actions will not solve the fundamental problem for most people and will often complicate the problem. Liberals tend to reject the critical need to teach young people to become responsible for them selves and accountable to the rest of us for the resources we have invested in their education! Liberals tend to see the circumstances a person suffers as a problem someone else is responsible for.

The conservative view does not suggest that those who have the resources to help those who cannot help themselves does not have a moral obligation to help. This is the compassionate and right approach. It is the American way and more importantly it is God's way! However, there is a vast difference between those who cannot help themselves and those who will not!

Government dependency will not solve the poverty problem and will ultimately lead the rest of the nation into poverty. It is the direction our government is taking us and we are moving down hill socially and economically at "warp" speed.

It should be clear to anyone who has any experience working with those who live on welfare that the socialistic welfare philosophy is bankrupt for reasons that should now be obvious. It is the doctrine of the deceived, a fools paradise, that seems good on the surface but once it captures its pray it destroys all who adopts its premise and enlists in its cause! It destroys the incentive to work. It destroys morality and removes liberty, democracy and religious faith. It destroys hope and the only winners in liberalism are those who know it is wrong, however, they use it and its people for their own political or economic gain.

In contrast, the conservative attitude tends to indorse opportunity and free enterprise, which are tied directly to individual responsibility and personal accountability. The conservative is a believer in the power of liberty and promotes its cause at every turn. The conservative sees government's mandate to protect the unalienable rights declared in founding documents and to offer equal opportunity in the marketplace of ideas, resources and justice.

The conservative mind believes essentially that it is up to the person to make the necessary choices to take advantage of the opportunities afforded to them and that it is not the governments, nor anyone else's, responsibility to take care of those who consistently make irresponsible and foolish choices. The conservative recognizes the wisdom and supports the public education of those who recognize the value of education and desire to prepare themselves to live disciplined, peaceful and productive lives.

The conservative recognizes that prosperity favors those who are able and willing to lead productive lives and they favor those programs that lead men to live productive and purposeful lives. They also typically lead man to recognize that it is his responsibility to prepare and provide for himself.

However, whether conservative or liberal, financing a college education for our children in liberal educational institutions to the tune of $35,000.00 per year student tuition costs is a recipe for social disaster. It is directly from the leadership of our universities that comes the lions share of the liberal thinking that brings America many of our most destructive social problems.

Conservatism demands the necessary social accountability of those who chose a life of indolence and/or evil over productive and accountable lives. Conservatism insists upon the necessary disciplines and the essential and appropriate economic and legal incentives, which provide the correct incentive to inspire men to productiveness and righteousness.

The liberal thinker is most comfortable and welcome in the democratic political party and the conservative thinker is typically republican, however, I do not hold up conservative or liberal thinking as necessarily Christian. When conservative thinking moves away from biblical principle it is just as Spiritually bankrupt and destructive as liberal thinking.

The problem of racial tension is exacerbated because the African American minority feels that because of past discrimination, they somehow have a right to expect preferential treatment in the work place, in our educational institutions and in virtually every arena of life in America. They believe the academic standards ought to be lowered to give them professional credibility without the knowledge to perform at the level the credential represents. The obvious answer to that is that those students effected need to be encouraged to work to meet the standard so they can compete in the work place and so that American industry can compete on the world market.

Many who read these remarks will be highly offended and label me a racist. I can understand their hurt and frustration, however, what I have said is true and can be easily confirmed by some research and observation.

Racial and gender related social problems cannot be fixed by a secular government! They are deep spiritual problems and God is the only one who can replace hate with love and heal this land. Denial of the problems by our society and/or our government will not solve the problem. However, when the emotion of racial tension is added in the mix of the political, economic, religious and the many social issues that face Americans the issues become confused and almost impossible for man to untangle. Only the lord can open eyes closed by deceit, bitterness and hate on every side of every issue.

Certainly it is right and according to God's will that those who He has given the means to care for the poor and needy are morally obligated to do so because it is the right thing to do in light of God's will for men. It expresses the mercy, love and charity of God and it is therefore the right and the humanitarian thing for any society of people to be committed to. A righteous and loving people are honor bound to provide financial help for those who are needy and honestly trying to provide for themselves and their family who are just not able due to circumstances beyond their immediate control. There is perhaps no more practical expression of love for our fellow man than to be willing and happy to help in the time of need. There is also no greater expression of true Christianity.

However, how is the rich man to respond to the poor man who is consistently poor because he acts foolishly and in rebellion squandering his money on foolish pleasures rather than caring for his and/or his families needs? Is the rich man responsible for continuing to provide support for the one who will never be willing to accept responsibility for himself and his family so long as someone else will do it.

How is a society to react to those who are just too lazy to work or to make any effort to prepare him or her self for the work place or to discipline himself to actively seek employment so he can care for himself and his family? Does such a man have any reason to expect the rich man, who by the way finances government and its welfare programs, to take care of him? Should society provide endless government financed welfare programs that tend to further perpetuate lethargy and dependence? The answers to these problems should be obvious! Government programs that perpetuate the dependence trap are a bad idea.

When we look for guidance to fix a broken fixture, appliance or machine we turn to the manufacturer who created it and knows how it works and what it takes to make it work the best.

Likewise, mans best hope for repairing human kind is the Creator. He knows how we work and has access to our deepest and most hidden problems. He can and will heal us if we seek after His wisdom and mercy. Mans next best hope is to gain wisdom and understanding and the only other hope is to be forced to suffer the consequences of his lethargy until he awakens to the need and decides he must change his ways if he is to survive. It usually takes the latter to see the wisdom of the former!

Men who do not and will not work will ultimately find himself consumed with introspection and trapped by dependence, which will destroy him and often those close to him. His poverty will never leave him, but rather, devour him. The writer of proverbs instructs us to **"look to the ant, o sluggard, observe her ways and be wise,...(she) prepares her food in the summer, and gathers her provision in the harvest. How long will you lie down, o sluggard? When will you arise from your sleep? A little sleep, a little slumber, a little folding of the hands to rest and your poverty will come in like a vagabond, and your need like an armed man." (Proverbs 6:6-11)**

In their deceit many of our government leaders they have seen fit to create massive and expensive social welfare give-away programs that inspire laziness and reward sloth. Some of these programs, and the people who create them, are directly responsible for rising up more and new welfare entitlement addicted generations. Many of our leaders fails to see that in essence what they are doing can be likened to giving drugs to drug addicts.

We have been foolish in our assessment of the foundational social problems of America and have therefore come up with wrong and destructive solutions. It is much easier for politicians to increase the tax on the productive workers in America and continue to dump more and more money into the giveaway programs than it is to tackle the real reasons for the welfare problem and correct domestic policy.

It took America at least 50 years and a lot of bad decisions to get here and it will take a long time and several good decisions to get out of here even if and after we decide we must turn our thinking around.

To help the poverty problem for some the minimum wage must be increased, however, it is also true that many who start and work at minimum wage are not worth even that wage. Many have never worked have no work ethic because they have been raised in an environment of indolence. Many are barely able to speak intelligently and some are not able to read and write above the third grade level. They are often not trustworthy, their social skills are non-existent and their moral conscience is seared. They often cannot interface with society and they simply do not produce enough to justify a higher wage. This may not be politically correct, however, it is nonetheless true.

Nevertheless, for men to begin to climb out of poverty they have to start somewhere and work to improve their lot. We have placed much of the blame on education, on the rich, on industry, on history, opportunity, the church etc. However, it goes much deeper than that. We have a deep generational and political problem that is Spiritual in nature. Many of the families of the poverty stricken minorities produce children that are victims of a rebellious and angry entitlement culture. These families are not able or willing to care for or train up children to prepare them for life in America or to have the disciplines and drive to grow and succeed either materially or spiritually.

Often the parents themselves are victims of the entitlement system and often second or third generations of families who have survived on welfare handouts and crime. They are isolated and alien to the society in which they live. They have little in common with society and the social skills and social acceptable values and attitudes common to society are not part of their living experience. They are often rebellious and angry and the knowledge they have has come from the street and their own appetites, pleasures and lusts. The world has taught them to hate. They perceive the rest of society as their enemy and they believe they have a right to take advantage of its charity. Many think their circumstance is some else's fault. They see themselves as the victim of everything and everyone. Many of them are constantly looking for an opportunity to play the race card to get some sort of advantage. Their hate, anger and rebellion are consuming them and they refuse the help they need to be delivered from their circumstance. Moral degeneracy is destroying them.

How can we approach such an impossible problem in a spiritually and politically divided society? Certainly equal opportunity is necessary, however, the problem is not simply opportunity it is the inability to function and compete in a social realm that has advanced beyond some of our people. Education is one of the answers, however, you cannot teach those who refuse to learn. Throwing unlimited material resources perpetuates the fundamental problem! Lowering the standard destroys the ability of the people to compete.

One of the things that are needed badly is wise leadership. Many of the social leaders of the African American culture in America are not providing the kind of leadership their people need. They are teaching their people to blame and strike out at the rest of society rather than truly leading their people, encouraging them and teaching them to assimilate into and compete in the society in which they must function if they are to succeed. Some of these leaders are not constructive guides, but rather destructive to the cause of raising the disenfranchised of their race so they might become integrated into society and compete for opportunity in the job market on their own merit. They tend to promote crutch idea's and attitudes like graduating minority students who fail to meet the educational standard that is designed to qualify them for a certificate of graduation rather than promoting the notion that education is vital and encouraging their race to pick up the vision and do the work.

Life is not a movie! Success requires achievement not image! Dragging the rest of Americas students down by introducing a lower standard does not help the student who is unable to meet the standard to compete in the world of ideas and jobs and destroys the inspiration for students to rise to the competitive edge our nation must maintain in the world market of products, services and ideas.

A better leadership strategy would be to begin to encourage the people to adopt the value system and character traits that bring wisdom, hope and charity. Our leaders must provide tangible programs that support efforts to educate and train people to meet the standard and live productive, fruitful and purposeful lives. We all must immediately reject the "victim" and entitlement mentality that sets the tone of some in the minority community. We must remove and incarcerate the evil and aggressive gang leaders that victimize and demoralize many of the minority communities. We must begin to actively enforce the law. Minorities must be lead to reject the recruiting efforts of Islam because its foundation and goal is not love but hate. Many minority youth tend to join its cause to gain a since of direction and purpose and some because its radical leaders impart a sense of vengeance and hate the flesh readily adopts. Its God is a God of judgment and its religious fervor is one of constantly trying to gain God's favor through religious ritual and works that can never be achieved by man. Its vision is evil and a lie and its internationally sponsored terrorist movement speaks loudly about its purpose and intention. We must begin to establish technical training centers and help fund the establishment of work centers that employ people in jobs that teach disciplined work habits and demand productive work. African American leaders must discourage the cultural gibberish or "jive" many speak and begin to teach their people to speak, articulate and enunciate the English language so they can assimilate into the American culture and compete for the jobs needed to lift them out of poverty and give their lives purpose and direction. Finally our leaders must introduce and demonstrate the character and charity of Christ.

I can already hear the screams that I am racist and attempting to destroy the cultures of the minorities they have a right to adopt, live and express. I am clearly not racist, however it is true that as long as a race of people insists upon retaining the things that keep them isolated and out of the mainstream of society they will find themselves isolated from that society and they will typically suffer the consequences of that choice.

Frankly, I agree with Bill Cosby and Walter Williams and other minority leaders who are telling their people they must begin to wake up and smell the coffee. Society has bent over backwards to right some of the wrongs suffered by African Americans and other minorities. However, society has decided the discrimination and victimization crutch is passed its usefulness

There must become a moral and Spiritual awakening and there must arise from within the culture strong, courageous and wise moral leaders to help lead the way. There are several African Americans that have raised their voices to encourage their race of people to wake up and smell the coffee so to speak. However, a few destructive leaders who promote entitlement and racial division negate their efforts.

Far too many waste their lives and productive energies by attempting to promote destructive activities such as legalizing drugs, the social acceptance of homosexuality, sexual promiscuity, getting God out of the classrooms and out of government and the public arena, promoting the radical women's rights movement, insisting upon socialistic economic schemes, exploitation of racial tensions, rebellion against decency and dignity and the spreading of hate and division. Such are foolish people with destructive notions that will always present themselves in any society of people, however, their ideas are wrong and destructive and they must be defeated and discredited if America or any society hopes to succeed.

The message that will be the most helpful to any people group is that any man who will work and walk humbly and honestly will be accepted eagerly in the work place and will advance in position, pay and responsibility regardless of his or her race. The message will not help, however, if the message is not true. However, he or she must be willing to begin somewhere and earn his or her way and demonstrate his value, confirm his character and the sincerity of his purpose if he or she hopes to advance in any society.

The time is passing when opportunity will be offered because of race or gender or minority or because he or she feels they deserve it because of past discrimination. The economic formula is simple and color blind. Until men recognize what makes it work they will not go very far in the work place. If you are to be hired by someone you must have something to offer that is valuable to the employer. If you are hired by someone to perform a task you must produce or you have no value to the employer. It is not simply a matter of race or gender. The idea that an employer owes you something beyond what you earn because of your race, gender or minority status is utter foolishness. He owes you nothing beyond what you earn working for him or promoting his interests. If your efforts do not offer tangible value to the company you work for you should be fired if the management of the company is doing its job properly. A company exists to make a profit and if you are not part of the formula that makes the company profitable they need to get someone who is!

Current government sponsored economic incentives guarantee's the rising up of an ever increasing number of people who's life-style is public welfare, poverty, crime and the promotion of hate, division and rebellion! Government entitlement teaches men to refuse to accept responsibility for themselves and their families because the government will guarantee them a living, an education and free medical care.

Race relations and equal opportunity is a long-term ideal worthy of our best efforts. Our best efforts must begin by electing wise leaders and providing the right guidance and proper incentives through laws that reflect God's will and wisdom. We must justly enforce and administer our laws impartially to the very best of our ability.

As a nation we must eliminate preference and quota programs and any other program that smacks of special treatment for special interest groups. The standard and the opportunity must be the same for all Americans.

In education America must expect and strive for academic excellence! The standard must not be lowered because it is difficult to attain. The goal must be the same for all and the measure of academic progress identical for every student that does not have a mental incapacity to learn. The goal of education is academic achievement, growth in character and self-discipline and preparation to compete in the market place of works and ideas. Schools are not day care centers and teachers are not paid to be baby sitters to undisciplined and unruly brats. The taxpayers pay dearly for every student that passes through the system! We do that because we understand the value of education to produce a society of people who can compete in the job market, who can communicate with each other, who understand and appreciate the value of the political and economic system in which they live, who have learned from the mistakes of past generations and who know their God. Our public education system is failing us!

Lowering the standard for any group eliminates them from the competition for the good paying jobs. It does not help anyone to lower the performance standard for a special group of people. It promotes even greater social division and tension. If we want to give a disenfranchised person or people group a "hand up" what we must do is encourage him to try harder, help the one who is trying hard and guarantee everyone in the race equal opportunity to compete for the prize.

Some of these groups have exploited the situation by discovering their ticket to ride is to organize and have their group labeled "minority" in order to qualify for special treatment an a free ride by government. The magic word in jurisprudence today is "minority"! However, the prize goes to the winner and the winner walks in faith in God and has figured out how to compete and dedicated himself to what it takes to compete.

A new key word has joined itself to the "discrimination" debate. That magic word is "hate"! If a crime is committed, particularly against anyone labeled as a minority, it is virtually pre- determined that the motive was "hate" and therefore carries penalties beyond the otherwise standard penalty prescribed by the law of the land for the crime committed. The ironic and almost amusing stupidity of this approach to protecting minorities from the evil majority is that most of the major crime in America against another person is committed by the minority races. Rarely do we hear of the African American prosecuted for performing a hate crime against a white man.

So the big "lawyer thing" today is to grab hold of three words and link them together to get a juicy settlement: those words are "discrimination, minority & hate"!

Separating out such people and labeling them as oppressed by the rest is not the way to help them. The laws of the land, just like the opportunities, need to be applied equally and justly to all men of all races.

The real people who are unjustly suffering from the "minority" legal status nonsense are those who work hard every day and pay their taxes, much of which is used to support this nonsense! So long as government continues to actively discriminate against the diligent and hard working Americans and continue to protect and take care of the lazy, the criminal, the morally degenerate and the many other so called "minorities" these people groups will never in this life have to become accountable for their action or inaction or will never have to work for a living and therefore most of them will never escape the victimization of entitlement nor will they ever change their life-style. They have every incentive to stay in the quagmire they are currently in.

That kind of discrimination is as it should be. Sometimes it has little to do with the color of the skin. Unfortunately, our jurisprudence and political system is not color blind!! The backlash of playing the race card has done much to polarize and divide our nation. Justice must become color blind!

If any man wants opportunity and acceptance in America, or any society, he must earn it!! He must work for it and fight for his rights under the constitution! It is not a gift given to a special few simply because of the color of their skin or because they at some point suffered unjust persecution, or even because they have a steeper hill to climb than others.

There are many very successful minority business, professional, and social leaders in American society. If you interview those who do not have a discrimination agenda of some sort my experience and associations tell me they will agree with the context of what I have said.

The keys to social and economic opportunity are preparing yourself and diligently working toward that goal. It requires men to become accountable for their actions and to recognize they alone are responsible for the welfare and the care of their family. Typically it requires trustworthiness, individual character and perseverance. Virtually every sincere and responsible thinking person of any society, even secular humanist societies, honor those qualities among men and will always look to those character traits for its business and social leaders.

The stigma you cannot overcome that victimizes every person in this world is a spiritual one. The world hates God and our redeemer Jesus Christ. He said in His word He suffers and therefore we who follow Him will also suffer because the world hates Him and therefore will also hate us! Throughout history Christians have been persecuted against, executed at the stake, and looked upon with a stigma that denied them economic, social and political opportunity.

Christians have to do the same things to prepare themselves to compete in the job market and in society as anyone else. So does every other American and that is as it should be!!

So what ought we to do? Surely we are to fight vigorously against injustice and racial or any other kind of unjustified discrimination and persecution. Clearly we must!

However, we must present the truth and expose the lie that perpetuates the creation of generations of people who continue to be raised up in an entitlement environment. Such an environment teaches people that other Americans owes them something special because they were born black, white, yellow or whatever. The best hope for those beneficiaries of affirmative action today is to remove the crutch and allow government to provide them the same opportunity as everyone else. They must recognize that the only deliverance available to them will only come once they become willing to work to deliver themselves.

Kindness, gentleness and charity must be a part of the fiber of life in our society; however, charity is not the guarantee that you can skate by effortlessly constantly depending on someone else to take care of you. We must remove the minority legal distinction! Its time of usefulness is passed and it has become a destructive force.

America must have a true spiritual awakening in which we all commit ourselves to loving our fellowman and praying for his spiritual awakening and deliverance.

Unfortunately a Godly perspective escapes those who do not have it. Truth and tough love are not politically popular in America. However, so long as we sort out special interest groups for special privilege we promote the problem not the solution. Truth and tough love when applied to racial or poverty issues and the related problems which are currently so prevalent among the minority communities in America takes more courage in our society than politicians and political appointee's have proven to be capable of!

This condition will continue so long as we continue to appoint and vote for unwise men and women to lead us. So long as we continue in our current direction we are destined to foster further division and more and stronger special interest minority groups who demand more from the rest of us!

Any serious or sincere effort to diagnose the problem and suggest solutions, which demand change in attitudes and activities, are considered in our current politically correct social quagmire as cruel and racist. Anyone who dares to bring to light the deceit that is at the bottom of many of our social problems is politically unpopular because it might offend a voting block of people or demand unpopular social change.

Passing new laws and bringing more class action lawsuits will not solve the problem regardless of the judgment that comes forth from such action. In fact these actions cause more division and bitterness.

How are we to respond to the past persecution and slavery? It was a bad deal! African slave traders sold African immigrants to Americans and others throughout the world, wherever the market for slaves was the best. America was an emerging nation and workers were needed and deceived Americans saw fit to buy another human being from a slave trader to help with the work. In some cases he was treated badly. The very slave status idea is beneath the dignity of a creature created by our Creator in His image. It is inexcusable in the site of God and it is hard to understand how man could justify to himself and to his Creator a publicly accepted and legally protected institution such as human slavery.

It is equally hard to understand that women would be considered as a second-class citizen owned and dominated by men who often treated them as bad and even worse than the slaves they owned.

However, slavery and women suffrage is behind us in America. It doesn't legally exist anymore in America. No one is born a slave today to anyone else and we are slowly working our way toward greater tolerance between the genders and races that comprise this diverse society we call America.

No one can fix history, however, we can learn from it! It was as it was and its only ability to help the future is to extract from it the lessons that can keep it from occurring again. Changing our history books does not change history. It only distorts the lessons that can be learned from it. America needs to turn to the creator and to repent of her past and present wickedness. As the Lord says to the sinner, *"go your way and sin no more"!* We need to begin to get on with living our lives as God has given them to us to live!

For most of us the problems we find ourselves constantly defeated by are often not someone else's fault. If the problem is going to get solved we are going to have to face up to it and begin working out wise solutions.

Economic opportunity isn't a civil right nor a gift served on a silver platter just because we were born of a certain race or have chosen to live in America or claim membership to some special interest group or because you profess to be Christian.

The only answer to the racial problems that arise in such a diverse society of people is the love of almighty God! God loves all peoples with the same kind and intensity of love and he calls upon us to do the same. However, men have fallen natures and they tend to do and think according to their own desires. They are willing to take what belongs to another to serve their own needs and pleasures. That is where we stand as a nation and until all men humble themselves before God and commit their lives to serving and obeying Him these injustices will plague us and every society.

For the oppressed God will surely have a special reward. It is necessary to recognize that prosperity is illusive and problematic at best and destructive at it's worst. Many will not attain it because God may have a greater purpose and more durable blessing in mind.

A society must and should be willing to help meet the needs of these peoples regardless of their color or gender. There are many truly needy in America. We must not hesitate to broaden our sense of justice and outreach of love to include the truly deprived, the forgotten, the persecuted and the oppressed. Truth is not the enemy but rather the friend of the truly needy.

We need to learn somehow to be filled with gratitude for the blessings so lavishly bestowed on this once great nation. Our humility must somehow be deepened in recognition of the resources, which are so commonly plentiful in our land and readily share them with those in need when the opportunity arises.

America's greatest need at this moment in history is to be awakened to recognize that if we get rid of God and his ways we shall surely perish and so will our nation. Secondly, we must be awakened to recognize the need to choose wise Godly leadership to help lead us out of darkness and into God's marvelous light. Third we need to be delivered from the deceit and the foolish lies that guide much of our thinking and govern many of our activities and attitudes in America today!

The only stigma that you cannot overcome in this world is a Spiritual one. The world hates God and our redeemer Jesus Christ. Jesus said in his word he suffered and therefore we who follow him will also suffer because the world hates him and therefore will also hate those who follow after Him!

God the Holy Spirit and His ambassador in the earth, the body of Christ, through which He works is not a secular humanist government bureaucracy. It offers America the best hope toward achieving national unity, racial equality and peace between the races and genders! The political, moral, racial and religious divisions among us are the diversity foolish men claim to be our strength. On the contrary they are the source of social, moral, political and religious confusion that destroys unity. If the spirit of the world, who continues to destroy our Spiritual unity, is allowed to continue in its quest to destroy us, America cannot survive. God, not secular government is mans and America's only hope! That hope will someday not be available to America or the world.

Our Lord must intervene and awaken the heart and soul of America.

A
Book
By
Charles D. Gaines

PERSPECTIVE

I Peter 5:12,17
"Do not be surprised at the fiery ordeal among you, which comes upon you for your testing, as though some strange thing were happening to you….For it is time for judgment to begin with the household of God; and if it begins with us first, what will be the outcome for those who do not obey the Gospel of God?"

SECTION V

A WAKEUP CALL

—⁓—

CHAPTER SIXTEEN

IS GOD SPEAKING TO AMERICA?

—∽—

"Hear this oh people, who have eyes, but see not;
who have ears, but hear not" (Jeremiah 5:21)

The scriptures teach us that God has somehow numbered every hair of our heads and that not one sparrow falls to the ground without the Father taking note. It's hard to imagine if these scriptures are true that God would not be speaking to us or that we would conclude a nation can rise, fall or struggle under spiritual attack without His notice. Neither can we conclude that a nation could exist without His approval.

Therefore, if God is alive and speaking to anyone on earth I would think we would agree he is surely speaking to the nation that claims 85% of its citizens believe in Him. There is no other such nation in this world. There has never been a nation in recorded history so blessed by God as this nation. America has been the most generous and therefore the most prosperous nation in the world. Americans contribute more toward the care of the peoples of other nations than all the rest of the nations in the world combined. That kind of charity is surely inspired by our Creator.

Many Americans were pleased to see a new political wind blowing in the Executive branch of our government in Washington D. C., particularly in the white house, after the election of George W. Bush as President in 2000. They reaffirmed their confidence in George W. Bush in the 2004 election with the greatest popular vote margin of any President in modern history. Many who support President Bush see his leadership as the result of the hand of God at work to awaken America. However, many Americans did not recognize God's hand or hear God's voice. As I am putting the finishing touches on "perspective" we are half way into the second term of George W. Bush and Vice President Dick Cheney. It is becoming clear to anyone paying attention that these are both men of great wisdom, courage and good moral character.

The Democrats lost in popular support and they cannot advance their agenda through the legislative process so they have dedicated themselves to advancing their agenda through the mandates of a secular judiciary and a liberal Supreme Court.

The Liberal democrats remain so distracted by their failure they have demonstrated they are unable to formulate a plan for positive movement forward on any domestic or foreign policy issue. Perhaps they did recognize the voice of God and they hated what they heard. At any rate, they have no vision or direction except to express their hatred for George Bush. The only plan they are totally dedicated to is the cause of destroying George Bush. Their attitude and actions have some very disturbing implications and ramifications. It appears their hate is a spiritual matter and their actions are dividing America and aiding and abetting the terrorists we are attempting to defeat.

It was revealing to watch the many liberal politicians jump on the Bush popularity train after 9-11 trying to somehow glean some political footing. They were willing to sacrifice their liberal loyalties for potential political support. As soon as the headlines ended so did their support of our President. They could not set aside their political cause and rise to the need to stand united against the fight against the enemy of America and the free world. A few democrats have seen the foolishness of their politically and spiritually bankrupt political base. However, the fair weather democrats chose to endorse the leadership of President Bush so long as his leadership was popular. When Iraq and Iran begin to require commitment, endurance and sacrifice they saw the popularity parade moving the other direction and they tried to run out in front of that parade pretending to be leading it.

New National leadership and the destruction of the twin towers of the world trade center in New York by Muslim terrorists awakened many of our Citizens to the nature of the evil of the world system. Their fears and insecurities caused them to rally behind the President and his administration. Many politicians who despise him and are intimidated by what he stands for found they must join the political parade because the people were applauding his leadership and they would have been burned politically at the stake if they chose not to. However, inside some of them were seething and their hate for his faith and courage infuriated them even further. As the time has passed since 9-11 that frustration and hate has become more evident to the point they are fully committed to destroying all that is good in America if that's what it takes to destroy George Bush.

Of course, on the international scene the world is intimidated and frightened by Mr. Bush and his administration. His response to the terrorists and his recognition of who the enemy is and his demonstrated determination to seek them out and destroy them has them running for cover. Many, perhaps most, of our enemies are busy building political bridges on an international level because they definitely don't want to be called into accountability by George Bush. They feel free to ignore the United Nations because its only force is to issue declarations. The only power and authority the United Nations can depend upon is the power and Authority of the United States. Therefore our President is not only dealing with a determined enemy of liberals within our nation attempting to destroy him he is confronting a determined terrorist enemy that are encouraged by the response of the liberal enemy within our society. This is discouraging to watch because it is a repeat of what defeated us in Vietnam. We were defeated by political cowardice and domestic disloyalty and in some cases treason. Neither our politicians nor our courts would touch the treason during the Vietnam War because of the politically uprisings and student rebellions in America.

The abortion activists, gay rights activists, NAACP, Civil Liberties Union, the Rainbow Coalition, the radical environmentalists, teachers and the government dependent big government supporters make up a majority of the membership of this liberal crowd. My initial thoughts are, what an incredibly pathetic group to be associated with

We are also beginning to recognize that secularism is not the answer to governing our people because it cannot deal with the fundamental problem of spiritual deceit and darkness. It cannot fix domestic social problems because selfish intention is the natural state of the fallen nature of man. No amount of legislative work will find the right combination of laws to make us better and more peaceful and no amount of work by the judiciary will change the nature of people.

Christians are beginning to recognize that George W. Bush may be the man God has raised up for the moment to lead America? Perhaps we have fallen so far it is too late for America to recover from her spiritual and moral freefall? We were all encouraged to observe a brief religious and patriotic flare after 9-11. Our people were united and of one mind and it seemed good to be an American for a time. Our national attitude seemed to be one of hope and determination to fight the common enemy that was attacking America. Church attendance increased and Americans became patriots again untied against a common enemy. However, we soon observed this like mindedness, religious observance and patriotic flare begin to die out as we all returned to our selfish interests and rebellious agenda's. But for a moment it was great!! We still have a common enemy that is far more dangerous than the terrorists. It is a spiritual enemy that is out to destroy us all. Many cannot perceive this enemy and unknowingly many Americans have joined forces with the enemy.

One of the great disappointments, and perhaps revelations for many, in the 9-11 experience was the scramble of the various charities for a seat at the table. They were all obviously exploiting the circumstances of many suffering people to attract naive donors to give till it hurts to help the families of the victims. That is not unusual or even necessarily wrong, however, it is wrong when they exploit the circumstance making the donors feel they are collecting money's for the express benefit of the 9-11 victims when that was not the case. They calculatingly and deliberately gave the impression the money collected would go to support victims of the trade center bombing when that was not their intent.

Beyond misleading the donors regarding the use of the money collected they gave the donors and the public the impression they were actively and aggressively involved in setting up an administrative and investigative process through which they intended to search out the victims and work diligently to distribute those much needed funds to the surviving 9-11 families. Nothing was further from the truth. Not one victim received a dime unless that victim went through the trouble of seeking out the charity and making and justifying their claim. The victims were left with the impression that these benevolent and popular charities in consort with the local governmental agencies would identify and contact them and make the necessary arrangements to distribute the money collected. That is not at all what they did. The politicians and the charities sought the spot light and when the cameras were off they were gone. It was a disappointing, disgusting and devastating revelation. Its like realizing at the age of 10 there is no Santa Claus.

The point of all this is simply to point out that evil and deceit has no limits. It is the norm!! The question is how are we who*" have ears to hear and eyes to see*" supposed to react to it or do about it?

Even though America's government has turned her back on God there is hope for America if our people can somehow see fit to humble themselves before our Creator and seek His forgiveness & mercy. There is no other remedy to the deceit, social disintegration, crime, hate, prejudice and perversion that is destroying millions of Americans and America's national identity as an ambassador for Christ and a light to a dark and hopeless world.

The beginning of deliverance requires a perspective that is divinely imparted to a humble, believing, God fearing people. Spiritual discernment is the only route to escape from the kind of deceit America is suffering under and it is only available to those who will humble themselves and become born of God's Spirit through an act of repentance and confession to God!

The exciting truth, which can be conveyed to any who have ears to hear, is the promise of the lord that it is his desire that none perish and all come to knowledge of the truth and be delivered from this terminal disease of deceit. His word says, ""**if my people who are called by my name humble themselves and pray, and seek my face and turn from their wicked ways, then I will hear from heaven, will forgive their sin, and will heal their land." (2 Chron 7 13-14)**

Bible students will recognize this message from the Lord as one recorded in the Old Testament scriptures to the apostate nation of Israel who had turned their backs in rebellion against God. However, despite the warnings Israel refused to humble themselves.

America is making the same choice. God has tried for many years to awaken us to the inevitable tragic end if we continue our current direction. He did so for Israel including crying out to them in warning through prophets such as Jeremiah, Ezekiel and several others. However, Israel would not listen and their national identity disappeared from the face of the earth and the people were scattered among the nations. Millions perished until almost 2000 years later when Israel became a recognized nation once again in 1948

We Americans are indeed arrogant fools to think that God will not allow a similar judgment to come upon the United States of America if we continue to refuse to humble ourselves and seek Him, His will and His wisdom to deliver and guide us once again.

The message of *"perspective"* is that God is speaking to America. He has been crying out to America to repent and return to the God of her founding fathers for many years.

His cry to us is similar to his cry to the Ephesians," **awake, sleeper, and arise from the dead, and Christ will shine on you. Therefore be careful how you walk, not as unwise men, but as wise, making the most of your time, because the days are evil. So then do not be foolish, but understand what the will of the Lord is." (Eph 5:14-17)**

Those who chose to humble themselves have great hope because the holy scriptures, which reflect the nature and character of a faithful and loving God, promise us, **"ask, and it shall be given to you; seek, and you shall find; knock, and it shall be opened to you. For everyone who asks receives, and he who seeks finds, and to him who knocks it shall be opened." (Matthew 7:7-8)**

Our only hope is the promise that He will remain eternally faithful to His promise to forgive the sin of individuals, people groups and of nations and will return to them the vision, inspiration and divine purpose He had in mind when He called and established them as a people and a nation.

From an eternal perspective His word tells us, **"it is a trustworthy statement; for if we died with Him, we shall also live with Him; if we endure, we shall also reign with Him; if we deny Him, He also will deny us; if we are faithless, He remains faithful; for He cannot deny himself."**

The choice is ours to make individually and collectively as a nation. Our national leadership must acknowledge our Spiritual problem and commit our nation towards a new direction wherein as a matter of public declaration that America is a Christian nation and we are a people and a government "Under God" and dedicated to the cause of Christ.

At some point the door will have been closed on America as well as other peoples throughout the world and Christ will knock no longer. The choice will no longer be there for us to make. God will not honor our religious or philosophical diversity. On the contrary, the bible clearly reveals that the choice to humble ourselves before our Creator must be made by each individual during this lifetime. The nation of people who humbles themselves before God can expect to have their land healed and blessed.

The scriptures also tell us the world and its followers will perish. My goal is not to work at cross-purposes with God by attempting to sustain what he has declared he will ultimately destroy. However, God has said that he will bless and protect those who will humble themselves before Him and accept the atoning death of His son Jesus Christ as an adequate sacrifice for their sin.

America is a nation of people who God gave a gift of liberty, wisdom, prosperity, authority and power among the nations for the distinct purpose to lead, guide and influence the world toward righteousness and charity and reveal to the world His glory. We Americans need to re-light that candle and set it on a high hill for our fellow citizens and the entire world to see that many might see and be redeemed. We need once again to become the salt of the earth in our efforts to preserve our faith, liberty and charity.

What will our people chose to do? More importantly what are you, the reader, going to do? Will we as individuals and collectively as a nation continue to reject His offer of love, acceptance, wisdom, blessing and deliverance or are we going to continue to reject Him and walk in rebellion against him and allow our deceit to destroy us?

We can rest assured that God is speaking to us; however, it doesn't make much difference what God is saying if America cannot hear His voice! The fact that many Americans cannot see His hand or hear his voice is self-condemning because He declares to us that *"My sheep hear my voice, and I know them, and they follow me; and I give eternal life to them, and they shall never perish; and no one shall snatch them out of my hand, My Father, who has given them to me, is greater than all; and no one is able to snatch them out of the Fathers hand." (John 10:27-29)*

America has become the only super power in the world and our President is indeed the leader of the free world. The decisions he makes impacts virtually every nation on earth. He is perceived by every nation as their best hope or their worst enemy. The economy of virtually every nation in the western world has its economic foundation ultimately based on the economy of America. Historically, America has been the leader and the primary nation engaged in fighting evil and injustice around the world.

Unfortunately the deceit of the liberal thinkers among us promotes the spin that the world's circumstance is America's fault. America's government, corporations and the Christians are blamed for every bad circumstance in the world and for every domestic deadbeat couch potato. The liberals have overlooked the fact that American business and our people finance and feed half the world. They also finance the welfare checks that go to the growing number of couch potato's among us.

Therefore, I believe we can safely say that if God is speaking to anyone in the world we would have to conclude He is speaking to the people of America who have historically been committed to doing His bidding in the world! If we are no longer hearing His voice it is not because He is not speaking to us! The issue of course is "who is listening" and "who is able to hear" and if any are listening why are they not hearing or recognizing His voice? Who is the person or people equipped to hear or perceive what he is saying and why are they silent? If He is speaking to America what is God saying to America that is critical to our future? Has our rebellious life-styles and evil deeds blinded us to the work of His hands and deafened us to His voice? Do we live in denial running from the voice and will of God? Have we become so deceived as a nation we no longer care whether God is speaking to America?

Finally, does God's Creation have the capacity to discern God's voice and why would that be important to us? Where would we turn to answer such profound questions as these?

Well, we can be sure we won't typically find the answer to our blindness on the nightly network television news or in the movies produced by Hollywood that fills our minds with nonsense and evil nor will we find His voice on the front page of most of America's newspapers. Unfortunately, neither will we find the answer in many of the main line denominational institutions of church and we definitely will not find his voice when we only listen to the voice of the world.

The scriptures warn us about listening to the world. ***"Do not be conformed to this world, but be transformed by the renewing of your mind, that you may prove what the will of God is, that which is good and acceptable and perfect." (Romans 12:2)***

The answer to the questions posed above begins to find their answer in something called faith! The revelation of God's voice is found in His word when we study it under the inspiration and tutoring of His Spirit.

His voice becomes clearer and His truth self evident through the study of His word, His creation and through the prophetic voices of the leaders of His church, of government and of society. Once we take the time to consider leaders and leadership and we begin to define for ourselves those beliefs, character traits and strengths that qualify a leader to lead a nation, a state, a community, a church, a family or even a publicly owned business, or for that matter a leader that leads anyone anywhere our eyes become opened to the implications of our choices.

Every sincere minded person with whom I have discussed government leaders and leadership has concluded that everyone wants elected and appointed leaders who are men of character, men of strong moral courage, men of integrity and wisdom whose word is their bond. They must be men of charity and vision who are heading somewhere!

Spiritual leaders are men of vision. Only a fool follows a leader who isn't going anywhere or is going in the wrong direction. Unfortunately, as a nation we are often divided on the right direction and so we are all looking to find men running for elected office or men who are being appointed to public office or to the judiciary who are going in the direction that is best for America and therefore best for us. Sometimes the way we want to go is not what is best for the rest of us because we sometimes don't see the big picture and sometimes we are simply so selfish we don't care about what is true and right but only what gets us what we want.

Leadership that leads a people in the right direction requires men of strong moral character, Spiritual wisdom, the knowledge of the truth and a clear communication channel with the Creator. Leaders must be men who are able to determine the right direction for us to go and then they must clearly have the capacity to lead us in that direction. Most of us would agree that God's direction for us, if we could know it, would clearly be the right direction for us to go in any and every circumstance! Those who would not agree with that are obviously foolish.

The person who walks in rebellion against his creator is obviously a very foolish person. He justifies his foolishness by denying there is a Creator. However, those who walk in utter rebellion against God are fully aware there is a God and they are instinctively aware of their foolish attitude and most of them know instinctively where there rebellion will ultimately lead them.

Deceit is a Spiritual problem and no amount of clever intellectual argument will convince anyone to give up his or her rebellious and evil ways unless and until God opens the vial of deceit that hides the truth and reveals the truth. Once through the grace of God the truth is revealed to someone God leaves it up to them to humble themselves and respond.

It should be obvious to any of us that leaders must therefore be people who know God, can discern His will, His wisdom and His voice and are committed to following after Him. Leaders must be men of faith who honor and trust our Creator! Why would we want a leader who could not hear or discern God's voice if we could have a leader who is humble before God and in fact can hear his voice? Good, just, courageous and righteous leaders of vision and purpose are leaders who know where they are going, why they are going there and they know who is really leading the way. They recognize the voice of the Spirit that is leading them.

The question posed by the American media is "is God speaking to America"? The answer is clearly yes, unfortunately, anyone who would dare suggest a yes answer will be labeled a bigot by our modern culture. Nevertheless, God is speaking loud and clear to the America who has eyes to see and ears to hear. However, one thing is self-evident, it really doesn't matter if God is speaking or what God is saying to America or to America's leaders if we/they can no longer hear His voice or recognize the work of His hands.

If we have become a nation of people in rebellion against God or if we have elected Spiritually blind leaders to govern us who have rejected God or who are walking in rebellion against God they cannot discern His voice or see His hand and our circumstance can be compared to blind people being lead by blind people.

The Scriptures teach us that God has revealed in His word that he has given His followers the capacity to see life, circumstances and events as the Lord sees them. Jesus said about those men and women who become followers ,**"and I will ask the Father, and He will give you another helper, that He may be with you forever; that is the Spirit of Truth, who the world cannot receive, because it does not behold Him or know Him, but you know Him because He abides with you and will be in You." (John 14:16-17).** He has said His followers have been given the Spirit of the living God and therefore they have the keen capacity to discern the truth and to observe what is going on around them Spiritually. He is also saying that the world, natural man, does not have that capacity.

Some accept the idea that God is not speaking to America as a nation because as a people we are no longer able to comprehend His voice or message. Have we become a people who do not know the God of the bible and we therefore cannot discern His voice or the work of His hands? Perhaps you need to answer that for yourself first and then consider the implications. The implications are indeed scary!!

In fact many, because of sin, have become so intimidated by the idea there is a God who sees and knows us and considers our every move, mood, deed and attitude they feel forced (and I might add justified) in adopting the position there is no God. Some have decided there is a God, however, some know God and fellowship with Him through His Spirit that resides within.

In either case many Americans reject the idea that God even speaks to us and if He speaks many have decided they don't want to hear it. Some have decided that God no longer cares about a nation of people own whom he bestowed the precious gift of human liberty and to whom he gave the mandate to be a light to the world, a nation under God with the mission of spreading liberty and justice to all who will receive it.

Perhaps our rejection of God is our acknowledgement that we are living in rebellion and deceit and that we are descending by choice into a worldly secular humanist cesspool of evil, perversion, hate and deceit inspired by Satan? Perhaps we don't have a clue about what we are doing and we are so deceived that we don't recognize who and what is leading us to our ultimate destruction? Perhaps???

Indeed there are two distinctly defined Spiritually based perspectives that lead people. These two perspectives have distinct foundational beliefs upon which the guiding principles that lead them are based. These two perspectives are diametrically opposed to each other. They are lead by different Spirits. One perspective is based on what is right and the other is based on what is wrong! The implications of a nation trapped into following after the wrong one is devastating to consider.

For those who are destined to make a difference for good in America I suggest a look at some very profound scriptures found in the Christian bible that deal with our ability to hear the voice of God and the implications of not being able to discern His voice or the work of His Hands.

In the scriptures (**John 3:3**) we see an account of Jesus ministering to the religious Pharisee Nicodemus, a ruler of the Jews. Listen carefully to what he tells Nicodemus, **"Truly, truly, I say to you, unless one is born again, he cannot see the Kingdom of God."** Jesus was revealing to Nicodemus that God is Spirit and he was unable to comprehend, and therefore was not a part of, Spiritual truth or Spiritual reality without the Spiritual eyes to see. (John 3:5) **"Truly, Truly, I say to you, unless one is born of water and the Spirit, he cannot enter into the kingdom of God. That which is born of the flesh is flesh, and that which is born of the Spirit is Spirit."**

The startling implications of these scriptures are profound indeed. Without having been somehow given the capacity to see spiritual reality Nicodemus, (and for that matter any of the rest of us) would never recognize the Kingdom or voice of God nor understand or appreciate His being, meaning, or activities. Without the Spiritual eyes to see, no matter how learned or worldly renowned, no matter our secular brilliance or worldly wisdom natural man is separated from the Spirit of God and cannot discern His voice because, **"That which is born of the Spirit is Spirit and that which is born of the flesh is flesh."**.

Jesus went on to explain to those who were not his followers; (John 6:26-29) **"You do not believe because you are not my followers. My sheep hear my voice and I know them and they follow me. I give eternal life to them and they shall never perish; and no one shall snatch them out of my hand. My father, who has given them to me, is greater than all; and no one is able to snatch them out of His hand."**

In speaking to his followers he explained **(Mark 4:11) You have been given the mystery of the kingdom of God."** The message that is vital to recognize and receive is that the Kingdom and the voice of Almighty God is revealed to the initiated, and I must add, only to the initiated. If and when God renders the hearts of rebellious people insensitive to His voice they find themselves in a condemned condition of deceit and they have no choice but to live in the darkness of the deceit of the world and the perversion of their fallen nature.

Is it possible that God, for His purposes, condemns or judges men and nations who rebel against Him by removing from them the capacity to hear or recognize His voice or the work of His hands? We can be sure of it! For example, Jesus told his disciples that the Jews of the prophet Isaiah's day were under that condemnation and could not therefore understand the voice of God. Listen to the context of the quote by Jesus from the command God gave to the prophet Isaiah to tell the nation of Israel. **(ISAIAH 6: 9-13), "and he said, Go, and tell this people; keep on listening, but do not perceive; keep on looking, but do not understand. Render the hearts of this people insensitive, their ears dull and their eyes dim, lest they see with their eyes and hear with their ears, understand with their hearts, and return and be healed."** The implications of such judgment are indeed a tragedy for those under that level of deceit.

This is a startling revelation of how God had decreed to a rebellious nation for His purposes at a time when the hearts of this people rejected Him and therefore would be rendered insensitive, their ears dull, and their eyes dim to Spiritual truth and to His voice. Therefore, in their seeing they would not recognize and in their hearing they would not understand, recognize, accept and therefore they would not and could not respond. God had brought judgment upon a rebellious nation by withdrawing Spiritual discernment from them. Could that happen to America? We have chosen to deny our Christian heritage, reject God as a culture, reject God and His ways as a government and adopt what is bad as good.

In Genesis 3:13-19 we see revealed the account of the judgment God brought against the rebellion of man against Him. He withdrew His Spirit from them and they would be earthly, or worldly creatures and would live their lives in pain and return to the earth from whence they came. The profound implications of this Scripture are that natural man, short of God's intervention, is spiritually dead and destined to perish.

Unredeemed man finds himself in a desperate condition that his deceit hides from him. It is a condition of the heart and soul and mind that leads to certain death 100% of the time without divine intervention. Because man would not listen and respond to the voice and will of his Creator he had condemned himself. He would reap what he sowed. God gave His people Israel the law to live by against which their actions would be judged. He gave them a system of law and animal sacrifices to periodically atone for the sins of those who recognized their sinfulness and were repentant and sought after His forgiveness. That system provided prophetically a picture of the ultimate sacrifice that would be made for the sin of the world by His son Jesus Christ.

The incredible news of the New Testament Scriptures, The Gospel of Jesus Christ, is that the prophecy came true and God made a new covenant with mankind that would deliver him from the curse of sin under which he lived. It is a covenant in which God would extend His grace to a sinful and evil world by sending His only begotten son as an atoning sacrifice for the sins of the world. That sacrifice would cover the sins of any and all men who would believe and accept by faith the atoning sacrifice of His son for their sin, that is, to those who would accept by faith His redeeming grace.

The curse was lifted from the lives of those who would hear, see and believe the good news that he sent Jesus Christ to pay the penalty for their sin through His atoning death. That curse is removed from those who repent of their rebellion against him and He declares them His children. One of the incredible expressions of His grace is "eternal life". The scriptures teach us that God is Spirit and when we accept his deliverance we became born of His Spirit. The scriptures say *"Christ in us, the hope of glory"!* His word says that He will only remove the penalty of death from the lives of those who through hearing His word see and place their trust in Christ having repented of their sin placing it under the atoning blood of the savior, making him Lord of their life.

However, eternal life is only one of the expressions of His love and grace according to the New Testament Scriptures. Another expression is Spiritual rebirth. As I explained above we become new creations in Christ Jesus because we become "born again" and thereafter a member of His kingdom once again. We are indwelt with the Spirit of God. It is a new Spiritual birth in which we become a new creation through Christ living under the new covenant of the grace of God having been removed from under the curse. We are from that point on eternally His Child. **(Romans 8:1-9) "There is therefore now no condemnation for those who are in Christ Jesus. For the law of the Spirit of life in Christ Jesus has set you free from the law of sin and death. For what the law could not do, weak as it**

was through the flesh, God did; sending His own son in the likeness of sinful flesh and as an offering for sin",

Can it be that our acknowledgement of our inability to recognize the work of His hand or to hear His voice is self-condemning? If so can our condition be corrected?

Has God written off America and turned America over to her perverseness or is He trying once again to awaken us to His voice and deliver us from the bondage of the deceit we have chosen to walk in? Is God still attempting to return America to her foundation and calling and to help bring salt and light to a lost and perishing world through the witness and charity of a nation under God? Perhaps you have never considered the implications of removing from our national symbols and our coins any acknowledgement of God?

The answer is that it can be corrected, but only if we want it corrected!!

A third manifestation of His grace is access to His wisdom. We are delivered from the devastating impact of deceit. If Gods word is true and He has given us His Spirit to fellowship with us and remind us of His love and His will then we must conclude that God Speaks to us through His Spirit and through His Word. The scriptures are crystal clear regarding the inability of those who do not believe to not hear His voice and they contrast that condition with the ability of Gods people, His Church, those who walk under His grace to hear His voice. Listen once again to these profound words; *"But you do not believe because you are not of My sheep. My sheep hear My voice, and I know them, and they follow me; and I give eternal life to them, and they shall never perish; and no one shall snatch them out of My hand. My father who has given them to Me, is greater than all, and no one is able to snatch them out of the Father's hand. I and the Father are one." (John 10:26-29)*

Therefore, my fellowman, If you do not belong to the body of Christ it is not likely that you will recognize God's Voice when He speaks and therefore you will most likely not understand or appreciate what He is saying. **(I Cor 2:14), "But natural man does not accept the things of the Spirit of God; for they are foolishness to him, and he cannot understand them because they are Spiritually appraised."**

As I suggested earlier, it doesn't make much difference what He is saying to you if you cannot hear his voice. I am confident that if you have read this far He is indeed speaking to your heart. In fact He has said it is His desire that none should perish.

If there is anyone in America that should be in a position to determine whether or not God is speaking to America it is His Church, the body of Christ. I don't recall hearing any discussions at top government levels about conferring with Spiritually reborn Church leaders regarding whether or not God is speaking to America and if He is speaking to America, what he is saying!

Where do you suppose our secular government is going to go to get access to Spiritual wisdom and truth? Our Supreme Court has chosen to go the opposite direction and declared itself to be secular. Our government has chosen to reject God and/or any reminder of Him or His will as a matter of public policy. We have chosen "secularism" as our national god. We will be trapped by the mind and reason of natural man. Our governing leaders, short of our current President and a few of his associates, bow to the god of secularism thinking that secularism is the objective way to approach governing. Our government has rejected God and His will so it also rejects His people, His message, and is therefore unable to discern His voice or the work of His hands. God is clearly speaking to America but most of America is not listening because they are unable to hear.

Unfortunately, I am not sure what the government would find if it turned to the world council of churches for council in spiritual matters because much of the organized church is in apostasy and much of the rest of the church has adopted the attitude "we better wrap ourselves in a Spiritual cocoon for our mutual protection and hold on until He comes for us". The mandate God has given His church is to be salt and light to a lost world. The organized church is not necessarily His Church. Some of the church has discovered that entertainment and emotionally driven inspiration is popular and attracts many. They are little more than people who gather together on Sunday and pretend to worship God, however, their faith does not essentially impact the way the live and the decisions they make.

We tend to have an incredible attitude of isolation from the heathens presuming they are going to perish anyway. Sometimes we tend to forget that Christ died for the sins of the world and not just the sins of Christians. His sacrifice was sufficient atonement for any or all that will accept it. His heart is for all men who will humble themselves and accept the atoning death of His son on the cross as payment for their sins. That's why God must be the consuming fire that is involved in every aspect of our individual and corporate lives. The issue America has to deal with is not our diversity but the single-mindedness of our faith if we wish to hear His voice and if we cannot hear His voice we will surely perish as a nation.

If you are indeed a believer lead by God's Spirit you cannot possibly accept for a minute the perspective of the apostate church or the isolationist attitude of remaining low profile or non-involvement by the church in the affairs of state and must reject outright the foolish declaration of separation of church and state.

God is crying out to the Church and to America to awaken, arise from the dead and walk courageously according to the leading of His Spirit. Church, if you are indeed a part of the body of Christ you just as well decide you are going to have to get in the worlds face because they are not going to go away. As our President is learning, evil cannot be appeased it must be fought at every turn and defeated wherever it is encountered. The world is not going to go away until its guiding spirit and perspective has destroyed everything good about America and every reminder of God and His will in the public arena. If the church would agree to not meet in public, would agree to not use the public airways, would agree not to print its message in public media the world would still not be satisfied. They have a death wish on Christ and His Church. They hate God and His Christ because they live in darkness and are dedicated to destroying the light.

Is God speaking to America? He certainly is and he is awaiting the answer of those Americans who are listening.

God's Church is His ambassador to the world to which he has given His Spirit to lead them in His purpose to bring salt and light to the world. Clearly God has declared that He wants His church to be salt and light and He has allowed the enemy to give America not only encouragement but warning shots across the bow when it is appropriate. The church needs to reflect Gods wisdom and the character and courage of men and women of faith. He is warning the church and all Americans who have ears to hear to awaken as a Christian people and engage the battle against deceit and evil that America might return to her Christian Heritage and the world might once again see the glory of God at work through the hearts and minds of His people.

Even though salvation is an individual matter, God has historically seen the character of the collective association of a people (Their national identity) as a relevant matter. God does not honor or support secular thinking and actions any more than he honors or supports evil thinking and actions. His word places them in the same category. God's obvious will for America is that it become a nation of people who love Him, honor His will, reflect his love, live according to His wisdom, practice His justice for all, love righteousness and mercy, have charitable hearts and display moral courage and character.

He wants the character of His people to reflect the fruit of His Spirit in their attitudes and actions because it is the measure of the character and Spiritual health of any people or person. God has historically dealt with nations or societies on the basis of the character and dominant thinking of the people who are citizens of that nation as well as on the basis of the humility of the people before Him.

Those people and nations who continue to grow and mature in their Spiritual health enjoy His blessing and protection. Those who rebel against Him, walk in the flesh and not in the Spirit. Those who ultimately reject Him and mach His glory become blinded by deceit and inevitably become a degenerate and confused people whose intentions become continually selfish and evil.

In essence as men turn their heads toward evil he turns them over to harvest the results of their evil ways by withdrawing His Spirit for a time or eternally. He allows men to suffer the consequences of their foolish choices and evil deeds so long as they continue in rebellion and evil.

Perhaps it is too early to judge whether America will awaken to her decaying Spiritual condition or how the people will react when the freedom they once enjoyed is no longer theirs to enjoy and the incredible luxury they have lived in is stripped from them and disease, poverty and Spiritual darkness takes over the land and the corporations and businesses that supply the tax revenues to finance our prosperity become bankrupt and the jobs disappear. Many will turn to the church and it will not be able to help them because it to has become spiritually bankrupt and it no longer hears the voice of God.

Perhaps God is telling America that it has been given another chance because He has sent to us a leader who stands as an ambassador of His Kingdom because he is a man sensitive to His Spirit and will. President Bush is currently serving his second term as president and we have had an opportunity to observe the vision, firmness and consistency of the faith that works within his heart. He and his administration has tried and continues to try to bring about the necessary changes to the administration of government to restore respect for God , promote free enterprise and alter the course of the ship of state back toward smaller government with a true constitutional focus.

His leadership in world affairs on a scale of 1 to 10 shines above every President we have had in the last 50 years for sure. His successes in the middle east would have to be considered miraculous even though they are criticized endlessly by the liberal contingency. His success in domestic affairs since 9-11 staggers the imagination. By every way success by a President can be measured the Bush Administration must be given a high mark.

Unfortunately our citizens are being fed lies and disinformation to promote another agenda and many of our people have been deceived by the lies and the people are confused, therefore, the Presidents job performance rating according to the media poles is approximately 40%. Jesus was not very popular either except when he was doing something miraculous for the people.

It is that trust in leadership that has recovered our economy after 9-11. One thing is sure, the public perception of our economic condition and what it takes to improve our debt driven economy has much to do with the true condition of our economy. .

Why is the national Survival of America important in the overall scheme of things?

The mere fact that the United States still exists as a major world power gives many reason to suspect that we somehow still bask in the fruit of God's past blessing and grace.

There is a remnant comprised of Christian believers who are identified in the bible as *the body of Christ* for whose presence every American can thank God. They hear God's voice and represent and uphold everything that is good about America and without their presence God would have no doubt destroyed America long ago. They are the only remaining remnant of God's wisdom and truth that remains as an influence for good in the midst of a morally degenerate and spiritually deceived secular humanist culture. The true Church is a gift of His incredible grace.

Today's American culture, most of which are humanists and materialists at heart even though the poles tell us that over 85% of Americans, believe in God. Unfortunately the majority of those who profess belief in God include the lukewarm moderates whose God is one of their own making rather than the sovereign God of the bible.

Moderates are mostly honest people who will go along with most anything so long as it is reasonably convenient, not terribly offensive and doesn't cost too much. They believe the principle purpose of life for them is the enjoyment of it; therefore, their focus is their pleasures and appetites. They see little they are willing to fight for when the going gets rough. As it pertains to evil and sin they see themselves as mostly good and as good as most. Moderates do not see sin and evil as a significant issue that must be dealt with on a personal or national or international level. Moderates, unfortunately, are looked upon by most of today's culture as the standard bearers of true American tradition and thinking. Typically they are neither for or against abortion, homosexuality, perversion, burning the flag, or any religious group, even Christianity, so long as they do not affect anything or become bothersome to them personally or to society. They promote the idea of separation of church and state.

They are the time honored moderates who are spiritually dead or sound asleep. They are a subtle enemy who destroys right and good in the name of reasonableness.. The moderate movement is much more dangerous to America, or any other society, than those groups who openly declare war on God and/or America.

Satan and his plans flourish in the environment of the spiritually muted moderate because they are unable to discern the implications of evil or good. If they do they proliferate the good with evil in their pious sense of compromise until good and evil are indistinguishable from each other. Many of them attend church regularly. I can't imagine what for! They are typically hypocrites of the first order and they create the environment where evil can flourish almost unnoticed. It is the term used to identify the higher ground of non-involvement and to justify most anything in the right circumstance for the sake of a humanistic unity. They will readily trade good for evil if compromise demands it and the price is right. Moderates work the middle ground between the two dividing worldviews that fashion and form the foundations of the thinking of American's. Those who hold to either of these contrasting views find greater conflict and more polarization as their views become exposed. Therefore, many find a hiding place from truth and reality in the moderate, politically correct, group and that group is becoming a larger segment of our society. In fact the moderate is the politically correct attitude in today's culture. It is foolishly considered to be the wise and honorable attitude to hold on most any issue.

At any rate, both political parties are busy courting the moderates of America in an attempt to buy their votes or get them to support their candidates. The public image trick today presented by both parties is called "spin"! It is what makes publicity departments in corporations necessary and public relations people in government important. It is the art of making consumers and voters think one thing when in fact they are saying or selling something different indeed. It is the ability to make a big deal out of nothing in order to distract us from seeing what is truly significant. It is the attempt to shuffle context so as to appeal to our deceit and selfish appetites. We seem to gobble it up as if it was an ice-cream sundae instead of recognizing the evil and deceit it truly is.

After the 911 incident Americans rallied around the flag because it reminded us of the threat against our national security. It brought into question the public perception of our invulnerability from outside our borders. Most Americans have believed that everyone loves America and Americans and no one would dare to confront or attack the most powerful nation on earth. We are a generation that is fat, dumb, and happy because we have ignored the danger we are in. We have never been face to face with tyranny nor have most Americans been forced to pay the price to protect the freedom's they enjoy.

At any rate, it is easy to become distracted by this tragedy and the fight against terrorism and forget another important battle, which is an even more devastating tragedy at work among us. That tragedy is the deceit that accepts secular humanism and materialism as our God. The secularists have decided they will not allow the salt and light of the church or the effective witness of the God of creation to survive in America's social life, in the halls of our government or in our schools! They were distracted for a moment, their agenda's put on hold and their voices quieted somewhat, however, in spite of the patriotic frenzy of 9-11 they remain alive and well as the enemy of God and those of His kingdom. Their relentless efforts at removing God from the public arena continue while a sleepy, distracted and indifferent society fails to discern the times and/or to react effectively to the danger!

Oh yes! God is speaking loud and clear!

CHAPTER SEVENTEEN

DOES GOD JUDGE NATIONS?

—⟋⟍—

"And this is the judgment, that the light is come into the world,
and men loved the darkness rather than the light;
for their deeds were evil." (John 3:19)

For if we go on sinning willfully after receiving the knowledge of the truth, there no
longer remains a sacrifice for sins, but a certain terrifying expectation of judgment,
and the fury of a fire which will consume the adversaries. Anyone who has set aside
the Law of Moses dies without mercy on the testimony of two or three witnesses.
How much severer punishment do you think he will deserve who has trampled under
foot the Son of God....For we know Him who said, "vengeance is mine, I will repay,
and again, "The Lord will judge His people." It is a terrifying thing to fall into
the hands of the living God." (Hebrews 10: 26-31)

I recently spent some time at our nations capitol. It is an impressive architectural wonder. Its symbolism and setting has a grandeur about it that reveals to all the divine hand of God at work in our history, our heritage, our values and the price in human lives it has taken to protect our liberty and our way of life. It is a memorial to liberty and to the once great hope of government of, for and by the people. The setting is grand and the positioning of each of the memorials symbolic. They stand proudly in a setting that symbolizes the divine appointment and heritage of this once great nation.

The people walking around the Washington memorial watching the walls being built were all amazed and frustrated by what they were observing. The prevailing comments revealed the general attitude that creating this kind of walled environment in the capitol city of the nation that symbolized liberty and freedom in the world went against everything in them. Not one person I visited with felt this was an acceptable solution to the security problem. They complained that these symbols of freedom must remain proudly displayed, readily accessible and clearly visible to every person visiting this grand park. It is part of the inheritance of every American citizen and its existence sends a message to the world that there is a place in the world where men do not live in fear of evil men who threaten our way of life.

It was as though America was disappearing before my eyes. We had seemingly surrendered our way of life to the dictates of evil men. Our faith, our way of life and our moral courage seemed to have surrendered to evil. The authorities of the National Park system have decided to build high cement wall barriers around these solid granite memorials that mark our history, our commitment to liberty and our national heritage in order to protect them from potential damage by terrorists.

When I observed the wall construction my first thought was that it was perhaps a good idea. However, the "Star Spangled Banner" by Francis Scott Key flooded my mind and heart and after I considered the implications of the attitude and philosophy of those who dreamed up this plan I was outraged at the very Idea. I wanted to get hold of whoever dreamed this up and shake him until he awakened to the vision of liberty that is the foundation and inspiration of America.

It brought to mind the impact and source of the anxiety that has taken over our lives and is destroying our way of life. Our good intentions and reaction to fear have promoted fear and announced to America that we have been defeated by terrorism. It brought home to me that the terrorist activities of 9-11 and elsewhere and at other times in the world is accomplishing exactly what the terrorist wanted them to do. We brave Americans were all the sudden confronted with whether or not we valued freedom above the prison of fear and these security measures that were previously foreign to our way of life. The hypocrisy of the words of our politicians who declared to America that we would not give in to threats of terrorism echoed through my head. I remembered the words of our President telling us that if we change the way we live we have surrendered liberty for security. He was right and we have surrendered and our enemy knows it!

If someone should decide to run into the Washington, Lincoln or Jefferson Memorial with a bomb he most likely would not be able to get close enough to them with a vehicle to cause much damage because they are elevated and surrounded with granite steps and walls. It would take an incredible bomb to damage them significantly since they are virtually solid granite. If that should happen we will simply rebuild them. More to the point they symbolize the liberty we have fought so hard to protect in two world wars plus several smaller wars over the last 100 years. Lets let them stand strong.

It seems to me the best way for us to honor the one or ones for whom the memorials were erected is to first protect the way of life and the living principles these men stood for. If someone bombs the Lincoln memorial we should simply rebuild it and then we should find the one, or ones, who did it and hang him or them in front of the new memorial and invite every television network in the world to record it. Building walls to protect these memorials from life and evil will not really protect them if someone wants to take them out any more than all the airport security procedures can protect airliners if someone really wants to destroy one.

We are abandoning our faith and building a prison of fear and anxiety and destroying the public testimony of our resolve to be a free people! Beyond that we are destroying the beauty of this setting that millions enjoy and are inspired every year to be better Americans.

It also reminded me of the fact that our airport security system, according to virtually every investigative report on its effectiveness, has not been very effective in helping secure airline travel. Unfortunately, what it has done is contribute significantly to the fear and anxiety of our citizens and bring bankruptcy upon the Airline industry. Tens of thousands of people have lost their jobs and families have been disrupted because of this action.

We have made the choice to give up our way of life and the relative freedom we have historically enjoyed because of the potential risk inherent in living out our freedom in a world that hates us for who we are and our way of life. Clearly life is risky and liberty is costly. I know because I have watched men die to protect it. We cannot build walls high enough to protect us from evil. We will have to confront it and live the unalienable right of liberty that God has given us. Clearly there is risk. However it is worth the risk and safety, although important, is not the god at whose alter we kneel. Men who are unwilling to take the risk and pay the price of liberty will never be a free people. We must fight aggressively and destroy readily any who threaten our liberty. Security is not possible and if it were the prison cell in which we would have to live is not so dear as the freedoms we have historically enjoyed. Americans have historically been willing to sacrifice guaranteed safety for freedom every day of the week. The price of freedom and liberty is a risky business but we decided to take the risk a long time ago. I think we ought to re-evaluate the cost and damage we have caused and begin to remove our overt security blankets that will not protect us and place our trust in God who can and will protect us.

We have become the worlds most powerful and intimidating nation both militarily and economically. God has provided us a good Leader and has blessed us as a nation because of the Spirit of men living in liberty who walk the walk of faith and it has protected us and produced unprecedented success. We have been a nation of rugged and brave individualists who do no cower when faced with the enemy. We are alert to his workings and we confront him and when he proves to be evil we destroy him. We do not cower! We know life is a risk in a world of evil among men with fallen natures. Our protector and provider is our Lord!

Unfortunately, more and more of our people are willing to sell out liberty for security. Historically, if you get in our face we will come after you. If you act like a gentlemen, pull your own weight, do good to your neighbor and keep your nose in your own business we are a people who have historically been willing to help support, protect and encourage you. Courage has always been the bunkmate of liberty. When we surrender to fear and anxiety the enemy wins and liberty loses. When we surrender to it we are telling the terrorists that terrorism works.

We have a secular contingency in our nation that is working to systematically destroy our liberty and our faith and trust in a living and sovereign God. They live in fear because they do not live and walk by faith. They lack courage and will never confront and defeat the enemy. They stand on the sidelines and "BOO" the men in the ring and criticize the way they are fighting the battle, however, they are not brave enough to get in the battle beside the rest of us and fight the enemy. They, by their attitude and actions aid and abet the enemy!

The United States of America is moving through a defining moment in its history. Sincere minded Christian patriots must awaken and begin to present a distinctive in our thoughts, attitudes, actions and words which displays a wisdom and moral authority of supernatural origin and glory if we hope to ever see America revived and returned to her divinely appointed direction, glory and destiny.

There are many examples in our society of how we have traded faith for fear and have acted foolishly destroying the joy and freedom of the very life we have struggled for two centuries to build. If there is nothing we are willing to die for there is certainly nothing we will find worth living for. Freedom is worth the risk and if we take the risk and trust in our Creator and Lord that's as good as it is going to get in this life!!!!!!!

It is hard to believe the governing wisdom and authority of our Creator has been rejected by America. The founding documents, The Declaration of Independence and our Constitution, which laid the foundation and established for posterity the principles on which this nation was to be born and sustained have been badly circumvented by foolish Supreme Court Judges and many of our political leaders.

To justify the devastating circumvention it became necessary for the judiciary to disregard the intention of our founding fathers and interpret the constitution as a living organism, an evolving constitution, rather than the foundational truth and governing authority upon which the principles that guide our nation stands.

The deliberate out of context spin of foolish and unprincipled men have led the court to interpret our founding documents to meet the perspective and the whims of a secular, deceived and fickle segment of our society. These men sacrificed principle to remove God and truth from government and to fulfill the inexhaustible supply of fleshly appetites.

As a culture we have denied our Creator and the fear that abides in the hearts and minds of those who are without faith is overtaking our society. It has revealed itself in our domestic reaction to terrorism after 9-11. It is not that men of faith live in reckless abandon and wade into disaster without considering the risk. On the contrary men of faith recognize the evil nature of the world in which we live and that our lives and our possessions are not our own. They recognize that we can never completely protect ourselves from the work of evil. We live in faith and trust in a sovereign Creator who is our protection and has determined the time of our end.

It is almost impossible to imagine how the highest court in the land would chose to attack the open public expression of our most holy faith expressed in the Christian bible. What spirit within them would inspire such evil? We Americans need to recognize the foundational principles that inspired and guided the hearts and minds of those who founded America have been rejected by the judicial branch of our government. Our Supreme Court, in its utter deceit, has sold out to the lie of secularism.

Therefore, the spiritual foundation that was the source of the inspiration, power, authority and wisdom that has historically been our guide and has established our legitimacy and values by its foundational principles no longer governs us. Our leaders and our people have chosen to selectively disregard, rather than protect, the constitutional guarantees, which give us individual liberty and freedom.

In abandoning the faith of our fathers we have removed Godly character as the true measure of a man. Instead we have chosen to define and recognize man's worth in terms of material possessions and/or popularity. In our collective lust for worldly things materialism has become our God and we have left America with a secular humanist religion and a credit card economy both deeply dependent on deceit.

To those who love America and want to preserve the guiding Spirit that made America great I salute you and add my voice to your efforts to bring salt and light to a nation who has lost the light and perspective to guide it. I join many in urging you to step up to bat armed with the wisdom, faith and the endurance to keep swinging until you hit a home run for our Lord and for America!

Liberty demands a price of alertness, focus, endurance and perseverance in the constant battle against deceit and the forces of evil. That price must be paid by every generation. Should we take our blessed gift of freedom for granted and trade it for government guaranteed security? If that continues to be our choice we will soon discover that security has become slavery and the divine Spirit that created, sustained and protected America will have left us to suffer the consequences of our foolishness and fear.

My hope is that many Americans will read *perspective*, test the spirit in which it is written and take up the cause to preserve truth, freedom and our precious faith. It is dedicated to the hope of awakening and inspiring men to seek after biblical truth, proclaim and courageously defend it at every opportunity and to the hope of inspiring many to seek after biblical truth and to walk humbly in its wisdom under the hand of a sovereign and loving God.

I am asking you to consider the thoughts presented in *perspective* with a sincerity that goes deeper than the "good idea" stage to a platform for action and performance of those good works and exemplary citizenship we are each called to!

I urge every citizen to stay alert to what is taking place in the halls of congress, in the courts, in the executive branch of our government, in our elections and in the church lest we wake up one day and find that we are living in a foreign land not at all like the land described in the constitution and we are worshipping a foreign God not at all like the Creator.

The measure and value of biblical character and the family and those Christian values once cherished and recognized as the essence of life in America are rapidly disappearing. The true measure of life is being measured by a different ruler. Character, love for your fellowman, biblical truth, spiritual values, national purpose and individual liberty are disappearing while we slumber.

If we fail to lead the fight to stop the destructive life that is arising in place of truth and liberty America will become a secular humanist nation of satanic origin and inspiration diametrically apposed to all that is true. It will be difficult to discern between human and animal rights. The penalties for disrupting nature will exceed the penalties of taking human life. The democratic process will have given way to the demands of a bureaucratic tyrannical government. Our capitalistic economic system will have been replaced by a socialistic economy. God will have been removed from the public arena and Christians will be considered enemies of the state and openly persecuted for their beliefs.

Americans have been duped into believing perhaps the most profound lie ever perpetrated on any people. It is a lie of satanic supernatural origin. It has blinded natural man to the truth, it denies mans sin, excuses his ungodliness, justifies his foolish actions and attitudes, and systematically destroys men and nations. **The same liar who presents it to all men today presented the same lie in the Garden of Eden! Satan said, "You shall not surely die".** The lie says that natural man is not a fallen creature but is naturally good and charitable without God. The lie tells us that man is not a sinner by nature and given the facts most men will make the right, honorable, just and wise choices even when it costs him dearly to make those tough choices.

Man has believed the lie rather than God and is trapped in the foolishness of his deceit and is condemned by his condition. He acts naturally according to the leading of his deceit. God reveals to every man the way of escape and offers to every man a perspective of truth and the power of supernatural wisdom to guide him if he will humble himself and receive it. If men reject that truth he is condemned by his deceit. The consequences and destiny of his deceit have current and eternal implications.

This incredible lie that darkens men's minds and hearts has deceived all men and it impacts every aspect of human life including our modern public education system, our government and its governing decisions, our public policies and programs, our value systems, our legal system and our national philosophy. It is a lie designed to convince man that he does not need God because he is not a fallen creature who will perish without God's saving grace and will destroy himself and his fellowman without God's guiding Spirit.

It is the foundational lie that has perpetuated the idea of "separation of Church and State". The deceit it fosters leads us and our governing leaders to believe we can indeed carry out faithfully, justly and righteously our responsibilities toward those we serve without the wisdom of God or the presence and protection of His guiding Spirit. The deceit of the foundational lie attempts to convince us we can live in peace without the charity or wisdom of God. It leads us to believe we don't need righteous leadership, Godly example, discipline, training or the right incentives to guide us toward righteousness and justice. It teaches us that what is right is what men say it is and not what God says it is! It brings a perspective that leads men to authorize and promote through legislative act any idea, act or activity that satisfies his fleshly appetites or otherwise pleases him. It deceives men into thinking that just because the majority of men approve of something it is right and just and suitable for society.

The idea that men of fallen natures who live and act out their deceit can somehow arrive at wise and just decisions in leading our nation is the foolish thinking of secular humanists. The premise of this deceived thinking, of course, is that man is not naturally deceived in his thinking. Therefore it denies the need for spiritual awakening. Natural man in his humanist deceit believes he can be depended upon to hold to that which is right and best for himself, his fellowman and his nation without the aid of Spiritual influence. The deceit of secular humanism is the most deadly disease facing mankind.

It is the deceit of unbelief.

Deceived thinking gives man the glory for his existence, his exploits and his environment. It leads men to believe they can separate character, who we truly are, from decisions, actions and responsibilities. It leads us to believe we can bring whatever wisdom we might need or that we can rise to any occasion and become whatever we need to be to bring about a righteous and just result whenever we are called upon to do so regardless of what we really believe. Deceived thinking promotes the idea that man is complete within himself and teaches man that he has it within himself to overcome most anything, even his deceit, if he really needs to, without God's guiding wisdom It teaches us that we can act impartial or even contrary to what we know to be true even in dealing with critical issues. It teaches us that even though men habitually live and act like heathens they can discern the need to act or judge and can indeed judge and act rightly when necessary.

The deceit of this incredible lie allows men without a moral compass or without the guidance of the Spirit of God to rightfully claim to be Children of God and to stand arrogantly in the light of his favor. It creates a culture which sees no tangible need for God and encourages us to appoint judges over us who believe they are capable of justice without the guidance of God simply because they have a diploma from a school of law which, at least since the schools have rejected the leadership of men like Blackstone, teaches the deceit they use as the foundation for their judgments! It further teaches us to trust in the justice, righteousness and wisdom of human government without the source of the wisdom of truth and righteousness or the disciplines that guide it. Last but not least humanism teaches us that most people are good and are therefore heaven bound due to their own merit and that ultimate truth and goodness, salvation and hell are lies created by religion to force men to adhere to its bigotry.

The Lord gave a very encouraging word to us regarding His judgment through the Gospel of John, chapter 3 verse 17 thru 21: " *For God did not send the Son into the world to judge the world, but that the world should be saved through Him. He who believes in Him is not judged; he who does not believe has been judged already, because he has not believed in the name of the only begotten Son of God. And this is the judgment, that the light is come into the world, and men loved the darkness rather than the light for their deeds were evil. For everyone who does evil hates the light, and does not come to the light, lest his deeds should be exposed. But he who practices truth comes unto the light, that his deeds may be manifested as having been wrought in God"*

God has revealed that every man will face judgment. All men will stand before God and answer for his sin and rebellion. When the believer stands before God He will say to him, 'your name is written in the lamb's book of life. Your sin has been forgiven. Enter into your inheritance thy good and faithful servant'. The scriptures teach that those who have humbled themselves before Him during this life have already been judged and declared righteous. However, they too will face a judgment in which their works are judged and their reward awarded them.

God has already judged mankind and His judgment is that man will suffer the consequences of his sin and his decisions and actions unless he repents of his sin and seeks the redemption God has provided through Jesus Christ His son. That provision for deliverance is the good news of the gospels of Jesus Christ.

The question is however, does God Judge nations of people beyond the judgments upon the spirit and soul of man discussed above? Does a nation of non-believers suffer any consequences during their life on earth for their rebellion and evil deeds? If God does Judge how does His judgment manifest itself here on earth?

First it is important to note that God is God and He can do whatever pleases Him. Putting Him in some kind of box is not possible and attempting to lead him where revelation does not lead us is not wise, however, His character is knowable through His word, which reveals how He has historically dealt with nations over several centuries. Secular history, to the extent it exists, confirms the historical record of the bible.

Second, we can interpret judgment for disciplinary action. The Lord says he disciplines those He loves.

It is clear that God does judge in the context that he is sovereign and all knowing and nothing happens in, with, by or to His creation that he is not aware of and either intervenes to stop or alter the course of or He allows it to take place. He may not always desire that it takes place but he has made a covenant in which he leaves the choices governing mans life up to each man or women. The problem we encounter is that when we chose to reject God's way we suffer the consequences of our choices.

However, His word reveals and our experience confirms that He actively intervenes in the lives and circumstances of people and particularly the body of Christ. His word also tells us His followers know Him, recognize and hear His voice and follow Him. *"My sheep hear my voice, and I know them, and they follow Me; and I give eternal life to them, and they shall never perish; and no one shall snatch them out of My hand. My Father who has given them to Me, is greater than all; and no one is able to snatch them out of My hand. I and the Father are one." (John 10:27-29)*

His word is clear that His Church has already been judged and they shall not perish in the ultimate sense of their eternal destiny, however, the bible does not promise that we will not suffer from His judgments of nations in which we live and serve, or from the decisions of governments or of leaders, employers, criminals or peoples who live in the same society in which we live. In that context He has said in His word the rain falls on the just and the unjust! He also goes to great length to teach us the importance of wisdom by which we can avoid much travail. Nevertheless, we are all impacted in some way by what any of us does or does not do. That is, many who live in America who are not followers of Christ will experience the blessing and protection of God simply because God's people live among them and God blesses His people. Many often share in the blessings God provides for His people.

If and when His church (His people) is removed from the earth that blessing and protection is removed according to the scriptures and men will suffer the consequences of their actions and the wrath of Satan. In that sense God judges or condemns those who refuse the offer of His saving grace.

Otherwise He has told us that those who do not know him, in the sense that they are not believers born of His Spirit, will suffer the consequences of their sin and will reap what they sow. *"Even so, every good tree bears good fruit; but the bad tree bears bad fruit. A good tree cannot produce bad fruit, nor can a bad tree produce good fruit. Every tree that does not bear good fruit is cut down and thrown into the fire. So then you will know them by their fruits." (Matthew 7:17-20)*

The scriptures are full of examples of God's judgment of individuals and nations who consistently performed blatantly evil deeds! In some instances entire cities and nations of people were destroyed because they had become predominantly perverse and evil people. The majority of these judgments occurred before the advent of the atonement.

Clearly people and nations in which evil reigns supreme and whose people rebel against God suffers judgments of God that extends beyond the judgment of being left to our own devices to reap what we sow.

The scriptures reveal that if we reject Him he will ultimately withdraw His Spirit from us and we will be left to our own evil devices. When that occurs the evil within will work its way among us until it destroys us. The application and implications of this kind of judgment is explained in **Romans 1:18-30 & Romans 2:2** *" For the wrath of God is revealed from*

Heaven against all ungodliness and unrighteousness of men, who suppress the truth in unrighteousness, because that which is known about God is evident within them; for God made it known to them. For since the creation of the world His invisible attributes, His eternal power and divine nature, have been clearly seen, being understood through what has been made, so that they are without excuse. For even though they knew God, they did not honor Him as God, or give thanks; but they became futile in there speculations; and their foolish heart was darkened. Professing to be wise, they became fools, and exchanged the glory of the incorruptible God for an image in the form of corruptible man and of birds and four-footed animals and crawling creatures. Therefore God gave them over in the lusts of their hearts to impurity, that their bodies might be dishonored among them. For they exchanged the truth of God for a lie, and worshiped and served the creature rather than the Creator, who is blessed forever. Amen. For this reason God gave them over to degrading passions; for their women exchanged the natural function for that which is unnatural, and in the same way also the men abandoned the natural function of the woman and burned in their desire toward one another, men with men committing indecent acts and receiving in their own persons the due penalty of their error. And just as they did not see fit to acknowledge God any longer, God gave them over to a depraved mind, to do those things which are not proper, being filled with all unrighteousness, wickedness, greed, evil; full of envy, murder, strife, deceit, malice; they are gossips, slanderers, haters of God, insolent, arrogant, boastful, inventors of evil, disobedient to parents, without understanding, untrustworthy, unloving, unmerciful; and, although they know the ordinance of god, that those who practice such things are worthy of death, they not only do the same, but also give hearty approval to those who practice them."

The Scriptures also teach us that God often blesses the lives, works and families of His children as well as those nations in which they live who walk according to His will in profound and powerful ways. The United States of America has historically been the world's foremost example of God's blessing upon a nation of people.

In order for God to bless He must make judgments about what, who and when he is going to bless, discipline or condemn. The scriptures teach us that God clearly makes judgments that impact men and nations on earth. The way in which God judges the nations and the peoples of the earth are as varied and profound as His wisdom and nature. The best advice for anyone who is contemplating an evil act that God has declared against His will is to attempt to avoid it.

The Scriptures teach us the nature of the judgment against those people who live by the law and ignore it: *"For if we go on sinning willfully after receiving the knowledge of the truth, there no longer remains a sacrifice for sins, but a certain terrifying expectation of judgment, and the fury of a fire which will consume the adversaries. Anyone who has set aside the law of Moses dies without mercy on the testimony of two or three witnesses."* (Hebrews 10:26-28)

The scriptures also tells those under the new covenant who he says are without excuse will be judged because he has revealed himself to them; *"How much severer punishment do you think he will deserve who has trampled under foot the Son of God, and has regarded as unclean the blood of the covenant by which he was sanctified, and has insulted the Spirit of Grace? For we know Him who said, Vengeance is Mine, I will repay" and again, "The lord will Judge His people" (Hebrews 10:29-31)*

The Scriptures also warn us not to mock God because God will Judge those who mock Him by withdrawing His grace that goes before us and prepares the way; *"Do not be deceived, God is not mocked; for whatever a man sows, this he will also reap. For the one who sows to his own flesh shall from the flesh reap corruption, but the one who sows to the Spirit shall from the Spirit reap eternal life." (Galatians 6:6-8)*

The point is that God is in the process of judging and blessing his creation constantly. According to the scriptures those judgments are separate from the judgment all men will face after physical death.

God has also historically judged nations by bringing about natural disasters that destroys individuals, groups, cities and even nations. The scriptures also reveal His use of heathen nations to destroy other heathen nations to accomplish His purpose or to protect His people. He has used heathen nations to bring discipline His own people when they have refused to be obedient. He has also judged nations through famine and economic collapse and sometimes he has disciplined a people by bringing wealth to a selfish people who foolishly spend it unwisely on their lusts and appetites until they become destitute in hopes they will be awakened.

God completely destroyed the cities of Sodom and Gomorrah because of the sin and perversion present in those cities. God destroyed Lott's wife because she failed to obey Him. He wiped the nation of Israel off the face of the earth and scattered the people among the nations for almost 2000 years because of their rebellion and disobedience. Israel once again became a nation in 1948.

According to the scriptures an opportunity exists for America, or any other people for that matter, to move spiritually back toward their spiritual moorings. That opportunity will exist until God removes His Spirit and His church. I believe the window of time is narrow and there is little on the current horizon to indicate that America is so inclined.

For America to reject secularism will require that we be awakened spiritually. For that to occur the church must once again become the salt and light it is called to be. Short of that America will self destroy and this nation will become a cesspool of evil, lust and greed and its testimony as the most honorable, just, industrious, prosperous and charitable people the earth has ever known will be lost just like the Roman Empire was lost.

Will God allow the destruction of America? Does God historically allow nations to destroy themselves due to their immorality and rebellion? The bible answers those questions clearly! God does and He will unless America repents and seeks His face and turns away from its perversion? If we mock Him and continue to reject and rebel against Him his word says he will turn us over to our own foolish ways and allow us to destroy ourselves if we chose to continue the course we are on!

The problem with America's deceit is that we no longer discern the hand of God at work and we can no longer discern his voice speaking to us. The implications of this are devastating because deceived men cannot be delivered from a disaster they cannot perceive is coming nor do they typically recognize the hand of God at work in the signs of the times.

Clearly an opportunity exists for America to move politically and spiritually back toward its moorings, however, based on the historical biblical model the window of time is surely very narrow. The church must become spiritually awakened and aggressively seize the opportunity to become the salt and light it is ordained and called to be.

America must move rapidly and aggressively both individually and collectively to repentance and seek the mercy and forgiveness of God. We must begin to act in faith to overturn those destructive Supreme Court judgments such as those that have created "Separation of church and state", and "abortion on demand", "taking prayer out of school ", "removing the ten commandments from public grounds" etc.

America must rise up and move immediately to stop government sponsorship of the abortion clinics and dismantle completely Planned Parenthood. We must move immediately and aggressively to overhaul our public education system. We must aggressively examine the qualification and character of those we hire to educate our children at every level. Anti-Christ communists, socialists, atheists, pagans, perverts and fools must be removed from the system of education.

The debate is long since over and America's survival is not dependent on the freedom of speech of our enemies and of perverts and fools who are aiding and abetting our enemies! Freedom of speech is the right of every American to state his belief regarding the governing process or regarding political activity or the right to support candidates without the government prosecuting him. It does not protect speech that destroys our way of life or that allows perverts to spread his or her perversion poisoning the minds and hearts of children or our people, nor does it guarantee that those who chose to speak unwisely will not suffer the consequences of his foolishness.

We must awaken to the danger of the direction our judiciary and our government has taken us. We must move aggressively to redirect and downsize the government bureaucracy at every level. We must make the government accountable to the people once again. We must impeach those Supreme Court justices who have the mistaken idea that they have the power to change the character of our nation, legislate their will and disregard the will of the people.

God does judge nations and He clearly speaks prophetically to nations to awaken and/or warn them of what is to come if they fail to listen and take action! The bible gives many examples of God judging nations for their evil and rebellion against his will. His chosen people Israel have paid a terrible price because of their rebellion against God and for their rejection and crucifixion of His Son Jesus Christ. That price will not be completely paid until the end of the great tribulation, *"the time of Jacob's trouble,"* is completed. Kingdom after kingdom throughout history has come to wield great political, economic and military power in the world and they have all died an agonizing death and many have disappeared from view because they failed to recognize or give thanks for God's blessing and they rebelled against God. Because of the evil in them he destroyed them.

The great atheistic nation of the Soviet Union was one of three of the world's greatest political, economic and military powers of our time only to become the latest nation whose government hated God. This secular and heathen union of nations has disappeared. God used America and other nations to bring her to her knees. However, their choice within to reject God caused God to leave them to suffer the devastation that comes forth from the fallen nature of man which brought about moral and economic disaster and in that sense their destruction was God's judgment. God allowed them to destroy themselves from within.

How naive we would have to be to believe that God will overlook America's national apostasy and rebellion against him when he has not done so for any other nation. It is more likely that our demise will be more agonizing than the others because we have tasted of his love and grace and we have enjoyed the abundance of great blessing, yet we foolishly allowed our Supreme Court to force government to turn its backs on Him who has made our prosperity and power possible.

We take great pride in our material prosperity and become very nervous when it is shaken by a downturn in the stock market or in any one of several economic indicators. However material prosperity is not necessarily a measure of national or individual spiritual progress or stability. Prosperity certainly appeals to the flesh of men but it also often destroys the character of the men it touches.

At any rate, history reveals that seasons of material prosperity come and pass in the lives of men and nations. This current season of material prosperity in America could well be an economic fairyland that is a house of cards built upon debt that could collapse in just a few hours. We observed how that collapse could work all most immediately after 9-11.

Our economic development and life style is built largely on a debt driven economic model. A debt driven economy mortgages the future of Americans and has given America a false sense of national and individual prosperity and material security which blinds our eyes to the precipice ahead and to our deep need for spiritual wisdom.

Could it be that the Creator has given America this time of material prosperity for our testing? The scriptures teach us that God is sovereign! I grant you that this is a hard concept to grasp. However, whether we believe it or like it or not I am convinced it is true. In His infinite wisdom He chooses people and nations to fulfill his purpose. Our failure to recognize and cooperate with His sovereign work and purpose will cause Americans much pain and suffering.

When the rejection of God becomes predominate and the conscience of the people will no longer draw our nation back to God the nation will soon find itself condemned by its deceit and rebellion. The nation soon finds itself immersed in perversion, divisiveness, confusion, turmoil and both material and Spiritual poverty.

Deceived men and nations rarely recognize how they got there, however, the bible teaches us their dilemma has overtaken them because they are living in rebellion against God's purposes and God has turned them over to suffer the consequences of their own foolish ways which historically has always lead men and nations to disaster and destruction.

The scriptures teach that the **"Deeds of the flesh are evident, which are: immorality, impurity, sensuality, idolatry, sorcery, enmities, strife, jealousy, outbursts of anger, disputes, dissensions, factions, envying, drunkenness, carousing, and things like these...."Gal 5:19-21**

The scriptures also teach that the, **"Fruit of the Spirit (of God) is love, joy, peace, patience, kindness, goodness, faithfulness, gentleness, self-control; " Gal 5:22-24**

Consider which of these environments describes the American culture? Which would you prefer to live in? Once again it's a "no-brainer" isn't it?

God has proven Himself to be long suffering always giving individuals and nations ample warning and often decades of time to awaken, repent and return to Him and His ways. Arrogance and deceit leads to all manner of evil, injustice and Spiritual poverty, which eventually overtakes us.

Mans natural inclination is to begin to congratulate himself for whatever prosperity or blessing he is enjoying and he tends to worship the blessing rather than the giver of the blessing. God eventually gives them over to their perverse thinking and moral degeneracy, which soon takes over, and men destroy themselves and nations.

Some of those rebellious people suffered under incredible tyranny for many years. Other nations disappeared and their people perished and /or were scattered to the four winds! Other nations barely survive and remain little more than a shell and a memory of what they once were. All that remains of some once great nations are memories and marble statues pointing back to a time of material prosperity that ended in spiritual as well as material poverty. Many fertile and productive nations and lands have become desolate places with little or no evidence, except for the historical record, that they ever existed.

It's ironic how men reject the lessons of history to their own destruction. A majority of sincere minded Americans agree that the social moral disintegration of America is our most serious national problem. However, there is not general understanding of the relationship between the cause and solution to the problem. Therefore the way of hope and healing escapes them. Our government has determined our best hope is a secular government. Our nation has become deeply divided between the Spiritually alive who look to God and His solution to our problems for direction and guidance, and the spiritually dead who look to secular fleshly minded men for the solution to America's problems.

I believe the great Apostle Paul captures the essence of America's problem best in his letter to the Galatians written almost 2000 years ago: *Galatians 6:7-8, "Do not be deceived, God is not mocked; for whatever a man sows, this he will also reap. For the one who sows to his own flesh shall from the flesh reap corruption, but the one who sows to the Spirit shall from the Spirit reap eternal life." Galatians 5:17, "For the flesh sets its desire against the Spirit, and the Spirit against the flesh; for these are in opposition to one another, so that you may not do the things that you please."*

The scriptures point to the utter foolishness of secular humanists that promote the idea that man, through his fleshly wisdom, can produce a utopian nation and world over time.

Perspective is written to remind us all of our incredible need for God and His wisdom if we are to individually or collectively survive and live in peace with each other and ourselves here and hereafter. The Governing of a people by secular law is obviously foolish. Once again the scriptures give us guidance: *Matthew 7:24-27, "Therefore everyone who hears these words of Mine, and acts upon them, may be compared to a wise man, who built his house upon the rock. And the rain descended, and the floods came, and the winds blew, and burst against that house; and yet it did not fall, for it had been founded upon the rock. And everyone who hears this word of mine, and does not act upon them, will be like a foolish man, who built his house upon the sand. And the rain descended, and the floods came, and the winds blew, and burst against that house; and it fell, and great was its fall."*

Fellow Americans isn't it past time that we take inventory of our grave circumstance, throw ourselves on God's mercy, repent of our sinful ways and foolish arrogance and actively begin to change our direction as individuals and as a nation.

We must awaken to the danger of the social direction we have taken as a nation and move aggressively to discourage government dependence though our system of education. We must teach our people that indolence is not a right and it is a selfish way of life that is destructive and evil.

God's sovereignty impacts a people in almost every arena of life, relationship, speech and action constantly. The problem is that the deterioration of a society is typically not linked to God's judgment upon a people as much as it is His willingness to allow a people to make their own choices and go there own way.

If America shall ever discover they need a deliverer, where will America look for deliverance? After over 200 years of depending on God we have decided to change and depend upon the secular mind of man to deliver us from the devastation we have sown with our rebellious lives. Clearly the web we are weaving with our foolishness is getting tighter. The problems that arise out of the hearts and minds of lost and selfish citizens become more and more complex and come at us faster than we can ever hope to deal with them. We are not wise enough to recognize the truth and deliver justice. Clearly America's deliverance will not come from some secular humanist intellectual think tank in Washington D. C. or from the halls of some secular humanist university or from secular minded political leaders!

The scriptures tell us to awaken to the only source of deliverance. It will only come from the Spirit of God working through the lives of humble and wise men. Meanwhile America continues to experience and witness the systematic destruction of the foundational values, institutions and principles of our nation and the accompanying pillars of our society such as the institution of Christian marriage.

We observe the wholesale endorsement of every kind of "live in" arrangement and our perverted life styles have brought us to the point of justifying abortion on demand, and the sanctioning of the most abominable lifestyles of sexual perversion. Two out of three births in America last year among African American's was born out of wedlock. One out of three of the rest of us were born out of wedlock. Both are disastrous for America. The sanctioned wholesale perversion is leading America down the slippery slope of destruction like so many nations before us.

The tragedy, of course, is that in their deceit many American families ignore the relevance of these things as though these are simply political issues rather than Spiritual issues. They consider them as having little or no real impact in the overall scheme of things and will somehow work themselves out or somehow go away. Evil is winning folks because the good among us are asleep! God is saying to America, evil does not have to win, but the choice is yours and you are making the wrong choices.

When God turns a people over to moral collapse and to the deteriorating character of people who have rejected God what we can expect to experience among that people is listed in 2 Timothy 3:2-7 **"for men will be lovers of self, lovers of money, boastful, arrogant, revilers, disobedient to parents, ungrateful, unholy, unloving, irreconcilable, malicious gossips, without self-control, brutal, haters of good, treacherous, reckless, conceited, lovers of pleasure rather than lovers of God; hold to a form of Godliness, although they have denied its power......always learning and never able to come to the knowledge of the truth."**

Our public education system is one of three vital core systems that form the fabric of the future of America that must be protected as sure as we protect the White House and our Nations Capitol. First as a people we must declare all out war on evil and deceit and on those who promote it. We must begin to protect our precious faith and heritage with a critical eye. Second we must reject the homosexual life style as the abomination our Lord declares that it is. We must move aggressively to define a family within the confines of the biblically based Judeo Christian worldview. Any attempt to dismantle or attach the family unit must be treated with the same contempt that we treat any evil and treacherous move against America. Third our national character and its traits must be defined legislatively by a moral code that expresses our highest beliefs and ideals. Fourth, the institution of church, must awaken to its calling to be salt and light.

For those who will scream, freedom of speech, let them scream because these are not freedom of speech issues. They are dead wrong and their screaming is out of their ignorance and clearly out of context with the constitutional protection of freedom of speech. It is time that we examine the freedom of speech issue within the context of the constitutional writing and the reasonable and obvious interpretation of its focus and meaning.

We must awaken to the danger of the liberal and unrestrained social direction we have taken as a nation and move aggressively to discourage government dependence, discontinue or limit socialistic economic programs that provide the wrong incentives. We must downsize the government bureaucracy at every level and last but not least we must put the people back in charge of government and move aggressively to educate and inspire our citizens to become alert and involved in governing.

The scriptures teach us that God is sovereign and that His ultimate goal is to draw all men unto Himself! It is your soul not your fortune that concerns Him. I grant you that this is a hard concept to grasp in a materialistic society. It can only be grasped and appreciated through faith. However, whether we believe it or like it or not I am convinced it remains true. Life becomes easier to accept and much easier to understand when we recognize the will and ways of our Lord. He is in complete control and He has told us His will and way will ultimately prevail regardless of our sin and rebellion. The difference is that if we rebel against Him we are isolated from the deliverance of His grace and the benefits of His spiritual wisdom when we walk in rebellion against Him.

With the possible exception of a few spiritually alive Christian believers most Americans fail to assess the foundational problem in the social moral decline in America as principally spiritual. Many deceived thinkers promote the idea that a nation can be moral without the influence of biblical truth and Spiritual wisdom and power. Fleshly men reject biblical morality because it flies in the face of everything that the fallen nature of man wants. Without the leading of the Spirit of God moral character is impossible for man to achieve with any consistency.

In essence we have an active anti-American political terrorism within our nation conducted by the liberal fringe, comprised mostly of secular humanist political operatives, college professors, attorneys, atheists, homo-sexual activists, cultic religious groups and socialists who impact secular thinking and politics.

They have attempted to attach themselves politically to the causes of the children, the poor, the disenfranchised, the indolent, the welfare groups, the illegal immigrants and the minority groups in our society. They sell the concept of government dependency and they have captured the imagination of many who have their hand out demanding that the government fill it.

This destructive anti-American group is poisoning the minds of our teachers and therefore our children, removing God from our government and our classrooms and destroying every vestige of our values, our liberty and our heritage. They are only dangerous because the rest of America refuses to confront their destructive lies. We need to get in their face with the truth and keep in their face until America begins to wake up.

The democratic party has, for the most part, embraced their lunacy giving their agenda a place at the table. In fact they have hi-jacked the Democratic political party destroying its legitimate role in the political process. The Democratic party now gives their treasonous liberalism a political platform. They have also captured the imagination of much of the judiciary and are unfortunately protected and supported in many of their causes by a deceived court system and a socialist and anti-God liberal education system that is conducting its own special war against God, our President and our Constitution.

CHAPTER 18

HOW MUST WE RESPOND?

—ɯ—

His word says, *"if my people who are called by my name humble themselves and pray, and seek my face and turn from their wicked ways, then I will hear from heaven, will forgive their sin, and will heal their land." (2 Chron 7 13-14)*

What happens to cause a nation to lose its spiritual sight and moral compass and what must happen to that nation to regain it?

A response by Americans that will change the direction of our nation as well as our individual and collective lives must be profound and divinely inspired. It must be a profound and radical response and it will have to begin with each one of us. The destiny of millions of Americans and of people all over the world depends on the response of a few Americans.

A prominent sociologist has suggested that it takes only 2% of the people in a society committed to and diligent in the pursuit of a cause to change the entire society. A case in point is that a few Christians changed the entire Roman Empire from paganism to Christianity in less than two centuries. If the Church was willing and committed to demonstrating what they profess they believe it could transform the United States of America, and for that matter, much of the western world in one decade. Change comes much faster through the demonstration of truth and charity than through a sales pitch or religious piety.

What kind of response to God's call upon America ought we expect? Certainly, we cannot expect those who do not have eyes to see and understand to respond to God's voice unless God somehow intervenes. Sometimes that awakening occurs because of answered prayer and sometimes it occurs because of a national tragedy that must occur to get our attention. History teaches us that the greatest growth of the Church has been in times of human tragedy and suffering. What we must begin to recognize is that it is not likely that more prosperity, security, leisure and luxury will inspire us to seek after God out of a spirit of gratitude. That would be the heart of God, however, it is not the heart of man. History teaches us that mans natural instinct is not thankfulness for what he has been given, but rather, one of greed and lust for what he does not have.

Perhaps prayer is where we ought to begin! The flesh of man is committed to the appetites and pleasures of man and that spirit inspires the perspective of the world. The spirit of the world hates God, Christ and Christians and those who follow after the spirit of the world will perish without God's positive response to the prayers and intervention of the church actively petitioning God to bring awakening to the lost.

However, it is not just the world that must be awakened. Luke warm Christians must be awakened and become actively engaged in the fight working, praying, voting, speaking out and living in the purpose of glorifying God in their walk and works that the world might see and many repent. The scriptures speak of the Church as being the salt and the light of the world. *"You are the salt of the earth; but if the salt has become tasteless, how will it be made salty again? It is good for nothing anymore, except to be thrown out and trampled under foot by men. You are the light of the world. A city set on a hill cannot be hidden. Nor do men light a lamp, and put it under the peck measure, but on the lamp-stand; and it gives light to all who are in the house. Let you light shine before men in such a way that they may see your good works, and glorify your Father who is in heaven." (Matthew 5:13-16)*

The Church was given to the world to act as a preservative of Spiritual life and to lend taste to that life. It was also sent to dispel darkness and the encroachment of evil. It is to be the purveyor of truth and righteousness. It's important to notice the last sentence in the above scripture verse. It reads, *"let your light shine before men is such a way that they may see your good works, and glorify your Father who is in heaven."* The point is that it is not so much our words as it is the demonstration of the truth and life through our good works that changes the perspectives of people. Our purpose is to be a demonstration of the glory of God. Our lives are to be a demonstration of charity, righteousness, wisdom, joy, peace, patience, kindness, goodness, faithfulness, gentleness and self-control.

The point I want to emphasize is that Jesus emphasized our good works more than our words. The Church has not been as faithful as it should have been in the demonstration of our profession. We have not been the salt and light we were called to be. If we hope to change America, or the world, we need to take a serious look at our walk and our strategy.

The scriptures teach us that the way to life is narrow and few will find it and the way is broad and many will follow the way of the world. We need not expect that all will respond favorably to our walk or our words. Nevertheless, our calling is to make a difference by the distinctiveness of the way we live our lives. Our success will not come as a result of our conformity to the ways of the world! The church is populated with those who are "new creations in Christ Jesus" sent into the world as ambassadors of the Kingdom of God to make a difference through the demonstration of our distinctiveness.

The irony the world does not appreciate is that the body of Christ is on their side and provides the greatest hope in this world of preserving the witness of God's grace, glory, power and charity. The incredible problem with the deceit of the world is that it is a Spiritual matter. Life is in the Spirit of God and is only imparted to men by God Himself. The bible says that no one comes to Christ unless the Father sends him.

Our prayer has to be for the church to become the demonstration of the glory of God and for God to send millions of Americans to Christ. As I mentioned earlier, the goal of *"perspective"* is not to make a heaven of America but to populate heaven with Americans.

The admonition of the scriptures is; *"Awake Sleeper, and arise from the dead, and Christ will shine on you. Therefore, be careful how you walk, not as unwise men, but as wise, making the most of your time, because the days are evil. So then do not be foolish, but understand what the will of the Lord is." (Ephesians 5:14-17)*

The scriptures bring stern warning to those people and nations that mock God and the grace He has brought through the atoning death of Jesus Christ. Listen carefully, *"For in the case of those who have once been enlightened and have tasted of the heavenly gift and have been made partakers of the Holy Spirit, and have tasted the good word of God and the powers of the age to come, and then have fallen away, it is impossible to renew them again to repentance, since they again crucify to themselves the Son of God, and put Him to open shame. For ground that drinks the rain which often falls upon it and brings forth vegetation useful to those for whose sake it is also tilled, receives a blessing from God; but if it yields thorns and thistles, its worthless and close to being cursed, and it ends up being burned." (Hebrews 6:4-8)*

These scriptures were written to the Hebrew nation, the chosen people of God, who had lived according to the law but had been granted the knowledge of the saving grace of God and accepted God's saving grace that comes as a gift. They were living their lives according to the law depending upon their own works and righteousness to earn them favor with God rather than accepting the atoning death of Christ as sufficient and full payment for their sin. Nevertheless, the essence of the scriptures applies to America in the sense that God has unlimited patience with those who try and fail but He has little patience with those who rebel and mock the atoning death of Christ.

To the believer who is born of His Spirit he declares them to be His sheep and has promised them some incredible things. Listen carefully once again as you read this; *"My sheep hear my voice, and I know them, and they follow Me; and I give eternal life to them, and they shall never perish; and no one shall snatch them out of My hand. I and the Father are one" (John 10:27-30)*

Can America be renewed? Only if her people become God's people somehow awakened Spiritually and we begin to walk according to our calling. Our nation and our nations leaders are but a reflection of our combined faith and character. We elect those who lead us and therefore, these leaders reflect the character and faith of those who elect them.

Whatever God will do to lead us back to humility is difficult to predict. However, one thing is sure. We will have to ask Him and those who reject His grace shall perish.

Dependence upon and obedience to Him will only come to pass if we, as a people chose to humble ourselves before the truth and before God Himself. The alternative for our nation and for us individually is tragic. God is indeed merciful, however, He has left the choice to us individually and collectively.

If we continue to allow our government to reject Him and remove the witness and testimony to our dependence upon Him as a nation His judgment upon our nation is inevitable. The bible tells us that we have two alternatives. The preferable alternative is to live under His saving grace where the price for our sin and rebellion has been paid by the sacrifice of His only begotten son Jesus Christ. We can also chose to reject His grace and live under the judgment of the law of God and suffer the consequences of our sin, our decisions and our rebellion.

As a very wise person once said, the question for America is not *"is God on our side, but rather are we on His side"*. If we chose to humble ourselves and walk according to His will he will deliver us from the delusion we walk in and he will bless and protect us as a nation. If we chose to stand against Him he will allow us to suffer the consequences of our choice.

The notion that we each have a responsibility to our fellowman to protect our liberty and secure our most precious faith and our way of life has become a foreign and unwelcome idea in our culture because of its implications.

The scriptures teach us that God will not strive with man forever. The resource of His Spirit will not be available to us forever. There must be a distinction made here between the true church, the body of Christ, and the religious institutions our society recognizes as the church. Not because there should be a difference but because there is! There is a remnant of believers and followers of Christ that comprise the true church. Jesus tells us that number is small in comparison with the number of people who are culturally Christian. The institution of Church tends to be institutions in which a majority of its membership are at least cultural Christians. The true church is typically found somewhere within the religious institutions we refer to as the church. They are the true salt and light of the world!

I continue to be inspired by courageous men like Darrell Scott, the father of Rachel Scott who was a victim of the columbine high school shootings, in Littleton, Colorado. His address on Thursday, may 27,1999 to the house judiciary subcommittee capture the painful truth of what has happened to our culture and our national leadership. It is a clarion testimony to our inability as a people to think clearly and act objectively in the context and light of the truth.

I have included the text of his message because I believe it captures the essence of our spiritual degeneration and public deceit. His message needs to be shouted from the housetops until every parent, teacher, politician, judge, sociologist, psychologist and every business and religious leader in America, hears its message.

Mr. Scott told the committee, *"we all contain the seeds of kindness or the seeds of violence. The death of my wonderful daughter, Rachel Joy Scott, and the deaths of that heroic teacher, and the other eleven children who died must not be in vain. Their blood cries out for answers."*

"The first recorded act of violence was when Cain slew his brother Abel out in a field. The villain was not the club he used. Nor was it the national club association. The true killer was Cain, and the reason for the murder could only be found in Cain's heart."

In the days that followed the Columbine tragedy, I was amazed at how quickly fingers began to be pointed at groups such as the NRA. I am not a member of the NRA. I am not a hunter. I do not even own a gun. I am not here to represent or defend the NRA because I don't believe they are responsible for my daughter's death. Therefore I do not believe they need to be defended. If I believed they had anything to do with Rachel's murder I would be their strongest opponent."

"I am here today to declare that Columbine was not just a tragedy – it was a Spiritual event that should be forcing us to look at where the real blame lies! Much of the blame lies here in this room. Much of the blame lies behind the pointing fingers of accusers themselves. I wrote a poem just four nights ago that expresses my feelings best. This was written before I knew I would be speaking here today."

> *"Your laws ignore our deepest needs,*
> *Your words are empty air.*
> *You've stripped away our heritage,*
> *You've outlawed simple prayer.*
> *Now gunshots fill our classrooms,*
> *And precious children die.*
> *You seek for answers everywhere,*
> *And ask the question "why"?*
> *You regulate restrictive laws,*
> *through legislative creed.*
> *And yet you fail to understand,*
> *That God is what we need!"*

"Men and women are three-part beings. We all consist of body, soul and spirit. When we refuse to acknowledge a third part of our makeup, we create a void that allows evil, prejudice, and hatred to rush in and wreak havoc. Spiritual influences were present within our educational systems for most of our nations history. Many of our major colleges began as theological seminaries. This is a historical fact. What has happened to us as a nation? We have refused to honor God, and in doing so, we open the doors to hatred and violence. And when something as terrible as Columbine's tragedy occurs

politicians immediately look for a scapegoat such as the NRA. They immediately seek to pass more restrictive laws that erode away our personal and private liberties. We do not need more restrictive laws. Metal detectors would not have stopped Eric and Dylan. No amount of gun laws can stop someone who spends months planning this type of massacre. The real villain lies within our hearts. Political posturing and restrictive legislation are not the answers.

The young people of our nation hold the key. There is a Spiritual awakening-taking place that will not be squelched! We do not need more religion. We do not need more gaudy television evangelist spewing out verbal religious garbage. We do not need more million dollar church buildings built while people with basic needs are being ignored. We do need a change of heart and a humble acknowledgement that this nation was founded on the principle of simple trust in God!"

"As my son Craig lay under that table in the school library and saw his two friends murdered before his very eyes he did not hesitate to pray in school. I defy any law or politician to deny him that right! I challenge every young person in America, and around the world, to realize that on April 20, 1999 at Columbine high school – prayer was brought back to our schools."

"Do not let the many prayers offered by those students be in vain. Dare to move into the new millennium with a sacred disregard for legislation that violates your God given right to communicate with him."

Darrell Scott, thank you for your leadership, courage and wisdom at this critical time in our nations history. This horrible tragedy was a Spiritual wake-up call to America. 9-11 was another, however, America did not recognize the call and respond to the message of either. Your expressed wisdom strikes a clear contrast to the deceit of our national leadership and our Judiciary.

What will be our response? Can the Spiritual deceit be corrected through any action that a secular nation can take or institute? According to the Scriptures there is only one remedy that can turn the ship of state, the church and the people around. "(If), *My people who are called by My name humble themselves and pray, and seek my face and turn from their wicked ways, then I will hear from heaven, will forgive their sin, and heal their land"* (II Chronicles 7:14)

We must respond with a full understanding of the nature of the battle we are in! The real conflict is (supernatural) spiritual not material. The book of Daniel reveals to us the nature of the spiritual world. Understanding that world and the implications of its existence is essential to victory over the battle with evil. Daniel received a vision, which left him devastated. He prayed and he received an answer to his prayer in the form of *"a certain man dressed in linen, whose waist was girded with a belt of pure gold of Uphaz. His body was like beryl, his face had the appearance of lightning, his eyes were like flaming torches, his arms and feet like the gleam of polished bronze, and the sound of his words like the sound of a tumult." (Daniel 10:5-6)*

This person was a Spiritual prince. Listen to Daniels words, *"Then he said to me, "Do not be afraid, Daniel, for from the first day that you set your heart on understanding this and on humbling yourself before your God, your words were heard, and I have come in response to your words. But the prince of the kingdom of Persia was with standing me for twenty-one days; then behold, Michael, one of the chief princes, came to help me, for I had been left there with the kings of Persia. Now I have come to give you and understanding of what will happen to your people in the latter days, for the vision pertains to the days yet future" "Then he said, Do you understand why I came to you? But I will return to fight against the prince of Persia; so I am going forth, and behold, the prince of Greece is about to come. However, I will tell you what is inscribed in the writing of truth. Yet there is no one who stands firmly with me against these forces except Michael your prince." (Daniel 10:5-21)*

Perhaps your response to these scriptures is "what do they have to do with me or America and today'? These scriptures only have relevance to us today in the fact that they reveal the conflict that is occurring in the spiritual realm between angelic creatures. In addition they reveal there are princes in the spiritual realm that have jurisdiction over nations and peoples that influence the attitudes, events, actions, life and character of those persons under their jurisdiction. In addition it reveals there are princes in the spiritual realm at war with God and are attempting to destroy His creation.

If this is true, it has incredible implications because it affects the lives and destinies of all men and nations. The church has overlooked the profound implications of the spiritual and therefore it has lost touch with the spiritual and has directed its focus on the material. The Scriptures of the new testament open to us the picture of the invisible world and its implications.

However, for a people to be awakened spiritually they must become aware of the spiritual. For our eyes to fully appreciate the implications of the spiritual nature of man and of the impact of the spiritual world on the attitudes and actions of the people and the events of the day demands that we become born of the Spirit of God. Our Spiritual rebirth delivers us from the deceit we once walked in when we followed after the Spirit of Satan thinking all the time that we were following after the truth!

Once we see the light we begin to recognize the implications of the Scriptures that reveal to us the meaning and manner of the evil one. *"Be sober of Spirit, be on the alert. Your adversary, the devil, prowls about like a roaring lion, seeking someone to devour." (I Peter 5: 8)* The scriptures warn us to put on the full armor of God, which is a spiritual armor, that we might be able to stand firm against the schemes of the devil. *"Finally, be strong in the Lord, and in the strength of His might. Put on the full armor of God, that you may be able to stand firm against the schemes of the devil. For our struggle is not against flesh and blood, but against the rulers, against, the powers, against the world forces of this darkness, against the spiritual forces of wickedness in the heavenly places." (Ephesians 6:10-12)*

Jesus reveals the reality of the two kingdoms in the scriptures and how one of those kingdoms hates him and do not believe. *"I told you, and you do not believe; the works that I do in My Fathers name, these bear witness of Me. But you do not believe because you are not of My sheep. My sheep hear My voice, and I know them, and they follow Me; and I give eternal life to them, and they shall never perish; and no one shall snatch them out of My hand. My Gather, who has given them to Me, is greater than all; and no one is able to snatch them out of the Father's hand. I and the Father are one." (John 10:25-30)*

"For God so loved the world, that He gave His only begotten Son, that whoever believes in Him should not perish, but have eternal life. For God did not send the Son into the world to judge the world, but that the world should be saved through Him. He who believes in Him is not judged; he who does not believe has been judged already, because he has not believed in the name of the only begotten Son of God. And this is the judgment, that he light is come into the world, and men loved the darkness rather than the light; for their deeds were evil. For everyone who does evil hates the light, and does not come to the light, lest his deeds be exposed. But he who practices the truth come to the light, that his deeds may be manifested as having been wrought in God." (John 3:16-21)

Truly, truly, I say to you, unless one is born again, he cannot see the kingdom of God…That which is born of the flesh is flesh, and that which is born of the Spirit is spirit. (John 3:3-6)

Much of the church is in disarray and apostasy because it has not really understood the implications of the sovereignty of God and the existence and implications of the battle that goes on constantly in the Spiritual realm for the lives of the people of this world.

The predominant thinking in the church is that the Spiritual implications of the death of Jesus on the cross are limited primarily to the promise of eternal life for those who believe. It ignores the implications of the spiritual battle in the heavenly's as it bears on the attitude and actions of people. It also ignores the spiritual authority of the church. Therefore, the church tends not to be effective in the battle against evil. Much of the church, and the entire world, are blinded to the impact of the spiritual darkness that effects the attitudes, actions, ideas and character of the world.

The destiny of the United States of America, along with the rest of the world, is inevitable according to the scriptures. However, there is much we ought to do before the end of this world, as we know it. The United States has a significant role to play in the time we have left. That role is to be salt and light to a lost world. We are a nation among all nations that have reason reflect our Lords glory and to be an example of liberty and hope to the oppressed. The message of His redeeming grace ought to be on the lips of every American

Christian and the heart to share it with the lost that are seeking His grace ought to be the driving inspiration of the church.

As a nation of people who have been given the opportunity to live and walk according to His Spirit we must stay strong in the battle. Keeping America strong provides a sanctuary in the world from which God can work through the hearts and minds of a people who have tasted of His grace and blessing. We will not be able to do so unless the church and a majority of our citizens are Spiritually awakened. Our role in that process, if we hope to be effective, is to understand the nature of the battle and become the salt and light we are called to be.

The battle between deceit and deliverance is a spiritual battle and it must be fought and won with spiritual weapons. Our elected and appointed leaders must be men born of the Spirit of God who fully appreciate the spiritual battle we are in and the nature of man without God. The laws and the social programs that are instituted must be made by wise men that fully recognize the evil that leads the world and directs the response of the fallen nature of men without God.

Social programs, kindness, money, or convenience will not heal the breach in the character of the creature whose nature is fallen and who responds to the voice of a spiritual leader who is committed to the cause of ultimately destroying him and his fellowman.

It is perhaps wishful thinking to hope that every congressman and/or senator might take note and be awakened to recognize the call and the immediate need to begin restoring America by honoring the sovereignty of her God, the fact of her Christian heritage, the constructionist interpretation and application of the constitutional guarantees, and a biblical perspective to our system of justice!

Clearly America needs a spiritual shower bath beginning with her political leaders, her judges and government bureaucrats and, last but not least, her people. The stench of political posturing to gain power, secular humanism and immorality in public affairs and particularly in the governing of our nation needs to be flushed back into the gutter from where it arose.

Every year we continue to educate millions and millions of children in secular humanist public schools lead by secular humanist teachers and we wonder why they are not growing up to be responsible, accountable adults with moral courage. Attempts by our President to bring responsibility, accountability and build quality back into our education system are rejected by the failing system he is attempting to rescue.

Over the past 50 years government has passed thousands of legislative acts that restrict individual liberty, increase the size and power of government over the affairs of Americans only to find the need continues to increase as the people become less dependent upon themselves and more dependent upon government to protect them and meet their every need. The government on whom they depend is slowly and systematically becoming their enemy and they do not recognize it.

Our supreme court has become a literal embarrassment to America as it relates to carrying out its constitutionally assigned responsibility. The liberal members of the court are busy usurping legislative power, removing God from the public forum, and second guessing legislation, which attempts to lead our nation back on course. I recommend the book entitled "Men in Black" by Mark Levin if you would like to gain greater insight into how the Supreme Court has become a destructive force in America.

We, like blind and indiscriminant men following a modern pied piper, have unwisely agreed to turn our back to God and his truth and place our trust and turn over our individual rights and authority over our lives, as well as our freedom and liberty, to a secular humanist government bureaucracy believing that in doing so we have done a good thing. Sounds crazy doesn't it? That's because it is crazy and we must somehow see to it that it is reversed or we will all become subjects of a totalitarian government.

The result of our inattentiveness and deceit is that we are becoming more irresponsible and ironically we feel more secure and less bothered. We have followed after blind guides and we have forgotten that liberty in a lost world requires alertness, awareness and a constant readiness to fight for it at the least hint of infraction! Living in blindness and deceit we have failed to realize what we were creating.

It may very well be too late to correct it, not because God is not willing, but because we are not willing. The price that those who follow after us will have to pay for our spiritual blindness, foolishness and irresponsible stewardship will be a price greater than we can possibly imagine unless we humble ourselves nationally before God and pray for His forgiveness.

From a spiritual perspective we have been conditioned by the secularists to accept and indorse the idea that our federal and state governments must be amoral and must pass amoral legislation. We somehow have reconciled that with the belief that you can trust government to be moral and fair and just while all the time insisting that it be secular and amoral. Sound preposterous? It is!!! How could intelligent honorable men get hood winked into such deceit?

We have been sold on the idea that justice must not be guided by Godly truth and principle. We, like sheep headed to the slaughter, follow cooperatively along in our deceit in a debt driven prosperity and a huge and growing government. Like a stroll through wonderland we march merrily, merrily down the path to our own utter individual and national destruction. We are totally pre-occupied with our pleasures and have forgotten the meaning and purpose of life.

For liberty and freedom to prevail, in the context of the constitutional guarantees, men must abandon the notion of government dependency and the attitude of entitlement. We must wake up and begin to recognize that we are accountable for our own individual welfare. Believe it or not, welfare is not the essential constitutional role of Government.

The national perspective regarding the role of government made a dramatic change in the 1960's. The moral character of Americans made a dramatic shift away from our Judeo Christian ethic and attitude. We openly rebelled against our Creator and we became willing to trade-off liberty for a ticket to ride and for what the people thought would be a utopia of free love and isolation from accountability and/or the responsibilities that accompanies liberty. We begin to demand free needles, abortion, access to other peoples resources, free medical care, special rights for sexual perverts, guaranteed physical and economic security, protection and provision for and from anything and everything.

If America does not reverse its almost total dependence on government and reverse the secular direction of government we will end up under a totalitarian atheistic governing bureaucracy that will soon usurp the only power we had as citizens to throw it out.

In America today we need courageous and honorable leaders who are willing to impeach Supreme Court justices, state and local justices and legislators.

Our senate and congress needs to be flushed out along with the "behind the scene" power system that forces freshmen senators and congressmen to fall in line and compromise themselves and their constituents for special interests. They soon find they have joined the rest of the house and the senate for a social swim in the big pool under the capitol called the sewer. Their forced compromise ultimately renders them harmless and helpless to bring true change to the system they are trapped in, let alone to America.

My commentary is intended to encourage change, sometimes-dramatic change, from some firmly established ways and attitudes that currently guide our government and our current culture. Such change necessarily demands pressure and light brought directly on those in positions of power, influence and leadership in the church as well as those in government, in the business community and in the home. Those on whom God has placed the mantel of leadership are clearly targeted in this writing!

"Perspective" is presented to bring light that will perhaps influence and ultimately help change the current perspective of those who read it toward a more biblical view of truth and justice and help Americans reflect on why and how we arrived where we are and how we are instructed to proceed from a biblical perspective!

Someone has said, "The problem with deceit is the effected are blind to his or her deceit". One who is deceived cannot see to rise above his deceit. Therein is the tragic circumstance the one who suffers deceit finds himself or herself in. The arrogance of our sinful and selfish nature sets a trap from which there is no power within or on earth that can provide us an escape! There is no human being, no public relations program, no television add, no government program, no politician, no drug or medication, nor any amount of higher or special secular education and there is no counseling that can deliver man from spiritual deceit or death.

Deceit is not a condition of the soul of man limited to the minds and hearts of a few. It is a curse shared by the fallen nature of the entire human race. It was inherited because man rebelled against God and God placed a curse upon all mankind. Deceit is a spiritual disease that separated 100% of the human race from God. God's Spirit is the Spirit of life and man rebelled against God and now only those who are born again of His Spirit inherit his life and will never perish according to His word. Those who chose His redemption are those who receive His redemptive gift.

Deceit is the irrefutable evidence of God's judgment and it is so powerful and devastating there is no escape. Deliverance from its grasp requires divine intervention. Deceit is a devastating profound spiritual dimension in which all natural men are trapped because of sin. Man has been judged and the penalty for his sin and deceit is eternal death. Intellectual knowledge cannot redeem man. Knowledge is helpful to a wise man that does not walk in deceit, however, it puffs up the mind of a fool that suffers from deceit and further deepens his deceit!! The Scriptures teach, *"And you were dead in your trespasses and sins, in which you formerly walked according to the prince of the power of the air, of the spirit that is now working in the sons of disobedience. Among them, we too all formerly lived in the lusts of our flesh, indulging the desires of the flesh and of the mind, and were by nature children of wrath, even as the rest. (Ephesians 2:1-3)* The scriptures say "ALL" and it is probably fair to say that includes you!!!

It is the nature of that very deceit that has inspired the Supreme Court to condemn our government and the public educational institutions of our nation to secularism. They have chosen to declare a *"separation between church and state"* that removes God from the governing process, from the public forum and from the classrooms of our public schools.

This tragic decision by deceived men will lead millions of America's young people to turn their back on God. The bible declares that mans greatest goal is to gain the knowledge of God! The supreme purpose of education is to raise our children in the nurture and admonition of the Lord that they might come to know and love God.

There is hope for America if God will have mercy upon us and choose to intervene in such and powerful and profound way that our leaders and our people become awakened and see fit to humble themselves before our Creator, seek His forgiveness and accept his deliverance from death and deceit.

God is the only remedy to the deceit, selfish introspection, social disintegration, crime, hate, prejudice and perversion that is destroying millions of Americans and systematically destroying the distinctive traditional national identity of America as an ambassador of light, hope and liberty to a dark and hopeless world.

God is our only hope! We cannot deliver ourselves! Some new legislation will not deliver us! A new Supreme Court will not deliver us! If we give all we have to the poor it will not deliver us. Our only hope for deliverance is the grace of God manifest through the Spiritual awakening of the Church and the people. It is our only hope. If we want to be a part of that we must humble ourselves individually and pray for the deliverance of America.

The exciting truth, which can be conveyed to any who have ears to hear, is the promise of the Lord that his desire is that none perish and all come to knowledge of the truth and be delivered from this terminal disease of deceit and eternal death

Bible students will quickly recognize the passage of scripture from 2 Chron 7:13-14 as a message from the Lord delivered by a prophet to the apostate nation of Israel who had turned their backs in rebellion against God. If Israel refused to respond they would perish. Those words speak to us prophetically today. *"(If) My people who are called by My name humble themselves and pray, and seek My face and turn from their wicked ways, then I will hear from heaven, will forgive their sin, and will heal their land."* However, despite the warnings of King Solomon and the prophets of God the people of Israel refused to humble themselves. God tried for many years to awaken them to the ultimate tragic end their rebellious direction would lead them to. A study of the prophets such as Jeremiah, Ezekiel and several others will reveal the efforts God was willing to expend in an attempt to awaken Israel.

The bible clearly reveals that the choice to humble our selves before our Creator must be made by each individual during this lifetime if he wishes to be forgiven and born of God's Spirit. He will then be delivered from the penalty of his sin and the deceit that he is otherwise trapped in and his life will become eternal.

The scriptures teach us that Spiritual rebirth delivers us from the power of the flesh and guarantee's us eternal life. *"There is therefore now no condemnation for those who are in Christ Jesus. For the law of the Spirit of life in Christ Jesus has set you free from the law of sin and of death. For what the Law could not do, weak as it was through the flesh, God did; sending His own Son in the likeness of sinful flesh and as an offering for sin, He condemned sin in the flesh, in order that the requirement of the Law might be fulfilled in us, who do not walk according to the flesh, but according to the Spirit. For those who are according to the flesh set their minds on the things of the flesh, but those whoa re according to the Spirit, the things of the Spirit. For the mind set on the flesh is death, but the mind set on the Spirit is life and peace, because the mind set on the flesh is hostile toward God; for it does not subject itself to the law of God, for it is not even able to do so; and those who are in the flesh cannot please God. However, you are not in the flesh but in the Spirit, if indeed the Spirit of God dwells in you. But if anyone does not have the Spirit of Christ, he does not belong to Him. And if Christ is in you, though the body is dead because of sin, yet the spirit is alive because of righteousness. But it the Spirit of Him who raised Jesus from the dead dwells in you, He who raised Christ Jesus from the dead will also give life to your mortal bodies through His Spirit who indwells you. …If you are living according to the flesh, you must die; but if by the Spirit you are putting to death the deeds of the body you will live. For all who are being led by the Spirit of God, these are sons of God."(Romans 8:1-14)*

What will you do in response to the truth of God's word? What will America do? What must our national leaders do? Will we as individuals and collectively as a nation continue to reject His offer of love, acceptance, wisdom and deliverance? Are we going to continue to reject Him and promote this secular humanist insanity that has taken over our government. Are we going to allow deceit to continue to guide and destroy our children and our nation? Frankly the choice is up to you and I!!! God is willing and able. I believe He is waiting patiently for our answer!

A way to understand our natural circumstance and what takes place at Spiritual rebirth is to consider what happens to you and I if water, food and air are taken away from us. Everyone knows we will die. Human life cannot be sustained without food, air and water. Likewise, God created us to require Spiritual life if our Spirit is to live. His Spirit is eternal and therefore we inherit eternal life when we are born of His Spirit. Our spiritual lives have been cutoff from God because of mans sin. The penalty for sin is spiritual death. God is life and when we reject God we reject Spiritual life. When we do that our Spirit dies. When His spirit resides within us we inherit His life. We become born again of the Spirit of God and we are a new creation in Christ. His Spirit is life and when spiritual rebirth occurs we inherit eternal life.

A spirit of humility before God always accompanies spiritual awakening! It has been historically accompanied by a general willingness to repent of sin and surrender our lives to Christ. Salvation takes on the profound recognition of the call of God upon one's life and a desire to respond to that call and move forward from this point with a new direction, focus and purpose that is in accord with the will and purpose of God.

Spiritual rebirth does not come because we are sorry our sin has been exposed or because you recognize we might be able avoid hell if we give Christianity a try. It is not a risk verses benefit plan. In fact for men to come to the light they must see the light. God has the light switch, so to speak! Christian witness is not attempting to point someone to a religious movement or a cultural way of life, but to the person of Jesus Christ.

Once we have responded to God's call upon our life God's Spirit comes to reside within us to inspire and guide us. Our sin and failures have been forgiven and as we live and grow in spiritual maturity our desire becomes to be like Jesus. We are called to be a *"fragrance of Christ to God among those who are being saved and among those who are perishing; to the one an aroma from death to death, to the other an aroma from life to life.." 2Cor 2:15) "Therefore, gird your minds for action, keep sober in spirit, fix your hope completely on the grace to be brought to you at the revelation of Jesus Christ. As obedient children, do not be conformed to the former lusts which were yours in your ignorance, but like the Holy One who called you, be holy yourselves also in all your behavior; because it is written, "You shall be Holy, for I am Holy. And if you address as Father the One who impartially judges according to each man's work, conduct yourselves in fear during the time of your stay upon earth; knowing that you were not redeemed with perishable things like silver or gold from your futile way of life inherited from your forefathers, but with precious blood, as of a lamb unblemished and spotless, the blood of Christ. For He was foreknown before the foundation of the world, but has appeared in these last times for the sake of you who through Him are believers in God, who raised Him from the dead and gave Him glory, so that your faith and hope are in God."*

The Scriptures teach us that not all who run the race win. Listen to the words of the Apostle Paul: *"Do you not know that those who run in a race all run, but only one receives the prize? Run in such a way that you may win. And everyone who competes in the games exercises self-control in all things. They then do it to receive a perishable wreath, but we an imperishable. Therefore I run in such a way as not without aim; I box in such a way as not beating the air; but I buffet my body and make it my slave, lest possibly, after I have preached to others, I myself should be disqualified. (I Cor 9:24-27)*

The Scriptures teach us that *"God causes all things to work together for good to those who love God, to those who are called according to His purpose" (Romans 8:28).* This promise alone is more than adequate for any people to seek after God and the blessing of His grace.

Listen to the privileged blessing of the elect! *"What then shall we say to these things? If God is for us, who is against us? He who did not spare His own son, but delivered Him up for us all, how will He not also with Him freely give us all things? Who will bring a charge against God's elect? God is the one who justifies; who is the one who condemns? Christ Jesus is He who died, yes, rather who was raised, who is at the right hand of God who also intercedes for us. Who shall separate us from the love of Christ? Shall tribulation, or distress, or persecution, or famine, or nakedness, or peril, or sword?....But in all these things we overwhelmingly conquer through Him who loved us. For I am convinced that neither death, nor life, nor angels, nor principalities, nor things present, nor things to come, now powers, nor height, nor depth, nor any other created thing, shall be able to separate us from the love of God, which is in Christ Jesus our Lord." (Romans 8:31-39)*

There is still hope for America if the poll taken recently by NBC is accurate. The question was "Do you believe in God"? The question was presented in an effort to determine the percentage of Americans that wanted to keep the words "In God we trust" on our coins and the Words "Under God" in the pledge of allegiance. The reported response was 86% was for keeping God in the pledge and In God we trust as our national motto.

I hope this is the case. Unfortunately many Americans don't reflect this belief in their actions nor at the election booth. Either we have a large number of people who say they believe in a Creator who are not Christians accept in the cultural sense of the word or they are spiritually blind and fail to see the spiritual battle that is part and parcel of their Christian walk.

America is now in the hands of a generation of Americans who are finding they are not adequately prepared for the responsibility to lead and govern this nation. As a nation we have not stayed alert and stood our ground and adequately prepared to fight the spiritual battle, nevertheless, the battle is now upon us. We have perceived ourselves as "fortress America" and have become so immersed in the battles to protect our interests outside our shores that we failed to see that the real battlefield is within the fortress.

Most of us don't recognize the enemy or the fact there is a continuous spiritual battle raging against truth, righteousness, liberty and justice. We had the arrogant notion that because we won WWII we didn't have to worry about anything or anyone taking our nation from us. We forgot the scriptures warning that the greatest enemy of all is the enemy from within that raises up and destroys by leading men to reject the one who protects our faith, values and liberty. Without that protection our values and our liberty is taken from us without a shot every fired. We were fools to drop our guard and allow the enemy to come in like a flood. Are we reaping what we have sowed?

Our greatness as a nation has been the result of the blessing and grace of Almighty God. Without His blessing and guidance we, like all other secular nations before us, will inevitably self-destruct. Spiritual polarization, hate and political division are systematically destroying America's perspective and moral character. Can we regain our collective soul, character and perspective? Can we once again become a light on a hill that demonstrates God's grace and enjoys His blessing?

I have attempted to present a brief look at our birth with a divine purpose and then the devastating social rebellion and spiritual attack that came against our nation during the decade of the sixties and seventies that changed our national perspective. We have never recovered. I have attempted to present the cause and effect of this rebellion and the spiritual darkness that is overtaking our nation as I have observed it. God has given us several wake-up calls that we have not recognized and not heeded. He gave America another wake-up call on 9-11 and He has sent us a new leader as His ambassador to help guide us back to Him. Many Americans have failed to respond to his leadership. The question now is how is America going to respond to the spiritual darkness that is overtaking us? During this past four years our nation has rebelled against our President rather than uniting behind him to fight the enemy that is out to destroy western civilization. The hate of at least half of America's citizens and many of our political leaders for God, His people and our President seems to be accelerating. In the meantime our Supreme Court has declared our Government, and therefore our nation, to be secular separating and isolating the affairs of state from the wisdom, charity and purpose of God. I will leave it to you to assess our national response thus far!!!!!!!!

Perspective is a compilation of my faith, experience, hopes and whatever wisdom God may have given me. My hope is that many will read *perspective*, test the spirit in which it is written and take up the cause to preserve truth, freedom, our precious faith and this once great island of liberty. It is dedicated to the hope of ultimately awakening and inspiring men to become salt and light in this darkness and begin to seek after biblical truth, proclaim and courageously defend it at every opportunity and to humble themselves under the mighty and loving hand of God. I have asked you to take a few hour to consider the thoughts presented in *perspective* with a sincerity that goes deeper than the "good idea" stage to a platform for action and performance of those good works and exemplary citizenship we are each called to!

If you are a citizen of the United States of America who loves God and liberty and you want to see it protected and kept vibrant and alive for the generations to come think about this! *'"NOW THE LORD IS THE SPIRIT; AND WHERE THE SPIRIT OF THE LORD IS, THERE IS LIBERTY."!! (2 Corinthians 3:17)*

Printed in the United States
68309LVS00005B/73-250